Ṣàngó in Africa and the African Diaspora

ṢÀNGÓ
in Africa and the African Diaspora

EDITED BY JOEL E. TISHKEN,
TÓYÌN FÁLỌLÁ, AND
AKÍNTÚNDÉ AKÍNYẸMÍ

Indiana University Press
Bloomington and Indianapolis

This book is a publication of
Indiana University Press
601 North Morton Street
Bloomington, IN 47404-3797 USA

www.iupress.indiana.edu

Telephone orders   800-842-6796
Fax orders   812-855-7931
Orders by e-mail   iuporder@indiana.edu

⊚ The paper used in this publication meets the minimum requirements of
American National Standard for Information Sciences—
Permanence of Paper for Printed Library Materials, ANSI Z39.48-1992.

Manufactured in the United States of America

LIBRARY OF CONGRESS CATALOGING-IN-PUBLICATION DATA

Tishken, Joel E., date
Sàngó in Africa and the African diaspora / edited by Joel E. Tishken, Toyin Falola,
and Akíntúndé Akínyẹmí.
p. cm. — (African expressive cultures)
Includes bibliographical references and index.
ISBN 978-0-253-35336-8 (cloth : alk. paper) —
ISBN 978-0-253-22094-3 (pbk. : alk. paper)
1. Shango (Yoruba deity) 2. Shango (Cult) 3. Yoruba (African people)—Religion. 4. Afro-Brazilian cults. 5. African diaspora. I. Falola, Toyin. II. Akínyẹmí, Akíntúndé. III. Title.
BL2532.S5T57 2009
299.6'833302113—dc22   2008055799

1 2 3 4 5 14 13 12 11 10 09

For Professor Joãs Reis,
an astute interpreter of the history
of the Yorùbá in Brazil

Contents

Acknowledgments

Chapter 5 originally appeared as Marc Schiltz, "Yoruba Thunder Deities and Sovereignty: Ara versus Sango," *Anthropos* 80, nos. 1–3 (1985): 67–84.

Portions of chapter 10 appear in Kamari Maxine Clarke, *Mapping Yoruba Networks: Power and Agency in the Making of Transnational Communities*, Durham, N.C.: Duke University Press, 2004.

Chapter 12 has also been printed as Luis Nicolau Parés, "Shango in Afro-Brazilian Religion: 'Aristocracy' and 'Syncretic' Interactions." *Religioni e Società* 54 (2006): 20–39.

CHAPTER ONE

Introduction

JOEL E. TISHKEN, TÓYÌN FÁLỌLÁ
AND AKÍNTÚNDÉ AKÍNYẸMÍ

There are not many deities in the world that are truly international in the scope of their worship. The Yorùbá *òrìṣà* Ṣàngó is one such deity. Worshippers of Ṣàngó may be found everywhere the Yorùbá people have had a cultural or demographic influence, and even beyond. Such influence encompasses several nations of West Africa and a good many of the nations of the Americas. Whether by trade associations, imperial expansion, the Atlantic slave trade, cultural exportation, or immigration, the Yorùbá people have left an undeniable and permanent imprint on many parts of the world.[1] This imprint includes Yorùbá religion and its pantheon of deities.

The Yorùbá religious system itself is extremely complex. Therefore, we can attempt only a tentative and exploratory treatment of it here. The religion is associated with some objects of worship known individually and collectively as the *òrìṣà*. There is a commonly accepted tradition among the Yorùbá people that there are 401 of these deities, although the count should be viewed as a sacred metaphor and not a scientific fact. If allowance is given for duplication of some deities in different localities under different names, the total number of recognized Yorùbá objects of worship would not be more than 200. Most of these *òrìṣà* are deified ancestors or personified natural forces classified into two broad groups by Drewal et al. as the cool, temperate, symbolically white deities (*òrìṣà funfun*) and the hot, temperamental deities (*òrìṣà gbígbóná*).[2] The former, such as Ọbàtálá, Ọ̀ṣun, Yemoja, Olókun, and Ọ̀sọ̀ọ̀sì tend to be gentle, soothing, calm, and reflective. On the other hand, many of the hot temperamental gods, such as Ògún, Ṣàngó, Òsanyìn / Ọbalúayé, and Ọya, are more harsh, demanding, aggressive, and quick-tempered.

This characterization of the òrìṣà Yorùbá into "cool" and "hot" has nothing to do with issues of good and evil. All Yorùbá deities, like humans, possess both positive and negative values. Furthermore, the deities are not ranked in any hierarchy. But, even so, the issue has been addressed by a good number of scholars, although they all have opposing views on the subject matter. The relative importance of any òrìṣà in any given part of Yorùbáland reflects the deity's relative local popularity, reputation, and influence. However, some of these deities are nevertheless worshipped globally. Among such deities are Ògún, Ṣàngó, Èṣù, Ifá, Ọbàtálá, Ọ̀ṣun, and Ọya to mention just a few. Ṣàngó is among the mightiest of deities within the Yorùbá pantheon, and this collection of chapters addresses the nature of Ṣàngó worship within Africa and from various perspectives within the African Diaspora.

The Cult of Ṣàngó

Ṣàngó is the most powerful and the most feared Yorùbá deity both in Africa and in the Diaspora. For instance, Ahye claims that Ṣàngó devotees in Trinidad speak of him affectionately as "Papa Ṣàngó." This, according to her, is not unconnected with the military might and prowess of the deity, and his association with two dreadful forces of nature, thunder and lightning. The cult of Ṣàngó is controlled by a set of priests known collectively as the *mọgbà*s among the African and diasporic worshippers of the deity. By virtue of their relationship with the deity, the *mọgbà*s are responsible for officiating at Ṣàngó rituals and for the selection and upkeep of his ritual paraphernalia. For instance, the worship of Ṣàngó in each of the modern Nigerian cities of Ẹdẹ and Ọ̀yọ́ is administered by a council of twelve *mọgbà*s, with the ọ̀nà-mọgbà as their leader. He is ably assisted by both the ọ̀túun-mọgbà and the òsì-mọgbà. Below these two *mọgbà*s are the other nine with the titles of the ẹkẹrin-mọgbà, the ẹkarùún-mọgbà, up to the ninth. In addition to the *mọgbà*s, there are other lesser priests of Ṣàngó, called the adóṣù and the ẹlẹ́gùn. These priests are charged with the responsibility of performing magical feats aimed at astonishing and enticing people into the cult; they also serve as mediums through which òrìṣà Ṣàngó is revealed and accessed.

Ṣàngó's paraphernalia, including charms and replicas, are kept by his devotees and placed as treasures on his altar. It is through these personal objects that Ṣàngó's devotees believe that they can commune with him, for they are of the view that he hears their supplications through these religious objects and blesses them. Usually, Ṣàngó's seat, a mortar (*odóo Ṣàngó*), and a fairly big pot (*ìkòkò àgbélé*) are at the center of the arrangement, and where the pot is absent, the mortar is positioned at the center with other personal items of Ṣàngó, such as double-edged axe (*osé*), thunderbolts (*ẹ̀dùn àrá*), kola nut (*obì*), gourd rattle (*ṣẹ́ẹ̀rẹ́*), sixteen cowries (*owó ẹyọ*), and other items, placed around it. A shrine custodian, usually a priest or priestess, often lives in the vicinity of the shrine, so that suppliants and devotees who call from time to time to consult Ṣàngó would meet him or her there. Ordinarily, whenever a Ṣàngó devotee is faced with any spiritual or physical problem that she or he cannot solve, the concerned individual consults the Ṣàngó Ẹ̀ẹ̀rìndínlógún divination system for a solution. This stems from the ability of Ṣàngó to resolve all kinds of human problems through his mysterious and mystical power.

There are two types of ritual processes among the devotees of Ṣàngó in Africa and the Diaspora, namely, periodic and annual rituals. The periodic ritual is usually very brief and takes place occasionally, usually once a week. This falls on Thursday or Friday in the Diaspora and on Jàkúta day (the last day of the traditional Yorùbá four-day week) in Africa, a day well known as Ṣàngó's day, when he fights with stone. The weekly ritual is mainly for singing praises to Ṣàngó (*Ṣàngó pípè*) and cleaning his shrine. The annual ritual, which is more elaborate, is a form of thanksgiving as well as a reactivation of the power of the deity. It lasts seven days, of which the first, the third, and the seventh days are the most important. The annual ritual of Ṣàngó takes place in early December in the Diaspora and anytime during the rainy season among the West African Yorùbá people. The choice of the rainy season for the annual worship of Ṣàngó probably stems from the attendance of thunder and lightning. However, the actual week for the annual festival is chosen by Ṣàngó devotees and their priests after consultation with Ṣàngó's Ẹ̀ẹ̀rìndínlógún diviners in their respective city. The celebration during the rainy season gave birth to the popular Yorùbá proverb: *ìgbà ara là ń búra, a kì í bú Ṣàngó lẹ̀ẹ̀rùn*, meaning "one should do the right thing at the right time, for Ṣàngó cannot be invoked in the dry season [when there is no thunder and lightning]."

On the first day of the annual celebration of the Ṣàngó festival in modern-day Ọ̀yọ́, for instance, the calabash containing the various paraphernalia of the *òrìṣà* is taken outside in preparation for the ceremonial religious bathing of *òrìṣà* Ṣàngó (*òrìṣà wíwè*). The cleaning is done with the herbal preparation made from the leaves of *eèsún* (*Pennisetum purperedum* Schum), *tẹ̀tẹ̀* (*Amaranthus hybridu* Linn), *òdúndún*

(*Bryophylliam*), and fresh water taken from the *ojúbọ* (the altar). This is done with incantations and praise songs to Ṣàngó. The calabash is also washed and painted with camwood powder (*osùn*). The paraphernalia are then put back into the calabash and placed on the mortar (*odóo* Ṣàngó). A sacrifice of a cock and a ram is made. The blood of those animals is allowed to pour on the paraphernalia. The essence of this blood, according to Drewal and others, is to feed and reactivate the power, which is the *òrìṣà* in them.[3] The flesh is then cooked for the devotees present to eat.

On the third day, referred to as *ìta*, another feast is made. On the seventh day, known as *ìje*, after feasting, the devotees dress up in any dress of their choice—usually the dress is specially sewn for the annual festival—with their red and white neck beads. The *ẹlẹ́gùn* puts on a reddish-purple tunic with appliqués of cowries called *ẹ̀wù owó*. The *wàbì*, the paneled skirt, is made from cloths of warm colors, and the *yẹrì-owó* (cowried skirt) is worn on top of the *wàbì*. The *ẹlẹ́gùn* carries the double-headed axe (*osé*) of Ṣàngó and a gourd rattle (*séẹ́rẹ́*). She or he might put on a tiara or a cap, however; whether the *ẹlẹ́gùn* is male or female, the hair is plaited and exposed so even the male devotee looks like a woman; the devotee rarely wears shoes or sandals during the celebrations. The *ẹlẹ́gùn* is referred to as Ṣàngó when he is possessed by the spirit of the deity and is greeted by everybody saying "*ká wóó!*" or "*kábíyèsí!*" (your majesty or royal highness). The devotees carry with them different symbols of the Ṣàngó cult, including a magical box. They go around the city singing melodious songs accompanied by *bàtá* drummers. Prayers are said to the ancestors by the *ẹlẹ́gùn* to bless their leaders (the *mọgbàs*), other priests and devotees of Ṣàngó, and the town at large. The celebration may be crowned with magical presentations by the *ẹlẹ́gùn* to entertain the spectators in an open place.

The Direction of This Study

This Ṣàngó collection contributes to knowledge in several meaningful ways. First, it builds upon a growing body of scholarship on Yorùbá-based religions and on the African Diaspora in general. In particular, it builds upon similar collections on the deities Ògún and Òṣun. The central purpose of each of these texts is to reveal the multidimensional nature of each of these *òrìṣà*.[4] This collection also echoes this theme of complexity regarding the multiple definitions of Ṣàngó. Prismatic definitions of a god or goddess are an intrinsic part of polytheistic religions, and there is nothing peculiar about Ṣàngó or any of the Yorùbá *òrìṣà* in this regard. However, as the worship of Ṣàngó has grown increasingly widespread and international, such definitional complexity has grown with it, as all of these contributions discuss.

Second, this collection contributes to a growing body of scholarship on so-called neopagan religions. Whether Yorùbá-based religions fit this category or not is a debatable point; the term "neopagan" is an elastic one that eludes easy definition.[5] But what appears unquestionable is that there is a growing interest in polytheistic religions throughout many parts of the world that were once predominantly Christian. Whether it is the worship of Thor from Norse religion, Diana from Roman religion, or Ṣàngó from Yorùbá religion, people throughout the Americas, Europe, Australia, and New Zealand are rediscovering a variety of polytheistic religions. The Yorùbá òrìṣà figure prominently in this growth of polytheistic religions, particularly among peoples of African descent—in this volume, Clarke, Glazier, Lovejoy, and Parés note the growth of Ṣàngó worship in the Disapora. The worship of Ṣàngó has hardly disappeared in West Africa, but neither is it growing. The strength of Christianity and Islam is militating against an increase in formal Ṣàngó worship, though the presence of the òrìṣà is constant within many facets of life in Nigeria, as revealed in this book by Adéjùmọ̀, Adélékè, Bádéjọ, Fọlárànmí, and Ajíbádé.

Third, this collection integrates two contributions from worshippers of Ṣàngó. This is certainly not customary practice within the academic study of religion and reflects the history of religious studies. Academics have tended to have a distrustful view of the faithful. Atheist and agnostic scholars have tended to see them as ignorant people who will worship anything that comes their way, while scholars of religion have tended to see them as uneducated rabble who cannot adequately express their religion within an academic setting as the trained scholar can. Neither of these perspectives does justice to those of faith in any religion and neglects the complex factors that lead a person to be faithful to any religion. The faithful are more than a herd of people gathering around an illusion, as some classic theorists of religion such as Freud, Durkheim, or Marx would have us think. And the faithful are quite capable of intelligent expressions of what their religion means to them without acquiring a Ph.D. Some works on Afro-Christianity in South Africa have recently begun to integrate the perspective of Afro-Christian leaders.[6] Integrating the perspective of worshippers does not turn an academic work into an exercise in religious propaganda. Rather it brings about a fuller view of the religion in question by making it a lived reality, in conjunction with the traditional approach of an intellectual abstraction. The reader thereby gains knowledge from both the inside and the outside in a much richer way than could be gained from a strictly academic perspective. Two contributions from a priestess and priest of Ṣàngó, Ọlọmọ, and Pichardo and Mason, provide us with just such a perspective on Ṣàngó.

Defining Ṣàngó within a Polytheistic Milieu

Attempting to define a deity with worship as widespread as that of Ṣàngó is no easy task. Within Yorùbá religion and Yoruba-based religions, Ṣàngó demonstrates a variety of definitions, or "many faces."[7] All the contributors in this volume in some way grapple with the complex definitions of Ṣàngó. In broad terms, such definitions of Ṣàngó include the mythic Ṣàngó, the historical Ṣàngó, and the syncretic Ṣàngó. These three general images of Ṣàngó reveal only a fraction of the complexity of the way in which Ṣàngó is defined, particularly in the Americas, as further pluralism is evident even within these categories. This introductory chapter will present the essentials of each of these categories to provide the reader with a basic understanding of Ṣàngó and his worship.

Deities with "many faces" are part of any polytheistic religion, and there is nothing peculiar about Ṣàngó in this regard. Within Greek religion, for instance, Zeus (literally Sky Father) was known as Zeus Kataibates (Descending, or of the Lightning), Zeus Kappotas (Downpourer), Zeus Anax (King), Zeus Herkeios (of Order), Zeus Eleutherios (Liberator), Zeus Ktesios (Protector of Property), Zeus Polieus (of the City), Zeus Gamelois (God of Marriage), Zeus Teleios (Giver of Completeness), Zeus Xenios (of Oaths), and Zeus Heraios (of Hera).[8] Zeus is most commonly known as the father of the gods or the dispenser of lightning, but his epithets indicate he is far more than this alone; he is also associated with the rule of law, society, and civilization as well.

Such variations in the definition of a deity stem from two central features of polytheistic religions. The first feature is the apportionment of the universe amongst a multiplicity of deities. Within polytheistic religions each god or goddess is assigned a particular domain. For instance, Zeus and Ṣàngó were both "in charge" of lightning according to Greek and Yorùbá mythology. However, the boundaries of these domains overlap, which means that the domain of one deity traverses a variety of other domains. Lightning intersects with thunder and air and even comes to earth and affects the terrestrial domain as well. Thus, lightning deities such as Ṣàngó and Zeus cannot do their "job" as the dispensers of lightning without also impacting other aspects of the universe. The other domains they impact are given varying degrees of importance depending upon the desires of the worshippers in different geographic locations.

The second feature of polytheism that encourages the development of a deity's "many faces" is the fact that polytheistic religions lack a center of orthodox enforcement. In other words, polytheistic religions lack a mechanism by which one region can regulate the theology of another. A local variation in the way in which a god or goddess is defined can flourish even when it is at odds with the definition of the deity in its place of origin. Even when a god or goddess has a central temple, like Zeus did at Olympia, the Japanese goddess Amaterasu did at Ise, and Ṣàngó did at Kòso, the priests and priestesses of that shrine lack the power to enforce beliefs on the population. That does not mean they lack any power over the population; they may be able to request sacrifices or rituals on behalf of the deity. But that power does not generally extend to policing the minds of the populace and enforcing a particular definition of the deity upon them, such as the power of excommunication provides the Catholic Church, for instance.

As the Schiltz article demonstrates, concerning the western reaches of Yorùbáland, Ṣàngó was defined in a much different way among the Kétu-Yorùbá and Sábẹ̀ẹ́-Yorùbá. Here Ṣàngó was defined as the wife of another thunder deity, Àrá. There was nothing that the priests of Ṣàngó at Kòso, or anywhere in the Ọ̀yọ́ heartland, could do to rectify the disjuncture between the definitions, presuming they even wished to. Polytheistic religions, because they believe that divinity exists in a multiplicity of forms, have historically been very accommodating to the ways in which a community defines gods and goddesses. Though one community may have different deities, or different definitions of well-known deities, than another, within polytheistic cultures that does not make them "wrong." Within a polytheistic milieu, worshippers would assume that the deity has chosen to reveal him/herself in that way for a reason, or perhaps that community has discovered a deity, or a facet of a deity, of which others were unaware. The concept of heresy, beliefs that are at variance with the most commonly accepted dogma, is largely a feature of monotheistic religions.[9] Polytheistic religions are not free of internal tension, but that tension rarely leads to purges within the same religion against "improper belief."

Thus, within a polytheistic mindset, there is nothing "right" or "wrong" in the multiple images of Ṣàngó; all Ṣàngó worshippers have been free to define Ṣàngó in the way most meaningful to them. However, though there may not be anything "right" or "wrong" about these definitions, there do exist tensions. This entire collection is dedicated to exploring the many ways in which Ṣàngó has been defined historically within Africa and the Americas. Let us now explore the basic characteristics of each on these "faces," and the tensions, as well as peaceful coexistence, among them.

Irúnmọlè: The Mythical Ṣàngó

According to oral literature contained in the *Ṣàngó pípè* and the *odù ifá*, the mythical Ṣàngó is a primordial divine entity. This Ṣàngó descended to earth from heaven with the rest of the *òrìṣà* and is said to have grown up with other primordial *òrìṣà* like Odùduwà, the creator of humans. Mythic Ṣàngó is the embodiment of thunder, lightning, and the fierceness of atmospheric power. So great was his power that other *òrìṣà* named one of the four days of the week in his honor, Jàkúta. So mighty was his power, and so great his virility, that Ṣàngó stole the goddess Ọya from Ògún, and Ọ̀sun from Ọ̀rúnmìlà. This Ṣàngó was never reported dead but simply disappeared from earth en route to Àtìbà. The mythic Ṣàngó was worshipped at Ilé-Ifẹ̀ as Ọ̀ràmfẹ̀ before the founding of Ọ̀yọ́; therefore the worship of this Ṣàngó probably has its roots in the formation of Yorùbá culture. In short, the image of the mythical Ṣàngó is grounded in his primordial nature that is equivalent to mighty *òrìṣà* such as Odùduwa, and perhaps greater than that of other *òrìṣà* such as Ògún and Ọ̀rúnmìlà. The divine power of Irúnmọlẹ̀ Ṣàngó would then derive from his pedigree of being among the original *òrìṣà*.

But as the contributions by Adéjùmọ̀ and Akínyẹmí note, this image of Ṣàngó has become less powerful than the historical image in the modern era. They argue that the historical image of Ṣàngó became the dominant image in popular culture because the historical Ṣàngó was textualized in writings by Yorùbá scholar Samuel Johnson and missionary A. L. Hethersett.[10] As the power of the written word came to dominate the oral one through Westernization and Christianization, so too did the image of Ṣàngó from written sources come to dominate that from oral sources. If one focuses solely on written sources, the mythic Ṣàngó is virtually invisible within them, aside from the role of dispenser of lightning.

Yet, Johnson and Hethersett did not make up the historical Ṣàngó. Both the mythic and the historical Ṣàngó are based on Yorùbá religious beliefs. In other words, both portray inherited historical images of Ṣàngó. Let us now examine the essentials of the image of the historical Ṣàngó.

Ọba Aláàfin: The Historical Ṣàngó

The historical Ṣàngó, the Ọba Aláàfin, is the more common image of Ṣàngó today due to the impact of a number of seminal publications on Yorùbá religion. In addition to Johnson and Hethersett, a number of other written works also reveal the historical Ṣàngó. This includes explorer A. B. Ellis, scholar J. Ọmọ́ṣadé Awólàlú, and anthropologists/folklorists Judith Gleason, Harold Courlander, and Ulli Beier.[11] All of them focus upon Ṣàngó as a deified ancestor (what is typically called a hero in many mythologies), rather than as a primordial entity, as with the image of the mythic Ṣàngó. Like in many other polytheistic religions, the worship of heroes is perfectly ordinary among the Yorùbá, and these deities were viewed as being as efficacious as any others.

Most historical traditions are in agreement that Ṣàngó was the fourth Aláàfin (emperor) of the Old Ọ̀yọ́ Empire.[12] The first ruler of Ọ̀yọ́ was held to be Odùduwà while the second was his son, Ọ̀rànmíyàn. The third was Ọ̀rànmíyàn's eldest son, Àjàká. Àjàká was deposed by the Ọ̀yọ́ Mèsì (group of seven nobles) who chose exile as the more cautious route, due to Àjàká's temper, and replaced him with Ọ̀rànmíyàn's second son, Ṣàngó.[13] There are some common themes one can identify concerning the sort of ruler the historical Ṣàngó was said to be. First, many tales tell of Ṣàngó's magical powers, particularly his ability to breathe fire (which he gained from a medicine created by Èṣù and carried by Ọya). Second, Ṣàngó's personality is repeatedly described as "hot," or in other words powerful, virile, and volatile. Many of the tales related to the historical Ṣàngó are not particularly flattering. Some stories have often been deemed false by Ṣàngó devotees, who insist it is Ṣàngó's jealous enemies who have spread such slanderous tales of his tyranny and violence. Ṣàngó's devotees insist Ṣàngó represents justice and fairness.[14]

Awólàlú has identified three variations in the story of Ṣàngó's deification. The first version states that Ṣàngó discovered a charm by which he could call down lightning. While testing the charm from a hilltop, Ṣàngó called lightning down atop his own palace through his own ignorance of, and inexperience with, the charm's power. So horrified was Ṣàngó that he had killed his own wives and children that he took his own life by hanging. The second account says that Ṣàngó was suffering from domestic troubles (quarrels among his wives Ọya, Ọṣun, and Ọbà) and constant complaints from his subjects about his heavy-handed rule. Weary from this constant squabbling and tension, he mounted his horse in anger and rode into the forest, where he ascended a chain into the sky. When his subjects tried to call him back, he declared, "I will not come back to you; I will now rule you unseen." Ever since, he has asserted his kingly rule through lightning and thunder. The most popular of the three tales of deification, however, tells of Ṣàngó as a powerful and tyrannical ruler versed in magical arts. When two of his courtiers, Tìmì and Gbọ̀nńkà, had grown too powerful, Ṣàngó craftily devised a plan where they were forced to fight one another. Ṣàngó's hope was that both might die in the struggle. Gbọ̀nńkà killed Tìmì but survived himself. When Gbọ̀nńkà continued to be an irritant to Ṣàngó, Ṣàngó had him tossed into a fire. However, Gbọ̀nńkà came from the fire unharmed and challenged Ṣàngó's right to rule. Ṣàngó was forced to abdicate the throne and flee the kingdom, and his followers slowly abandoned him, including his wives, except ever-loyal Ọya. To preserve his remaining honor, Ṣàngó decided to "play the man" and hung himself from a tree.[15]

In a more detailed version of this deification story of Ṣàngó, Samuel Johnson reported that some time after Ṣàngó's death, a few of his supporters went to his maternal home land in Ìbàrìbá (Nupeland) to acquire magical charms so they could use them, as Ṣàngó did. Upon their return, these followers of Ṣàngó ravaged the community with their newly acquired power, invoking thunder and lightning on Ṣàngó's detractors. Each time the lightning and thunderstorm abated, Ṣàngó's devotees would tell the people that the misfortune was caused by the wrath of Ṣàngó, whose demise was announced with contempt. As a remedy, the victims were often told to contact the *mọgbàs* (Ṣàngó's friends, who had constituted themselves into his high priests) to prepare sacrifices to Ṣàngó. The victims were not allowed to cry or weep over their loss, but were made to chant Ṣàngó's praises instead. The *mọgbàs* soon became so powerful that all the people were afraid of them, resulting in many of the people seeking protection from the attacks of Ṣàngó from the *mọgbàs*. The Ṣàngó rituals were, therefore, a panacea—although in the first instance, they were meant to be punishment for Ṣàngó's detractors. The cult later gained more devotees, and, as time went on, Ṣàngó rituals become firmly rooted and institutionalized in Ọ̀yọ́. They were no longer seen as punishment, but rather as a re-enactment with gestures of supplication and gratification.

Therefore, as Akínyẹmí argues in the opening chapter of this collection, the celebration of the deity Ṣàngó, at Old Ọ̀yọ́ and modern Ọ̀yọ́, is not just an important religious festival; it is essentially associated with royal power. According to Akínyẹmí, the shrine in modern Ọ̀yọ́ is considered to be a royal mausoleum where any Aláàfin-elect goes to worship Ṣàngó as an integral part of the installation rites. Each Aláàfin is also expected to participate actively during any Ṣàngó ritual or festival, as such Ṣàngó rituals are treated as state religion in Ọ̀yọ́. In Old Ọ̀yọ́, where Ṣàngó was used as an instrument of governance, his lesser priests (*adósù* or *ẹlẹ́gùn*) were sent as envoys of the Aláàfin to different villages to maintain the king's jurisdiction. Through these priests, the worship of Ṣàngó spread north, south, east, and west of Old Ọ̀yọ́, and thus it was established mostly in those Yorùbá areas that were under the imperial rule of Ọ̀yọ́ before its collapse in the nineteenth century. This explains why the religion is principally confined to present-day Ọ̀yọ́ town and its environs up to Ìbàdàn, Ọ̀yọ́ north, and Ọ̀ṣun regions of Yorùbáland. Later, Ṣàngó rituals spread to the New World and the United States of America through the Ọ̀yọ́ Yoruba slaves brought to the Americas during trans-Atlantic slavery.

As we have seen, many of the stories of the historical Ṣàngó do not assign terribly flattering characteristics to Ṣàngó. Tyranny and sorcery are generally not attributes one would expect devotees to assign to their deity. Akínyẹmí argues that the tales of the historical Ṣàngó are largely legends of the fourth Aláàfin of Ọ̀yọ́, and over time the human Aláàfin was conflated with the primordial Ṣàngó revealed in oral literature. Thus, contrary to Isola's claim, tales of the historical Ṣàngó cannot be simply dismissed as the erroneous recordings of foreign observers who did not truly understand Yorùbá religion, or as propagandist efforts by Christians to present traditional Yorùbá religion in an unflattering manner.[16] Tales of the historical Ṣàngó do represent the Ṣàngó of the Yorùbá political past, but they likely do not represent the Ṣàngó that emerged in the early roots of Yorùbá culture. This Ṣàngó, the mythic Ṣàngó, seems best represented in oral literature.

Syncretic Ṣàngó

Today, we see the manifestations of Ṣàngó among the descendants of the Yorùbá in the Diaspora: Brazil, Cuba, Haiti, Trinidad, Puerto Rico, and the United States. Therefore, the worship of Ṣàngó is global in the sense that it is transnational. As Ṣàngó worship spread, both within Africa and to various parts of the Americas, Ṣàngó was combined with a variety of new, often non-Yoruba, characteristics. Among his Brazilian worshippers, for instance, the deity has two sacred numbers, four and six. This tradition is completely absent in Africa. Also, Ṣàngó's favorite meal among his Nigerian worshippers is *àmàlà* and *gbẹ̀gìrì*, but in the Diaspora his offerings consist of cornmeal, okra, green banana, and red apple. However, the same Ṣàngó carries his double-headed axe (*osé*) on both sides of the Atlantic, where he dances to the rhythm of *bàtá* drum music in a virile, warlike, dignified, and kingly fashion. Ṣàngó devotees in general are also not allowed to touch *sèsé* seeds (*phaseolus lunatus* Linn), as it is believed that the seed will negate the *àṣẹ Ṣàngó* (Ṣàngó's power) vested in them.

The ẹlẹ́gùn and the adósù should also not eat certain types of animals, such as òkété (big bush rat), ààgó (a kind of bush rat), ọ̀kẹ́rẹ́ (squirrel), and èsúró (antelope).

The process of syncretism, or religious blending, is a ubiquitous feature of religions. All religions change across both time and space and become influenced by other religions as they spread.[17] Catholicism, for example, is practiced differently in Gabon, Mexico, Poland, and the Philippines. The variations in practice may be attributed to syncretism as Catholicism became combined with local religious practices in each of those locations. The essence of Catholicism remained, but worshippers adapted the religion to best suit their religious and cultural needs and local milieu. So too is the same process evidenced in Ṣàngó worship. The essence of Ṣàngó as a deity of lightning remains in all locations. However, regional variations due to syncretism are demonstrated.

Even within Yorùbáland itself, syncretism can be found. Schiltz demonstrates how the definition of the historical Ṣàngó was closely tied to the power of Ọ̀yọ́. In the border kingdoms of Sábẹ̀ẹ̀ and Kétu, a compromise was created between the royal cult of Ṣàngó and that of the preexisting thunder deity, Àrá. But just as the control of Ọ̀yọ́ over Sábẹ̀ẹ̀ and Kétu was not total and complete, so too did the dominion of Ṣàngó over Àrá remain incomplete. In Sábẹ̀ẹ̀ and Kétu, Ṣàngó was defined as the wife of Àrá, a religious marriage of convenience precipitated by Ọ̀yọ́ imperialism.

But it is within the African Diaspora that the greatest syncretism may be observed. In Brazil and various parts of the Caribbean (and later in other parts of the Americas as African-derived religions such as Santería and Candomblé spread beyond their place of origin) Ṣàngó has been combined with Saint Barbara. According to legend Barbara lived near Nicomedia in Asia Minor at a time when Christianity was still outlawed within the Roman Empire. She had converted to Christianity against the wishes of her jealous father, Dioscorus, who had previously imprisoned her in a tower. Around 235 CE, Dioscorus learned of her conversion and brought her before the prefect, who decreed that she be tortured and decapitated. Dioscorus carried out the decapitation himself, and was struck by lightning on his way home and his body consumed by fire. Barbara later became the patron saint of towers and fortifications (due to her imprisonment) and the protector from thunderstorms and fire.[18]

Scholars disagree over the reasons why Catholic saints were combined with African deities in the Americas. But as Clarke indicates, the most commonly accepted explanation asserts it was due to the criminalization of African deities within plantation societies. Peoples of African descent in places like Cuba, Trinidad, and Brazil practiced their religion on two stages: the public stage where they appeared to honor Catholic saints, and the private stage where they continued the worship of various African deities, particularly Yorùbá *òrìṣà* like Ṣàngó. In time the lines separating the two practices became blurred, and soon Catholic saints and Yorùbá *òrìṣà* became viewed as two names for the same divine beings. Saint Barbara, because of her association with lightning, was associated with Ṣàngó. That one being was female and the other male was not of significance, as divine beings are not limited by form. It is also possible, as Glazier discusses, that syncretism was due to the religious needs of the worshippers, who knowingly and willingly engaged in the practice of two religions simultaneously. Ultimately, asking the question of why syncretism occurred may reveal more about the agenda of the researchers asking the question than it will reveal of the religious past. Perhaps we might be better off asking how syncretism transpired than why.

Ṣàngó played such a significant role in the process of syncretization that the African-based religion of Trinidad became known as Ṣàngó. As Glazier examines, there is an effort among some practitioners of Afro-Trinidadian religion today to refer to general "Òrìṣà work," rather than Ṣàngó. Nonetheless, Ṣàngó continues to hold a very prominent place in many shrines across Trinidad, and may in fact be increasing in popularity. Ṣàngó was equally popular in Brazil. Parés discusses all of the "qualities" that Ṣàngó manifests across Afro-Brazilian religions, thereby illustrating Ṣàngó's prominence in a variety of forms.

There appears little question that the historical Ṣàngó had a more profound influence on the Americas than the mythic Ṣàngó did. As Clarke, Glazier, and Parés all reveal, the Ṣàngó of Òrìṣà, Afro-Trinidadian religion, and Afro-Brazilian religions is known for his violence, fierceness, and impulsiveness, just as is the historical Ṣàngó. However, as these authors discuss, there is interest among some contemporary devotees of Ṣàngó in the Americas to create a more authentically Yorùbá, more "African," definition of Ṣàngó. To these worshippers, that means purging Ṣàngó of his syncretic associations with Saint Barbara. The perspective here is that removing the Catholic elements from deities such as Ṣàngó will reveal the "proper" Yorùbá *òrìṣà* beneath. Yet interestingly, this process of Africanization that is evident within African-derived religions of the Americas is not advocating a return to a definition of Ṣàngó more like the mythic one revealed in the *Ṣàngó pípè* and the *odù ifá*. It may be that the discontinuity in Yorùbá oral literature and language in the Americas largely militates against that.

However, in her contribution, Ṣàngó priestess Olóyè Àìná Olomọ advocates an emphasis on Ṣàngó as a divine essence. She denies the image of the historical Ṣàngó and attributes tales of his virility and violence to patriarchy and male stereotypes. Since men glorified these attributes, they assigned them to their male deities. But Ọlọmọ insists that this distorts the true fundamental nature of Ṣàngó as a deity of lightning and thunder. She instead says that the real Ṣàngó is naturally manifested around us. We perceive Ṣàngó as light (lightning), sound (thunder), and even in our bodily processes (libido, or sexual impulses, and the electrical impulse that is life). Ọlọmọ advocates an image of Ṣàngó that only partly depends on Yorùbá mythology. This "face" of Ṣàngó is not syncretic or historical but is based on Ṣàngó as a divine natural essence.

Rectifying the Many "Faces" of Ṣàngó

Among the many images of Ṣàngó one can find both tension and peaceful coexistence. No one image is more "correct" or "authentic" than another because no group of Ṣàngó worshippers is more "correct" or "authentic" than another. Every image of Ṣàngó is legitimate because there are worshippers who pay reverence to that image. As discussed in the first section, Yorùbá and Yorùbá-based religions lack a means to police orthodoxy. This means that worshippers are free to define deities in the way that is most meaningful to them. However, even though worshippers have the ability to do this, this does not mean that worshippers agree with the images that other groups of worshippers have created.

Theological tension can even be identified in the common phrase *Ọba kò so* (The king did not hang), one of the most commonly uttered phrases of Ṣàngó worship that can be found on both sides of the Atlantic. According to the legend of the historical Ṣàngó, the beleaguered Ṣàngó decided to "play the man" by hanging himself. The enemies of Ṣàngó, those who had suffered at the hands of his tyrannical rule, defamed his reputation by repeating that he was a hung king. Ṣàngó's supporters countered with the phrase *Ọba kò so,* to show that, for them, Ṣàngó the great king did in fact not hang, but became deified and ascended into the heavens. Thus, the phrase reveals tension between Ṣàngó as a mere defeated historical actor and Ṣàngó as a glorious defied hero. Every contributor to this volume in some way addresses the multiple definitions, or the many "faces," of Ṣàngó.

This collection begins with the contribution of Akíntúndé Akínyẹmí on the place of Ṣàngó in the Yorùbá pantheon. The chapter discusses the prestigious position occupied by Ṣàngó among the Yorùbá, and postulates reasons why the deity is still worshipped and admired by devotees on both sides of the Atlantic to the present day. Akínyẹmí argues that the elevated position of Ṣàngó stemmed from the deity's association with Ọ̀yọ́ kingship institution and royalty, his ability to resolve human problems, spiritual and physical, through a specialized system of divination, his commitment to social justice, his supernatural power and association with thunder and lightning, his military might, and his pursuit of the two main themes of a warrior: prowess and honor.

The first part of Àrìnpé Adéjùmọ̀'s chapter questions the validity of the popular myths surrounding the historical Ṣàngó. She reveals that the historical Ṣàngó was the image of Ṣàngó reflected by written accounts from A. L. Hethersett and Samuel Johnson, not the image of mythological Ṣàngó presented in Yorùbá oral literature like the *ẹsẹ ifá*. In the second section of her contribution, Adéjùmọ̀ discusses the worship of Ṣàngó in present-day Nigeria. The section reveals that Ṣàngó is not a god of the past but that he is still relevant in the contemporary Yorùbá society, where the worship of the deity is still nearly as potent as it was in the past. Because of Ṣàngó's popularity in present day Yorùbáland, Adéjùmọ̀ submits that many literary works are being created regularly around his myths and history.

Olúṣọlá Ajíbádé investigates the Ṣàngó Ẹẹ̀rìndínlógún divinatory system, and his conclusions are twofold. First, Ajíbádé asserts that even with the growth of Islam and Christianity, divination among the Yorùbá is alive and well. Diviners are agents of memory who preserve history and reshape the present and future through their use of the past. Because diviners address such a vital concern of the community, the practice of divination has continued to the present. Second, the *odù* of Ṣàngó place a great deal of emphasis upon Ṣàngó's masculinity. In this way, the virility of the image of the historical Ṣàngó is reinforced.

Alternative representations of Ṣàngó within Yorùbáland are examined in the chapter of Marc Schiltz. Schiltz argues that the worship of Ṣàngó was tightly connected with the power of Ọ̀yọ́. The worship of Ṣàngó, as the patron deity of Ọ̀yọ́ royalty, was seen as a statement of loyalty by conquered communities. In essence, the worship of Ṣàngó was imposed upon border communities, such as Sábẹ̀ẹ́ and Kétu, that were outside the Ọ̀yọ́ heartland. However, a compromise was created between the royal cult of Ṣàngó and that of the preexisting thunder deity, Àrá. In Sábẹ̀ẹ́ and Kétu, Ṣàngó was defined as the wife of Àrá, a religious marriage of convenience precipitated by Ọ̀yọ́ imperialism. In this way Sábẹ̀ẹ́ and Kétu could demonstrate their loyalty to Ọ̀yọ́ through their worship of Ṣàngó, yet simultaneously maintain a sense of their own religious, and thereby political, autonomy through the continued worship of their indigenous thunder deity Àrá.

Diedre L. Bádéjọ considers the gender relationships of Ṣàngó mythology. She argues that the Ṣàngó embodied in Yorùbá oral tradition demonstrates the contradictory, though complementary, nature of the human condition. Tales of Ṣàngó demonstrate both dominance and submission, patriarchy and matriarchy. Such contradictions are an inherent feature of the universe, and one part of the pairing cannot exist without the other. Male cannot exist without female, just as Ṣàngó cannot live without his wives. This is naturally manifested as lightning and thunder (Ṣàngó) goes with rain and wind (Ọya). While Ṣàngó may be dominant at some moments, at other moments it is his wives who preempt him. One may see this in nature as rain and wind precede lightning and thunder.

The contribution of Dúrótoyè Adélékè examines images of Ṣàngó through the medium of film. Dúró Ládipọ̀'s *Ọba Kòso*, Wálé Ògúnyẹmí's *Ṣàngó*, Afọlábí Adésànyà's *Oṣé(e) Ṣàngó*, and Lérè Pàímọ́'s *Lákáayé*, represent both the mythic Ṣàngó and the historical Ṣàngó on the big screen. Adélékè interprets these counter-images as evidence of Ṣàngó's duality in accordance with Yorùbá cosmological thought. He argues that Ṣàngó can embody benevolence and destruction or justice and healing simultaneously. Thus, perhaps the mythic Ṣàngó and historical Ṣàngó can coexist simultaneously as well, without tension but rather complementation.

The art of Ṣàngó is investigated in the chapter by Stephen Fọlárànmí. Fọlárànmí illustrates the centrality of Ṣàngó in Yorùbá artistic production, both past and present. In precolonial and colonial Yorùbáland, Ṣàngó was among the *òrìṣà* whose shrines were overflowing with sacrificial objects, statuary, wands, ritual pots, mortars, and other symbols. This sort of ritualistic artistic production has continued in the postcolonial period, though on a reduced scale. In recent decades Yorùbá art has expanded into new media and found new non-ritualistic purposes. Numerous examples of such art can be found on both sides of the Atlantic, featuring Ṣàngó as the central, or sole, object of depiction. That Ṣàngó continues to inspire artists, even those who do not practice Yorùbá religion, is a testament to the importance and power of Ṣàngó.

The ambivalent images of Ṣàngó are addressed in another contribution from Akíntúndé Akínyẹmí through an examination of the *Ṣàngó pípè* and *odù ifá*. He concludes that the Ṣàngó represented in Yorùbá oral literature is the mythic Ṣàngó whose definition goes back to the roots of Yorùbá culture. Stories of the tyrannical and violent historical Ṣàngó do not come from Yorùbá oral mythology but are rather tales of the historical figure and Ọba Ṣàngó. This individual so identified with Ṣàngó that he adopted the name and attributes of his patron deity. Because of the Ọ̀yọ́ custom to deify an Aláàfin upon his death, the deified Aláàfin Ṣàngó was conflated with the deity Ṣàngó. This conflation became even deeper through the power of the written word when figures such as Johnson and Hethersett recorded tales of the historical Ṣàngó as that of the mythic one.

Yorùbá revivalism is evident within the religious practices of Ọ̀yọ́túnjí Village in the United States and is discussed in the chapter of Kamari Clarke. Clarke asserts that the Internet is playing a central role in how religious practitioners define authenticity and their religious practice. The syncretic Ṣàngó of Santería has had a significant impact on the image of Ṣàngó in the United States. But the transnational linkages brought by Internet communities have led to a process of Africanization within the United States. This process of Africanization has led some practitioners to purge Ṣàngó of his syncretic associations with Saint Barbara, arguing that this is not in compliance with the original and "true" definition of Ṣàngó within Yorùbá religion. This "sanitized" image of Ṣàngó can be reified through Internet contacts with Africa, something that people of African descent in the Americas were unable to do in previous eras.

The position of Ṣàngó in Trinidad is the subject of Stephen Glazier's contribution. Glazier demonstrates that Ṣàngó is becoming less significant in Trinidad than general "Òrìṣà work," or at least this is how it might appear in the public image of Trinidadian Òrìṣà worship. However, within the shrines themselves, a resurgence of Ṣàngó worship is in evidence. The issue of authenticity and syncretism has grown increasingly important. While scholars have debated the nature of New World African syncretism for decades, the tone and forum for such debate has shifted in recent years. Now worshippers themselves are heatedly debating what is the "purest" and most "authentic" image of Ṣàngó, what syncretic associations are acceptable, and which must be purged.

Ṣàngó, as Luis Nicolau Parés analyzes, is a central part of Afro-Brazilian religion for several reasons. First, because of the large number of Ọ̀yọ́ Yorùbá who were brought to Brazil, the *òrìṣà* most favored by the Ọ̀yọ́ Yorùbá became the most important deities in Brazil. Second, the priests and priestesses of Ṣàngó demonstrated a great deal of initiative and charisma in their dedication to Ṣàngó in Brazil. But third, one cannot discount the important theological issue of Ṣàngó's associations. Many Brazilians were, and continue to be, drawn to Ṣàngó because of his control of thunder, lightning, fire, justice, and royalty, which appeals to many worshippers. Within Afro-Brazilian religion Ṣàngó is said to have many qualities—some say twelve in accordance with his sacred number.

Laura Edmunds's chapter discusses the literary manifestation of Ṣàngó in Esmeralda Ribeiro's short story titled "A procura de uma Borboleta Preta" (In search of a black butterfly), published in a collection of short stories written by eight Brazilian women writers. According to Edmunds, a specific set of signs associated with Ṣàngó, such as the color red, stone celts or thunderbolts, and a double-headed axe, are well represented in

Esmeralda Ribeiro's story. For instance, she argues that the manifestation of Ṣàngó's association with the color red is symbolized in the red blouse, red sandals, red braids, and the flowing of blood down the legs of Leila, the lead character in the story. As for the importance given to the butterfly in "A procura de uma Borboleta Preta," Edmunds interprets this as an artistic representation of Ṣàngó's double-headed axe, which has a butterfly shape, as well as the thunderbolts used in his worship in Bahia.

Henry B. Lovejoy discusses the importation of *bàtá*—Ṣàngó's favorite drum—to Cuba by West African Yorùbá slaves. The time frame for his study begins with the uprising at Ìlọrin circa 1817 and ends when the last documented slave ship arrived in Cuba in 1867. Lovejoy contends that the twenty years before and after Ọ̀yọ́'s disintegration (c. 1836) coincided with many Yorùbá wars, shifting political alliances, and a continuous movement of people from West Africa to Cuba. He argues further that the largest influx of slaves of Yorùbá descent leaving the Bight of Benin for the Americas occurred in the first half of the nineteenth century. According to him, a sizable proportion of those enslaved Yorùbá who went to Cuba arguably came from Ọ̀yọ́, which can be demonstrated on the basis of surviving cultural practices and historical evidence associated with *bàtá* drums. Consequently, Lovejoy submits that, as an artifact and a cultural icon, the sizes, shapes, and components of the *bàtá* drum genre can be documented rather systematically. He concludes that, directly or indirectly, *bàtá* drums can serve as a model that can be projected backward into references of terms, such as *drum, batuque,* or *tambor,* found in early nineteenth-century documentation from Cuba and West Africa.

Ṣàngó priestess Olóyè Àìná Ọlọmọ provides us with a worshipper's perspective from the modern African Diaspora. Ọlọmọ argues that it is human-generated mythologies that have added false images to the true divine essence of Ṣàngó. Patriarchy has caused men to assign tales of virility to Ṣàngó's oral legends. In turn, this affects the gender roles of Ṣàngó's worshippers and priests/priestesses. However, we perceive Ṣàngó's divine might as light, sound, and bodily processes, and these natural manifestations of Ṣàngó occur outside of human social constructions. Ọlọmọ argues that tales of Ṣàngó's virility and womanizing should be rejected for the patriarchal stories they are.

In an interview with Michael Mason, Ṣàngó *olóshà* (priest) Ernesto Pichardo discusses his views of Ṣàngó and the *òrìṣà*. Pichardo has played a historic role in the development of *òrìṣà* worship within the United States. Pichardo argues that one may not truly know Ṣàngó. His mighty divine nature reflects manifestations beyond our counting. One's understanding of Ṣàngó is an ongoing process that can never cease as Ṣàngó continues to develop new ways to reveal himself. In this way, many definitions of Ṣàngó are superficial, Pichardo contends, because they are based only upon glimpses of Ṣàngó, not upon detailed nuanced understandings accumulated over an extended period of time. Even then, such a long-term understanding still remains incomplete.

———

As all our contributors reveal, the many images of Ṣàngó have produced an intense discussion among both scholars and practitioners. The mythic, historical, and syncretic Ṣàngó coexist in both peaceful and contentious fashions on both sides of the Atlantic. What is at stake in the debate is the quest for authenticity and legitimacy as peoples grapple with the legacy of slavery, colonialism, changes in identity, and the spread of Islam and Christianity. One might also say that it is a quest to (re)define the ambiguous terms of tradition and modernity and challenge common understandings of progress and stasis.[19] That a resurgence of polytheism is underway across the Atlantic world seems unquestionable, and Yorùbá religion figures quite prominently in this. As both our scholars and practitioners assembled here demonstrate, the worship of Ṣàngó is increasing and is truly global in scale. This is a testament to the strength of Yorùbá religion on both sides of the Atlantic and to the importance of Ṣàngó within it.

NOTES

1. Tóyìn Fálọlá and Matt D. Childs, eds. *The Yorùbá Diaspora in the Atlantic World* (Bloomington: Indiana University Press, 2004).

2. Henry John Drewal and John Pemberton with Rowland Abiodun, *Yorùbá: Nine Centuries of African Art and Thought* (New York: Harry N. Abrahams, 1989), 26.

3. Ibid., 26.

4. Sandra T. Barnes, ed., *Africa's Ògún: Old World and New* (Bloomington: Indiana University Press, 1989), 3, and Joseph M. Murphy and Mei-Mei Sanford, eds., *Òṣun across the Waters: A Yorùbá Goddess in Africa and the Americas* (Bloomington: Indiana University Press, 2001), 1.

5. Joyce Higginbotham and River Higginbotham, *Paganism: An Introduction to Earth-Centered Religions* (St. Paul: Llewellyn Publications, 2002), 6–7.

6. See I. Dlamini, "Zionist Churches from the Perspective of a Zionist Leader," in *Religion Alive,* ed. G. C. Oosthuizen (Johannesburg: Hodder and Stoughton, 1986), 209–10, and I. Dlamini, *Speaking for Ourselves* (Braamfontein, South Africa: Institute for Contextual Theology, 1985).

7. Barnes, *Africa's Ògún*, 1–26, uses this phrase in the introduction to her edited collection.

8. Walter Burkert, *Greek Religion*, trans. John Raffan (Cambridge, Mass.: Harvard University Press, 1985), 126–30, and C. Kerenyi, *The Gods of the Greeks* (1951) (London: Thames and Hudson, 2000), 116–17.

9. Jonathan Kirsch, *God against the Gods: The History of the War between Monotheism and Polytheism* (New York: Viking Compass, 2004), 7–12.

10. Samuel Johnson, *The History of the Yorùbás: From Earliest Times to the Beginning of the British Protectorate* (1921), O. Johnson, ed. (London: Routledge and Kegan Paul, 1966), 34–36; and A. L. Hethersett, *Ìwé Kíkà Ẹ̀kẹrin Lí Èdè Yorùbá* (Lagos, Nigeria: Church Missionary Society, 1941), 50–55.

11. A. B. Ellis, *The Yorùbá-Speaking Peoples of the Slave Coast of West Africa: Their Religion, Manners, Customs, Laws, Language, Etc.* (1894) (Oosterhout, Netherlands: Anthropological Publications, 1970), 46–56; J. Ọmọ́ṣadé Awólàlú, *Yorùbá Beliefs and Sacrificial Rites* (1979) (Brooklyn: Athelia Henrietta Press, 2001), 33–38; Judith Gleason, *Òrìshà Yorùbáland* (New York: Atheneum, 1971), 58–78; Harold Courlander, *Tales of Yorùbá Gods and Heroes* (New York: Crown, 1973), 79–82, 91–100, 193–95; Harold Courlander, *A Treasury of African Folklore* (New York: Crown, 1975), 201–10; and Ulli Beier, *Yoruba Myths* (Cambridge: Cambridge University Press, 1980), 20–32.

12. Some traditions do not count Odùduwà as the founder of Ọ̀yọ́, thus making Ṣàngó the third Aláàfin. See Funso Afolayan, "Kingdoms of West Africa: Benin, Ọ̀yọ́, and Asante," in *Africa*: vol. 1, *African History before 1885*, ed. Toyin Falola (Durham, N.C.: Carolina Academic Press, 2000), 171–72.

13. Gleason, *Òrìshà*, 60–61.

14. Awólàlú, *Yorùbá Beliefs*, 35.

15. Ibid., 34.

16. Akínwùmí Ìsòlá, "Religious Politics and the Myth of Ṣango," in *African Traditional Religion in Contemporary Society*, ed. Jacob K. Olupona (New York: Paragon, 1991), 93–99.

17. Joel E. Tishken, "Ethnic vs. Evangelical Religions: Beyond Teaching the World Religions Approach," *History Teacher* 33, no. 3 (May 2000): 315.

18. St. Barbara was removed from the Catholic calendar and her cults suppressed in 1969 in acknowledgment that "pious fiction was mistaken for history." Catholic Community Forum, "Patron Saints Index: Saint Barbara," N.d. (Jan. 30, 2005) http://www.catholic-forum.com/saints/saintb01.htm.

19. Jacob K. Olupona, "Introduction," in *Beyond Primitivism: Indigenous Religions and Modernity*, ed. Jacob K. Olupona (New York: Routledge, 2004), 2.

PART ONE

Ṣàngó in West Africa

CHAPTER TWO

The Place of Ṣàngó in the Yorùbá Pantheon

AKÍNTÚNDÉ AKÍNYẸMÍ

Òòṣà tí Ṣàngó ò le nà
Aré kọ́ ló le sá;
Ó mobìí f' Ólúkòso ni
Àjà 'nbà, ọba àwọn òòṣà

If any deity would escape being thrashed by Ṣàngó
It would not be because s/he was fast in running away
It must be because s/he knows how to appease Olúkòso
The mighty ruler, king of all (Yorùbá) divinities.

The above excerpt may be so ambiguous that it will be necessary right from the beginning of this chapter to define what I do *not* intend to do in this work, and then explain what I am really interested in doing. The purpose of this chapter is not to present Ṣàngó as the most important deity in Yorùbáland; neither is it my intention to determine the seniority of the Yorùbá deities. That issue has been addressed by a number of scholars, although they all have opposing views on the subject. For instance, while Bọ́lájí Ìdòwú holds the view that Òrìṣà-ńlá is the "supreme divinity" of Yorùbáland, N. A. Fádípẹ̀ sees Ifá as the "most universal . . . *òrìṣà* in Yorùbáland."[1] Bádé Àjùwọ̀n, for his part, presents Ògún as "First Among Equals" in the Yorùbá pantheon.[2]

If, on the other hand, one asks the worshippers of each of the other major Yorùbá deities which is the most popular of all Yorùbá deities, one finds that each group claims that its own deity is the most important one. Unfortunately, there is no common saying among the people which designates a particular divinity as the most important, except for the claim of their mythological stories that some sixteen Yorùbá divinities descended to earth.[3] Having said that, however, there are certain Yorùbá divinities which are generally acclaimed as more important than the others, and these might be called the major deities. According to Fadipe, the following divinities are universally worshipped everywhere in Yorùbáland on an annual basis: Èṣù, Ifá, Ọbàtálá, Ògún, Òrìṣà Oko, Ọṣun, Ṣàngó, Ṣànpọ̀nná, and Yemọja.[4] Since the order of seniority among these major deities is not very clear, I do not intend to contribute to the controversy by presenting Ṣàngó as the supreme Yorùbá deity.

What I intend to do, instead, is to discuss the elevated position occupied by Ṣàngó in the pantheon of the Yorùbá, and explore the reasons why the deity has been so popular not only in Nigeria but also among diasporic Africans in the New World. The chapter argues that the prestigious position that Ṣàngó occupies among the Yorùbá people stemmed from his association with Ọ̀yọ́ royalty and the institution of kingship, his specialized divination system made of sixteen sacred cowries (known as Ẹẹ́rìndínlógún), his commitment to social justice, his association with thunder and lightning, his military might and pursuit of the two main themes of a warrior culture—prowess and honor: the former being his attribute and the latter his aim—both of which his devotees believed were part of the reason he did an enormous variety of things toward their improvement and for humanity in general.

Ṣàngó is so much a part of Yorùbá life in general that, whether one likes it or not, one comes across his influence every day, in spite of his recognition as a purely Ọ̀yọ́ Yorùbá hero-deity. Leo Frobenius argues that the association of the deity with thunder and lightning is largely responsible for this, claiming that the deity is fearfully eulogized as "the Hurler of thunderbolts, the Lord of the Storm, the God who burns down compounds and cities, the Render of trees and the Slayer of men."[5] The evidence of Ṣàngó's dreadful nature is further documented in the following Yorùbá saying, which describes the sociopolitical position of the deity among the people:

Túláàsì la fi í fẹ̀ràn-an Ṣàngó,
   Túláàsì la fi í fẹ̀ràn
   ẹni tó bá ju ni lọ.
Ẹni tó bá bínú osùn,
Àfi tó bá fẹ́ẹ́ kun ata.

It is by force that one loves Ṣàngó,
  It is by force that one loves a person
  greater than oneself.
One who hates camwood ointment,
Is left with no other choice than to rub pepper over his/her body.[6]

Ṣàngó must have acquired this enviable position because of his strong link with Ọ̀yọ́ royalty and kingship. For instance, Ṣàngó was the state religion of the Old Ọ̀yọ́ Empire and the guiding deity of its political head, his royal majesty, the Aláàfin. Even in present day Ọ̀yọ́, the relevance of Ṣàngó to the success of the Aláàfin's administration cannot be overlooked. The Aláàfin himself is the chief celebrant in the daily worship of the deity as well as during the annual Ṣàngó festival.[7] The importance of the deity in Ọ̀yọ́ town compels every reigning Aláàfin to keep priestesses and priests of Ṣàngó in his palace, where the deity is regarded as the "father" of the king. For instance, the incumbent Aláàfin is praised by his royal bards as the "offspring of Ṣàngó":

Àjùwọ̀n, ọmọọ Ṣàngó
Aláàfin, èlè.
Ọba lọmọọ Adéyẹmí,
Ọmọ òòṣà.

Àjùwọ̀n, offspring of Ṣàngó
Aláàfin, gently.
Child of Adéyẹmí is the king,
offspring of the deity [Ṣàngó].[8]

The association of Ṣàngó with Ọ̀yọ́ royalty has thus spread the cult of the deity across the entire territory under the control of the Aláàfin, where he is regarded as a sacred and divine king. There is a clear similarity between the sacred and divine power of the Aláàfin, as epitomized in this aspect of his eulogy: *Ikú, bàbá-yèyé, aláṣẹ, èkejì òrìṣà* (Death, the-almighty-ruler, commander-and-wielder-of-authority, next in rank to the divinities) and the royal status of Ṣàngó, documented in the following excerpt of his praise names: *Olúwaà mi ò, ọba nirúnmọlè o ò, ọba tíí pọbaá jẹ* (My lord, this deity is a king, a king who has power to kill other kings).[9]

There is also the line of chiefs in the political setup of Ọ̀yọ́ town, under the Aláàfin, who are closely connected with the cult of Ṣàngó. At the head of the line is one of the high chiefs of Ọ̀yọ́—the ọtún èfà. The chiefs have dual roles: they are politically responsible to the Aláàfin, and, at the same time, they are fully involved in the affairs of the cult of Ṣàngó.[10] There is also a special priestess of Ṣàngó in the palace of the Aláàfin—*ìyá nàso*—who is charged with palace worship of the deity, and her assistant—*Ìyá Aàfin Ikú*—who is responsible for Ṣàngó's sacred ram (the horns of which are poetically compared to the thrust and parry of the thunderbolt).[11] According to Thompson, these palace customs reach climax at the annual *Bẹẹrẹ* festival[12] when a masked priest, said to represent Ṣàngó's own ancestral spirit, *Alákoro,* "perambulates the palace walls while gesticulating and, his robe of blazing red and shining mask of polished brass, looking like a crimson ghost. Before each of the main gates to the Aláàfin's palace he gestures to heaven and then to earth, to heaven and earth again, and moves on to the next point of blessing."[13]

Apart from those chiefs and royal priestesses of the Aláàfin, there are also the proper Ṣàngó title holders who are, strictly speaking, not politically connected with Ọ̀yọ́ royalty directly, but who are nonetheless highly respected in the community. They are the priests and priestesses of the deity—known generally as *adósù*—who handle all matters connected with Ṣàngó worship. Their leader, who is the chief priest of the cult, is known as *baálẹ̀ Ṣàngó*. There is also the Ọdẹ́jìn (known also as *Ayòòṣà* in some Yorùbá communities) who represents the deity Ṣàngó on earth. It is pertinent to note that the exclusive royal greeting of the Aláàfin—"*Kábíyèsí*"—(meaning literally: no-one-dare-challenge-or-question-your-authority) is also used for the Ọdẹ́jìn when he walks in the streets of Ọ̀yọ́.

Even in the Diaspora, where Ṣàngó is syncretized as Saint Barbara (as in Cuba) or as Saint Jeronimo (as in Brazil), his association with Ọ̀yọ́ royalty is still recognized, and he is subsequently accorded royal respect.[14] Ṣàngó is one of the most important Yorùbá divinities that has survived in the Diaspora up till today. He is regarded as a divinity of thunder and lightning in the Diaspora as in Nigeria, and he dances to the rhythm of *bàtá* drum beaten in a virile, warlike, dignified, and kingly fashion. Wande Abímbọ́lá has rightly observed that the cult of Ṣàngó dominates the Brazilian pantheon of divinities in Bahia.[15] According to him, the fact that the title of *ìyá nàso* (high priestess who keeps the royal temple of Ṣàngó in the palace of the Aláàfin at Ọ̀yọ́) was taken to Brazil and borne by several of the original Brazilian devotees of Ṣàngó clearly shows that the Ṣàngó that the Yorùbá slaves took to Bahia was from the palace temple at Old Ọ̀yọ́. The prominent divisions of the Bahian devotees of Ṣàngó—*Òpó Àṣẹ Àfọ̀njá* and *Òpó Àṣẹ Aganjú*—also emphasize the Ọ̀yọ́ origin of the Brazilian Xàngó. For instance, Aganjú was a prominent Aláàfin in Old Ọ̀yọ́ who strongly promoted the worship of Ṣàngó during his reign. In Brazil, the deity is hailed as "*Kábíèsílẹ̀*" like all the kings of Ọ̀yọ́:

Káwo, Kábíèsílẹ̀
   Emire míre sòroó be
Ẹ jẹ́ kóba bẹ̀nà wò.
Òréré baba
Ẹ jẹ́ kóba bẹ̀nà wò.
Ìlú ìlú sòro ó bé
   E jẹ́ kóba bẹ̀nà wò.
Òréré baba
Ẹ jẹ́ kóba bẹ̀nà wò.
   Káwo Kábíèsílẹ̀!

All hail your royal majesty
   A strange land is difficult to live in
Let the king keep watch over the streets.
The good father
Let the king keep watch over the streets.
This city is difficult to live in
   Let the king keep watch over the streets.
The good father
Let the king keep watch over the streets.
   All hail your royal majesty[116]

The integration of the cult of Ṣàngó into the political system of Ọ̀yọ́ probably dates back to the reign of the fourth ruler of Old Ọ̀yọ́, Aláàfin Ìtíolú Olúfinràn also known as Aláàfin Ṣàngó. This highly impetuous and warlike king was said to be responsible for the effective consolidation of the nascent Ọ̀yọ́ kingdom.[17] First, he refused to pay tribute that the Olówu of Òwu had demanded from his predecessor in office (Aláàfin Àjàká). Instead, he routed the Òwu army and proceeded to destroy the Òwu kingdom. Thereafter, Aláàfin Ṣàngó moved the capital of the emerging Ọ̀yọ́ kingdom from Òkò to Ọ̀yọ́-Ilé. This powerful king was described as a strong adherent of an earlier Yorùbá solar divinity, to whom lightning and thunder have been attributed. The name of that deity is Jàkúta, which means, "one-who-fights-with-stones" or "one-who-hurls-stones." It might be difficult to state categorically how Ṣàngó eventually became a Yorùbá divinity because of the discrepancies in the various versions of legends surrounding its deification. For instance, a reconstructed version of some of these legends claims that Aláàfin Ṣàngó was a powerful, self-willed, cruel, and tyrannical ruler, who was very well respected by his subjects.[18] In the end people became tired of his tyranny: his authority was challenged and his purpose thwarted by two of his courtiers. Out of frustration and annoyance, that version of oral tradition claims further, the king committed suicide by hanging himself on an *àáyán* tree. His opponents then taunted his supporters that the king had hanged himself. This led the supporters to seek the means of saving their faces: they went and procured some preparation by which lightning could be attracted. They set to work with this, with the result that lightning became frequent in and around Ọ̀yọ́: compounds and houses were often in conflagrations, and there were losses of lives and property. People became panic-stricken, and so were prepared for the next move by the supporters of Aláàfin Ṣàngó, who then came out with the story that the Aláàfin did not hang himself, he had only ascended to heaven, and that the resulting calamities from lightning were vengeance which Ṣàngó sent upon those who slandered him by saying that he hanged himself. As a consequence of this, a shrine was constructed for him, and later a temple was built for his worship on the traditional spot where he was said to have hanged himself, which was renamed Kòso (He-did-not-hang).

However, Ṣàngó devotees and the priestly house of Kòso in Ọ̀yọ́ have always argued against the version of oral tradition reconstructed above. Their own version of the deification of Aláàfin Ṣàngó states that the Aláàfin ascended to heaven by a chain which sprang from an *àáyán* tree in reaction to a few complaints from his subjects concerning his tyranny and high-handedness. They argue that, from heaven, Aláàfin Ṣàngó has since manifested his kingly authority with lightning and thunder. One may argue, therefore, that it was by a clever stroke that the identification between Jàkúta and Ṣàngó was registered in such a way that Aláàfin Ṣàngó practically usurped the place of Jàkúta in the Yorùbá pantheon. Some priests of strong, imposing character, perhaps someone who found a chance of replacing an indigenous divinity with an imperialistic one, must have been working upon the credulity of the people. Today, the sacred day of Jàkúta is still observed regularly by the devotees of Ṣàngó in Ọ̀yọ́, although this is done in connection with the worship of the deity Ṣàngó.

The cult of Ṣàngó was probably introduced to other parts of Yorùbáland from Ọ̀yọ́ during the sixteenth through eighteenth centuries with the expansion of the Aláàfinate's control. The Ọ̀yọ́ kingdom expanded steadily during the reigns of four succeeding Aláàfin (Àjàká, Aganjú, Olúàso, and Kọ̀rí), even though the internal conflict that Old Ọ̀yọ́ experienced later stopped the expansion abruptly. However, that was not until the kingdom had reached the banks of the river Niger in the north and extended a hundred miles south to Benin. When Old Ọ̀yọ́ was eventually invaded, the reigning Aláàfin Onígbogí and his people fled northward; and finally found refuge among friends in the Borgu region. Many others dispersed southward, where they established or augmented several towns throughout the Upper Ògùn river valley. Thus began approximately seventy-five years of exile, during which six Aláàfin reigned; a period that Smith has carefully reconstructed.[19] Repeatedly harassed and brought to their wits' ends while in exile, the Ọ̀yọ́ rulers realized that to survive amidst hostile neighbors, they must depend on their fighting strength and diplomatic alliances. Ọ̀yọ́ therefore developed a cavalry force which, by the late sixteenth century, had become the most important characteristic of its army. From this time until early in the nineteenth century, Ọ̀yọ́ kingdom expanded to its greatest power and size despite extreme internal political instability. It conquered portions of Borgu and the Nupe to the north and Dahomey to the southwest, and extended its influence over many southern kingdoms. The army directed its attention southwestward into the grassland, where it imposed the authority of the Aláàfin on the people of Ẹ̀gbádò, Ẹ̀gbá, Kétu, Weme, and Àjàṣẹ́ (Porto Novo). The early eighteenth century witnessed the subjection of the Fon kingdom of Dahomey to tributary status. By the 1750s, even the Asante kingdom came to feel the impact of the Ọ̀yọ́ imperial push. In northwestern Yorùbáland, the army of the Aláàfin also invaded the Ìbọ̀lọ́ and the greater part of Ìgbómìnà. By the second half of the nineteenth century, the new Ọ̀yọ́ Empire had reached its zenith of power. According to J. A. Àtàndá, the empire was "territorially the largest and politically the strongest kingdom ever established by a Yoruba potentate."[20]

The power of the Aláàfin thus transcended the city of Ọ̀yọ́ to the numerous provincial towns and villages in the expansive empire, where all his political and economic policies were regressed in religious terms. In this sense, the Aláàfin made leaders of the conquered towns and villages to realize that they derived their political authority from his divine power as the head of the empire. The cult of Ṣàngó, the state religion of Ọ̀yọ́ kingdom and the patron deity of the Aláàfin, its leader, must have been imposed on the provincial towns during the conquest. That was probably how the worship of Ṣàngó spread to other parts of Yorùbáland from Ọ̀yọ́, its original home. But for the extensive power of the Aláàfin and his control over the numerous provincial towns and villages, Ṣàngó might have remained an ordinary Ọ̀yọ́ historical figure, or at best, a little domestic divinity of Ọ̀yọ́.

One other factor that enhanced the popularity of the cult of Ṣàngó in Yorùbá society was the ability of the deity to resolve human problems through a system of divination known as Ẹẹrìndínlógún, which involves the casting of sixteen sacred cowries.[21] The Yorùbá are a deeply religious people and therefore have a strong belief in the existence of supernatural powers. These supernatural powers are believed to affect the everyday life of humans for good or ill. The Yorùbá conceive the supernatural powers as being of two types, good and evil. The good supernatural powers aid humans in their daily lives. They are, however, sometimes angry with a human if he/she neglects his/her duty either to his/her fellow human or to the supernatural powers. Therefore, to the Yorùbá people, the only way to find out when and for what reason the supernatural powers are angry is through divination. When the supernatural powers are angry, they can always be appeased with one form of sacrifice or another as pre-scribed by trained diviners.[22]

Ifá is the most popular Yorùbá system of divination.[23] With his great wisdom, knowledge and understanding, it is believed that Ifá coordi-nates human daily activities and the work of all the divinities through divination. In other words, Ifá serves as a middleman between the other divinities and the people, and between the people and their ancestors. If a man is being punished by any of the divinities, it is believed that the most logical thing to do is to turn to Ifá diviners for assistance. If a whole community is to make sacrifice to one of the divinities, this can be revealed only by Ifá. On the contrary, however, whenever a Ṣàngó devotee is faced with any problem that she/he cannot solve, she/he con-sults the Ẹẹrìndínlógún divination system of Ṣàngó, not Ifá. The Ṣàngó Ẹẹrìndínlógún divination system is very similar to the Ifá in several ways. It has its own *odù,* twelve in number, and each *odù* has its many verses (known as *ẹsẹ*). Although the whole corpus of Ẹẹrìndínlógún is not as large as the Ifá corpus, the services are nevertheless as effective. Com-pared to Ifá divination with its manipulation of sixteen sacred palm nuts or even the casting of its divining chain, sixteen-cowry divination is much simpler. However, memorizing the verses is as difficult and time consum-ing as learning those of Ifá.

Sixteen-cowry divination (Ẹẹrìndínlógún) is also popular among the descendants of Yorùbá slaves transported to the New World during the trans-Atlantic slave trade period. Although the system of divination is simpler than Ifá and held in less esteem among the West African Yorùbá, it is more important, more widely known, and more frequently employed than Ifá in the New World, where it is known as *Dínlógún.* This may be due to its relative simplicity; to the popularity of Ṣàngó, Yemọja, Òṣun, Èṣù, Oya, Ọbà, and other Yorùbá deities with whom sixteen cowries is associated, and to the fact that it can be practiced not only by men, but by women, who outnumber men in these cults in the New World, whereas only men can practice Ifá in West Africa. The cowries are cast on a woven tray (àtẹ) by the diviner, and the number of shells facing mouth-up are counted to determine the right odù through which Ṣàngó has decided to communicate with the client. Once the odù has been determined by the first toss of the cowries, the diviner begins to recite the verses that are associated with it. The verses contain the predictions and the sacrifices to be made, based on the case of a mythological client which serves as a precedent. Unless the diviner is stopped by the client, she/he recites all the verses that she/he has learned for that odù. As in Ifá divination, it is the client who selects the verse that is applicable to his/her own case; and, as in Ifá, more specific information can be obtained by making additional casts of the cowries to choose between specific alternatives (ìbò)[24] on the basis of the rank order of the odù that appeared.

Each of the various types of Ẹẹrìndínlógún systems of divination follows a tripartite process of prognostication, explanation, and control, which corresponds to the modern medical practice of diagnosis, prescription, and medication.[25] Through the Ẹẹrìndínlógún divination system, Ṣàngó is also able to resolve the crises and conflicts brought about on his devotees in particular, and humanity in general, by the interactions of benevolent and malevolent spiritual beings. Thus, he has the spiritual capability and competence to make great achievements in a way that would surpass the Ifá's. Through this divination practice, it is believed, Ṣàngó can manipulate, capture, and condense the complexities involved in the ordering of the universe. This is attested to by this aspect of Ṣàngó pípè (Ṣàngó praise poetry):

> Atáyéṣe-bí-olú,
>> N ò rí ọ lóde, n ò jẹ́ ròde.
>> Iré bá mi délé,
>> Ire n mo wá tọrọ.
>> Ire lèmi wá tọrọ lódòọ Ṣàngó.
>> Ire gbogbo tí n ó níí láyé
>> N bẹ lódòọ Ṣàngó
>> A-lànà-tẹẹ́rẹ́-wáyé
>> A-lànà-téẹ́rẹ́-kòrun
> Èyẹ òṣùpá lójúu sánmọ̀ ló wà.
>> Jẹ́ kó yẹ mí, Ṣàngó, Baálẹẹ Kòso.
> Àrẹ̀mú, Baálẹ̀ Agbòràndùn;
>> O ó gbọ̀ràn mi dùn,
>> Dákun má yà mí.

O-tóó-rọra-níjó-kan-ìpónjú,
Ọ̀já ìgbàlà o fi pọ̀n mí, má mà tú u.

One-who-mends-the-world-as-the-creator,
   I cannot embark on a journey without you.
   Success abides with me,
   Success is all I am here for.
   I am here to plead for success from Ṣàngó.
   All the good things of life that I will have
   Are within the reach of Ṣàngó
   He who makes a narrow path to the earth
   He who makes a narrow path to heaven
The beauty of the moon dominates the sky.
   Let me be favored, Ṣángó, lord of Kòso.
Àrẹ̀mú, the great avenger;
   Avenge for me,
   Please do not forsake me.
   It's you alone who can perfectly protect me in my trouble days,
Please do not remove the protection with which you covered me.[26]

The ability of Ṣàngó to resolve all kinds of human problems (both spiritual and physical) through his mysterious and mystical power is well documented in many verses of Ẹ̀ẹ̀rìndínlógún and Ifá. In the *Odù Òdí Mejì* of the Ẹ̀ẹ̀rìndínlógún corpus, for instance, a verse recalls how the Crocodile who could not deliver her children herself consulted Ṣàngó for assistance.[27] Ṣàngó shouted and all the children were born sooner than later. Another verse of the same *odù* recalls how Ṣàngó drove away the mysterious animal that had been killing the citizens of Ìjàgbà town, and became the deity that the people of Ìjàgbà worship today. Also, in *Odù Èjìlá Ṣẹ́bora* of the same Ẹ̀ẹ̀rìndínlógún corpus, it was reported that Ṣàngó opened the door of water a little and rain fell for seven days, causing leafless trees to sprout, dry rivers to flow again, and the people of Ìrè to prosper.[28] The following verse, taken from *Odù Ìrosùn Méjì* of Ifá literary corpus, confirms the extent to which Ṣàngó will go to protect his followers. The verse summarizes how the deity helped a man known as Ọlọ́gbun Àyíkú to conquer his enemies by throwing thunderbolts at them:

Irinó efọ̀n,
Ẹgbẹ̀rin ìwo;
Ònlénú efọ̀n
   Níí rìn wàràwàrà létí ọpa.

A díá fún Ọlọ́gbun Àyíkú.
Wọ́n ní kí ó rúbọ;
Wọ́n ní àwọn ọ̀tá ẹ̀
Fẹ́ pa á lọ́dún náà.
Wọ́n ní ó lọ dì mọ́ Ṣàngó.
Ó sì ṣe gbogbo rẹ̀.
Ibi tí àwọn ọ̀ta rẹ̀ gbé ń pètepèrò
Pé àwọn ó pa á,
Ni Ṣàngó bá lọ sọ ẹdùn àrá
sí ààrin wọn.
Ìgbà tí ó ṣẹ́gun àwọn ọ̀tá rẹ̀ tán,
Ó wá ń jó,
Ó n yọ̀.
Ó ní bẹ́ẹ̀ gẹ́gẹ́
Ni àwọn awo òún wí:
Irinó efọ̀n,
Ẹgbèrin ìwo;
Ònlénú efọ̀n
Níí rìn wàràwàrà létí ọpa.
A díá fún Ọlọ́gbun Àyíkú;
Èyí tí ó d'Ọlọ́gbun Àyílà.
gbirigbiri lórí ọ̀tá
Èrò Ìpo,
Èrò Ọ̀fà,
Ẹ wá bá ni láìkú kangiri.
Àìkú kangiri làá bọ̀kè.

Four hundred bush-cows,
Eight hundred horns;
Two hundred and eighty bush-cows
    Walk confidently near a snare.
    Divination was performed for Ọlọ́gbun Àyíkú.[29]
    He was asked to perform a sacrifice;
    He was told that his enemies
    wanted to kill him during that year.
    He was told to go and cling to Ṣàngó for protection.
And he did everything.
    As his enemies were conspiring together
    In order to kill him,
    Ṣàngó went and dropped thunderbolts
        in their midst.

After he had conquered his enemies,
He started to dance
He started to rejoice.
He said that was exactly
    what his diviners had predicted:
    Four hundred bush-cows,
Eight hundred horns;
Two hundred and eighty bush-cows
    Walk confidently near a snare.
    Divination was performed for *Ọlọ́gbun Àyíkú;*
Who would become *Ọlọ́gbun Àyílà.*[30]
    on top of stone
Travellers to *Ìpo*
Travellers to *Ọ̀fà*
Come and meet us alive and in good health.
One always finds the hill alive and in good health.[31]

The protective power of Ṣàngó is also well recognized and appreciated by his devotees in the Diaspora. Since Ṣàngó worshippers in the New World developed from a background of slavery in an atmosphere of bondage and suffering, the deity is often called upon in their chants as an instrument of deliverance. Thus we have in the following excerpt, a call to Ṣàngó by descendants of African slaves in Brazil for help:

Éníyé ọba sáré wá.
    Olúwa mi àrọ̀sẹ̀ẹ̀sẹ̀.
    Tòkò tòkò lọ́mọdéè Rèsé,
Ọba sáré wá.
    Olúwa mi àrọ̀sẹ̀ẹ̀sẹ̀.
    Tòkò tòkò lọ́mọdéè Rèsé,
Ọba sáré wá.
    Sáré wá bà mí o
Èrùjèjè, ọba sáré wá.
    Kábéèsí,
    Emire míre sòro bé e
E jẹ́ kóba bẹ̀nà wo.
Òréré baba,
Ìlú ìlú sòro ó bé.
E jẹ́ kóba bẹ̀nà wò.
Òréré baba,
    Kábéèsí.

O! king, hasten here
   My lord of the ceaseless rain
   Come with thunder stones to the aid of the children of *Ìrèsé,*
O! king, hasten here
   My lord of the ceaseless rain
   Come with thunder stones to the aid of the children of *Ìrèsé,*
O! king, hasten here
   Come and deliver me,
The fearful king, hasten here.
   Your royal majesty,
   A strange land is difficult to live in
Let the king keep watch over the streets.
The good father,
This city is difficult to live in.
Let the king keep watch over the streets.
The good father,
   Your royal majesty.[32]

Ṣàngó is presented in the above as an agent of deliverance of a people who have been deprived of their freedom but whose faith in the power of the deity to shelter and care for his own followers remains unshaken even in a foreign land. The worship of Ṣàngó in the New World has thus become a strategy for survival and for freedom. Therefore, the deity is seen in the Diaspora as a national heroic symbol as well as a protective spiritual leader.

The absolute control that Ṣàngó has over two forces of nature—thunder and lightning—and his ability to spit out fire from his mouth without being hurt have also contributed to his elevated status in the Yorùbá pantheon. Ṣàngó's magical power and association with fire is very well captured in the following lines of his praise name:

Iná lójú, iná lẹnu;
   A-gbéná-jó
   Adójúlé-kan-jà-lógun
   Abo ló mọnú ẹ, kó wá wí
   A-kunlé-polè.

He who spits out fire in his mouth and eyes;
   He who dangles a touch of fire while dancing
   One-who-singles-out-a-house-to-wage-war-with-it

If there is a woman who understands you, let her say so
One-who-burns-down-the-house-to-kill-the-thief.[33]

Also, in the Diaspora, the image of a metaphoric fire balanced on the head of devotees of Ṣàngó traveled with Yorùbá slaves to the New World, where actual dancing with loads of fire has been reported in Bahia, Brazil, by Vivaldo da Costa Lima:

> In the cycle of festival for Shàngó in the shrine of Sao Goncalo there is an impressive ceremony, only realized there, wherein the daughters of Shàngó, possessed by their orisha, dance with a vessel that contains material in flames, upon their heads. The fire does not harm them, nor does it burn the hands with which they secure the burning vessel. Later, while still moving in the dance, they eat flaming balls of cotton dipped in oil.[34]

Thompson has described the above comments as "miracles" to convince followers of Ṣàngó that spirit possession of his priests and priestesses is actual, not a sham.[35] Ṣàngó is a particularly powerful but difficult Yorùbá deity. An excerpt of his praise poetry testifies to his turbulent, violent, and unpredictable nature this way:

Lásán là ń bá o rìn
  A ò monú.
  Ako ló monú e, kó wá wí;
  Adójúlé-kan-jà-lógun.
  Abo ló monú e, kó wá wí;
  Akunlé-polè.

We are merely moving with you
  We do not know your thoughts.
  If there is a man who understands you, let him say so;
  One-who-singles-out-a-house-to-wage-war-with-it.
  If there is a woman who understands you, let her say so;
  One-who-burns-down-the-house-to-kill-the-thief.[36]

These aspects of Ṣàngó's nature demonstrate to his devotees as well as other members of the community what kind of deity he is, and therefore what he would normally expect of his followers. However, laws are not laws unless they are enforced. Only very few people would voluntarily obey laws the breach of which carries no reprisals. So, Ṣàngó's attributes also show his ability to enforce his own laws. Hence, we come across aspects of Ṣàngó's epithets such as the following:

Òkun ò ṣe é kojú ìjà sí
    Baálèè mi,
    Ta ló lè ko Ṣàngó lójú?
Èmi ò ní kò ọ́ lójú;
    Odò-nlá-tíí-gbónígèrè-tẹjatẹja.
    Alémọrẹrẹ-bí-eégún;
    Agbọ́mọ-lójú-yọkun-nímú;
    Abínú-falágbèdẹ-bọ̀gún;
    Ejò, abìjàwàrà.
    Atúnfun-àjé-ṣe-lógán,
    Afêtímọ́-bẹjú-èké-wò.

No one can confront the ocean
    My lord,
    Who can confront Ṣàngó?
I dare not confront you;
    The-mighty-river-that-drowned-the-master-fisherman-along-with-his-catch.
    He-who-pursues-a-child-like-the-Masquerade;
    He-who-slaps-a-child-violently;
    He-sacrifices-the-blacksmith-to-the-deity-Ògún-out-of-annoyance;
    The-snake-that-is-quick-to-fight.
    He-who-quickly-rearranges-the-intestines-of-the-witches,
    He-who-uses-lightning-to-expose-the-lair.[37]

The above is a conscious attempt by Ṣàngó praise singers to lift their deity onto a realm that would make him higher than other Yorùbá divinities.[38] He is presented, therefore, as a deity that is so powerful that no other divinities can share in his privileges. This is also a calculated attempt to make Ṣàngó's superhuman nature more complex.

This superhuman nature of Ṣàngo is further demonstrated in his military might and the ability to provide physical protection for his followers. The deified Aláàfin Ṣàngó was said to be a military genius. Oral tradition recalls that he personally led numerous military expeditions to expand the territory of his kingdom.[39] Being a great warrior, Aláàfin Ṣàngó never attacked his enemies when he was underprepared, and never attacked when on equal terms with them. He took time to train his own soldiers before leading them into the battlefield, and with every victory he was more firmly established on the throne. Nothing, however, could show Ṣàngó's military excellence and fame better than this aspect of his attributes:

Ọbaa Kòso!
    Bó bá fojú kan ogun,
    Gbàù, ni ó yìnbọn jẹ.
Ẹ̀tù tán, ẹ̀tù ò tán
Ọbaa Kòso,
    Máa dágọ̀ọ́ yìnbọn.
Ò-fagada-bọ̀dí-jagun.
    Bó bá jí, ara ogun níí pa.
Ò-fagada-buwọ́ọ̀jà-mọ́dọ̀;
    Agada pénpé
    ni fií béégún Alápiti lórí;
    Onísèkèrè̀ oògùn.
    A-bìta-mọ́ra-bí-ahéré;
    Fàì-bá-wọn-jà-kọni-lóminú;
    A-dì-ṣaka-ṣìkì-lọọọbi-ìjà;
Ọkùnrin-jógun-ó-sinmi;
    A-dé-kógun-ó-ró.
    Kò mọ̀ọ̀yàn nígbà ìjà.
    Abéléri-bẹ́rí, ọmọ Yemọja.
Ọbalúbẹ-tíí-dóoyin-ta-gbogbo-wọn.
Ọ̀wàrà-òjò-tíí-ṣú-pẹgbèje-èèyàn.

The king who reigned at Kòso!
    When he is confronted in war,
    He becomes a marksman.
He's not bothered about the availability of gun-powder or the non-availability of it
The king who reigned at Kòso,
    Just continue to take your shots.
He-who-stuck-cudgel-in-his-side-waist-to-wage-war.
    When he wakes up, he prepares for war.
He-who-swings-cudgel-to-fight-in-war;
    He uses a short cudgel
    to cut off the head of the *Alápiti* masquerade;
    One-who-has-his-charms-in-the-rattle.
    One-who-has-charms-and-armlets-stuck-all-over-his-body;
    You don't need to wage a war to create fear in the minds of your enemies;

One-who-is-fully-armed-when-going-to-battle;
The-mighty-man-who-silenced-the-war;
One-whose-arrival-in-battle-changes-the-course-of-war.
He has respect for nobody when in war.
He-who-helps-to-behead, child of Yemọja.
The-great-fighter-who-stings-everyone-like-bees.
The-mighty-storm-that-soaked-fourteen-hundred-people.[40]

While we may trace the enormous achievements of Ṣàngó in the military and spiritual spheres to his natural endowment, his pursuit of justice and fairness on earth was the result of his love for honor. To him, human existence on earth involved more than spiritual satisfaction and military protection. The most important article of need, worthy of being possessed by everyone on earth, is moral power—which one uses to strike a balance in all of one's social relations with the other members of the community to guarantee honesty, peace, and harmony on earth. It is for this reason that Ṣàngó is said to forbid lying and stealing, two offences that are against the Yorùbá ethical system. Ṣàngó loves the truth, but he hates liars, thieves, and other criminals. It is this ability of his to enforce truthfulness and good behavior that makes him a force to be reckoned with among the Yorùbá up till today. This is because people respect more readily any deity that can deal with practical problems quickly, efficiently, and effectively. Perhaps, it is only Ògún who shares this attribute with Ṣàngó in the Yorùbá pantheon.[41] Ṣàngó's commitment to truthfulness is presented by one of his praise singers this way:

Èbí sọ́sọ́ níí ṣe léyìn asòdodo,
   Ọkọ ìyáà mi.
   A-kò-má-tìkà-léyìn,
   A-kò-má-gbẹbọ-èké-rú.
   A-fàgbàná-runwó-èké-dànù;
   A-kunlé-polè;
   Ògírígirì,
   Ẹkùn-a-ṣeke.
   Onímú ń ṣímú, èké ń sá.
   Ṣàngó, a-kò-má-tìkà-léyìn.

He stands solidly behind a truthful person,
   My lord.
   He-who-refuses-to-support-the-wicked,
   He-who-refuses-to-accept-the-sacrifice-offered-by-the-liar.

He-who-makes-the-liar-bankrupt;
He-who-burns-down-a-house-to-kill-the-thief;
The terrible, rumbling one;
The leopard that devours the liar.
The owner of the nose turns up his nose, the liar trembles.
Ṣàngó, he-who-refuses-to-support-the-wicked-ones.[42]

It is a fact that has been proved often enough in Yorùbá society that Ṣàngó priests still have the secret power of directing lightning to identify and strike a thief or criminal. Therefore, today, people still use the secret power of Ṣàngó on critical occasions. For instance, if something very important is stolen, and every effort to locate the item through conventional means has failed, some people often go to Ṣàngó priests for help and quick resolution of their problems. Even when it comes to swearing or taking an oath in contemporary Yorùbá society, many people will think twice before using any of the symbols of Ṣàngó or Ògún. Such people will probably be more comfortable using either the Qur'an or the Bible. This is because only Ṣàngó and Ògún rule the minds of this people when it comes to swearing about serious matters in Yorùbá society. One may conclude therefore, that Ṣàngó will continue to retain his prestigious position in the Yorùbá pantheon for as long as he continues to rule and guard the conscience of those who believe in him.

What I have done in this chapter is to discuss the elevated position occupied by Ṣàngó in the Yorùbá pantheon. I have shown that Ṣàngó is one of the most powerful and universally worshipped Yorùbá deities both in Nigeria and in the Diaspora. The chapter has argued that the divinity owes this popularity to a number of variables. This has included, but has not been limited to, his association with Ọ̀yọ́ royalty and the institution of kingship, his magical power and ability to resolve human problems through a specialized divination system which involves the manipulation of sixteen cowries, his pursuit of justice and fairness, and ability to enforce truthfulness and good behavior, his military might and prowess, and his association with two dreadful forces of nature—thunder and lightning. These factors, and many more, have made Ṣàngó one of the foremost and highly respected Yorùbá divinities not only in Nigeria but also among descendants of African slaves in the Diaspora.

NOTES

1. See E. B. Idowu, *Olódùmarè: God in Yorùbá Belief* (New York: Frederick A. Praeger Publisher, 1963), 71; and N. A. Fadipe, *The Sociology of the Yorùbá* (Ibadan, Nigeria: Ibadan University Press, 1970; reprint 1991, 262.

2. Bádé Àjùwọ̀n, "Ògún: Premus Inter Pares," in *Proceedings of the First World Conference on Òrìṣà Tradition,* ed.Wándé Abímbọ́lá, held at the University of Ifẹ̀ (now Ọbáfẹ́mi Awólọ́wọ̀ University, Ilé-Ifẹ̀, Nigeria June 1–7, 1981), 449.

3. Oral traditions often give a confusing impression of the exact number of Yoruba divinities: sometimes they speak of *Ẹ̀rùnlójọ irúnmọlẹ̀* (700 divinities). We are told also that there are *igba irúnmọlẹ̀ ojùkòtún, igba irúnmọlẹ̀ ojùkòsì* (200 divinities of the right hand, and 200 divinities of the left hand—making 400) or *òkànlénú irúnmọlẹ̀* (401 divinities). There are still *òjìlélẹ́gbèje irúnmọlẹ̀ tí wọ́n ń lu ẹdan fún* (1,440 divinities for whom metal rods are sounded). See Idowu, *Olódù-marè,* 67–68.

4. Fadipe, *The Sociology of the Yorùbá,* 261–62.

5. Leo Frobenius, *The Voice of Africa,* vol. 1 (London: Hutchinson, 1913), 205.

6. Excerpt from Ṣàngó chant collected by the writer in Ọ̀yọ́ town, Nigeria, between 1989 and 1990.

7. See Akíntúndé Akínyẹmí, *Yorùbá Royal Poetry: A Sociohistorical Exposition and Annotated Translation,* Bayreuth African Studies Series (BASS), number 71 (Bayreuth, Germany: University of Bayreuth, 2004), 62–66, and Samuel Johnson, *The History of the Yorùbás from the Earliest Times to the Beginning of the British Protectorate* (London: Routledge, 1921), 34–36 and 149–52.

8. Excerpt taken from the praise names of the Aláàfin in Akínyẹmí, *Yorùbá Royal Poetry,* 360.

9. Excerpt from Ṣàngó chant collected by the writer in Ẹdẹ town, Nigeria, between 1989 and 1990.

10. See J. A. Atanda, *The New Ọ̀yọ́ Empire* (London: Longman Group, 1973), 20–21.

11. See Johnson, *The History of the Yorùbás,* 65, and Akínyẹmí, *Yorùbá Royal Poetry,* 70.

12. *Bẹẹrẹ* served as an annual festival to commemorate the re-thatching of the Aláàfin's palace. *Bẹẹrẹ* itself is a common savannah grass (*anadelphia arrecta*), but the ceremony by that name became an annual festival in Ọ̀yọ́ as a result of the need for leaders of provincial towns and villages to re-thatch the Aláàfin's palace annually as a symbol of their obedience to the authority of the Aláàfin. For details on the festival, see S. O. Babayemi, "Bẹẹrẹ Festival in Ọ̀yọ́," *Journal of Historical Society of Nigeria* 7, no. 1 (1973): 121–23.

13. Robert Farris Thompson, *Flash of the Spirit: African and Afro-American Art and Philosophy* (New York: Vintage Books, 1984), 85.

14. According to Christine Ayorinde, in Toyin Falola and Matt D. Childs, eds., *The Yorùbá Diaspora in the Atlantic World* (Bloomington: Indiana University

Press, 2004), 219, "Chàngó . . . is linked to the virgin Santa Bárbara" in Cuba. She argues that an examination of the saint's legend reveals the logic behind this: Santa Bárbara chose martyrdom, and her father was struck dead by lightning as a punishment for killing her when she refused to give up her Christian faith. Catholic lithographs depict Santa Bárbara wearing a red cloak and crown, and carrying sword. The author concludes that the saint's connection with royalty and valor identifies her with the Aláàfin of Ọ̀yọ́, among whose attributes are the color red, a sword, and a lightning stone.

15. Wande Abimbola, "The Yorùbá Traditional Religion in Brazil: Problems and Prospects," in *Seminar Series,* Number 1.1 (Ilé-Ifẹ̀, Nigeria: Department of African Languages and Literatures, University of Ifẹ̀, 1976–77), 15.

16. Ibid., 33–34.

17. Johnson, *The History of the Yorùbás,* 149.

18. Idowu, *Olódùmarè,* 90.

19. R. S. Smith, *Kingdoms of the Yorùbá* (London: Methuen, 1969), 25–58.

20. Atanda, *The New Ọ̀yọ́ Empire,* 12–13.

21. For details on this system of divination, see William Bascom, *Sixteen Cowries: Yorùbá Divination from Africa to the New World* (Bloomington: Indiana University Press, 1980).

22. See Wande Abimbola, *Ifá: An Exposition of Ifá Literary Corpus* (Ibadan, Nigeria: Oxford University Press, 1976), 151–94.

23. For more information on *Ifá,* see Abimbola, *Ifá,* and William Bascom, *Ifá Divination: Communication between Gods and Men in West Africa* (Bloomington: Indiana University Press, 1969).

24. The *ibò* are used by diviners to translate their broad pronouncement into concrete details. The *ibò* are mere lots based on the two opposite alternatives of "yes" and "no." It is the belief of the diviners that their client's inner *orí* (destiny) will make the right choice of alternatives for him/her when lots are cast. The commonest and simplest form of *ibò* is a pair of cowry shells tied together and a piece of animal bone. Generally speaking, the cowry shell stands for "yes" while the piece of bone stands for "no."

25. David Ogungbile, "Ẹẹ̀rìndínlógún: The Seeing Eyes of Sacred Shells and Stones," in *Ọ̀ṣun across the Waters: A Yorùbá God in Africa and the Americas,* ed. Joseph M. Murphy and Mei-Mei Sanford (Bloomington: Indiana University Press, 2001), 190.

26. Excerpt from Ṣàngó chant collected by the writer in Ọ̀yọ́ town, Nigeria, between 1989 and 1990.

27. Bascom, *Sixteen Cowries,* 582–665.

28. Ibid., 733–36.

29. This name literally means "the owner of the deep pit into which one rolls and dies."

30. The new name literally means "owner of the deep pit into which one rolls but not to perdition." The ability of Ṣàngó to protect his devotees is reflected in

the name change when he saved his client, Ọlọ́gbun Àyíkú, who was going to be killed by his enemies. To commemorate that, Ifá changed the name of the man to Ọlọ́gbun Àyílà.

31. Abimbola, *Ifá*, 155–56.

32. Abimbola, "The Yorùbá Traditional Religion in Brazil," 34–35.

33. Excerpt from Ṣàngó chant collected by the writer in Ẹdẹ town, Nigeria, between 1989 and 1990.

34. Quoted by Thompson, *Flash of the Spirit,* 87.

35. Ibid.

36. Excerpt from Ṣàngó chant collected by the writer in Ẹdẹ town, Nigeria, between 1989 and 1990.

37. Ibid.

38. This is a common trend in polytheism, i.e., Yahweh's ascendency in Jewish religion and Hare Krishna in Hinduism.

39. Johnson, *The History of the Yorùbás,* 149.

40. Excerpt from Ṣàngó chant collected by the writer in Ọ̀yọ́ town, Nigeria, between 1989 and 1990.

41. Ajuwon, "Ògún: Premus Inter Pares," 441–44.

42. Excerpt from Ṣàngó chant collected by the writer in Ọ̀yọ́ town, Nigeria, between 1989 and 1990.

CHAPTER THREE

The Practice and Worship of Ṣàngó in Contemporary Yorùbáland

ÀRÌNPÉ GBẸ́KẸ̀LÓLÚ ADÉJÙMỌ̀

The Origin of Ṣàngó

Ṣàngó, the god of thunder, is one of the major deities worshipped among the Yorùbá people of southwestern Nigeria and their descendants in the diaspora. According to Isola,[1] different types and modes of worship of Ṣàngó have emerged as the deity has been transported from one region of the world to another. The myth of the origin of Ṣàngó itself is controversial. The first school of thought about the origin of Ṣàngó claims that Ṣàngó was one of the primordial deities that descended from heaven. Notable among scholars in this school of thought are Adeoye[2] and Isola.[3] Adeoye asserts that Ṣàngó's origin cannot be pinned down to mortal parentage but to the Ifá divinatory verse, Ọ̀yẹ̀kú-Méjì, that brought Ṣàngó to the earth.[4] Adeoye claims that the primordial Ṣàngó is also referred to as Ayílégbẹ̀ẹ́-Ọ̀run, who is worshipped on Jàkúta day, the fifth day of the Yorùbá traditional week.

The second school of thought claims that Ṣàngó was a human being deified as a god. Notable among scholars in this school of thought are Herthersett, Johnson, Ogunbowale, Daramola, Ladipo, and Canizares. They claim that Ṣàngó was the fourth Aláàfin of Ọ̀yọ́, who later hanged himself, and as a result, he was deified by his followers. This was Aláàfin Ìtíolú, the son of Ọ̀rányàn.[5] According to Isola, Herthersett's position about Ṣàngó, which was later embraced by almost all scholars who wrote after him, was born out of Christian sentiment. Though Adeoye

44

highlights eight major differences between the primordial Ṣàngó and Aláàfin Ìtíolú who was later deified as Ṣàngó, in Òyó many people still mix up the two.[6] Isola brings to the fore the reasons why Aláàfin Ìtíolú was deified as Ṣàngó.[7] In his own account, Aláàfin Ìtíolú of Òyó-Ilé (Old Òyó) had the same disposition to life as the primordial Ṣàngó, hence, the name Ṣàngó became his cognomen. However, it is apparent through our findings that Herthersett's meaning of Ọba Kò so (the king did not hang) is quite different from the devotees' meaning of Olúkòso, that is, Olú of Kòso, an area where the Aláàfin later departed to the world beyond.[8]

Herthersett's opinion about Ṣàngó's myth seems sentimental, probably because of his status as a missionary of the Christian Missionary Society (C.M.S.), whose main aim was to propagate Christianity and present anything that is opposed to Christian doctrines as evil. Hence, in order to present Ṣàngó as evil, Herthersett perhaps distorted the myth to bring out his own view. Thus, Baba Canizares, commenting on the worship of Ṣàngó in Cuba, also claims that the fourth Aláàfin of Òyó, who was apotheosized as a deity, is being worshipped in Cuba as "Chàngó."[9] But in Nigeria where Ṣàngó takes it root, our research findings show that Ṣàngó, the god of thunder, predated Aláàfin Ìtíolú, the fourth Aláàfin of Òyó.

Ṣàngó is worshipped all over Yorùbáland, but the data for this research were drawn from four major towns where he is still worshipped as a prominent or the most prominent deity. The towns are Òyó, Ẹdẹ, Ìbàdàn, and Ìṣẹ́yìn. In an interview with one Ṣàngó priest, the Ẹlẹ́gùn of Òyó, Chief Ṣàngórìndé Ibúọmọ, It was claimed that the two mythologies about the origin of Ṣàngó are true, but he opined that the worship of Ṣàngó, the god of thunder, predated the birth of Aláàfin Ìtíolú who later was deified as Ṣàngó. According to all our informants, the primordial Ṣàngó came with other primordial gods. He was worshipped on Jàkúta day, the day assigned to him by the assembly of Yorùbá gods. The primordial Ṣàngó was a troublesome and fierce god.[10] He was in charge of justice. He fought the mischievous and the wicked ones with stones, which Olódùmarè (God, the Creator) gave to him as his own power. Though our informants claimed that the primordial Ṣàngó was in charge of lightning, the control of thunder and lightning was later hijacked by the deified Ṣàngó, to whom everybody now ascribed the power to rain thunder and brimstone on his perceived enemies.[11] The chief priest of Ṣàngó, interviewed at Òyó, claimed that the use of thunder and fire to combat an enemy came as a result of the attempt made by Aláàfin Ìtíolú, the apotheosized Ṣàngó, to stop Ṣàngó's enemies from spreading the rumor that Ṣàngó hanged from a tree. As Ṣàngó's friends retaliated by sending thunder and fire to his enemies, enemies in turn ran to the friends for help, and the usual slogan then was *Baba, ẹ gbà wá o!* ("Father, save-us"), which was later nominalized as "*Baba mọgbà*." Even today, the priests of Sango are referred to as *Baba mọgbà* in all Yorùbá regions where Ṣàngó is worshipped.

Origin of Ṣàngó Worship: Our Submission

From the foregoing, it is apparent that there are some beliefs about a primordial Ṣàngó and his status as a god. First, it is believed that Ṣàngó is the god of thunder and lightning. Second, there was a primordial Ṣàngó in the mythologies, who came with a chain from heaven to earth in the midst of other gods and goddesses. If the myth of the creation of the earth reported by Adeoye[12] is to be considered, each of the primordial gods, including the primordial Ṣàngó, has his or her own devotees allotted to him or her by Ọ̀rúnmìlà. Third, the myth about the relationship of Ṣàngó with the other gods such as Ọ̀rúnmìlà, as narrated in *Odù Òtúá-Oríkọ̀, Ọ̀wọ́nrínyẹ̀kú, Ìká-Méjì,* and *Òkànràn-Méjì,* shows that Ṣàngó had something in common with the other primordial gods. This corroborates the fact that Ṣàngó as a god predated Aláàfin Ṣàngó, referred to by Herthersett and other scholars in the same school of thought with him. For instance, the myth about the relationship between Ṣàngó and Ọ̀rúnmìlà says that there is a covenant between Ṣàngó and Ọ̀rúnmìlà. Similarly, the myth about the enmity between Ṣàngó and Ògún regarding how Ṣàngó deceitfully snatched Ọya, Ògún's favorite wife, because of Ṣàngó finesse, corroborates the fact that Ṣàngó existed before Aláàfin Ìtíolú. This myth also encapsulates the source of Ṣàngó's power over lightning.

The fifth point to be considered about the origin of Ṣàngó is the existence of Aláàfin Ṣàngó. All our informants agreed that one Aláàfin Ṣàngó existed in Old Ọ̀yọ́ and that he was a devotee of Ṣàngó. The general belief is that the Aláàfin exhibited the attributes of Ṣàngó; hence, he was given the *oríkì inagijẹ* (sobriquet) Ṣàngó.[13] But the controversial issue about this myth is the mystery behind his death. Herthersett, Canizares, and Ogunbowale, in their individual accounts, say that he died hanging on an *àáyán* tree in Kòso before his friends deified him.[14] But according to oral tradition, Aláàfin Ṣàngó never hanged himself, but simply disappeared mysteriously because he could not bear the shame of being rejected by his relatives and subjects.

Be that as it may, the myths about all Yorùbá gods and goddesses always associate them with one particular Yorùbá town or another at a point in their life. For instance, the Yorùbá will always trace Ọya to Irá town, while Ògún is traced to Ìrè. Hence the saying,

   i. *Ọya wọlẹ̀ nílé Irá*
      ii. *Ìrè kì í ṣelé Ògún*
      Ó yà débẹ̀ mẹmu ni
   i. Ọya disappeared into mother earth in Ira
      ii. Ìrè is not Ògún's home of origin
      He only stops there for palm-wine

One may infer, therefore, that while the primordial Ṣàngó sojourned on earth, he was in Ọ̀yọ́ at a particular time, where he was worshipped as the royal god of the Aláàfin. Even today Ṣàngó is still one of the famous gods being worshipped and linked to the Aláàfin royal lineage. Because of this, one Aláàfin who took after Ṣàngó's attributes is now metaphorically addressed as Ṣàngó. He also was a devotee of Ṣàngó. Considering the fierce attitude of the fourth Aláàfin and the circumstances surrounding his death, it is not surprising that he too was deified and turned to an object of worship. The above action finds a corroboration in Adelugba's view that man has the tendency to anthropomorphize and that the defensive impulse of man is to concretize and make the invisible visible.[15]

From the foregoing, the argument about Ọ̀yọ́ as the origin of Ṣàngó the god of thunder could be perceived in two ways. One, the primordial Ṣàngó perhaps ended his sojourn on earth at Ọ̀yọ́. Two, the fourth Aláàfin, who was later deified as a devotee of Ṣàngó, was the one who later made the worship of Ṣàngó to become more elaborate because of his control over lightning, fire and thunder, and the use of weapons against his enemies after he was deified. Hence, the opinion that Ṣàngó could not be worshipped without being linked to Aláàfin Ṣàngó will be upheld.

However, the practice and worship of Ṣàngó differ from place to place. One of our informants, Chief Ṣàngórìndé Ibúọmọ, has this to say: *Ẹ mọ̀ pé mo sọ pé Ṣàngó kanlẹ̀ máa ń lọ fara han ẹlẹ́gùn pé ohun ti ẹ ó ṣe nìyí. Bí ó ṣe ń fara han ẹnikọ̀ọ̀kan ní ìlú kọ̀ọ̀kan yàtọ̀.* ("You know I have said that Ṣàngó deliberately reveals himself to his spirit-carrier and tells him what to do. The way he reveals himself to the spirit-carrier in each town is different.") This statement accounts for some of the noticeable differences in the mode of practice and worship of Ṣàngó in places where he is worshipped today.

The Worship of Ṣàngó

The annual worship of Ṣàngó takes place in a shrine, which is believed to be sacred to Ṣàngó worshippers. It is worthy of note that both the initiates and the non-initiates can worship Ṣàngó. But the non-initiates are mere spectators who are felicitating with friends and loved ones who are Ṣàngó devotees. The sacred aspect of the worship of Ṣàngó is restricted to the *adósù Ṣàngó* (Ṣàngó priest / priestess). The *adósù*s are initiated into the cult of Ṣàngó, and they are usually dedicated worshippers. Therefore, they are normally referred to as *ìyàwóo Ṣàngó* (Ṣàngó's wives). At all levels of worship, an ordinary devotee cannot take active part in the worship of Ṣàngó. He or she could only be a nominal participant.

Ṣàngó could be worshipped at five different levels, namely: the early-morning worship, the Jàkúta-day worship, the revelation worship, the twenty-one-day worship, and the annual Ṣàngó festival. The early-morning worship is essentially an individual affair. A priest who has a shrine in his house does this with his family members. The Jàkúta-day worship is done every fifth day, also by individual priest, but in a more elaborate way than the early-morning worship. The twenty-one-day worship is also an elaborate worship which marks the day that primordial Ṣàngó disappeared from Ifẹ̀ Oòyè en route to Àtìbà.[16] The revelation worship is another form of individualized worship. Ṣàngó may decide to reveal himself to someone through dream or in his or her adventure on earth. If this happens, it is compulsory for such an individual to worship Ṣàngó. Ṣàngó will dictate the items of sacrifice to the individual, and when the objects should be sacrificed to him. The annual festival is an event that brings together all Ṣàngó worshippers in a particular town. Our research has also revealed that Sango could be personalized. For instance, in each of the royal families of Ẹ̀dẹ town, Ilé Dáódù, Ilé Dúródọlá, Ilé Ọ̀jẹ́tìmí, and Ilé Babańlá, the Ṣàngó shrine is erected in the family compound. The generalized objects usually found at the shrine are:

1. *apèrè*, a wooden bowl in which thunderbolts are kept;
2. *odó*, a mortar;
3. *arugbá*, a carved female figure, in kneeling posture carrying a bowl;
4. *osé*, a wooden axe having two blades;
5. *ìkòkò*, an ornamented clay pot;
6. *ṣẹ́ẹ́rẹ́*, a small long-necked gourd containing seeds of the *canna* plant, used as a rattle; and
7. *ìwo*, a horn.

We, however, observed that the objects of worship vary from shrine to shrine. For instance, at the shrine of Ọbabìnrin Ṣàngó, Kẹ́hìndé Òjó, a priestess of Ṣàngó based in Ìbàdàn, we also noticed the following objects in addition to the items previously listed:

1. *ère àkùkọ*—a carved cock;
2. Ṣàngó's painting on the wall;
3. mat;
4. different types of mask;
5. a magical box;
6. red cloth;
7. bottles; and
8. gourd of water.

Personalized Worship

The personalized worship of Ṣàngó is peculiar to Ṣàngó priests, priest-esses, and devotees. Each *mọgbà* and priest/priestess makes sure he/she worships Ṣàngó every day with *orógbó* (bitter kola). Although the daily worship is not elaborate, it always involves chanting (*Ṣàngó pípè*).[17] The priest/priestess salutes Ṣàngó and pays homage to him during this time, and hands over his/her life and all that he/she is going to do daily to Ṣàngó. An account is given by Isola[18] of Ọdéjìn, a priest of Ṣàngó at Ọ̀yọ́, who worshiped Ṣàngó in his presence:

O gbọ́ Ṣàngó
   Bá a bá jí, Olú là á kí
   Bàbáyèyé!
   O jíire ọmọ Òòṣàásè̩
   O jíire, Ṣàngó
   O jíire, Bàbáyèyé . . .
   Ìbà è é hunmọ
   Má jẹ̀ẹ́ kó hun mí o
   Àṣẹ iná niná fi í múgi o
   Fàṣẹ sí mi lẹ́nu Ṣàngó
   Àṣẹ oòrùn loòrùn fi í là
   Fàṣẹ sí mi lẹ́nu ọmọ Òòṣàásè̩.

I trust you are hearing me, Ṣàngó
When we wake up, we salute the Lord

The Almighty
Good morning, son of Òòṣàásẹ̀
Good morning Ṣàngó
Good morning, the Almighty . . .
He who pays due homage is safe
May I be safe too.
It is by its peculiar power that fire consumes the wood
Put the magic power of utterance—fulfillment
On my tongue, Ṣàngó
It is by its peculiar power that the sun rises
Put the magic power of utterance—fulfillment
On my tongue, son of Òòṣàásẹ̀.[19]

After the homage, sacrifice of *orógbó* will be offered to Sango, and then the priest can continue the day's activity, believing all is going to be well. But when a Ṣàngó priest invites other priests and devotees to come and worship with him, the audience will be feasted with Ṣàngó's favorite food: *àmàlà* (yam flour pudding) and *gbẹ̀gìrì* soup (peanut soup) with *àkùkọ* (rooster). The personalized worship of Ṣàngó can also extend to the worship made on behalf of the child of a devotee who is getting married. Even in contemporary society, there have been cases of such worship, especially in the Ọ̀yọ́-speaking area of Yorùbáland. This act of worship transcends the educational status of such devotees.

The Revelation Worship

Adeoye claims that if Ṣàngó has revealed himself to a particular individual, such a revelation can lead to a type of Ṣàngó worship.[20] Ṣàngó devotees also can provoke a revelation appearance or visitation through worship. This type of worship is peculiar to some parts of Ọ̀yọ́-speaking areas of Yorùbáland. For instance, in Òtu, a town in Ọ̀yọ́ north, the devotees believe that Ṣàngó visits his devotees every three years. Therefore, at a certain period, the *Ẹlẹ́gùn* will be secluded in a thick forest.[21] There, he will make sacrifices and worship Ṣàngó. The *Ẹlẹ́gùn* will be there for seven days, during which Ṣàngó might reveal himself. On the seventh day, the devotees will now go and receive the *Ẹlẹ́gùn* at the entrance of the forest; they will then dance round the town for seven days as the *Ẹlẹ́gùn* prays for everybody he meets on his way.

Jàkúta-Day Worship

According to our findings, the Jàkúta-day worship is always very elaborate. This takes place every fifth day. In the worship of Ṣàngó on a particular Jàkúta-day which I participated in, the different aspects of worship were painstakingly performed by the priestess of Ṣàngó, Ọbabìnrin Ṣàngó, Kéhìndé Òjó. It should be stressed that it is an abomination for a devotee to pass through the shrine of Ṣàngó without paying homage to the god of thunder. The mere sight of the shrine and object that symbolize Ṣàngó calls for salutation and homage. Therefore, the first aspect of worship on Jàkúta-day entails salute or homage to Ṣàngó, followed by prayer or supplication. The excerpt below is a priestess's salute to Ṣàngó at the time of this research:

Bọ́mọ ó bá lahùn
  Baba níí kọ́ perí
  Mo júbà baba mi Olúòso
  Òna-mọ nílagbà ikú
  Ẹlẹ́gbèrún àkáábá
  Kábíyèsí, ọkọọ̀ mi
  Ṣàngó, Olúkòso arẹ̀kújayé
  O ò jíire bí o?
  Ṣàngó, gbè mí lónìi o
  Ewélérè, ọkọọ̀ mi
  Má jóde òní ó hun mí
  Jẹ́ ó yẹ mi kalẹ́ tọmọtọmọ.

  If a child wants to talk
  He first calls on his father
  I salute you my father Olúòso
  One-who-beats-a-child to death with the *ilagbà* whip
  The one with one thousand charmed padlock
  Kábíyèsí, my husband
  Ṣàngó, Olúkòso who wears the mask all-about
  Good morning
  Ṣàngó be in my support today
  Ewélérè,[22] my lord
  Do not let me fall into trouble today
  Let it be well with me and my children.

Immediately after this, the priestess throws nine pieces of *orógbó* on the floor as a way of knowing whether she should continue with the sacrifice or not. The moment Ṣàngó confirms that the sacrifice should continue, other aspects of the ritual performance then follow.

The metamorphosis stage is the second phase of the salute/homage aspect of worship. The sacrificial items will be picked and shown to Ṣàngó one after another. Libation now follows as the priest slaughters the sacrificial ram, and its blood poured on the thunderbolt in the *apẹ̀rẹ̀*. The blood is to appease Ṣàngó. The belief is that Ṣàngó visits his devotees during worship and that the moment he sights the blood of the ram, he will be pleased to bless them.

The theatrical aspect of worship is the stage when the spirit of Ṣàngó is seriously invoked through the chanting of *Ṣàngó pípè*. This aspect of worship brings to the fore the glamorous attributes of Ṣàngó. As Sango is praised, the *Ẹlẹ́gùn* (spirit-medium) will be possessed. There are times that a non-initiate may be possessed, but usually if a non-initiate is possessed, palm oil will be given to him or her as an antidote. Dancing and drumming of *bàtá* music also form an integral part of this theatrical stage. The Jàkúta-day worship usually ends with a time of music, dancing, and feasting. As the people are dancing, they always remember to bring their heart's desires to Ṣàngó in form of prayer.

The Annual Worship

The annual worship takes place during either the dry season or the rainy season. However, the most elaborate is the rainy season festival. There are six features of the annual festival as highlighted by Isola:[23]

1. The period of the festival is long.
2. Sacrifices are offered at the different shrines.
3. There are sumptuous feasting.
4. There is prolonged chanting of *Ṣàngó pípè*.
5. There is elaborate dancing to *bàtá* drums.
6. There is usually a magical display by the *Ẹlẹ́gùn*.

The period of the festival differs from one place to another. For instance, the annual worship of Ṣàngó at Ọ̀yọ́, which normally takes place over a long period, has been subsumed to a day. A week is now dedicated to the worship of all deities in Ọ̀yọ́, and Ṣàngó is given just a day. One thing that is common to the worship, whether it is going to be for a day or longer, is that the worship must start on a Jàkúta day. The annual worship of

Ṣàngó in Ìṣéyìn and Ọ̀yọ́ takes place in a location called Kòso, the place where the apotheosized Ṣàngó departed from the earth.

Contrary to the above, the annual worship of Ṣàngó is still elaborately celebrated in Ẹdẹ town. The celebration runs through a week. The announcement of the annual worship usually takes place twenty-one days before the festival. The long notice allows Ṣàngó devotees and their relations in the Diaspora to come home for the festival. Apart from this, there are some preparations that must be made by the *baálẹ̀* or *mógàjí* of every compound in the town. The preparation involves all the high chiefs, clan chiefs (*mógàjí*), and the Tìmì, the paramount ruler of Ẹdẹ himself. The *mógàjís*, on behalf of members of their compounds, must go and present gifts in cash and kinds to the king. Food items and rams are usually part of such gifts.

Stages in the Annual Worship of Ṣàngó in Present Day Ẹdẹ

Day 1: *The Dipping Day*

This is the beginning of the festival. The *mogbà* goes to River Ọ̀ṣun and dips a calabash into it to fetch water. The River Ọ̀ṣun is specifically chosen because Ọ̀ṣun was one of the wives of the primordial Ṣàngó. This act is usually referred to as *Ojọ́ ìtagbè bodò* ("The day of dipping the gourd into the river"). There is the belief that rain will fall only after this ceremony. The fetched water is medicinal. Immediately the water is brought to the shrine of the *Ìyápọ̀* (spirit-medium), who is possessed on the first day of festival; women who desire children from Ṣàngó will come and drink of it.

Day 2: *The Sacrifice Day*

The second day is earmarked for a more elaborate worship of Ṣàngó. This day is set aside for priests and priestesses to offer sacrifices to Ṣàngó in their respective shrines situated in their compounds. The day is dedicated to making rituals to one's father and mother. Generally, Ṣàngó is believed to be their father, while Ọya is taken to be their mother. Hence, the praise of Ọya is also a major component of the epithet rendered in praise of Ṣàngó.

The various aspects of sacrifice on Jàkúta-day worship are religiously followed, but rams are killed, and their blood poured as libation on *ẹdùn àrá*, the symbol of Ṣàngó. Salutation/homage, metamorphosis, chanting of *Ṣàngó pípè,* and rhythmic dancing to a *bàtá* ensemble always accompany the worship. After the individual worship by the priests, the priests now proceed to the palace. The paramount ruler of the city, the Tìmì of Ẹdẹ himself, will receive them in his palace, and give them lots of rams and cows to be sacrificed on behalf of his subjects. After being slaughtered, the cows and rams given by the Tìmì will be roasted, and all the devotees will partake in the eating of the roasted meat. The significance of this is the belief that once you have been a partaker, no curse or ill wishes will have effects on you. This notable aspect of Ṣàngó's annual worship is the *aképè* (curse-negator) ceremony. The feasting of *aképè* meat marks the end of day two ceremonies.

Days 3–7: Feasting, Dancing, and Magical Feat Days

The third to the seventh days are for feasting, dancing, chanting, and performance of magical feats. The devotees, priests, and priestesses will assemble at the front of the palace to dance to *bàtá* music. Songs depicting the physique, nature, and attributes of Ṣàngó are sung. Such songs include the following:

1. *Ewélérè, ọbaa Kòso*
   Má mà jáyé ó parẹ
   Má mà jáyé ó parẹ
   Má mà jáyé ó parẹ
   Ewélérè, ọbaa Kòso
   Má mà jáyé ó pare.

   Ewélérè, the king of Kòso
   Do not let the world go into oblivion
   Do not let the world go into oblivion
   Do not let the world go into oblivion
   Ewélérè, the king of Kòso
   Do not let the world go into oblivion.

2. *Ẹ bá n gbé Ṣàngó*
   Òòṣà ẹni làá gbé gẹgẹ
   Ẹ bá n gbé Ṣàngó o
   Òòṣà ẹni làá gbé gẹgẹ.

   Lift Sango up
   It's one deity that one lifts up
   Lift Sango up
   It's one deity that one lifts up.

3. *Ṣàngó dé*
   Orò, ọkọ Ọya
   A-gbéná-gẹngẹ
   A-fèké-lẹ́nu-ya.

Ṣàngó is here
The bullroarer, husband of Ọya
One-who-carries-the-fire-high-up
One-who-tears-the-mouth-of-the-mischievous-person.

As the devotees dance and jubilate, the *Ẹ̀lẹ́gùn* is distinctively recognized through his costume. He dresses in a red blouse and skirt known respectively as *gbéri* and *làbà*. Two carved images are usually in front of the *gbéri* and a carved image at the back. The hand props on the *Ẹ̀lẹ́gun* are *osée Ṣàngó* (Ṣàngó wand) and a big red handkerchief called *òdòdóo-Ṣàngó*. The neck/ankle prop is *kele* (a mixture of red and white beads which are alternatively sown together). According to Canizares,[24] the mixture of white and red is a sign of Ọbàtálá's cooling effect on Ṣàngó's red hot temper. But one of our informants, a Ṣàngó princess, claims that it is a depiction of Ṣàngó's finesse and fierceness. The red symbolizes Ṣàngó's fierceness and heartlessness, while the white is cooling down the fierceness and danger associated with the wrath of Ṣàngó. The *Ẹ̀lẹ́gùn* now sits on *odóo-Ṣàngó* (Ṣàngó mortar), which is the stage prop. The moment he is on the mortar, he is referred to as Ṣàngó, because he is now the god-hero.

Chanting and a dancing spree now fill the air. The following excerpt is a recorded text of performance on an annual festival of Ṣàngó:

Ṣàngó o o o
   Olúkoooori o o o
   Olójú orógbó
   Ẹlẹ́ẹ̀kẹ́ obì o ò
   Kábíyèsí, Ewélérè ọkọ̀ mi
   Subúlutú tíí jí mu tábà oògùn
   Iná lój'u
   Iná lẹ́nu
   Iná lóòlée páànù
   Jogbo bí Orò o ò
   Jogbo bí orógbó o o
   Ẹlẹ́ẹ̀kẹ́ obì o o o
   Ó pègbọ́n, ó gbé e rùbúrò

Ó pàyàwó ó gbé e rùyáálé
Irúnmọlẹ̀ abìjàwàrà
Ó bá baálé jiyán ìgángán tán
Ó pọmọ ẹ̀ síloro
Ó ní báa bá ṣeni lóore
Ọpẹ́ làá dú
Abẹ́mọlórí fi ìyókù jinni
Àyánrán iná
Àkàtà yẹrìyẹrì
Ewe e e e e e
Ewélérè o ò
Ṣàngó
Olúkoórì.

The-man-with-the-bitter-kola-eye
The-man-with-the-kola-nut-chin
Kábíyèsí, Ewélérè my husband
Subúlutú[25] that sniff medicinal tobacco
Early in the morning
His eye emits fire
His mouth emits fire
He is the fire in the roof
He is as bitter as the bullroarer
He is as bitter as the bitter-kola
The man with the kola nut chin
He kills the elder brother and put his corpse
On his younger brother's head
He kills the young wife and put her corpse
On the elderly wife
One-thousand-demons that fight scowlingly
He eats pounded-yam with the head of a compound
And kills his son at the forecourt
He says when you are kind to someone
You must give thanks
One-who-beheaded-a-child
And left the corpse
The mighty fire, the great lightning
Ewé é é é
Ewélérè.

As the chanting goes on, the spirit of Ṣàngó will be descending on the devotees. It is therefore a taboo to stand at the entrance of the shrine and obstruct Sango from coming in at will.[26] At this point, the Ẹlẹ́gùn becomes possessed and can also fall into a trance. His movement becomes erratic as he jumps and suddenly becomes dizzy.[27] He will then start prophesying.[28] This now leads to the next stage of performance, which is the magical feat.

The Magical Performance Aspect of Ṣàngó Worship

Investigation shows that the metaphysical aspect of performance is that aspect of worship that links Ẹlẹ́gùn to Ṣàngó. In his time, Ṣàngó is believed to have charms, and he could do mysterious things with this magical power. One of the feats he was known for was carrying fire with his bare hands. This is re-enacted again as the Ẹlẹ́gùn, even in this contemporary time, also carries a bowl of fire with his/her hands. The Ẹlẹ́gùn can also call forth anything she/he desires, or the devotees desire, through magical power. The magical aspect of performance is an integral part of the annual worship, for without it the festival is incomplete.

The Magical Feat

The stage props for the magical performance are odóo-Ṣàngó (Ṣàngó's mortar), the magical box, a black wrapper, and òdòdóo-Ṣàngó (Ṣàngó's red handkerchief). At the point of performance, the Ẹlẹ́gùn sits on the mortar. The magical box, which is rectangular in shape, is drawn close to him/her. The box has both a wooden and a glass cover. The Ẹlẹ́gùn covers the box with the black wrapper and the red handkerchief. As he covers the box, he begins to make an incantation in order to send the spirit on errand. The spirit will now bring whatsoever is the desire of the Ẹlẹ́gùn.[29]

The Ancestral Worship in Ṣàngó Festival

The ancestral worship is a vital aspect of Ṣàngó festival in Ẹdẹ. The masquerades are called Egúngún-un Ṣàngó (Ṣàngó's masquerades). Egúngún and Ṣàngó are believed to be brothers, Egúngún being the elder one. The reason for this is not far-fetched because, according to two of our informants, the Odù Ifá that brought both of them to the earth is Òyẹ̀ kú-Méjì.[30] Therefore, anytime Ṣàngó is worshipped in Ẹdẹ, Egúngún is also propitiated. The sacrificial items for Egúngún include wine, kola nuts, and cocks. Investigation shows that the spirit of Egúngún is gentle, so it is necessary to feature it in order to calm the fiery force of Ṣàngó.[31]

Ridicule: An Aspect of Ṣàngó Worship

The act of worship of Ṣàngó by his devotees is beyond the five realms of worship discussed above. The devotees worship with their actions and ways of life because Ṣàngó hates evil and mischief. No adherent will ever wish to incur the wrath of Ṣàngó through living an indecent way of life or being an aberrant to the norms of the society.[32] Ṣàngó, according to Idowu, is a "manifestation of the wrath of Olódùmarè" against men and their evil acts.[33] Thus, Ṣàngó is believed to be the god of justice. He speedily judges anybody that commits a heinous offense. In his attack, he knows no bounds. Thus, he is praised as *a-jà-má-màà là* (he-who-fights-without-moderation). In his rage, he does not limit the punishment to the offender. Neighbors and co-tenants may share in such punishment.

Ṣàngó employs ridicule as one of the weapons of his attack. In the past, and even in recent times, offenders who have stolen or committed evils are openly disgraced by sudden deaths through thunderbolts with the stolen items placed on their chests. Adeoye states that when this happens, the *mo̩gbà* will be consulted immediately. The *mo̩gbà*'s role is twofold:[34] one, to remove the thunderbolt from the dead, and two, to propitiate the spirit of Ṣàngó. As the propitiation is going on, satirical songs are sung, and everybody at that spot, including the relatives of the dead culprit, must dance to the song.

The Yorùbá culture values the "shame culture." No one wants to bring shame to his or her family. The family of the deceased has been given a bad name already, and on top of it they must dance to the satirical songs rendered. The excerpts below are examples of such songs:

1. *Ṣàngó, má pa mí o*
   N ò bá wo̩n pomo je̩
   Òòrá-bàbà-sánmo̩-lábàrá,
   Ṣàngó, má pa mí o
   N ò bá wo̩n pomo je̩.

   Ṣàngó, do not kill me
   I am not among those that kill children
   One-who-hovers-to-slap, you've arrived
   Ṣàngó, do not kill me
   I am not among those that kill children.

2. *Kádóṣù ó róde lọ*
   Kádóṣù ó róde lọ
   Ṣàngó, ròjò kóo polè
   Kádóṣù ó róde lọ.

So that the priest might go out to officiate
So that the priest might go out to officiate
Sango let rain fall and kill the thief
So that the priest might go out to officiate.

Although the song is in praise of Ṣàngó, it is an indirect way of mocking the person that has stolen. However, the butt of the ridicule is no longer the dead but his relatives, who are compelled to dance and praise Ṣàngó for his acts of justice. This is contrary to the Yorùbá attitude toward death, especially if it is the death of a young person. The occasion that is supposed to be for mourning the deceased will now be a joyous moment, as it is a taboo for the relatives of the victim of Ṣàngó's attack to mourn. To add more to the ridicule, they must also provide lots of food items (*àmàlà* with *gbègìrì* soup) and ram for the *adóṣù* and *mọgbà*. In short, they are at the mercy of the *mọgbà,* because any amount demanded from them must be provided; hence, Ṣàngó is referred to as "*a-lápa-dúpẹ́*" (one-that-kills-and-you-still-thank him). This retributive aspect of Ṣàngó's worship is a subtle way of satirizing the wicked in order to bring sanity to the society. This simple act of worship is so dreadful that no one will want to be a subject of shame in society.

Taboos Surrounding the Worship of Ṣàngó

There are some taboos associated with the worship of Ṣàngó. These include the following:

1. A devotee must not smoke, for this may amount to imitating Ṣàngó.
2. A devotee must eat neither the *àgó* (rat) nor the *èṣúró* (red flanked duiker).
3. It is an abomination for a female *adóṣù* and a male *adóṣù* to marry each other.
4. It is forbidden for Ṣàngó devotees to eat *èwà sèsé* (cowpeas).
5. It is also a taboo for Ṣàngó devotees to eat *ẹmi dìẹ* (a type of vegetable).[35]

Different reasons are adduced for not eating *àgó* rat and *èsúró*. They are both portrayed as disloyal beings who betrayed Ṣàngó, who consequently turned them into animals. In addition, the moment a devotee is initiated as a priest or priestess, he or she automatically becomes Ṣàngó's wife. Thus, it is an abomination for two of Ṣàngó's wives to marry. The reason adduced for not eating *ẹ̀wà sèsé* lies in the belief that the fourth Aláàfin ate it, and it caused stomach disorder. Since then, Ṣàngó devotees abhor it. Also, the taboo on *ẹmi dìẹ* is integrated to Ṣàngó worship from Yemọja worship. Yemọja was Ṣàngó's foster mother. Yemọja did not eat *ẹmi dìẹ,* and Ṣàngó adopted this habit. It is also discovered that anytime Ṣàngó is worshipped, it is a taboo for devotees or non-initiates to stand by the door. The reason for this is that as the invocation goes on through the chanting of *Ṣàngó pípè* and throughout the worship session, Ṣàngó's spirit will be present. Therefore, if he intends to come in, he may not like to be obstructed.

Conclusion

This chapter has elucidated the various aspects of Ṣàngó worship in southwestern Nigeria. Contributing to the debate about the origin of Ṣàngó worship, we conclude that though the fourth Aláàfin of Old Ọ̀yọ́ was apotheosized as Ṣàngó, the primordial Ṣàngó predated him. Therefore, the Ṣàngó which is worshipped in southwestern Nigeria is the primordial Ṣàngó, whose fame was spread and is still being spread by devotees who follow him. Also, the satirical aspect of Ṣàngó worship is still present.

In sum, it is considered that Ṣàngó, as a god, is not a god of the past but is still relevant in contemporary Yorùbá culture and religion. The practice of Ṣàngó worship is still as potent in some places as it was in the past. Ṣàngó is worshipped as ritual performance, and its myth has given birth to many artistic, poetic, and dramatic works. For instance, Bamidele gives an account of the potency of Ṣàngó worship as he mentions the ways some priests/priestesses make a god-hero of Ṣàngó.[36] According to him, they roam about in streets and markets to pray for people, who in return give them gifts. The people's actions corroborate the fact that they have faith in Ṣàngó, who, as a god, has not been de-supernaturalized in spite of the activities of radical Christians and Muslims.

Finally, the recent trend of the depiction of the Ṣàngó myth in literary works, as revealed by Bamidele,[37] attests to the fact that Ṣàngó (as well as his worship) is still real. The list of dramatic works on Ṣàngó's myth demonstrates his popularity.[38] Today, a popular actor is referred to as

Ṣàngó. He always plays the god-hero in his plays as he emits fire from his mouth and engages in all the magical feats which were attributed to the apotheosized Ṣàngó in his days. A feeling of the impulse of his audience shows that the actor is popular because he brings to the fore this fierce god and his supernatural prowess even in this jet age.[39]

NOTES

1. Akinwumi Isola, "Èdè-àiyedè tí ó rò mó orírun Ṣàngó," in *O Pegedé: Àkójo pò Àwon Àròkọ Akadá fún yíyònbó òjògbón Adébóyè Babalọlá,* ed. Omotayo Olutoye. (Lagos: Longman Nigeria, 2000), 113–19.

2. C. L. Adeoye, *Ìgbàgbó àti Èsìn Yorùbá* (Ibadan, Nigeria: Evans Publishers, 1985), 285–88.

3. Isola, "Èdè Àìyedè," 113.

4. Adeoye, *Ìgbàgbó àti Èsìn,* 285.

5. Isola, "Èdè Àìyedè," 114.

6. Adeoye, *Ìgbàgbó àti Èsìn,* 288.

7. Isola, "Èdè Àìyedè," 114.

8. Ibid., 113.

9. B. R. Canizares, *Shàngó: Santeria and the Òrìshà of Thunder* (Plainview, N.Y.: Original Publications, 2000), 1.

10. Adeoye, *Ìgbàgbó àti Èsìn,* 285–86.

11. Akinwumi Isola, "Ṣàngó-pípè: One Type of Yoruba Oral Poetry," M.A. thesis, University of Lagos, 1973, 1.

12. Adeoye, *Ìgbàgbó àti Èsìn,* 80–85.

13. Adeoye, *Ìgbàgbó àti Èsìn,* 287, and Isola, "Èdè Àìyedè," 114.

14. A. L. Hethersett, "Ìtàn Ṣàngó," in *Ìwe Kíkú Èhọrin Lá Èdè Yorùbá,* ed. A. L. Hethersett (Lagos: Church Missionary Society, 1941), 51; Canizares, *Shàngó,* 1; and P. O. Ogunbowale, *Àwọn Irúnmọlè Ilè Yorùbá* (Ibadan, Nigeria: Evans Publishers, 1962), 33.

15. D. Adelugba, "Trance and Theatre: The Nigerian Experience," in *Drama and Theatre in Nigeria: A Critical Source Book,* ed. Yemi Ogunbiyi. (Lagos: *Nigeria Magazine,* 1981), 183.

16. Adeoye, *Ìgbàgbó àti Èsìn,* 296.

17. Ṣàngó pípè is one type of Yorùbá traditional oral poetry that is chanted in praise of Ṣàngó.

18. Isola, "Ṣàngó-pípè," 14–17.

19. Ibid., 17.

20. Adeoye, *Ìgbàgbó àti Èsìn,* 294.

21. The Elégùn is the spirit-carrier/medium who is the god-hero. The moment the Elégùn is possessed he is no more his person but Ṣàngó.

22. Ewélérè means "The art of herbal medicine is profitable." It is one of Ṣàngó's sobriquets, to confirm his knowledge of herbal medicine.

23. Isola, "S̩àngó-pípè," 21.

24. Canizares, *Shàngó*, 13.

25. Súbúlutú is one of S̩àngó's sobriquets that has lost its etymological meaning.

26. In the course of this research, one of my research assistants stood at the entrance of the shrine where Jàkúta-day worship was being performed. He was possessed and palm oil was given to him as an antidote before he came round.

27. This was witnessed at the worship of S̩àngó in the shrine of O̩babìnrin S̩àngó, Princess Ké̩hìndé Òjó at Ibadan.

28. Ogunbowale, *Àwo̩n Irúnmo̩lè̩*, 34.

29. An example of this is a magical feat performed at the worship of S̩àngó in the shrine of O̩babìnrin S̩àngó in Ibadan. The *E̩lé̩gùn* used her magical prowess to produce sweets and biscuits for the audience.

30. The information collected from S̩àngó's chief priest at E̩de̩ and Princess Ké̩hìndé Òjó attests to this. Adeoye, *Ìgbàgbó̩ àti È̩sìn*, 288–89, also collaborates the fact that ò̩ye̩kú-Méjì brought S̩àngó to earth.

31. The ancestral worship is not limited to E̩de̩. Even in Jàkúta worship of S̩àngó a priest may decide to worship the ancestors. A case of this is recorded at the worship of S̩àngó at O̩babìnrin Ké̩hìndé Òjó S̩àngó's shrine in Ibadan.

32. Ogunbowale, *Àwo̩n Irúnmo̩lè̩*, 33; Isola, "S̩àngó-pípè," 22–24; and Adeoye, *Ìgbàgbó̩ àti È̩sìn*, 300.

33. E. Bolaji Idowu, *Olódùmarè God in Yorùbá Belief* (London: Longman, 1962), 88.

34. Adeoye, *Ìgbàgbó̩ àti È̩sìn*, 294.

35. Isola, "S̩àngó-pípè," 221, and Adeoye, *Ìgbàgbó̩ àti È̩sìn*, 294.

36. L. Bamidele, "S̩àngó Myth and Its Challenges in Science, Art and Religion," in *IBA: Essays on African Literature in Honour of Oyin Ogunba*, ed. W. Ogundele and O. Adeoti. (Ifè̩, Nigeria: Obafemi Awolowo University Press, 2003), 185.

37. Ibid., 178–86.

38. The list of such works according to ibid., 182–83, include:

    a. *Bamgbose S̩àngó* by Esinkinni Olusanyin;

    b. *Ose S̩àngó* by Afolabi Adesanya;

    c. *Àrá* by Femi Anikulapo Kuti;

    d. *O̩ba Kò So* by Duro Ladipo;

    e. *S̩àngó* by Wale Ogunyemi;

    f. *Ìbínú S̩àngó* by Wale Ogunyemi; and

    g. *Many Colours Make The Thunder King* by Femi Osofisan.

39. The actor is one of Jimoh Aliu's sons, nicknamed S̩àngó. According to Tai Oguntayo's story titled "Ekiti Agog As Àwòrò and Fáyó̩s̩é Get Awards," in *Saturday Tribune*, March 12, 2005, one of the events slated to thrill the audience at the Award Ceremony is the magical feat. He says "S̩àngó will again cut into pieces different parts of human beings in the full glare of viewers and then join them together again."

CHAPTER FOUR

Ṣàngó's Ẹẹ̀rìndínlógún Divinatory System

GEORGE OLÚṢỌLÁ AJÍBÁDÉ

This chapter examines the divinatory system of the cult of Ṣàngó among the Yorùbá of southwestern Nigeria. I discuss the pluralistic nature of the divinatory system in this cult and its place in Yorùbá cosmology in time and space, opening with discussion of the essence of the divinatory system among the Yorùbá and different ways by which they decipher information about futuristic events in order to forestall impending dangers.

Virtually all Yorùbá deities, apart from Òrúnmìlà, use Ẹẹ̀rìndínlógún to decipher information about futuristic events and to learn what to do to avert ongoing and impending disasters. The deducible reason for this is that Òrúnmìlà is the deity who has given Ẹẹ̀rìndínlógún divinatory objects and method to other deities through Òṣun. This chapter deals with the acquisition of Ẹẹ̀rìndínlógún divinatory system, the *odù* of Ṣàngó and its general interpretations, and the content of Ṣàngó divination literature, as well as identifies gender traits in the divinatory system of Ṣàngó showing a bias for the masculinity of Ṣàngó. The study concludes with the effects of globalization on the divinatory system of the cult of Ṣàngó.

Divination and Its Essence among the Yorùbá

For most sub-Saharan African peoples, divination rites are an essential part of daily life. An individual casts pieces of a kola nut or addresses questions to a friction oracle in the morning in order to determine what to do to make his or her way successful through the day. A family may consult a diviner to learn why death is repeatedly taking a mother's new-born children or to know the will of the ancestors for resolving conflicts within the household. A king seeks the knowledge of his diviners to make his position of authority secure. Diviners are agents of memory, the pre-servers of people's history, or, in times of crisis, the creators of a past or a vision by which the living may endure.[1]

To the Yorùbá, divination is an essential part of their normal daily life. Divination among them is in diverse forms. In a traditional Yorùbá soci-ety, the type of dreams an individual has, the first person an individual meets when he or she wakes up, repeated occurrence of an incidence, which leg an individual hits on a rock or stump, all these are signs of carefulness, and in short they are passing one message or the other on to the person. From these and many other means, an individual person can know about what is going to happen to him, to befall her. Also, kola nuts are used as a way of knowing the future, and various interpretations are given to each of the results of each cast, that is, when the lobes of kola-nuts are thrown. It all depends on what appears and what interpretations are given to it by the diviner. Through divination, human beings know what they should do and what they should not. They know the deity to offer sacrifice to and when they are to offer the sacrifice. In essence, divi-nation is a cautionary measure which the people employ in order to live a desired and meaningful life of blessings, longevity, prosperity, and sound health. It is the prayer of Yorùbá that "what we are not thinking should not destroy what we are thinking" (*Ohun tí a ò ró kó má ba ohun tí àń rò jé*). This connotes that the Yorùbá people plan for unforeseen contingen-cies, but they are aware that much of the future is menacingly unknown. They have to seek to penetrate the unknown by different means. Promi-nent among the means used is divination. Hence the saying "*Bónií ti rí òla kì í rí bẹ́ẹ̀, lo ń mu kí babaláwo máa dífá oròorún*" (Today's happen-ings might not be the same as that of tomorrow prompts the diviner to make weekly divination). The Yorùbá believe that the world in which they live is influenced by certain forces—witches, sorcerers, the ancestral spirits, and malevolent forces. Therefore, they believe that it is wise and expedient for them to have these powers on their side for favor and mer-cies, and they are convinced that the diviner can reveal what these forces are planning and what men can do to forestall, propitiate, and humor them. Thus, divination is a means by which divine will and directives are ascertained.[2] Through divination, the Yorùbá make effort to find an answer to the mystery of creation.

Yorùbá Divinatory Systems

There are many divinatory systems among the Yorùbá people, and it is not only in the Ifá cult that the issue of divination exists. Divination takes various forms depending on the cult, purpose, and the means by which it is made. Divination has been defined as the art or skill of divining (by the use of divinity or deity) that which is unknown—for example, the future, the identity of culprits, the location of lost items, the best partner for marriage, and so on. Divination could be by dreams, presentiments, body actions, ordeals, animals or parts of the dead animals, mechanical means using objects, patterns in nature, or observing other patterns.[3] This is an indication that the issue of divination is not a restricted one. It has been recorded that almost every deity in Yorùbáland has a separate means of divination. Also, there are various divination systems among them. These include Agbigba, Awẹrẹ, Ikin, Ìbò dídì, Òpèlè, Ọwó wíwò, Ẹẹrìndínlógún, and so forth.

Sixteen cowries, or Ẹẹrìndínlógún, is a form of divinatory method employed by most deities among the Yorùbá to gain an insight into the unknown by looking into some history and myths. It is very popular among the adherents of Ṣàngó, Òṣun, Yemọja, Ọbàtálá, and many others.[4] But the focus of this chapter is on the Ẹẹrìndínlógún system of divination that is associated with Ṣàngó. Literally, "Ẹẹrìndínlógún" means sixteen. It has its source from *"ọwó ẹyọ mẹrìndínlógún"*—sixteen cowry shells. Hence, this divinatory method of using the charmed sixteen cowries is called Eérìndínlógún. The users of this method of divination call it Ìránṣẹ Ṣàngó—the Messenger or the Servant of Ṣàngó

Training of the Diviner

The training of the Ẹẹrìndínlógún diviner requires time, patience, and concentration, but it is not as cumbersome and time consuming as the Ifá divinatory system, which takes about sixteen years. The simplicity of Ẹẹrìndínlógún makes more people prefer it to Ifá and other means of divination in Yorùbáland. This divinatory method is mostly female-dominated. In most cases the diviner passes it down to his/her children. It requires about three or four years of training. The apprentice begins with the learning of verses (*odù*) and stories associated with each *odù* by heart. The mastery of the *odù* depends so much on retentive and recapitulative stamina, the capability of the apprentice, and also on the years of training. Besides this, many apprentices make use of traditional medicine to aid their retentive memory. This is called *òògùn ìsòyè* (literally, the medicine that wakes people's understanding). At times it may be reciting of a particular incantation known as *ọfọ ìsòyè* (literally, incantation that wakes people's understanding). In most cases, it is the combination of the two. The essence of this is for the apprentice, or diviner in training, to learn many *odù* by heart so that it will be easier to recall when divining for clients.

After it has been observed by the master of the apprentice that the latter has mastered the art, the diviner-in-training will be tested before she or he is allowed to practice. There are two major steps with regard to this. The apprentice will be asked to make divination for the master, the success of which is judged by the ability to toss the cowries, interpret them, and narrate a fitting and appropriate *odù*. When an apprentice has been assessed as a capable diviner, she or he will be given the cowries. This is the second stage. It is called *ifinimawo* (initiation into cult). It takes place in the divining room of the master. On this day, the cowries will be religiously washed. This connotes the purity and sacredness of the cowries because they are no longer ordinary but ritualized. This process gives the cowries the potency to see beyond the physical; they can project into the spiritual and psychological arena in solving the clients' problems. This initiation rite and ceremony is highly significant to our understanding of Yorùbá cosmology and worldview, especially in relation to their deities. During the initiation rites of the apprentice, homage is paid to many deities in Yorùbáland. This shows the interrelation of the deities in the Yorùbá pantheon. The ceremony is witnessed by other invited Ẹẹrìndínlógún diviners and the relatives of the new initiate. The initiation is also marked with eating and drinking. After this rite the initiate has the freedom to make divination. The initiation process in Ṣàngó's Ẹẹrìndínlógún is simpler than that of Ifá, which takes several weeks and processes. That is why many people, especially women, are found practicing it.

The Ṣàngó's Ẹẹrìndínlógún Divinatory System

The divinatory system in Ṣàngó's Ẹẹrìndínlógún could be regarded as a binary pentagon. It centers on positive and negative issues; this could be either good/blessing or bad/evil as illustrated below:

Good/Blessing	Bad/Evil
Owó (Money/Wealth)	*Òfò* (Loss)
Ọmọ (Children)	*Ikú* (Death)

Àìkú (Long life)   *Àrùn* (Disease)
Obìnrin (Women/marriage)   *Ìjà* (Fighting)
Ibùjókòó rere (Peaceful settlement)   *Òràn* (Problems)

Its binary nature has to do with its two focuses of good and evil and negative and positive. This reveals Yorùbá philosophy of their cosmography as a world of binary complementarities; that *tibi-tire la dá ilé ayé*—the world is created with good and evil. Also, the pentagonal attribute centers on the fact that there are five areas of the good/positive side and five areas of the bad/negative side, as arranged above.

Ṣàngó literature provides some insight into the operation of the Ṣàngó divinatory system. It stresses the interrelations of people with the past, that is, the embodiment of humans' past, present, and future. Therefore, Ṣàngó literature, especially the *odù*, cannot be separated from the divinatory system.

When the *odù* has been determined by the toss of the cowries, the diviner begins to chant that *odù*. From the *odù*, predictions, sacrifices to be made, and various taboos are relayed to the client, based on a mythological or historical story that serves as precedent. It is the duty of the client to choose the exact *odù* that is applicable to his or her own situation when recited.

The cowries are cast on a mat (*àtẹ*) which is flat in nature. The tossing of these cowries takes place on this mat (*àtẹ*) to determine the *odù* that apply to each client. The *odù* are historical analogies in a prescribed form. They encapsulate statements of human beings' troubles, wishes, hopes, aspirations, and testimonies to how each historical or mythical client has reacted to these problems, in a time perspective. To the Yorùbá, human vitality in the universe revolves round three things: the blessings of money, children, and longevity. In order to achieve these, they consult diviner to know what to do and what not to do. For instance, the *odù* below is from Èjìlá Aṣébọra, and is the *odù* of Ṣàngó as a deity. It is used in this chapter to illustrate the content of *odù* in Ṣàngó's Ẹẹrìndínlógún.

Òòṣà sọ pé "ire ajé."
   Irúnmọlè sọ pé "ire ọmọ."
Òòṣà sọ pé "ire àìkú."
Níbi tí a ti dá Èjìlá Aṣébọra,
Òòṣà ní kí a lọ bọ Ṣàngó;
Kí a sì lọ bọ òrìṣà oko.
Nítorii kín ni?

Fìkànfìkàn, awo ayé;
Dùgbẹ̀dùgbẹ̀ awo ọ̀run;
Ló dá fún Ọ̀nì waaka;
Tó lóyún tí ò lè bí i.
Tí Ọ̀nì waaka bá lóyún,
Tó bá tó àkókò ìbímọ,
Ni kò bá ní rí oyún mọ́.
Ọ̀nì waaka ní báwo lòun
     ó ti ṣe é tí òun ó fi dọlọ́mọ láyé.
Ó káwọ́ lérí ó tẹ mọlẹ̀.
Òkè ìpọ̀nrí rẹ̀ ń gbèjè,
Òkè ìpọ̀nrí rẹ̀ń pe ẹ̀ẹ̀rìndínlógún,
Kò rí ẹlòmíràn
Ẹni ńlá ló rí.
Wọ́n ni ẹbọ ni kó rú.
Ó ní kín ni òun yóò rú lẹ́bọ?
Wọ́n ni kó rú ẹgbàà méjìlá,
Wọ́n ni kó rú àkùkọ adìẹ méjì,
Wọ́n ni kó rú ẹyẹlé méjì,
Wọ́n ni kó rú àmàlà méjìlá,
Orógbó méjìlá,
Wọ́n ni kó lọ fún Ṣàngó.
Wọ́n ni kí Ọ̀nì rú aṣọ pátapàta.
Ọ̀nì kó ẹbọ, ó rú ẹbọ,
Ọ̀nì kó èrù, ó tù,
Ọ̀nì bọ òkè ìpọ̀nrí rẹ̀
     pẹ̀lú jíjẹ mímu
Nígbà tó yá, Ọ̀nì yún bí tíí yún.
Nígbà tó tó àkókò, ni Ṣàngó bá ké.
Ìgbà tí Ṣàngó kọ lẹ́ẹ̀kan,
Gbogbo ọmọ Ọ̀nì ló jade;
Wọ́n sì bá àgbàrá lọ sínú odò.
Báyìí ni Ọ̀nì bẹ̀rẹ̀ sí ní bímọ;
Ni ọmọ Ọ̀nì kò wá lè run mọ́.
Ọ̀nì ń jó, Ọ̀nì ń yọ̀;
Ni Ọ̀nì wá ń yin àwọn awo;
Ni àwọn awo náà ń yin Ṣàngó.
Pé, bẹ́ẹ̀ ni àwọn awo ṣe ṣẹnu rere wí:
Fìkànfìkàn awo ayé,
Dùgbẹ̀dùgbẹ̀ awo ọ̀run,
Ló dá fún Ọ̀nì waaka,

Tó lóyún tí ò lè bí i.
Ó ní, "a gbọ rírú ẹbọ a rú,"
A gbọ èrù àtòkèṣù ó sù,
Kò ì pé, kò ì jìnnà,
Ẹ ò rí mi ní jèbútú ọmọ.
Ọpẹlọpẹ Òòṣà tí ń bẹ lókè
Ló jẹ n bímọ
Níbi tí àrá ń pa kí,
Ọmọ Ònì tó jade.
Òòṣà pé ire ọmọ rí bẹ nù un.

The Deity says "blessing of money."
    The gods say "blessing of children."
    The Deity says "blessing of long life."
    Where Èjìlá Aṣébọra is cast,
    The Deity says we should go and sacrifice to Sango;
    And we should go and sacrifice to *òrìṣà* Oko.
    Because of what?
    Zigzag, the diviner of earth;
    Instability, the diviner of heaven;
    Were the ones who cast for Crocodile;
    She was pregnant but could not give birth.
    Whenever the Crocodile was pregnant,
    When it was her time to deliver,
    She won't see the pregnancy any more.
    The Crocodile lamented on what she could
        do to have children in my life.
    She puts her hands on her head and consulted the Diviner.
    His head was showing seven,
    His head was showing sixteen,
    She didn't see anyone else
    She saw an important person [Ṣàngó].
    She was told to offer a sacrifice.
    She asked for the materials she would offer?
    She was told to offer 24,000 cowries,
    She was told to offer two roosters,
    She was told to offer two pigeons,
    She was told to offer twelve wraps of *àmàlà,*
    Twelve bitter kola nuts,
    She was told to go and give them to Ṣàngó.
    Crocodile was told to offer a speckled cloth.

The Crocodile gathered the materials and offered them,
She performed rituals to the deities,
The Crocodile worshipped her head
   with dining and the wining.
Later on, the Crocodile was pregnant as before.
When it was time, Ṣàngó shouted.
Sango shouted once,
All Crocodile's children came out;
And were carried into the river by a torrent.
And so, Crocodile began to procreate;
And Crocodile's Children could not perish anymore.
The Crocodile was dancing and rejoicing;
And Crocodile was commending her diviners;
And the diviners were commending Ṣàngó.
That the diviners were speaking the truth:
Zigzag, the diviner of earth,
Instability, the diviner of heaven,
Were the ones who cast for Crocodile,
She was pregnant but could not give birth.
She said, "We've been told to offer sacrifice and we offered it,"
We were told to appease to Èṣù and we did,
Not too long, not too far away,
Don't you see me amidst plentiful children.
Thanks be to the Deity above
Who made me to bear children.
That is where the thunder cracks before,
Crocodile's children come out.
The Deity says there is a blessing of children in it.

This *odù* reveals many sociological issues, as it were, in the Yorùbá cosmology. In Ṣàngó divination as seen in the above *odù* (which is a typical one), twelve major steps are identified. They are, firstly, the introductory lines that contain the message of hope for the client, as we can see in lines 1–3. This step could be seen as the summary of the whole text. It prepares the client for a hopeful venture to the diviner and it stabilizes him/her from emotional and psychological trauma that his/her problem might have created. This idea is captured by a Yorùbá proverb that "*A kì í gbọ́ búburú lẹ́nu abọrẹ̀*"—We don't hear any evil from the diviner/priest. The rest of the text could be regarded as the historical narration that authenticates the message that has been conveyed to the client.

The second step is the name of the *odù,* which appears to the client as seen in line 4 of the above example. What the client should do is in the next step. In the above case, Ṣàngó and Òrìṣàòko should be worshipped in order to have breakthrough. The fourth step is the names of the mythical or historical diviners. In most cases, this is usually abstract nouns. In the above *odù*, Fìkànfikàn (Zigzag) and Dùgbẹ̀dùgbẹ̀ (Instability) (lines 10 and 11), diviners of earth and heaven respectively, are the historical diviners who made divination for the Crocodile. These two are just qualifiers. They are describing the physique of a pregnant woman. Besides the fact that they are abstract ideas, they are used to give a pictorial or imagistic code of pregnancy. It is therefore a prognostic idea of presenting divination literature in Ẹẹrìndínlógún.

The next step (fifth step) is the name of the mythical/historical client that serves as precedent. In the above example, Crocodile is the mythical client (line 12). This method of divination is just revealing the Yorùbá worldview about social interaction and psychotherapeutic ethics. The Yorùbá hold the belief that "*a kì í tojú oníka mẹ́sàn-án kà á*"—we must not count the fingers of a person with nine fingers in his presence. This is just a way of alleviating the psychological trauma that the problems of the client might have created. Also, a mythical figure that is not a human being was used to create ambiguity and remove suspicion of a client. But, "Crocodile" in this context is used by the diviner as a form of synecdoche to symbolize all clients in the past, present, and the future. The ultimate aim of the client at this moment is to know the outcome of the divination made for the mythical client, putting himself/herself in a similar situation.

The next step in Ṣàngó's divinatory method, after the mythical client has been mentioned, is the reason(s) why the client has gone to the diviner for consultation. The reasons are in diverse forms as the case may be. In the above excerpt from Ṣàngó's Ẹẹrìndínlógún it is the inability of Crocodile to deliver a baby whenever pregnant. In other words she had miscarriages (lines 13–17). She was troubled because of her inability to procreate. It has been observed that one of the major reasons why many women in Yorùbáland consult various diviners is the problem of infertility. This is because a barren woman in the society is condemned and stigmatized. Therefore, every married woman prays and seeks a solution to have children in order to remove the stigma. Whatever might be the physical or spiritual problem of the client who has gone for divination, such a client would feel comfortable that she has taken a right step in consulting the diviner.

After the client has made her problem known to the diviner, the latter will consult the Ẹẹrìndínlógún to know the way out, as seen in lines 17–20. This step is followed by what the client needs to do, as done by the mythical client, to achieve the desired result. This step involves the articles of sacrifice and rituals. I observed that in most cases, the steps to be taken by the client usually involve rituals and sacrifice as illuminated in the above example (lines 21–29, 31). The step after this reveals the recipients of the sacrifice to be offered. From observation, the prescribed sacrifice is usually attributed to a particular deity or some deities. In the above excerpt, Ṣàngó is the recipient of the Crocodile's sacrifice and rituals (line 30). The next step is the protagonist or the client's reaction or attitude toward the diviner's prescription (lines 32–34). He/she can obey or disobey. In most cases, the clients do obey the diviner. The way out of the client's problems and calamities rests solely on her obedience to the prescription by the divine and the power of the deity who receives the sacrifice. The diviner's instructions are highly regarded and adhered to because violation hinders the client's requests.

The diviner will then inform his/her client of the mythical client's reaction to the prescribed sacrifice. In the above example, the Crocodile was obedient to the prescription. Therefore, she offered sacrifice to Ṣàngó and worshipped her head (*orí inú*) too as the diviner had instructed her. At times, the mythical client can disobey or disregard the diviner's instruction, the result of which he/she will regret. Everything is just to forewarn the client that he/she must honor and obey the diviner's prescription. It is important to state that in every condition of any client, the diviner emphasizes the support of one's personal head for good health, long life, and prosperity. This is because, it is believed that one's head is a "god" or deity; and that "good or ill fortune attends one, according to the will or decree of this god; hence it is propitiated in order that good luck might be the share of the votary."[5] To the Yorùbá, the physical head is the insignia or outer symbol of the inner head (*orí inú*) that must be worshipped for various accomplishments in life. This worldview is also captured in *Odù Ifá Ọ̀sẹ́tùúrá* that "It is the personal head that favors one; it is rather the *orí* that should be worshipped and not gods."[6]

The last step is usually the outcome of the mythical client's reaction to the diviner's instructions and prescriptions (lines 35–41). Obedience to the instructions usually results in alleviation of the client's problems, while disobedience leads to regret and sorrow. In the above example, Crocodile was obedient, and she reaped the fruits of obedience. She was helped by Ṣàngó through his thunder to deliver her children, and barrenness was removed from her (lines 35–41). This helps to stimulate conformity with the diviner's prescription. Also, the outcome of this obedience made Crocodile to appreciate the diviner, and the diviner in return ascribed the glory to the deity (Ṣàngó) who did the work (lines 42–56).

This kind of historical excursus in Ṣàngó divinatory literature gives assurance to the client that her problems will be solved. It gives joy and peace to the client so that she puts herself in the position of the mythical client who got a solution to her problem. This *odù* also reveals Ṣàngó as a powerful, brave, and dependable deity. It shows his masculine traits, power, and prowess, which he exhibits through lightning and thunder. One of my respondents, Ifátóògùn Adébóyè Babalọlá, even remarked that:

Yàtò sí Ẹẹrìndínlógún gẹgẹ bí ìlànà yẹmíwò èyí tí Ṣàngó ń lò; ìlànà sísán àrá pa olè tàbí àwọn ọdaràn nínú àwùjọ tún jẹ ọkan lára ọnà tí Ṣàngó ń gbà láti ṣàwárí ohun tó bá farasin fún àwọn ènìyàn àwùjọ. Alágbára àti akíkanjú Ìbọ ni Ṣàngó jẹ láwùjọ òrìṣà ilẹ Yorùbá.[7]

(Apart from the Ẹẹrìndínlógún as a divinatory method used by Ṣàngó; the method of killing thieves and culprits in the society with thunderbolt is one of the ways that Ṣàngó uses to expose the secret things in the community. Ṣàngó is a powerful and brave deity among the Yorùbá pantheon.)

One can link the work of lightning and thunder, and how it exposed the children (fetus) inside the belly of Crocodile in the above divinatory literature, to the ways Ṣàngó exposes thieves and culprits in the society. He has the power of second sight, which he bestows upon his devotees, including the diviners. It is pertinent to say that the steps in this mode of divination are different in structure from that of Ifá divination. That of Ifá has been previously argued to contain three, eight, and seven steps.[8] But it is clearly evident that there are twelve steps in the structure of Ẹẹrìndínlógún divinatory literature.

The *Odù* of Ṣàngó and Their Interpretations

The sixteen cowries are put inside the diviner's right hand palm, and they are tossed at once to determine the *odù* that appears for the clients. In Table 1, "O" represents the cowry shells facing up while "C" represents the cowry shells facing down.

The sixteen *odù* of Ẹẹrìndínlógún divination have names, and their names are cognates of names of *odù* in Ifá divination. Each *odù* has its meaning and fits into different situations of various clients. We present below a synopsis of the meaning of each *odù*.

TABLE 1. Codes of *Odù* in Ṣàngó's Ẹẹ̀rìndínlógún

Òkànràn	O C C C	Èjì Òkò	O O C C
	C C C C		C C C C
	C C C C		C C C C
	C C C C		C C C C
Ògúndá	O O O C	Ìrosùn	O O O C
	C C C C		C C C C
	C C C C		C C C C
	C C C C		C C C C
Ọṣẹ́	O O O O	Ọ̀bàrà	O O O O
	O C C C		O O C C
	C C C C		C C C C
	C C C C		C C C C
Òdí	O O O O	Èjì Ogbè	O O O O
	O O O C		O O O O
	C C C C		C C C C
	C C C C		C C C C
Ọ̀sá	O O O O	Òfún	O O O O
	O O O O		O O O O
	O C C C		O O C C
	C C C C		C C C C
Ọ̀wọ́nrín	O O O O	Èjìlá	O O O O
	O O O O	Asébọra	O O O O
	O O O C		O O O O
	C C C C		C C C C
Ìká	O O O O	Òtúrúpọ̀n	O O O O
	O O O O		O O O O
	O O O O		O O O O
	O C C C		O O C C
Èjì	O O O O	Ìrẹtẹ̀	O O O O
Ọlọgbọ́n	O O O O		O O O O
	O O O O		O O O O
	O O O C		O O O O

Òkànràn—The concave side of one out of the sixteen cowry shells faces up and others are facing down. This *odù* means that there will be an enigmatic success after a series of adversities and opposition, provided the client performs the prescribed sacrifice. The sacrifice for each client may differ, depending on the message from the priest.

Èjí Òkò—The concave sides of two cowry shells face up and others are facing down. This *odù* signifies timely success and productivity. It is the *odù* for marriage and productive friendship.

Ògúndá—Three cowry shells face up while thirteen face down. This *odù* means that the client will be elevated to a position of honor and authority after much labor and struggle.

Ìrosùn—Four cowry shells face up while twelve face down. If this *odù* appears to a client, it means that he or she will face many difficulties and problems in life. But if the client can adhere to the prescriptions and sacrifices, there will be a prosperous future.

Òsẹ́—Five cowries face up while eleven face down. It means that the client will pass through terrible constraint, shocks, adversity, and calamities unless he or she adheres to the prescribed sacrifice. If the *odù* appears to a client, such a person must prepare for hostility, antagonism, and resentment.

Òbàrà—Six cowry shells face up while ten face down. This *odù* means that the client or the relations may suffer loss of properties. But if they can offer the prescribed sacrifice, there will be unparalleled prosperity and blessings.

Òdí—The convex sides of seven out of the sixteen cowry shells face up and the rest have their concave sides facing up. If this *odù* appears to a client, it means that the client will experience lasting prosperity and abundant riches in a short time. It is the *odù* of success and breakthrough if the client can exercise patience and endurance.

Èjì Ogbè—This is the *odù* that appears when the concave sides of eight out of the sixteen cowry shells face up and other eight are facing down. It is the *odù* of sound health and long life. It brings joy and comfort to the client.

Òsá—Nine cowries shell face up while seven face down. This is the *odù* of the witches. It means that if the client will succeed in his or her endeavor, the client will work very hard after the prescribed sacrifice has been offered. It is the *odù* to inform the client that he/she needs to get prepared for any form of hardship that might befall him or her.

Òfún—Ten cowries face up while six face down. It is the *odù* of giving. The client must sacrifice a lot of things in order to succeed in his or her enterprises in life.

Ọ̀wọ́nrín—Eleven cowries face up while five face down. This *odù* calls for patience by the client. All obstacles and calamities facing the client should be seen as "scar that will turn into star" if the client can be patient and obedient to the prescribed sacrifice.

Èjìlá Aṣẹ́bọra—Twelve cowries face up while four face down. This is the *odù* of Ṣàngó. If it appears to a client, he or she needs to be extraordinarily careful so that he or she will not have a bad ending, even when they have a good beginning.

Ìká—Thirteen cowries shell face up while three face down. This *odù* warns against disasters and mishaps. It warns the clients to be very careful of dealing with others so that they will not harm him or her. It also warns the client not to take any rash decisions about anything; he/she must act carefully with great endurance and perseverance. There will be a great success at the end of calamities and struggle.

Òtúrúpọ̀n—Fourteen cowries face up while two face down. This *odù* means blessings of spouse and children. If it appears to somebody, the person should be expectant for the blessing of wife and children after adhering to the prescribed sacrifices and prescriptions.

Èjì Ọlọgbọ́n—Fifteen cowries face up while one faces down. This means that somebody has supplanted the client in order to acquire success. Therefore, the client must be wise in recovering his/her lots or properties besides the sacrifices he/she has to offer.

Ìrẹtẹ̀—All the sixteen cowries face up. If this *odù* appears to a client it means that the person will become rich if he can adhere to the injunction of the diviner. It is all about prosperity, vitality, and fertility. Hence the saying "*Ìrẹtẹ̀ tẹ méjì látèlà, ó tẹ méjì ó là yẹbẹyẹbẹ*" (Ìrẹ tẹ̀ steps on two and becomes very rich, he steps on two and become acutely wealthy).

It is evident that most of the *odù* in Ẹẹ̀rìndínlógún are variants of the *odù* in the Ifá divinatory system.[9] The deducible reason is that according to Yorùbá religion, Ifá is the one who taught Ẹẹ̀rìndínlógún divination to the other deities who are using it. Though there are many things common to *odù* in Ifá and Ṣàngó's Ẹẹ̀rìndínlógún, their presentations are different. The usual opening thematic statement in Ifá is "*a dífá fún* . . ."—Ifá divination was made for . . . , but that of Ẹẹ̀rìndínlógún is "*òòṣà sọ pé* . . ."—the deity says that . . . Also, there is no order of seniority of the *odù* as we have it in Ifá; though most of the *odù* in Ṣàngó's Ẹẹ̀rìndínlógún revolve round Ṣàngó.

Conclusion

Divination rites are an essential part of daily life to the Yorùbá people. Ṣàngó's Ẹẹrìndínlógún system of divination cannot be underrated in this humanitarian work. This shows that Ṣàngó, as a deity, occupies an enviable space and place in Yorùbá cosmography. Ṣàngó's Ẹẹrìndínlógún diviners are agents of memory, preservers of people's history, and in the period of calamities the users of past events to reshape the present and the future. Even in the face of the incursion of civilizations and foreign religions, Ṣàngó's Ẹẹrìndínlógún divinatory system still finds its place in modern Yorùbá life. But this is not to deny the fact that many diviners have abandoned the practice for the new faith. However, some are still faithful to this divinatory system and have many clients, some of whom are even adherents of the new religions, Christianity and Islam.

NOTES

1. John Pemberton III, "Divination in Sub-Saharan Africa," in *African Art and Rituals of Divination,* ed. Alisa LaGamma (New York: Metropolitan Museum of Art, 2000), 10.

2. J. Omosade Awolalu, *Yorùbá Beliefs and Sacrificial Rites* (Brooklyn: Athelia Henrietta Press, 1979), 120–21.

3. John Browker, ed., *The Oxford Dictionary of World Religions* (New York: Oxford University Press, 1997).

4. William Bascom, *Sixteen Cowries: Yorùbá Divination from Africa to the New World* (Bloomington: Indiana University Press, 1980), 3.

5. Samuel Johnson, *The History of the Yorùbás* (1921) (Lagos: C.S.S., Bookshop, 1976), 27.

6. Wande Abimbola, *Ifá: An Exposition of Ifá Literary Corpus* (Ibadan, Nigeria: Oxford University Press, 1976).

7. Excerpt from the interviews held with an Ifẹ priest/diviner, Ifatoogun Adeboye Babalola, on April 16, 2001.

8. Raymond Prince, *Ifá: Yorùbá Divination and Sacrifice* (Ibadan, Nigeria: Ibadan University Press, 1964), 2–6, argues that there are four sections in each *ẹsẹ ifá;* William Bascom, *Ifá Divination: Communication between Gods and Men in West Africa* (Bloomington: Indiana University Press, 1969), 122–27, opines that each *ẹsẹ ifá* consists of three sections; Abimbola, *Ifá: An Exposition,* 43–62, posits eight sections for each *ẹsẹ ifá;* and Olatunde O. Olatunji, *Features of Yorùbá Oral Poetry* (Ibadan, Nigeria: University Press, 1984), 127–38, maintains that there are seven sections in each *ẹsẹ ifá.*

9. Compare the above discussion on *Ẹẹrìndínlógún* to that of *Ifá* in Wande Abimbola, *Ifá: An Exposition,* 150.

CHAPTER FIVE

Yorùbá Thunder Deities and Sovereignty

Àrá versus Ṣàngó

MARC SCHILTZ

One of the most popular and widespread *òrìṣà* cults among the Yorùbá of southwestern Nigeria is undoubtedly that of Ṣàngó, the deity of thunder and lightning. As a personification of this natural force, Ṣàngó is said to have been the fourth Aláàfin of Ọ̀yọ́.[1] In various myths Ṣàngó is described as a great magician who could eject fire from his mouth (*onínà-l'ẹ́nu*) and kill his enemies with lightning from heaven.[2] As Ọ̀yọ́'s power expanded in Yorùbáland and among various non-Yorùbá-speaking peoples in the seventeenth and eighteenth centuries, the Aláàfin's control over the Ṣàngó cult became an instrument for asserting his sovereignty all over the empire.[3]

Ṣàngó is not the only thunder deity among the Yorùbá. *Àrá* is the Yorùbá word for thunder (lightning is *ìmọ̀nàmọ́ná*), and the personification of this force is variously known as the *òrìṣà*, Òràmfẹ̀ in Ifẹ̀ and Àrá or Àrá-gbígbóná (lit., hot-*Àrá*)[4] in the western kingdoms of Ṣábẹ́ and Kétu (now in the Republic of Benin), as well as in the related town of Ìlárá (now on the Nigerian side of the border). Among these western Yorùbá-speaking peoples we note that outside the Ọ̀yọ́ kingdom, in Ṣábẹ́ and Kétu, the Aláàfin's cult of Ṣàngó became established alongside the earlier local Àrá cults. This cult-diffusion was no doubt linked to the rise of Ọ̀yọ́ as an imperial power in the seventeenth and eighteenth centuries. But if such coexistence of the Ṣàngó and Àrá thunder cults was possible outside the Ọ̀yọ́ kingdom, should we expect to find the presence of Àrá also in Ṣàngó's own kingdom of Ọ̀yọ́? As far as my investigations in the western Ọ̀yọ́ town of Ìgànná are concerned, I hasten to state that there

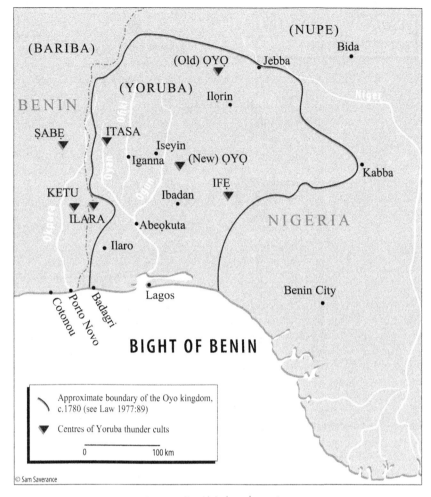

MAP 1. Yorùbá thunder cults.

also I found Àrá shrines in several compounds. Evidently, these Àrá cults functioned only for the benefit of their own lineage members,[5] whereas the Ṣàngó cult with its many devotees, annual festival celebrations, and possession priests (*ẹlẹ́gùn Ṣàngó*) functioned for the protection and prosperity of the whole town.[6]

However, in contrast to this typically tolerant Yorùbá attitude toward cultural diversity, I found in the nearby town of Ìtàsá (thirteen miles west of Ìgànná) a most unusual thunder-cult scenario of Ṣàngó exclusion and Àrá hegemony. It is on this rather perplexing Ṣàngó exclusion in Ìtàsá within the Ọ̀yọ́ kingdom, in contrast with the coexistence of Àrá and Ṣàngó in the Ṣàbẹ́ and Kétu kingdoms, that I propose to focus my discussion.

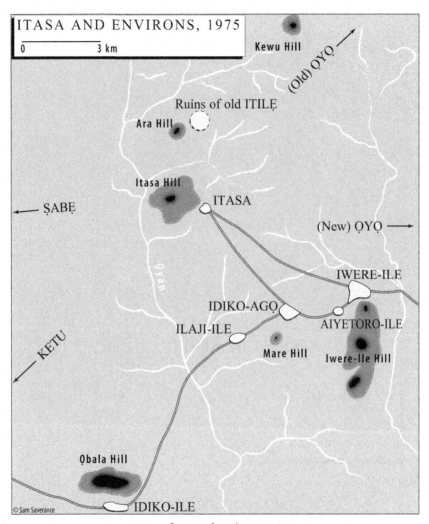

ITASA AND ENVIRONS, 1975

0   3 km

Kewu Hill

(Old) OYO

Ruins of old ITILE

Ara Hill

Itasa Hill

ITASA

ṢABE

(New) OYO

Oyan

IWERE-ILE

IDIKO-AGO

ILAJI-ILE

AIYETORO-ILE

KETU

Mare Hill

Iwere-Ile Hill

Ọbala Hill

© Sam Saverance

IDIKO-ILE

MAP 2. Itasa and environs, 1975.

Studies of traditional Yorùbá religion have often shown a tendency to hypostatize the òrìṣà within an overall cosmological model, applicable to the whole of Yorùbáland throughout history.[7] What this approach overlooks is that the relative rank, social functions, and popularity of the òrìṣà are contingent upon scenarios played out by certain individuals and groups in specific historical situations, especially those in which sovereignty was at stake, as in the cases to be discussed here of thunder cults associated with a royal lineage. Consequently, it is in the context of cult organizations in specific localities that we must approach the study of Yorùbá religion, rather than by making generalizations about the òrìṣà on the basis of some formal characteristics abstracted from their sociohistorical contexts. By applying this approach to a comparison of the Àrá and Ṣàngó cults in Ṣábẹ, Kétu, Ìlárá, and Ìtàsá, I hope to account for some of the variations in the myths, the cult organizations and the ritual symbolisms encountered in these different localities. First, I will comment briefly on the political momentum of the Ṣàngó cult within the context of the Ọ̀yọ́ empire. This will be followed by more detailed discussions of the thunder cults in the Ṣábẹ and Kétu kingdoms. Finally, these data will be contrasted with the exclusiveness of the Àrá cult in Ìtàsá.

Ṣàngó and Ọ̀yọ́ Imperialism

Various authors have commented on the important role played by the cult of Ṣàngó in sanctioning the Aláàfin's authority in the Ọ̀yọ́ empire.[8] Biobaku has even suggested that this cult assumed something of the force of emperor worship in the later Roman empire.[9] Possession priests of Ṣàngó had to come to Ọ̀yọ́ for the final stages of their initiatory training, and wherever a lightning catastrophe occurred, the local king had to go to the spot and pay homage to Ṣàngó, who was thought to have visited the world.[10] Moreover, for retrieving the *ẹdùn àrá* (stone celts taken for thunderbolts) which Ṣàngó was supposed to have hurled down from heaven on those who had incurred his displeasure, the Ṣàngó priests were authorized to collect ruinously high purification fees.[11] The Aláàfin also made use of the powers of Ṣàngó in the Ọ̀yọ́ empire. His strategy of appointing initiated Ṣàngó priests as governors (*ajẹ́lẹ̀*) along the Atlantic trade route further illustrates this.

Since lightning was an ever present danger everywhere (Yorùbáland and adjoining areas are reported to have among the highest lightning frequencies in the world),[12] a royal cult associated with this terrifying natural force was put in possession of an "extremely powerful medium for asserting the king's sovereignty." As attributes of divine kingship, thunder and lightning were in themselves effective symbols for communicating royal wrath, especially as this was coupled with a powerful corporation of Ṣàngó priests with representatives far and wide, who were capable of interpreting the divine messages and of taking disciplinary action when required.

Obviously, the administration of the Ọ̀yọ́ empire depended on more than the Aláàfin's control over the cult of Ṣàngó. Of great importance was Ọ̀yọ́'s military strength for the expansion and policing of the empire. At least as important was the Aláàfin's diplomatic skill in securing the loyalty of the provincial kings within the Ọ̀yọ́ kingdom, and in making alliances with the rulers of more distant areas.

With regard to the degree of dependence of Kétu and Ṣábẹ̀ on Ọ̀yọ́, Law comments that while friendly relations with Ọ̀yọ́ prevailed for most of the time during the imperial period, there is conflicting evidence as to whether these western kingdoms ever paid tribute to the Aláàfin.[13] But even if tribute was paid at times, the kings of Kétu and Ṣábẹ̀ seem to have retained much of their autonomy in controlling the internal affairs of their kingdoms. Moreover, the fact that the Atlantic trade route to Badagry, the lifeline of landlocked Ọ̀yọ́ after 1736, bypassed their territories suggests that the Aláàfin could not, or chose not to, depend on their loyalties.[14] For these reasons, I would suggest that the juxtaposition of the Aláàfin's cult of Ṣàngó and the local cults of Àrá in these western kingdoms reflects how sovereignty was divided, and largely the outcome of compromise arrangements, as I will illustrate below.

Within the Ọ̀yọ́ kingdom, the Aláàfin's rule was established more rigorously. Nevertheless, my own data on the fringe area west of Ìgànná and the nearby Atlantic trade route (that is, the area adjoining the Ṣábẹ̀ kingdom) reveal that local loyalties were not always guaranteed. This frontier land seems to have been weakly administered. While some local rulers were loyal to Ọ̀yọ́, there were others who lorded it over petty kingdoms in which local interests, rather than those of the Aláàfin, often prevailed. The Àrá enclave of Ìtàsá, which I will discuss in the last section of this chapter, was one such place. The ineffectiveness of Ọ̀yọ́'s rule there is reflected in the absence of the cult of Ṣàngó. Moreover, Ìtàsá's Àrá cult differs noticeably from Ṣábẹ̀'s and Kétu's, even though it was from these last two areas that the cult spread to the western Ọ̀yọ́ towns. This unique identity of Ìtàsá's Àrá is, at least in part, explained by its opposition to Ọ̀yọ́'s Ṣàngó; but before discussing this development I will compare the Àrá cults in Ṣábẹ̀, Kétu, and Ìlárá, and examine their relationship to the cult of Ṣàngó.

Àrá, the Wandering Stranger, and Ṣàngó, the Independent Senior Wife: Two Thunder Deities in a Marriage of Convenience

In the western Yorùbá kingdoms of Ṣábẹ̀ and Kétu, where we find the cults of Àrá and Ṣàngó alongside each other, we note that the formula for their apparent peaceful coexistence was worked out at the cost of a conceptual reversal and compromise arrangements between the two fierce thunder gods. Essentially, this formula consists in a sex change for

Ṣàngó, who is said to be Àrá's senior wife, as well as in a division of labor between the priests of the two cults with regard to the purification rituals after lightning catastrophes. Unlike the cult of Ṣàngó, which was centralized under the Aláàfin's control, neither the Alákétu nor the Oníṣàbẹ́ seems to have revered Àrá as his lineage *òrìṣà*, and thus used the powers of Àrá directly for buttressing royal authority. The different towns have their own versions of how Àrá came to them, and a comparison of these will provide some insights into the local variations of the thunder cult.

The stories of the origin of the cult describe Àrá as a wandering man of unspecified abode. They concur in locating a hunter's camp within the kingdom of Kétu as the place where the cult of Àrá originated. Eventually this settlement grew in size, and later became known as the "town of Àrá," Ìlárá (from *ilú-àrá*). From Ìlárá the cult spread in various directions, including to the towns of Kétu and Ṣàbẹ́. I will first give a Ṣàbẹ́ version of the story of Àrá before making a comparison of the cult with Kétu and Ìlárá.

Àrá was introduced to Ṣàbẹ́ by a man called Gou. This man, who was a native of Ṣàbẹ́ , was afflicted by *àbíkú* spirits, with the result that his children kept dying in infancy. After being told about the cause of the deaths he decided to leave Ṣàbẹ́ . He stopped in many hunters' camps along the route he traveled, but none of the hunters he met was capable of curing his affliction. Eventually he reached a camp where he was welcomed by a hunter and his wife. This hunter was a great magician called Ogodo. He promised Gou to solve his problem if he came to live with him. Gou accepted, and his hosts gave him their daughter in marriage, as well as a powerful charm to overcome the *àbíkú* affliction.

A few years later Àrá came to their camp. He appeared as an ordinary man, and asked if he could stay. He was welcomed, and Gou immediately became his close friend, always praising him for his mighty deeds. As the reputation of Àrá spread, more people flocked to the settlement to join in the worship of Àrá. In the end, the place grew to such a size that they called it ìlú-Àrá, or Ìlárá.

Some years later Àrá decided to proceed with his journey, but before leaving he gave to Gou some irons and thunderbolts to remember him by. After Àrá left, Gou built him a shrine, in which he placed the sacred objects. Then he prayed to Àrá and asked him what he would like to receive. Àrá answered his prayer and revealed that at the altar (*ojúbọ*) of the sacred objects he wanted to receive a ram, a hen, kola nuts, and cold maize gruel (*èkọ tútù*). Àrá also promised to help those who came to worship him.

When Gou had fathered many sons and daughters, and none of them had died, he decided to take them back to Ṣábẹ́ in order to show his people the great blessing that had befallen him. He took with him some of the irons and thunderbolts, and during his stay in Ṣábẹ́ he taught his people there how to worship Àrá.

Later he returned to Ìlárá, where he died. But when the news of his death reached Ṣábẹ́ his people went to Ìlárá and brought his body back home and buried it near the Àrá shrine.

The main Àrá shrine in Ṣábẹ́ is located in an enclosed area. Access to the sanctuary is gained through a small gatehouse along the fence. A thatched-roof building in the center of the open space is the Àrá shrine, in which the irons and stone celts that symbolize Àrá are kept. Nearby are altars for Òsọ́ọ̀sì and Amọde, two hunter deities who in the Ṣábẹ́ tradition are said to be Àrá's wives. Another small building within the enclosure serves as a dwelling for the chief priest of Àrá and his wife. Once installed as head of the cult, the chief priest lives there for the rest of his life. Also kept within the enclosure are the sacred ram, which is tethered to a post, the Àrá drums and gongs, and a large inverted pot, which is adorned with relief designs. Near the Àrá shrine is Gou's tomb, while further away is a cooking area used by the *aláàrá* (Àrá worshippers) on festive occasions.

A comparison of the Àrá cult story and ritual arrangements between Ṣábẹ́ , Kétu, and Ìlárá shows that the main differences concern the personages involved in the thunder god's drama, that is, differences in their identities, actions, and peregrinations, and in the way they interrelate with each other. Inasmuch as myth can be rationalized as "a charter for action," one may note local concerns with town, identity, inter-town rivalry over the control of the powers of Àrá, and other mundane affairs underpinning these differences.

The stories from Kétu and Ìlárá stated that Àrá originally came from Ṣábẹ́ through a man called Agbọn. This man, like Gou in the Ṣábẹ́ version, was said to have left his hometown because he was troubled by *àbíkú* spirits. But whereas Gou met Àrá in the hunters' camp that later became Ìlárá, and afterward returned to Ṣábẹ́ in order to introduce the Àrá cult there, Agbọn appears as a man who already had Àrá before leaving Ṣábẹ́. This does not affect the fact that Àrá himself remains a somehow timeless and mysterious figure whose origin is not probed, and who, after his encounter with the ancestors, goes his way, perhaps to die somewhere in the way other men die, or perhaps to live on. In any event, his power to bless or punish lives on through the ministry of his initiated followers who guard the irons and the thunderbolts. In the case of Kétu and Ìlárá, there is the acknowledgment that Àrá came to them through a man from Ṣábẹ́, but that the cult itself began only in a hunters' camp, which later became renowned as the "town of Àrá," in Ìlárá.

At this point, however, the different versions begin to diverge, and local interests prevail. First there is the question of the identity of the lone hunter who invited the Ṣábẹ́ refugee to settle with him, and then saved him from his *àbíkú* affliction. In the Ṣábẹ́ story the hunter was called Ògòdò, and did not belong to any town in particular. Ògòdò is the Yorùbá word for yaws, and the name here suggests the *òrìṣà* that personifies this disease. But in one of the Kétu versions the name of the hunter is Adare, and he is identified as one of the royals of the Alákétu's *ìdílé* (lineage), who had set up his camp on Kétuland. Adare then gave his daughter Kọbọla in marriage to the Ṣábẹ́ settler. The couple had a son who was named Ewégbèmí ("the leaf saves me"), indicating that Adare's magic had overcome the *àbíkú* threat. When Ewégbèmí grew up he had a son who became popularly known as Bàbá Aláàrá ("father of the Àrá worshippers"), as by then the cult had gathered a large following.

Our Ìlárá story also mentions Agbọn, who brought Àrá from Ṣábẹ́. But contrary to the Kétu claims that the site of the hunter's camp was on the Alákétu's land, and that the hunter was a royal kinsman, the Ìlárá version leaves out the question of land ownership and states that the first settlers were two Ṣábẹ́ hunters, Ọ̀sọ́ọ̀sì and Ògòdò. As mentioned earlier, these two personages are themselves *òrìṣà*, and in Ṣábẹ́ the former is revered as one of Àrá's wives. A look around the shrines in Kétu and Ìlárá shows, however, that the setup of Àrá's household there is different from Ṣábẹ́'s. In Kétu the Àrá cult is located in two compounds, Abiya's and Ògòdò's, who worship the deity on different days. Abiya's compound claims to have obtained the cult through Iná-akọ, a woman who, after visiting relatives in Ìlárá, brought back the sacred objects. Later she passed some on to her sister, Afẹyin/a-Àyìnké, who lived in the compound of Ògòdò. In these Kétu shrines the *òrìṣà* revered as Àrá's wife is Orojafin. Also present, though not as wives, are Ọ̀sọ́ọ̀sì and Àbíkú. Both are represented by pots from which the worshippers can draw water to protect themselves from various afflictions. In Ìlárá the main Àrá shrine is located in an enclosed area on the fringe of the town, adjoining a sacred bush. There also, Orojafin is revered as Àrá's wife, but the *òrìṣà* most closely associated with them is the ubiquitous Yorùbá trickster Èṣù.

Despite these differences which bring out the specific ways in which each town has integrated Àrá within its own cult organization, the similarities between Kétu's Àrá and Ìlárá's Àrá are greater than those between either of these and Ṣábẹ́. This may be explained by the geographical and historical proximity of Kétu and Ìlárá, although now they are located on opposite sides of the international boundary. But if there were such close links, why should Ìlárá's story of origin of the Àrá cult say that the first settlers were hunters from Ṣábẹ́ and fail to mention Adare, the Alákétu's kinsman? I would suggest that the answer here is provided by Ìlárá's concern to control its Àrá cult (and possibly other affairs as well) independently of Kétu. A clue to this can be found in the following two accounts from Ìlárá.

> After Agbọn had settled in the hunting camp of Ọ̀sọ́sì and Ògòdò, other people also joined the settlement when they heard about the great deeds of Àrá. Some years later, however, death came to the area and Agbọn ran away to Lie-down, another hunter's camp where he had spent some time after leaving Ṣábẹ́. He stayed there for many years, and during that time the Àrá shrine in Ìlárá gradually fell to ruins. It was not until Agbọn had grown old that he called his son Ewégbèmí and told him how he had brought Àrá to Ìlárá, and how from there he had run away to Ilé-ẹdu. When Ewégbèmí heard this he was very grieved that he had been left in the dark about how to worship Àrá. Then suddenly he became possessed by his father's *òrìṣà,* and he brought Àrá back from Ilẹ̀-edu to Ìlárá. He did not know how to worship Àrá, but he did as the *òrìṣà* directed him. That was why the people of Kétu always sang his praises, saying: "Ewégbèmí made the *òrìṣà,* Ewégbèmí had no *olúwo.*" (That is, he had no head of the cult above him). Therefore, all the powers of Àrá to strike with lightning were given to Ewégbèmí before his father's death.

From this Ìlárá account, then, it would seem that what gives Ìlárá the edge over Kétu is Àrá's direct intervention in taking possession of Ewégbèmí. This headship of the cult, the account states, was fully acknowledged by the Kétu people in the past. But later things changed, and by some accident of history the Àrá worshippers from Kétu managed to pull the wool over the Ìlárá people's eyes and seize control of the cult. This rivalry between the two towns is further expressed in the second Ìlárá account, which deals with the more rewarding aspects of the rights to conduct the purification rituals (*ètùtù*) after a lightning catastrophe has occurred.

> After the *olúwo* (that is, Ewégbèmí) who brought Àrá to Ìlárá died, the townspeople did not know that Àrá had been introduced to Kétu from their town. They thought that it was from Kétu that Àrá had come to

them. Therefore, whenever Àrá struck anyone or destroyed any property, all the fees collected for removing the thunderbolts were sent to Kétu. This went on for many years, until one day an old man sang a Gèlèdé song in which he told the people that after Agbọn had gone to Ilèedu and his descendants had forgotten about the cult of Àrá, Ewégbèmí reinstated the òrìṣà through his own bravery and zeal. This song was a real eye-opener for the people of Ìlárá, and they immediately challenged the Kétus about who was to be in charge of the cult. The dispute was serious, and in the end the Alákétu called the Àrá worshippers from the two towns in order to seek a settlement. After listening to both sides, he ruled that when lightning struck in Ìlárá the ètùtù would be carried out by the people of Ìlárá, whereas when lightning struck in Kétu the ètùtù would be carried out by Kétu Àrá worshippers.

The implication of this Ìlárá account is that the Alákétu had jurisdiction over the affairs of Ìlárá, since he could sit in judgment over a dispute involving the Aláàrá of Kétu and Ìlárá. But the account implies also that, unlike the Aláàfin, who could control the Ṣàngó cult in every tributary town, neither the Alákétu nor the Aláàrá in Kétu town had overall control of the Àrá cult. Such control, the Ìlárá people felt, should have been accorded to their own olúwo, hence the reference to Ewégbèmí, to whom the Kétu people originally used to address their praise songs. Therefore, the Alákétu's verdict that the Aláàrá from Kétu could no longer receive purification fees from Ìlárá victims of lightning was fair, but it fell short of acknowledging Ìlárá's claim of supremacy for their olúwo.

From the data reviewed so far it is clear that the Àrá cults in Ṣábẹ, Kétu, and Ìlárá share a common tradition. Ṣàngó did not feature at all in this, neither in the stories of origin nor among the òrìṣà worshipped in association with Àrá. Yet in these three towns the Ṣàngó cult took root. We have no historical data to ascertain when or how Ṣàngó got there; but, as everywhere else, the people acknowledge that the cult came from Òyó and was named after the legendary Aláàfin Ṣàngó. On the other hand, Ṣàngó in these western towns is revered as a female òrìṣà who is said to have been Àrá's senior wife. How are we to reconcile these apparently incompatible and contradictory claims with what has been stated earlier?

In trying to clarify this I will first examine the claim that Ṣàngó is a female òrìṣà, and secondly, why she is said to be Àrá's wife. From the way people expressed their thoughts on this question it seemed that a neat distinction was made between the name of the cult and the òrìṣà that personifies thunder and lightning. One man in Kétu had this version of one of the well-known myths about Ṣàngó:

In the old days "Ṣàngó" was not such a fearsome name as it has become now. Many people bore that name. So it was, until one Aláàfin of Òyó called Ṣàngó fell out with his people. When he realized that they had rejected him he went to the bush and hanged himself from a tree. When the people of Òyó heard that he died, they started spreading the word that he had committed suicide, saying "*oba so,* the king has hanged himself." But those still loyal to Ṣàngó were much incensed when they heard this "*oba so,*" and tried unsuccessfully to stop the rumor of this ignoble death. Eventually they went to Ìbàrìbáland, where they obtained a dangerous and powerful charm made with gun powder. At the time of a thunderstorm, any house at which they deposited this charm would attract lightning and burn down. Back home, they planted this charm on the houses of all those whom they wanted to punish. These people then had to pay heavy fines for Ṣàngó's followers to come and perform the *ètùtù* and remove the thunderbolts. As fear of punishment spread, the people tried to please the Ṣàngó followers by retracting the previous rumors, saying instead: "*oba kò so,* the king did not hang himself." This is why, to this day, they call Ṣàngó "Ọba Kòso."

This story, then, claims that the power to direct lightning was not really the legendary king Ṣàngó's, but was imported by Ṣàngó's follow-ers from Ìbàrìbáland, west of Old Òyó. Similar stories which trace the origin of the Ṣàngó cult to that area[15] outside Yorùbáland had already been recorded by Frobenius in the early part of this century.[16] In fact the Àrá cult may also have originated in Ìbàrìbáland or elsewhere, but what concerns us here is that ultimately the decision about, or perception of, the sex of an *òrìṣà* rests with the worshippers. In Òyó it is said that Ṣàngó himself could direct lightning, before his followers learned the secret, therefore he is the *òrìṣà,* and obviously male. However, in this Kétu ver-sion of Ṣàngó the situation is different. Here, the cult that developed in Òyó is specifically named after the legendary Aláàfin Ṣàngó, but the sex of the *òrìṣà* personifying thunder and lightning remains unspecified.

What makes Ṣàngó a female *òrìṣà* in the Ṣábẹ́ Kétu tradition can best be understood in light of the accounts which describe the relationship between Àrá and Ṣàngó as one between husband and senior wife. This is how one Ìlárá man explained it.

This Ṣàngó was just like any other woman. But when Àrá learned that she had some powerful charms (*òògùn,* "medicine") he thought that he might help him in his work. He married her, and whenever his enemies tried to harm him Ṣàngó would come to his aid and kill them. She did this for many years and Àrá was very pleased with her. Since he had married many junior wives, he rewarded Ṣàngó by giving her the freedom to live on her own. She gratefully accepted this, but later she returned to him and implored him to give her his powers. After many requests, he eventually gave her some of his powers. Whenever lightning struck in the places which Ṣàngó had acquired, Àrá would tell his followers to let her perform the *ètùtù*. But when Àrá struck, only his followers could perform the *ètùtù*. However, even in her own territories Ṣàngó could not remove the thunderbolts without invoking and honoring (*ìjúbà*) Àrá.

The main effect of this conceptualization of the relationship between Àrá and Ṣàngó as a marital one is, ipso facto, an acknowledgment of a rank and role differential between two fierce personalities who are essentially equals. In Yorùbá society, no matter how wealthy or powerful a woman may be, she is expected to acknowledge her husband's authority in domestic matters (although not in her business dealings), and more generally she must always show respect and praise him publicly. However, this conceptualization of Ṣàngó as Àrá's senior wife euphemizes in the idiom of ordered domestic relations a pragmatic solution to what appears to have been a potentially dangerous power confrontation at the time the Ṣàngó cult spread to the Ṣábé-Kétu areas. What we have, then, is an assertion of the primacy of Àrá, if not politically then at least morally. (Ṣàngó priests cannot perform the *ètùtù* if they do not first honor Àrá.) Secondly, the story provides a justification for the spatial and organizational separation of the two thunder cults; in each town the shrines of Àrá and Ṣàngó are located in different compounds, and each cult has its own internal organization. Similarly, senior wives of wealthy polygynists often live away from their husbands and junior co-wives. This arrangement gives such women more freedom and scope to pursue their own business activities. Thirdly, this story accounts for the ritual division of labor between the two cults with regard to the public function of conducting the purification rituals after lightning has struck. How each town practically sorted out this question may have varied, but data from Ṣábé indicate that formerly divinatory procedures after a lightning catastrophe decided whether the Àrá or Sàngó priests should perform the *ètùtù*.

To what extent the Ṣàngó cult backed up the Aláàfin's sovereignty in the Ṣábé and Kétu kingdoms in the days of Òyó imperialism requires further investigation. Whether the challenge which the Ṣàngó cult presented to the preexisting Àrá cult owed its muscle to its grassroots popularity or to the direct influence of the Aláàfin is not clear. What the data reveal, however, is that the conceptual linkage of the two thunder deities in a marital union was the outcome of a marriage of convenience which most likely had been precipitated by the rise of Ọ̀yọ́ imperialism.

Ìtàsá's Àrá: "When Two Rams Clash, One Must Give Way"[17]

Unlike the Kétu and Ṣábẹ̀ kingdoms, where compromise arrangements made the coexistence of the Àrá and Ṣàngó cults possible, Ìtàsá presents us with a history in which no such overt allowances were made. In this western outlier of the greater Ọ̀yọ́ kingdom, the Aláàfin's Ṣàngó cult was kept at bay by the Àrá, cult which was directly controlled by the local rulers. Clearly, the story of Ìtàsá's Àrá is intimately linked to the story of the town itself. I will begin the discussion with the latter story, so as to bring out more clearly the sovereignty issue behind the "clash of the gods."

Ìtílé was the original name of Ìtàsá, and *onítílé* was the title of its kings. Ìtílé town was sacked and abandoned in the course of the nineteenth century, and the present village of Ìtàsá was rebuilt about 1 ½ miles south of the site of the old ruins by some returnees after the establishment of Pax Britannica in the 1890s. Under the colonial and post-colonial administrations, the headman of Ìtàsá ranked as *baálẹ̀* (chief of settlement), whereas in precolonial times the *onítílé* of Ìtílé had established themselves as *ọba* (kings) in the area. In what follows I shall use the name Ìtílé, unless the data indicate that I am dealing with the more recent settlement of Ìtàsá.

The starting point of the story of Ìtílé is Old Ọ̀yọ́ at a time when two princes were contesting the succession to the throne. The contest must have been a fierce one, and resulted in the defeat of Ilẹ̀mọ́là, the junior aspirant to the throne. Rather than pledge loyalty to his senior brother as the new Aláàfin, the angered Ilẹ̀mọ́là and his supporters decided to leave Ọ̀yọ́ and found a town of their own.[18] They trekked over a hundred miles in a southwesterly direction until they settled at a site called Agbolé, near the Ọ̀yán river (a tributary of the Ògùn). Many were said to have followed Ilẹ̀mọ́là. After they had settled, the chiefs and people of the settlements in the area chose to serve the leader of the Ọ̀yọ́ exiles. In one account, 143 towns were involved, but the late Baálẹ̀ Oyèdòkun gave the more likely figure of seven. When Ìtílé was sacked by the Fulani in the 1830s, and by the Dahomeans around 1880, all its subordinate towns were also destroyed according to the stories. These settlements were probably located to the north and west of Ìtílé (as, for instance, old-Kéwú, whose chiefly descendants now hold the Básàmú chieftaincy in nearby Ìgànná). Certainly none of the remaining towns in the area, from Ìwéré to Ìjìò (which were also sacked, but later rebuilt), seems to have been subordinate to the *onítílé*. What the Ìtàsá stories say, then, is that when the Ọ̀yọ́ exiles had settled, "Ilèmọ́là ordered the towns in the area to serve the Aláàfin no longer, but to serve him alone. Because of this order they called the king of the place where they lived 'the one who owns the land' [*eni t'ó ní ilé*]. This was the meaning of *onítílé*."

This etymology sets up a taunting contrast with the title of Ilèmọ́là's senior brother who acceded to the Ọ̀yọ́ throne, that is, Aláàfin, which means "the one who owns the palace." And to make sure that the negation of the new Aláàfin was not just a one-off angry outburst, Ilèmọ́là is said to have sworn (*búra*) that "He and his senior brother who is king must never again meet each other face to face. If they were to see each other again and Ilèmọ́là too had the great honor of being king, something extraordinary would happen [*gọngọ yóò sọ*]."

Later I will mention one thunderous occasion during the colonial period when the two brothers almost met. Meanwhile, the question about the origin of Ìtílé that remains unanswered is, when was the town founded? Unfortunately the stories of origin do not provide the information needed to establish this date. From the list of kings, it seems that Ilè mọ́là founded his kingdom in the early part of the eighteenth century. But it is likely that Ìtílé is older than this, since in stories of origin genealogies often become telescoped and names forgotten. In any event, the Ìtílé kings must have been ruling over their insubordinate petty enclave in the Ọ̀yọ́ kingdom at the time the Aláàfin's power was at its highest during the eighteenth century.[19]

Ìtílé is not the only town in Yorùbáland whose kings claim descent from the royal house in Ọ̀yọ́. One other case is Ìdìkó (now split into two small settlements, Ìdìkó-ilé and Ìdìkó-àgó), which is situated about eight miles southwest of Ìtílé. The founder of Ìdìkó is said to have been an Ọ̀yọ́ prince who went into exile with his followers after his brother had usurped his right to accede to the Aláàfin's throne. The Onídìkó (kings of Ìdìkó), however, have no history of a lasting grievance (at least overtly) with the Aláàfin. According to custom, shortly after a new Onídìkó is installed as king, he must go to Ọ̀yọ́ to pay his respects to the Aláàfin. Afterward, the two "brothers" are never to meet again face to face. But apart from this personal avoidance relationship, Ìdìkó seems to have been loyal to Ọ̀yọ́, including during the time the Àrá cult spread to the area, as I will discuss in the following paragraphs.

What emerges from our Ìtílé data, however, is that by adopting Àrá as their own *òrìṣà* the *onítílé* institutionalized their taunting of the ideology

underpinning the Aláàfin's sovereignty, namely his rule by the power of
Ṣàngó. This is how Àrá is said to have come to Ìtílé:

> Àrá was a wanderer. We heard that before he lived in the land of Saworo
> [here referring to Ṣábẹ́]. Wherever he stayed he was in the habit of leav-
> ing one or two of his wives as well as some of his power, in order to show
> the people how strong he was. In the course of his wanderings we heard
> that he went to Ìdìkó and asked if he could stay. They asked him what
> kind of food he wanted to eat. He told them he liked roasted yams and
> the meat of dogs and cows. But before eating any of these, he said he had
> to eat the king's firstborn son. On hearing this the Ìdìkó people refused
> him as a visitor. As Àrá did not know where his journey would take him,
> he was worried that the lack of food would be too great a hardship for
> the two wives who were traveling with him. He therefore asked the peo-
> ple of Ìdìkó to keep one of them. The name of that wife was Ọbálá.

In Ìdìkó the stories of origin confirm that when Àrá first called on
them the people were afraid and would not allow him to stay. He was
put up for the night, but on the second day the Onídìkó took him to
Ìtílé where he was welcomed and worshipped. Historically, Ìdìkó's fear
of Àrá may have been coupled with fear of incurring the wrath of Ṣàngó,
their Ọ̀yọ́ overlord's òrìṣà. Another reason why Àrá was not welcomed
may have been because Ọbálá was already established as the town's òrìṣà.
This Ọbálá was not Àrá's wife, as according to the Ìtílé story, but the deified ancestor of the original inhabitants of the area.[20] By making Ọbálá
Àrá's wife, the Ìtílé people seem to imply that Ìdìkó became subordinate
to them, that is, inasmuch as Àrá, the husband, is free to go and visit his
wives at any time and in any place. But to the people of Ìdìkó this is not
at all the case. It is true that adjoining the main Ọbálá shrine in Ìdìkó
there is another shrine for Àrá, and that whenever they worship the former, offerings will be made also to the latter. This ritual linking of Ọbálá
and Àrá is played down, however. The reason why Àrá is worshipped,
the Ìdìkó people explained, is because he once visited them. Then they
hastened to say that they had nothing to do with the Àrá worship in Ìtàsà
(that is, old Ìtílé), that they never even attended the annual festival of the
thunder deity there. In this way the people of Ìdìkó asserted their own
local sovereignty vis-à-vis Ìtílé, while the fact of simply commemorating
Àrá's visit, without accepting his cult for the town, could hardly be interpreted as an act of disloyalty toward Ọ̀yọ́.

The story of Àrá's coming to Ìtílé continues with his visit to the town
of Ìwéré. There also the people were afraid and unwilling to meet his

demands. It was afterward that he made his way to Ìtílé. Who the *onítílé* was at the time is not specified,[21] but the story says that the king trembled with fear when Àrá explained that, in order to stay with him and his people, he demanded the sacrifice of his *àrèmọ* (firstborn son). Àrá promised that if his requests were met he would assist the king with all his extraordinary powers. The king, however, insisted that he could not give up his son. Finally he called his town chiefs and asked for their advice. The chiefs reminded the king that his firstborn son was mad, and that whenever he was allowed out he wandered from town to town until search parties were sent out to bring him back home. For this reason the chiefs advised the king to sacrifice his son, saying, "It would be better that one heard 'he died' than 'the king's son got lost'" (*ó kúkú sàn kí á gbọ́ wí pé ó kú ju ọmọ ọba nù lọ*). After thinking this over the king finally agreed to allow Àrá to stay and to sacrifice his son to him, provided it would be a one and only occasion. This condition was accepted, and they agreed that from that time on they would sacrifice a dog to Àrá every year.

The story continues to narrate how after receiving the king's son and the other sacrificial offerings Àrá retired to the small hill on the edge of Ìtílé town. Before taking his leave, Àrá told the king to come and visit him the following day, but when early in the morning the king called all the townspeople and asked who would go and see the stranger on his behalf, nobody volunteered for fear that Àrá would kill and eat whoever went up. Finally, when the king announced that he himself would go if nobody else went, his two affines, Babalàlè and Babẹgbé, decided to go. The story continues as follows:

On the way Babalàlè walked in front and Babẹgbé followed, carrying the calabash with maize gruel which he wanted to give to the stranger. While they were walking Babalàlè looked up and saw in the distance Àrá, who was eating the head of the king's firstborn son. Babalàlè was struck with fear and fell to the ground. Babẹgbé did not know what had happened, and asked Babalàlè what the matter was. But Babalàlè was so terrified he could not speak. Instead, Àrá raised his voice and shouted to Babalàlè "Your chest which has touched the ground, keep it down and come here crawling,[22] and let Babẹgbé come to me upright as he is now." That was how Babẹgbé went forward with his calabash of maize gruel. When he came to Àrá he was told to put the calabash down. Then Àrá began to pluck many different kinds of leaves and put them in the calabash. He explained to Babẹgbé that the calabash would remain as a propitiatory calabash [*koto amèrò*] whenever a place fell victim to his wrath. Then he ordered Babalàlè to stand up from his prostrating posture and go and sit on a tree near where he was lying, which they had cut short. He did as he was told and that is the reason why, to this day, when Àrá strikes somewhere [jà nibikan], Babalalè must get a stool and sit down until they have removed the òrìsà 's wrath. Finally, Àrá gave Babalalè a ceremonial staff [òpá idásà]. Then he sent Babalalè and Babẹgbé back to the king to give him his (Àrá's) promise that in all his needs he would stand by him.

As in the stories from Kétu and Ṣábẹ, here also Àrá is characterized as a wandering stranger who did not foist himself upon the local people but always asked to be given hospitality. But what is new in the Ìtílé account is that on arrival in a town Àrá always confronts the sovereignty issue. He goes straight to the king, from whom he demands the ultimate sacrifice, namely the latter's àrèmọ, or firstborn son, in return for his promise of protection and assistance. No such demands on the kings were mentioned in the Ṣábẹ-Kétu traditions. But we should bear in mind that at the time the Àrá cult spread to the Ọ̀yọ́ kingdom, the Aláàfin's Ṣàngó cult was already organized empire-wide. Therefore it would seem that no provincial king could accept the Àrá cult, with its own priests who were specialized in conducting the purification rituals after lightning catastrophes, without bringing into question his loyalty to the Aláàfin. In Ìtílé it is clear that the sovereignty issue was central to the introduction of Àrá. Not only did the onítílé accept Àrá as yet another cult in the way that Yorùbá kings used to welcome new òrìsà cults when exiles and refugees asked to settle in their towns,[23] but he actually made Àrá into his own royal cult and an instrument for asserting his sovereignty in the area over which he ruled.

First, by sacrificing his firstborn son to Àrá, the onítílé entered into a lasting pact with the òrìsà. In this way he was believed to participate in Àrá's power to direct lightning and strike his enemies, in the same way that the Aláàfin was said to act through Ṣàngó. Before giving up his son, however, the king had consulted his chiefs and followed their counsel. Therefore, in the eyes of the people, his action was not only legitimate but beneficial for all of them. Secondly, having acted on behalf of the people, the onítílé retained direct control over the Àrá cult by having its priesthood vested in the lineages of his non-chiefly affines, Babalalè and Babẹgbé, rather than in the lineages of town chiefs or non-affinal commoners. The onítílé's strategy of relying on his affines to carry out the dangerous mission to Àrá is referred to in the following words in the accounts: "Such was our custom in the old days, of entrusting the hardest and most risky obligations to our affines."

Moreover, the fact that they were under such a constant affinal obliga-
tion prevented Babalalè and Babẹgbé from usurping the *onítílê*'s right to
control the Àrá cult, even though as priests they were fully initiated in its
secret powers. Normally affinal relations are ego-focused, but in this case
we note that this relationship became institutionalized, so that to this day
in Ìtàsá the lineages of Babalalè and Babẹgbé stand in an affinal relationship to the royal lineage.[24]

The *onítílê*'s anxiety to be the sole controller of the power to direct
lightning can perhaps best be illustrated in the following incidents. In the
first two cases, the anxiety concerns the threat that someone else might
manipulate this power to harm the king, while the last two cases illustrate the king's anxiety to maintain law and order in the face of threats
by townspeople, as well as by strangers.

> In 1962 the late Oyèdòkun Ágànná was installed as *baálè* of Ìtàsá. Dur-
> ing the days preparatory to the installation, the king-elect organized
> a hunting party so that large quantities of meat could be made avail-
> able for the coming festivities. One night while he and the other hunt-
> ers were camping in the bush it started to rain heavily. They all ran for
> shelter to a hut in a nearby farm. While they were sitting round the fire,
> Oyèdòkun narrated stories of his predecessors. Suddenly there was a ter-
> rific thunderclap, and a flash of lightning struck a huge tree, which came
> crashing down on top of the hut. Everybody inside was knocked out,
> some men being pinned down by the branches on top of the open fire.
> Oyèdòkun was also hit on the head, but he managed to bring his entire
> party out from under the debris. The men spent the rest of the night in
> the pouring rain, suffering from their injuries and surrounded by lurking
> hyenas and other wild animals. Throughout that time the *onítílê*-elect
> could be heard praying to his forefathers to save him and his men, and
> not allow his enemies to rejoice over his death before he was made king.

The king-elect and his men saw this attack by lightning as an obvious
challenge to the *onítílê*'s sovereignty. But because he and his men survived
the attack he proved that Àrá was on his side and that no rival had succeeded in turning the *òrìṣà*'s power against him. Moreover, if the attack
had been the work of the Aláàfin's Ṣàngó, he had proof that Àrá's power
(in protecting him) was stronger. Asserting the supremacy of Àrá over
Ṣàngó has indeed remained a matter of concern for the *onítílê*, especially
after the establishment of the colonial administration, when their royal
title was no longer recognized and they were made ordinary *bálè* under
the Aláàfin. It was this demotion which led to the following incident.

When Abíóyè was *baálè* of Ìtàsá, the Aláàfin ordered that all the kings visit him, including the *onítílé*. The order came notwithstanding the fact that Ilèmólà (the founder of Ìtílé) had sworn that he and his senior brother (the Aláàfin) would never see each other again. As soon as the *onítílé* and his party of followers set out on their journey to Òyó the rain started to pour and there was thunder and lightning. Yet the elements did not affect the king and his party. On arrival in Òyó they stayed at Ìsokùn. While they were there the thunderstorm continued with increasing intensity for nine days. The Aláàfin then enquired who was the king who had arrived in Òyó. They told him that it was the *onítílé*. As soon as he heard this he sent a giant-sized fowl and the following message of apology: That the king who greets with thunder (*àrá*) should not be angry with him, the Aláàfin, any longer. Àrá himself has had to chase him away, compulsorily, because the *onítílé* should never see the face of the king of Òyó, and what is more, the *onítílé* should never prostrate to any king.

This incident is now alluded to in a song sung by the women of Babalalè's compound on the day of the annual festival of Àrá in Ìtàsá:

Àkùkọ Àr(ì)rà kọ d'Òyò-ó,
  Gbangba l'a ń gbó l'óko.

The cock of Àrá crowed as far as Òyó,
  The news of it reached all of us in the farm.

In his book *The New Òyó Empire,* Atanda has cogently argued that an unprecedented, authoritarian regime of Native Administration developed in Òyó under Aláàfin Ládùgbòlù between 1906 and 1944. Backed by the British Resident, Captain Ross, the Aláàfin made visits to Òyó by provincial kings mandatory at the occasion of the annual *bèèrè* festival.[25] Since it demoted the *onítílé* to the rank of one of the many village chiefs within the Native Authority system, the flouting of the age-old avoidance relationship between the Aláàfin and the *onítílé* was bound to spark off a "clash of the gods."

For the *onítílé*, the importance of asserting his sovereignty by the power of Àrá centered not only on legitimizing himself in office, or securing his personal protection, but also on playing his role as ruler of his people. From the following two accounts we will see how the Àrá cult functioned in sanctioning certain types of antisocial behavior.

When a man was planning to harm someone by using sorcery (which is different from witchcraft), something would happen so that the king learned of the man's sinister plans, and also about the location in the bush where the sorcerer kept the secret of his evil medicines. First the king would send his messenger through the town to announce to the people that a sorcerer was about to harm someone. Then the sorcerer would be given a warning that if he did not stop his evil plans he would die a certain death and his name would be made public.[26] If the man in question did not immediately repent, Àrá would strike suddenly. The man would be found dead and his secret grove burnt to ashes by lightning, even though not a drop of rain fell from the sky.

If such was Àrá's punishment for criminals within the community, his treatment of outsiders who threatened the peace and livelihood of his people was equally devastating. The following anecdote illustrates this:

> Àrá protected the town also from outside dangers, especially by punishing marauders. One day [in 1957] some thieves came to Ìtàsá and stole all the property of Chief Jagun and his sons. The theft took place during the night, and the thieves left the town immediately. The following morning the king called some of the hunters and told them that Àrá had revealed to him that the thieves had taken their loot to one particular bush. Eight hunters went out to the assigned place at ten o'clock, and by three in the afternoon they returned to the town with all the stolen goods. As for the marauders, Àrá's wrath had killed them all.

The question of sovereignty not only centers around the cult of the royal òrìsà itself, but includes also the structural arrangements between this and other related cults within a town's social organization, as well as the way in which particular òrìsà are worshipped. The specificity of these arrangements (which defies generalizations about the òrìsà for the whole of Yorùbáland at all times) is tied in with a town's history and gives expression to its identity and claim to sovereignty in contrast with other towns. Earlier I discussed this question by comparing the Àrá and related òrìsà cults in Ṣábé, Kétu, and Ìlárá. In the case of Ìtílé we are once again confronted with a different configuration of the way in which Àrá interrelates with the other town òrìsà and the ways in which these deities are worshipped. I will restrict my comments to the òrìsà most directly related to Àrá in the ritual drama which is enacted at the annual festival celebrated on the Àrá hill near Ìtàsá.

Unlike Ṣábẹ́-Kétu, where the Àrá festival is timed as a new yam festival in September or October, Ìtàsá celebrates its Àrá festival after the
first maize harvest, around June. The day of the festival is the only day in
the year when the people are allowed to climb the Àrá hill.[27] Perched on
the rocky outcrop on the top of this hill are three shrines. In the center
stands the Àrá shrine, consisting of a hut in which the sacred stone celts
(ẹdùn àrá) are kept. Nearest to Àrá is a shrine for Ògún, the òrìṣà of
hunters and blacksmiths. Ògún is said to have wrought the ẹdùn àrá, and
is worshipped as the onítílé's titular deity. His shrine consists of just an
upright stone. The third shrine, which stands behind Àrá's, is for Ọbájí.
According to the baálẹ̀ of Ìtàsá, the Babalalẹ̀, and the chiefs Ṣóbalójú and
Ìkólàbà, Ọbájí is not Àrá's wife, as some Ìtàsá people first told me, but
Àrá's senior brother. He came to visit Àrá, and on the invitation of the
townspeople agreed to stay. In the Ìtílé tradition Àrá's wife is Ọ̀ṣun. Her
main shrine is located not on the Àrá hill, but in a grove nearer to the
present town of Ìtàsá.

This entourage of Àrá is different from the ones discussed earlier in
the Ṣábẹ́-Kétu area. Over there no òrìṣà was roped in to play the part of
Àrá's brother, but those that were there in other capacities did not make
their reappearance in Ìtílé, least of all Ṣàngó. Structurally, however, the
position of Ọ̀ṣun in Ìtílé, as Àrá's wife who lives away from her husband,
is similar to the position of Ṣàngó as Àrá's senior wife in the Ṣábẹ́-Kétu
tradition. But from the Ọ̀yọ́ point of view Àrá's marriage to Ọ̀ṣun in Ìtílé
is tantamount to "wife snatching," since many hold that Ọ̀ṣun is one of
Ṣàngó's wives.

The presence of Ògún, the hunter-blacksmith, on the Àrá hill can be
seen to parallel the presence of the hunters' òrìṣà Ọ̀ṣóòsì and Amọdẹ in
the Àrá shrine at Ṣábẹ́. That Ògún should occupy a place of importance
in the Ìtílé tradition seems logical, as to this day most men devote much
of their time to hunting. Nevertheless, unlike hunters in neighboring
towns who celebrate their annual festival in honor of Ògún, the Ìtílé
hunters assert their separate identity by honoring Agẹmọ instead.[28]

Unknown outside the Ìtílé tradition is Ọbájí, the third òrìṣà on the
hill, who is worshipped by the town chiefs as representatives of the nonroyal lineages. This unparalleled appearance of an òrìṣà as Àrá's senior
brother makes Ọbájí look like the joker in the pack. Except, perhaps,
when we interpret his presence in the light of Ìtílé's story of origin.
There we saw that the town owed its foundation to a feud between their
ancestor Ilẹ̀mọ́là and his senior brother, who was said to have usurped
Ilẹ̀mọ́là's right to become Aláàfin. Viewed from this angle, I would suggest that structurally Ọbájí 's appearance on the Ìtílé scene is a form of

sublimation for the Aláàfin's Ṣàngó. By sacrificing to Ọbájí, the towns-people (as represented by their chiefs) mediate, subconsciously, between Àrá/*onítílé* and Ṣàngó/Aláàfin.

There are both general and specific ethnographic reasons for support-ing this structural interpretation. Mediation is pervasive in Yorùbá social practices, especially in the context of disputes. Conflict management almost invariably results in triadic arrangements because the parties to the conflict, or other interested parties, will soon call on elders or a chief to help reach a settlement.[29] Above all, it is through the medium of sac-rifice (following arbitration by the Ifá oracle) that people try to restore peaceful relations with angered *òrìṣà* or other spiritual powers. The *onítí-lé*'s refusal to honor the Aláàfin irrevocably implicated all the people of Ìtílé once Àrá was institutionalized as town *òrìṣà* and Ṣàngó was rejected, and created in effect the deadlock situation. Practically, Ìtílé could not ignore the Aláàfin's overlordship. Spatially and politically, Ìtílé was still part of the Ọ̀yọ́ kingdom, even though it was situated on the periph-ery. There is evidence, for example, that when the Àrá priests conducted purification rituals the Aláàfin sent a delegation to receive part of the fees collected. It would seem, then, that the contradiction between negating Ṣàngó ideologically and honoring him politically by paying tribute to the Aláàfin (the *onítílé*'s senior brother) was resolved ritually in the people's sacrifice to Ọbájí (Àrá's senior brother).

Further to this examination of the enigmatic identity of Ọbájí, I should point out that this *òrìṣà*'s name literally means "the king (Ọba) rose," or "stood up" (*jí*). For example, a boy born after his father has died is often named Babá-tún-jí, "father has again risen." Similarly, Ọbájí could here be interpreted as a sublimation of the king of Ọ̀yọ, who has reappeared.

Finally, it is in the rituals that surround Àrá, Ògún, and Ọbájí during the annual festival that Ìtílé gives further expression to its separate iden-tity from both Ṣábẹ̀-Kétu's Àrá and Ọ̀yọ́'s Ṣàngó. The animal sacrificed to Ògún is a cock (presented by the *onítílé*), while a dog (also presented by the *onítílé*) is sacrificed to Àrá. Elsewhere in Yorùbáland these animals are considered to be favored by Ògún—the dog, however, more than the cock. But since here Àrá takes precedence over Ògún, it seems appropri-ate that the former receives the dog and the latter the cock. Nevertheless, from the Ṣábẹ̀-Kétu point of view Àrá's choice of a dog in Ìtílé is most unorthodox, as in their area the thunder god receives a ram. Why Ìtílé's Àrá wants a dog may have an ad hoc explanation, but what stands out structurally is Ìtílé's assertion that its thunder god is unlike Ṣábẹ̀-Kétu's as well as Ọ̀yọ́'s, since the ram is also sacred to Ṣàngó.

FIGURE 5.1. Àrá shrine, Babẹgbẹ́'s compound, Itasa, 1975.
Photo by Marilyn Hammersley Houlberg.

FIGURE 5.2. Àrá hill, annual Àrá Festival, Itasa, 1975.
Photo by Marilyn Hammersley Houlberg.

FIGURE 5.3. Sacrificing a ram to Ọbajì atop Àrá hill, Itasa, 1975.
Photo by Marilyn Hammersley Houlberg.

FIGURE 5.4. Sacrificing a dog to Àrá atop Àrá hill, Itasa, 1975.
Photo by Marilyn Hammersley Houlberg.

FIGURE 5.5. Babalalè, priest of Àrá, annual Àrá Festival, Itasa, 1975.
Photo by Marilyn Hammersley Houlberg.

The distinctiveness of Ìtílé's Àrá is expressed also in the way these ani-mals are sacrificed. In the Ìtàsá area, hunters kill dogs or cocks in honor of Ògún by holding the animal outstretched in midair while one man severs the head with a stroke of the cutlass. In contrast to this method, the cock sacrificed to Ògún on the Àrá hill is killed in the common fash-ion of killing a fowl at ancestral groves or *òrìṣà* shrines: by keeping the head pressed on the ground with the toe and pulling the body away. The second contrast is in the way of killing Àrá's dog, which is actually clubbed to death (without spilling the blood)[30] in the way New Guinea Highlanders kill their pigs—a rather unusual method among the Yorùbá. Most disconcerting, however, is the animal demanded in sacrifice by the enigmatic Ọbájí. In his honor the town chiefs kill a ram, the sacred ani-mal for thunder gods elsewhere, including Àràmfẹ̀ in Ifẹ̀. If, as I sug-gested earlier, Ọbájí is here a sublimated representation of Ṣàngó, then the sacrificial ram is no longer disconcerting but most orthodox. Also the manner in which the ram is killed is orthodox: first it is smothered, then its throat is slashed with a knife.

One final question: How did Ìtílé get away with its taunting of the Aláàfin's rule by opposing Àrá to Ṣàngó? Or did it? None of the histories recorded suggests that Ọ̀yọ́ ever took disciplinary measures, military or otherwise, against Ìtílé. Perhaps it was the sibling relationship between the Aláàfin and the *onítílé* which precluded any potentially fratricidal action. Perhaps unruly petty kings such as the *onítílé* were too unimportant for the Aláàfin to take much notice of, as long as they did not engage in subversive activities. Perhaps also, as I suggested earlier, the Ọ̀yọ́ rulers found it unworkable to secure effective control and loyalties in a frontier area such as the one between the rivers Òfikì and Okpara.[31]

But whatever reasons Ọ̀yọ́ may have had for not taking direct action against Ìtílé, it is worth noting that when the western frontier began to fall prey to foreign invaders (Fulani ruled Ilorin and Dahomey) in the nineteenth century, the Aláàfin did not take special action to protect Ìtílé, while in loyal Ìdìkó he posted a governor (*ajẹ́lẹ̀*). This Aláàfin strongman set up camp on the Onídìkó's land on the banks of the Ọ̀yán river (this town is now known as Ìlaji). Ìtílé accounts do not mention this development, but they cite an incident that occurred during that period which made the *onítílé* obliterate the last vestiges of his royal Ọ̀yọ́ descent. Until that time, boys born into the *onítílé*'s lineage had the same facial marks cut as those of the Aláàfin's house (that is, six cuts on each cheek, *àbàjà méfà*). One day when Olúgbọlá was the *onítílé*, a catastrophe occurred when 143 boys who had had their faces cut died when the wounds became infected. Afterward Olúgbọlá ordered that no one of the royal house be given the *àbàjà méfà* marks.[32] The figure of 143 casualties which ends this story is remarkable, because it is the same story that began by stating that, at the foundation of Ìtílé, 143 towns in the area decided to serve the *onítílé*. Whatever the number of towns was, the fact remains that eventually all of them, including Ìtílé, were sacked and reduced to ruins by Dahomey, never to be rebuilt again. The village of Ìtàsá, rebuilt at a new site at the turn of the century, is the only reminder of this Àrá enclave within the Ọ̀yọ́ kingdom. So perhaps this abandonment and dispersal was the ultimate price that had to be paid by Ilèmọ̀là's descendants for preferring Àrá to Ṣàngó.

———

This discussion of Yorùbá thunder gods has been largely an exercise in writing ethno-history. Further research will be needed to fill the gaps in our knowledge, and, possibly, revise our understanding of history in Yorùbáland. Meanwhile, this approach has tried to heed Horton's call to study traditional Yorùbá religion in action.[33] This implies, as I have argued, that religious beliefs and ritual symbolisms must be studied in the context of group concerns with identity and the exercise of power. In the case of royal cults, these concerns centered around the assertion of sovereignty in both the internal and the external affairs of the kingdom. We saw that in the western kingdoms where Àrá was not a royal cult, the imposition of the imperial Ṣàngó cult led to compromise arrangements between the two thunder cults, while local variations in the Àrá cult persisted as a result of the circumstances under which that cult had developed originally. The failure to reach such a compromise in Ìtílé could therefore not be explained by the argument that Àrá and Ṣàngó are in themselves mutually exclusive spiritual forces. On the contrary, what the history of this petty kingdom revealed was that its uncompromising stance toward the Ṣàngó cult found its rationale in the original feud between their king-founder and his senior brother, the Aláàfin of Òyó. Therefore, by adopting Àrá as their lineage *òrìṣà*, the *onítílé* secured for themselves the instrument for asserting their exclusiveness and sovereignty vis-à-vis Òyó's imperialism. Finally, concerning the claim that the cult of Ṣàngó buttressed the Aláàfin's authority empire-wide, our findings in some western Yorùbá towns suggest that historically this was realized only inasmuch as Òyó's rule had already been established effectively in a particular area.

Postscript—"Where is Àrá nowadays?"

Almost two decades after my 1970s fieldwork in the Ìtàsá area, my old friend and lifelong correspondent, Paul Ọládélé, wrote to me with a startling question about Àrá's whereabouts. "I often wonder where Àrá is nowadays?" is how he raised the issue. By then, in 1992, he and his family had been living in Lagos for about fifteen years. At that time all his business ventures had come to naught, and his marriage seemed to be heading for the rocks. Returning home to Ìtàsá to farm or do business seemed hardly an option because of his fear of secret enemies (witches/sorcerers). Implied in this perception was an awareness, it seems, that missionary conversion and modernity may have scored a victory over paganism by the demise of the *òrìṣà* cults, including Ìtàsá's royal cult of Àrá. But the backlash has been that, nowadays, in Paul's and other people's minds, any evil-minded man or woman can dabble in witchcraft and sorcery with impunity. Paul's comment on his questioning of Àrá's whereabouts was phrased thus:

In the olden days, if a hunter in Ìtàsá broke Àrá's taboo and brought gunpowder inside the town near the òrìṣà's shrine, there would be a sudden flash of lightning which would burn down the man's house. Also, when the king learnt that a man was secretly preparing evil medicine [jùjú] in the bush in order to harm someone, he would send out his town crier to warn people of the impending danger. And if the sorcerer did not immediately abandon his evil plan, Àrá would strike him dead and burn his jùjú grove to ashes. However, nowadays things have fallen apart, and everyone just does what he or she pleases.

I know that Àrá no longer dwells on the sacred hill near our town. . . . I discussed this with Babalalè [the old Àrá priest]. He said that civilization had spoiled everything. Anyway, he had no answer to my question where Àrá is to be found nowadays. He himself, he assured me, has always carried out the daily propitiatory rites [ètùtù] for Àrá, and responded to all the òrìṣà's requests throughout his life. Likewise, at every annual festival he has led the townspeople up the Àrá hill and offered the sacrifice of a dog on behalf of the king. Yet near the Àrá hill, where none was ever allowed to farm, one of our townspeople is now growing tobacco for the Nigerian Tobacco Company. It is pity that the spirit is no longer to be found where he used to dwell. Who is Àrá? Where did he come from? Where is he now? No one can answer these questions.

Having known Paul Ọládélé for many years, I sensed that this was not an academic question about Àrá's whereabouts, but an existential one. What had prompted it was his awareness of being at the mercy of forces beyond his control in a failed nation state (Nigeria) and in a dysfunctional hometown without Àrá. Controlling these occult forces has now become a growing industry in Nigeria, foremost among born-again Christians and Pentecostals, who profess to confront these alleged minions of Satan with the power of the Holy Spirit, often during spectacular show exorcisms in front of thousands of worshippers. However, speaking as a one-time missionary in the Catholic diocese of Ọ̀yọ́, and a belated convert to anthropology, I should caution that preaching such a holy war against the occult powers of evil is not unproblematic. On the one hand, the effect of this war on today's faithful—as Paul Ọládélé intimates—is that many of them become even more paralyzed by fear of witches and wizards than their forebears were, in so far as the latter believed that their personal and town òrìṣà offered the best protection against occult enemies. On the other hand, whipping up frenzy against witches and wizards, rather than promoting sociality, trust, and goodwill in one's neighborhood, tends to heighten fear and hatred of the "other," since she or he may, after all, be a witch or a wizard disguised as an ordinary woman or man. Finally, by pinning the blame for people's suffering on satanic agents, this holy war tends to cloud people's vision of the near and long-lasting repercussions of their own actions or failures to act, and, consequently, of how their agency impacts, for better or worse, on other people's lives.

NOTES

The research on which this chapter is based was conducted in the Òkèhò-Ìgànná Council area in the Ọ̀yọ́ state of Nigeria in 1974–75. For the data on the Àrá cult in Ìtàsá and in the Republic of Benin I am especially indebted to Mr. Julius B. Oyésòro of Baálẹ̀ Agbòjò's compound in Ìtàsá. I also wish to express my gratitude to the late Father Múléró of Kétu, who kindly allowed me to consult his field notes on the Àrá traditions in Kétu and Ìlárá, as I was unable to obtain a visa for entering Benin at the time. Mr. Oyésòro, who did manage to get across the border, was greatly helped in carrying out my investigations, thanks to the letters of introduction Father Múléró provided in all the Àrá cult centers. This I wish to recall as a tribute to a great Yorùbá historiographer and pastor.

The editors wish to thank editor in chief Professor Dr. Othmar Gachter and the Anthropos-Institute for permission to reprint Marc Schiltz, "Yorùbá Thunder Deities and Sovereignty: Àrá versus Ṣàngó," *Anthropos* 80, nos. 1–3 (1985): 67–84.

1. Although *ọba* is the generic term for crowned monarchs, it is a Yorùbá custom to refer to a particular *ọba* by the title attached to his dynasty (see Samuel Johnson, *The History of the Yorùbás*, London: Routledge, 1921), 34. Hence, we speak of the Aláàfin of Ọ̀yọ́, the Onítìlé of Ìtílé, the Onídìko of Ìdìko, the Alákétu of Kétu, and the Oníṣábẹ́ẹ́ of Ṣábẹ́.

2. See J. O. Lucas, *The Religion of the Yorùbás* (Lagos: C. M. S., 1948), 104.

3. P. Morton-Williams, "An Outline of the Cosmology and Cult Organization of the Ọ̀yọ́ Yorùbá," *Africa* 34 (1964): 255.

4. In Ṣábẹ́ and Kétu, Àrá is also associated with the disease of smallpox, which, in Yorùbá, is referred to as *igbóná*, or *ilẹ̀-gbígbóná*, i.e., "hot earth." Elsewhere, Sònpònná is the *òrìṣà* that personifies this affliction.

5. The lineage who owned an Àrá shrine in Ìgànná invariably attributed its provenance to a long-dead ancestor who had first erected it. In one case the cult had been brought by refugees from the coastal kingdom of Àjàṣẹ́ (Porto-Novo). In the other cases the origin stories recalled an ancestor who at one time had serendipitously chanced upon an *ẹdùn àrá* ([pre-Yorùbá] stone celt, believed to be a thunderbolt), and on returning home had erected an Àrá shrine in the courtyard where the thunderbolt was kept in an earthen pot.

6. J. Lorand Matory, *Sex and the Empire That Is No More : Gender and the*

Politics of Metaphor in Oyo Yoruba Religion (Minneapolis : University of Minnesota Press, 1994).

7. See E. B. Idowu, *Olódùmarè: God in Yorùbá Belief* (London: Longmans, 1962), and Lucas, *The Religion of the Yorùbás.*

8. See Morton-Williams, "An Outline," 255, and R. Law, *The Ọ̀yọ́ Empire* c. *1600-c.1836* (Oxford: Clarendon Press, 1977), 140.

9. S. O. Biobaku, *The Ẹ̀gbá and Their Neighbours 1842–1872* (Oxford: Oxford University Press, 1975), 8.

10. Johnson, *The History of the Yorùbás,* 35.

11. Morton-Williams, "An Outline," 255.

12. G. J. A. Ojo, *Yorùbá Culture,* (London: University of Ifẹ̀ and University of London Press, 1966), 171.

13. Law, *The Ọ̀yọ́ Empire,* 141–42.

14. Ibid., 217–18.

15. Johnson, *The History of the Yorùbás,* 159; 263–71 also mentions the Ìbàrìbá people as military allies of the Ọ̀yọ́. King Eléduwè, the Ìbàrìbá war leader, is the hero whose name is still remembered in Ìgànná accounts of the battle of Ìlọrin prior to the destruction of Old Ọ̀yọ́ in the 1830s.

16. Idowu, *Olódùmarè,* 90.

17. Yorùbá proverb: *àgbò méjì kì í kàn kí ọ̀kan má yẹ̀.*

18. As in many other foundation stories of Yorùbá towns, the king-founder of Ìtílé is said to have left his town of origin as a result of a succession dispute with a brother. The recurring theme of these stories is that the junior brother usurped the succession right, causing the senior to go into exile in anger. The pattern is so common that some Ìtàsá informants told me their story of origin in similar fashion. It was not until I recorded this "more official" account from the *baálẹ̀* and some chiefs and Àrá priests that to my surprise I noted that the pattern had been reversed: Ilèmọ́là was junior to the brother who became Aláàfin. It is in the light of this version that I suggest below my interpretation of the identity of the *òrìṣà* called Ọbájí.

19. Law, *The Ọ̀yọ́ Empire,* 89.

20. Ọbálá is the sacred python, worshipped on the hill (Òkè Ilé) overlooking Ìdìkó. He is the personified ancestor of the original inhabitants of Ìdìkó. Traditionally he was also worshipped as the local smallpox *òrìṣà* in the way Àrá is associated with this disease in Kétu and Ṣábẹ́. In nearby Ìgànná, Òrìṣàálá was the smallpox *òrìṣà* before the foundation of the town.

21. When I asked for the name of the Onítìlé who introduced the Àrá cult, I was told it was Ilèmọ́là. Whether or not the beginnings of the Àrá cult coincided with Ìtílé's foundation, the reply underscores the point I made in the beginning, that the story of Ìtílé and that of Àrá are two sides of the same coin as far as the sovereignty issue is concerned.

22. *Àyà rẹ tí o dà délẹ̀ náà ni kí o máa fi lalẹ̀ bọ̀ wá.* From these words, i.e., *lalẹ̀,* to crawl or split the ground in two, is construed the etymology of *babalalẹ̀.*

23. In some towns this resulted in the reduplication of the same *òrìṣà* cults,

especially during the nineteenth century wars, when refugees took their ancestral cults with them to the towns where they resettled. In Ìgànná, for instance, we noticed three centers for the Ọ̀ṣun cult, as well as three different Orò cults.

24. In Ìdìkó the priests of Ọbaálá also stand in an affinal relationship to the Onídìko.

25. Johnson, *The History of the Yorùbás,* 49–51.

26. The punishment for sorcery was thus not just an ignoble death at the hands of Àrá; the stigma of the criminal also became attached to the sorcerer's *ìdílé* (descent group). His sorcery puts at risk the renown, or "symbolic capital," of his *ìdílé*. For a discussion of the centrality of this concept in Yorùbá social organization, see Marc Schiltz, "Habitus and Peasantization in Nigeria: A Yorùbá Case Study," *Man* new series 17 (1982): 728–46, and "Rural-Urban Migration in Ìgànná," Ph.D. thesis, University of London, 1980.

27. It is said that a long time ago a man returned to the hill after the ceremonies were over in order to retrieve his cap and pipe. On arrival at the top he confronted the *òrìṣà* who were holding their own celebrations. They got hold of him and killed him. His skull inside the Àrá shrine is a reminder of the seriousness of the taboo.

28. Agẹmọ occupies a central place among the southern Ìjèbú (Yorùbá). This cult is not common among the (northwestern) Ọ̀yọ́. Moreover, Ìtàsá's Agẹmọ cult is very different from Ìjèbú's.

29. K.-F. Koch, *War and Peace in Jalemo* (Cambridge, Mass.: Harvard University Press, 1974).

30. Even a few drops of blood spilled on the rock are immediately covered with earth to ensure the entire dog substitute of Ilèmọ́là's first-born is Àrá's.

31. I have argued elsewhere ("Rural-Urban Migration in Ìgànná.") that Ìgànná was Aláàfin's most western stronghold on the Òfikì river.

32. Girls, however, are given *pélé* marks in remembrance of an ancestress who was a native of Ṣábẹ́.

33. R. Horton, "African Conversion," *Africa* 41 (1971): 99.

PART TWO

Representations of Ṣàngó in Oral and Written Popular Cultures

CHAPTER SIX

Ṣàngó and the Elements

Gender and Cultural Discourses

DIEDRE L. BÁDÉJỌ

A man walks in front of his wife, and he walks behind his mother.
(Ọkùnrin níí ṣíwájú aya rẹ̀, tí tún tọ̀'yáa rẹ̀ lẹ́yìn.)
Ọya, the woman who is stronger than her husband.
(Ọya, obìnrin tó rorò j'ọkọ lọ)
If a man sees a snake, and a woman kills it, it does not matter.
What matters is that the snake is dead.
(Bí ọkùnrin rí ejò tí obìnrin pa á, kí ejò má sáà ti lọ.)[1]

Methodologies in Ṣàngó Discourses

Worldview, irony, vision, contradiction, ambiguity, historicism, and cultural wisdom: these are the cornerstones of many African proverbs, including those of the Yorùbá people. In fact, Yorùbá verbal, visual, and performance arts capture part of their historical essence and cultural knowledge in the pithy, metaphorically charged language of the proverb. The pathway, therefore, to discerning a Yorùbá perspective relies, in part, on the intertextuality and discourses found within the cultural nuances of proverbs and expressively articulated among oral, written, and performative resources. Spoken word and performance arts are inscribed on the papyrus of Yorùbá texts, which include drums, clothing, and visual arts. Yorùbá cultural literacy, we may assert, evolves from a knowledge and understanding of a cornucopia of these arts reverberating throughout its icons and polysemic verbal discourses, and, most importantly, within its complex cosmology that orders and re-orders the world and its inhabitants. Within these concentric spheres is found a distinctive Yorùbá perspective and logic that frames its cultural behavior and the human response to it. It is this Yorùbá sensibility which guides this chapter.

Seeking the Elements

Like most West African perspectives, the Yorùbá worldview is found in the power of the word, which can be spoken, drummed, danced, worn, carved, and inscribed. Yorùbá perspective lies in the accoutrements of art, attire, and verve alluded to in literature and performance; in *oríkì* and *ìtàn;* in shrines; and with the keepers of its cornucopia of cultural treasures. Those treasures are inscribed with hyperbole and mystery in the *òrìṣà* narratives and historiographies that intersect Yorùbá knowledge and identity. Like the roads that *òrìṣà* themselves follow, the pathways to that treasure may be cut by Ògún, but can often become obscured at the crossroads of understanding where Èṣù presides. In short, it takes more than one road to reach Yorùbá nirvana. My chapter walks along many roads in its journey toward understanding Ṣàngó and the elements that shape his narrated existence. One road that we will consider is how his parental, spousal/familial, cultural/spiritual/political elements suggest an engendered discourse with respect to Ṣàngó narrative space in Yorùbá thought.

The Gender Matrix in Yorùbá Cultural Discourse

In the perambulatory image in the first proverb above, an explicit gender order is implied by the relationship between the wife and her husband. Certainly, in a male-dominated, hierarchal society like the Yorùbá, it may not seem unusual for a woman to walk behind her husband. In today's world, the first phrase of the proverb is undoubtedly disquieting, as we bristle at the way in which it sanctions an apparent gender inequity and subordination of women. Yet, in typical proverbial fashion, this assumption is contradicted by the juxtaposition of the female roles when the husband then follows his own mother. We are told that the wife, *aya/ìyàwó,* follows the husband, *ọkọ,* who then follows his own mother, *ìyá,* the wife of his own father, in what conceptually may be the natural, infinite, and circuitous order of things Yorùbá. It may appear that the wife is subservient to the husband until we consider the husband's perennial position as a son who walks behind his own mother. It is also possible to surmise that women surround men in their more pedestrian activities. In fact, we may suggest that this unusual proverb seems to subvert male dominance in this very patriarchal culture by suggesting that women are the agents of men's mobility: that is, their comings and goings in the world. The prominent roles of Ọya and Ọ̀ṣun in Yorùbá cosmology, as well as the wives to Ṣàngó, seem to suggest that there may be an element of truth here.

We may ponder through these gendered paradoxes until we consider the second quote from an *oríkì Ọya*, which suggests that Ọya is stronger than Ṣàngó. In this case, we now are faced with yet another dilemma, which arises when we consider that Ṣàngó in his manifestation as deity of thunder and lightning precedes Ọya as deity of strong winds and torrential rainfalls. To fully appreciate this, a brief retreat to Nigeria's climatic realities is necessary. My days in Zaria during the Harmattan season sensitized me to the symbiotic relationship between Ṣàngó and Ọya. From my family room window, I overlooked a valley to my right and the expansive boundaries of the savannah to my left, between which meandered the various footpaths and roads that snaked through Ahmadu Bello University's campus and our living quarters. Often, from my sunny kitchen, I could hear the boisterous crack of thunder in the distance although there was no rain in sight. Its approach was, nonetheless, so awesome and processional that one could almost gauge its distance from the length of intervals between its echoing sounds. Without the sun abating, the thunder and lightning strikes would continue, and I would wonder which trees had been struck by Ṣàngó's ire. This phenomenon of thunder and lightning performing while the sun shone brightly reminded me of my New York childhood. From that kitchen window where the sun also shone brightly during its summer thunderstorms, my Maryland born great-grandmother, Nana, would say that the devil was beating his wife with a hambone. I can hardly imagine Ọya suffering the same fate! On the contrary, it was the roaring winds of Ọya that sent my children in search of their parents as we hurriedly secured the windows and the doors. It was Ọya's pounding rains whipped around by her furious winds that caused us to gather in a huddle in the middle of the house. That is how I understood that Ọya was, at least metaphorically, stronger than Ṣàngó. As an element of nature, Ọya follows Ṣàngó across the Sahelian terrain as his most loyal and equally fearsome companion. Truly, she too walks *behind* her husband as her *oríkì* below states, and as Ládipọ̀ captures in *Ọba Kòso*.[2]

And yet, the supposedly unyielding posture of gender hierarchy is challenged in the third proverb as we weigh the matter of familial security. In considering the danger posed by a snake in their midst, the clear purpose of preventing catastrophe seems to override the purported gender hierarchy in favor of more tangible problems of survival. The response to this dangerous situation seems less a function of some specious notion of propriety and more a sense of need and circumstance. The third quote above also suggests that the wife is not expected to feign timidity or weakness, but she is expected to attend to the business at hand with strength and authority. No time for fainting or the faint of heart here! From this we may glean that strength of character and of action is a human rather than a gender-specific expectation captured in the notion of *ìwà-pèlé*. Arguably, the consternation regarding gender ideology in Yorùbá thought is again confounded in the term *ìwà-pèlé*, which is usually associated with the female deity Ìwà, but applicable to both male and female. So from a critical point of view, it seems that there may be some circularity surrounding the question of gender itself. But I propose that this is not so. Rather we are faced with a gender ideology that dances to its own polyrhythmic philosophical constructs. The key principles in the rhythm of that construct rest upon a set of perspectives that can be broadly defined as functionality, shaped by a Yorùbá notion of wisdom as articulated by seniority or age, and biological sex. With respect to the later, the productive and reproductive realities of male and female function in an esoteric meta-language as metaphors for social-cultural and economic-political engagement. Yorùbá cultural caretakers, therefore, are viewed as the interpreters and specialists of that esoteric knowledge. Through their guardianship or covenant of Yorùbá hermeneutic gender concepts, the corporate body, at diverse levels and under fluid circumstances, are organized, deconstructed, and reconstituted as the need arises. This constant dynamic is apparent in the plethora of mythic narratives and contradictions that are embedded in Yorùbá oral traditions.

Sociocultural Reconstruction and the Yorùbá Body Politic

The counterpoising dynamic between women and men alluded to in the first quote demonstrates that Yorùbá gender ideology and its conceptual framework have their own logic. Obviously, that logic defies linearity and directness in favor of circularity and commutability, a matrix whose mantra is transformation and adaptability.[3] Yorùbá logic intimates a certain predilection for the rotund—like the womb, the earth, and the *opón Ifá*, all of which hold its most profound esoteric secrets, the *awo* of life and death. Envisioning the womb of Òsun as matrix, Yorùbá logic infuses the inscrutability of Èsù, the fallibility of Obàtálá's hands, and the *àse* of Olódùmarè. Within this worldview inheres a dynamic archetypal vortex or vibrant black hole, a drawing in of the stuff of life, gestating its disparate parts within the Yorùbá cultural *àṣẹ* before birthing a newly adorned *orí* in its own unique cultural modalities, attire, and accoutrements.[4] Within that matrix lies the cultural logic that sorts out and rearranges the roles and responsibilities of the human beings, *ènìyàn,* and deities, *òrìṣà,* who occupy and define its essences. The logic of that sorting and rearranging is found in the last proverb above, which emphasizes *what matters:* that is, that life continues unabated.

The dynamic relationships among mother, son, and wife exemplify this deep reverence for circularity as a metaphor of immortality and eternity. The inversion, transformation, and transmutability of gender roles envisioned here plays out in a plethora of Yorùbá rituals, festival dramas, fine arts, and oral narratives. It is obvious in Ṣàngó's cosmogenesis, for example, that Ọya and Òṣun function as metaphors of such transmutability and mythico-political power. When we (re)place the subject in Yorùbá discourse, it becomes evident that with Ọya as the *iyálé* of Ṣàngó's court, and Òṣun as his political and spiritual countervailing ruler, Ṣàngó's narrative articulates an indigenous model of power transfer and cultural transformation that dominated West Africa for almost a thousand years. Ọya, Òṣun, and Ọbà as Ṣàngó's wives, along with Yemọja as his mother, elevate his role in Yorùbá political and cosmological systems. Their presence in his narrative links the patriarchal legitimacy bequeathed to him by his father, Òrányàn, to the reproductive metaphor of political power and empire building ascribed to him by his mother and wives. From this perspective, Ṣàngó's meta-narrative enshrines key concepts in Yorùbá gender ideology as well as the role of this "King of the Mightiest Kings" within its cultural and historical universe.

Cosmology and the Transformation of Power: Ṣàngó and Ọya

This proverbial inversion and transmutability of gender roles suggests a more complicated meaning in the relationship between Ṣàngó and Ọya. Again in the second proverb, we are made to be swayed by the winds of Ọya, who, it seems, can displace the unnamed husband, Ṣàngó. In a bit of coyness and irony, this *oríkì* implies that the thunderous voice and awesome lightning strikes of Ṣàngó are nothing compared to the tumultuous winds and rains of Ọya. This is quite a claim since in the following excerpt from an *oríkì Ṣàngó,* it is Ṣàngó who inspires fear. Certainly, if one lives in the Harmattan regions of northern and western Nigeria as noted earlier, Ọya's elemental forces are particularly relevant, especially since the Saharan winds whip up blinding dust and pour down torrential rains. In some ways, Ṣàngó's thunderous cracks and lightning strikes seem to pale by comparison. However, we are confounded to again consider how the third quote disarms the first two, and speaks to the immediacy, sensibility, and essence of the male/female relationships; that is, the preservation of the home or community. One could posit that together these proverbs and the *oríkì* present a logical endoskeleton of roles, responsibilities, and engendered associative metaphors interlocked by cultural nuances, beliefs, and practices. That logical endoskeleton lies in a spatial matrix symbolized ideologically by the womb, a space defined by awe and mystery (*awo*). As I wish to reveal in this chapter, the cultural logic expressed by these proverbs is critical to understanding Ṣàngó's mythical and historical relevance in Yorùbá thought, where we find three elements of his story—parentage, conquest, and gender ideology.

Ṣàngó's Parentage as an Element of Cultural Historicism and Identity

Ṣàngó owes much of his intricacy to his parentage. According to oral traditions, Ṣàngó was the son of Ọ̀rányàn, a son or grandson of Odùduwà, and of Yemọja, a Nupe princess and daughter of Eléṅpe, a powerful chieftain north of the Niger river bend. Apparently, Ọ̀rányàn was sent on an expedition to secure Ifẹ̀'s influences and territories, which led him to the Nupe kingdom. Although the details are sketchy, tradition does confirm that the birth of Ṣàngó was one tangible outcome of Ọ̀rányàn's ventures. Briefly, according to Idowu, Ṣàngó grew up in Nupe, and later traveled across the Niger into his fatherland.[5] After proving himself in warfare, he became the ruler of Ọ̀yọ́ North, that is, Old Ọ̀yọ́, which was located in close proximity to Nupe itself. Although Nupe and Ọ̀yọ́ North were literally separated by the Niger river, we should point out these areas were united by the river as well. Historically speaking, the relationship between the territories north and south of the Niger river reaches far back into the earlier empires of Kanem-Bornu, Borgu, and Nupe itself. Trade and resettlement of communities affected by drought, wars, and population growth were among those factors that affected the interactions between these regions. In fact, Ṣàngó's grandfather/grandmother, Odùduwà, was an explorer and leader of the Yorùbá people in Ilé-Ifẹ̀, a fact that further implicates these north-south, and indeed east-west, ties.[6]

It seems that Ṣàngó's parentage, especially in this era, indicates a vision of the region's leadership that included expansion, unification, or perhaps cooperation among its various entities. This is certainly the case with Ṣàngó's grandfather, Odùduwà, and his father, Ọ̀rányàn. Viewing this with respect to the history of West African regional migration and resettlement, we can suggest that, at least metaphorically speaking, Ṣàngó walked behind his northern-born Nupe mother, Yemoja, and in front of his cosmo-political wives, Ọya and Òṣun. Regardless, it is crucial to remember that it is Òrányàn who gives Ṣàngó legitimacy among the Yorùbá crowned princes. The *oríkì Òrìṣà Ṣàngó* from S. A. Babalola's classic work on Yorùbá Ìjálá,[7] along with the *oríkì Ṣàngó Ọkọ Ọya;* and the *oríkì Ọya* from the Òṣun shrine in Òṣogbo,[8] open the way to comprehending Ṣàngó's mythico-political and spiritual configuration. Together, the oral narratives below inundate us with references to, and images of, Ṣàngó that reinforce a reputation for fierceness in his rule of Òyó, as well as his connection with the lands to the north and south of the Niger River. The several allusions to Ọya and Ṣàngó in their reciprocal poems are particularly noteworthy in this regard.

Oríkì Rising: Construction and Reconstruction in the West African Body Politic

The mythology and historiography of Ṣàngó is emblematic of the shifting political intrigues and realities of the West African region. In this *oríkì* (praise poem) to Ṣàngó, we are first introduced to a series of praise names, also known as *oríkì,* which allude to his rulership of Kòso. Other place names such as Òwu, Ifẹ̀, and Gudugbu town indicate political alliances or conquest. The poem also gives us an indication of Ṣàngó's relationships among townspeople who feared him. Allusion to his wife, Ọya, is expressed in two lines which are discussed below. This brief *oríkì* collected by Babalola introduces us to the element of fear that Ṣàngó inspired among his subjects, and I daresay, his family members.[9]

Oríkì Orìṣà Ṣàngó
Olúfínràn,
Ọba Kòso
Ọba Asángiri
Alàgiri Òlàgirikakaka-kọmọkùnrin-bọ̀.
Ṣàngó.
Ekuru gbágbá l'òdàá.
Ilẹ̀ gbogbo àkùrọ̀ l'ójò
Èniyàn tí a bú lẹ́hìn t'ó sì mọ̀.
Èniyàn tí a bú lẹ́hìn t'ó sì gbọ́
Ogunlabi
Etí lu kára bí ajere
Má bú u

Má sá a
Má s'òrò rè léhìn.
Baba Bámkólé.
N ò lo l'ónà ibèun
Ṣàngó o!
A-ru-òwú-r'Òwu.
Ó-ru-fèèfẹẹ-re'Fè.
Ó-ru-gudugbu tà ní Gudugbu.
Láì sòmò ẹranko kelebe
Ṣàngó o!
Dégòkè!
Àrèmú!

Salute to Ṣàngó

Olúfinràn, the king did not hang himself.
The king who cracks the wall.
Who splits the wall.
He who splits the wall here and there and curls up young men.
Ṣàngó.
Dust, dust, and dust again in the dry season,
Every inch of ground like marshy farm soil in the wet season.
A man who comes to know who has spoken ill of him behind his back.
A man who hears all that is said of him behind his back.
Ògúnlabí.
There are ears all over his body like holes in a colander.
Don't abuse him.
Don't hack him.
Don't back bite him.
Father of Bámkólé.
I'll say more of him.
O Ṣàngó!
The man who carried raw cotton to Òwu.
The man who carried *fèèfẹẹ* [fresh?] yam flour to Ifè.
The man who carried gudugbu yam tubers and sold them at Gudugbu town.
Whereas he wasn't a small goat.
O Ṣàngó!
Dégòkè!
Àrèmú!

The allusion to Ọya in this *oríkì* draws our attention to Ṣàngó's interrelationship with the northern region, transformation, and powerful women. *"Dust, dust, and dust again in the dry season,/ Every inch of ground like marshy farm soil in the wet season,"* alludes to the long reach of the Harmattan winds, which blow from the northeastern regions of Africa across the Sahara Desert into the western reaches of the continent and across the Atlantic Ocean. Read in the context of West African regional and cultural history, the allusion also refers to trade and migration patterns as well as cultural and religious ideologies that moved across the region in a similar pattern. Certainly, the Muslim traders and jihadists who migrated to the area during the early days of the Ghana, Mali, and Songhai empires as well as the Hausa and Kanem-Borno empires are implicated here. As these kingdoms evolved and disintegrated, scattered remnants of their people migrated around the region, often closer toward the fertile forest regions and trading centers of the West African hinterland. The movement of Odùduwà and his/her descendants across the savannah to Ilé-Ifẹ̀, then to Nupe, and later to Old Ọ̀yọ́ represents the dynamics of empire-building and political reconstruction that dominated the region well into the eighteenth century.

Ṣàngó's relationship to Ọya, while mystical and dramatic on one hand, more significantly reveals the role of intermarriage in the formation of regencies in the expansion of the Yorùbá empirical network. While Ọ̀rányàn's bloodline validates Ṣàngó's Yorùbá identity, it is the marriages of both father and son to Yemọja and Ọya respectively that help to expand the Yorùbá empirical reach. There are two possible perspectives here—first, as Olupona suggests,[10] the transfer of political power from female to male, as intimated in both marriages, reestablishes and expands the authority of the royal lineages; and second, given the frequency of these marriages in the oral narratives, such exogamous arrangements are a paradigmatic of regional expansion of political power. In either case, these marriages had the effect of consolidating enough power and force to forestall the Hausa-Fulani intrusion from the upper northern regions of the Niger-Benue confluence as well as to hedge the European intrusion from the Atlantic region in the south until the collapse of Ọ̀yọ́ in the nineteenth century.

In comparing the two lines referring to the transition from the dry to the wet season, we glean not only a change in seasons which affect farming cycles, but also a readiness of the soil for planting that points out the significance of fecundity as a theme in the poetry. Unfortunately, while we acknowledge this theme, little or no attention is paid to it because it is read solely as a female concern without placing it within its proper cultural context. A good life for the Yorùbá is defined by children, good health, wealth, and longevity. Here, fecundity implies fruitfulness and abundance, which speaks to longevity, sustainability, a good life, and independence. By contrast, in agricultural as well as the urban communities, the dry seasons brought certain drought and hunger, which frequently ushered in local land feuds, pawning, and feudal oppression. The allusions to times of feast and famine, of overlordship and dependency, are couched in the references to Òwu, whose town is also the name for cotton, to Ifẹ̀, which is the cradle of Yorùbá civilization, and to Gudugbu town, which, as Babalola notes, Ṣàngó provoked into war.[11] Indeed, we should consider the vacillating periods between peaceful reigns and political upheavals as characteristic of the Western Africa region between the tenth and the nineteenth centuries. Such vacillation created, and was created by, trade and expansion, enslavement, drought, and disease, all of which affected the population of the region. In the case of Old Ọ̀yọ́, these allusions refer to a shift of power from Òwu to Ifẹ̀ and then to itself. As Atanda notes, Ṣàngó completed the task of his father by liberating Old Ọ̀yọ́ from the grip of Òwu and creating a rivalry between itself and Ifẹ̀.[12]

We may add that in Ṣàngó's case, trade is less explicit than political expansion as a thematic element in his narrative. Nonetheless, it is undeniable that Ọ̀yọ́ grew under his tutelage, in part because of its control over such outposts as Ọ̀sogbo, the home of Ọ̀sun, to its south, and as Nupe, his motherland, to its north. Furthermore, as Law notes, the introduction of horses from the north into the Ọ̀yọ́ military made the regency a formidable foe.[13] Women controlled much of the regional marketplaces as *iyálójà* (lit., mother of the marketplace or president of the marketplace), and in conjunction with, and with the support of, the *iyálóde* (lit., mother of the outer spaces or chief ambassador for the Ògbóni). In conjunction with powerful military men, they maintained the regional trade routes and wielded considerable power in the political stability of the region, thus implying that marriage was more than a social-cultural contract. In fact, it may imply that marriage, especially among the ruling classes, was intentionally a more political and economic contract. The fact that Ṣàngó's mother was a Nupe princess and his father was an Ifẹ̀ prince substantiates this assertion, and contributes to our understanding of his ability to forge cooperation between both sides of the Niger river bend. Ọya's role as *iyálóde* underscores her ambassadorial role in the region. Her role as *iyálé* in Ṣàngó's house and court, as well as her influence among his sub-regions and within its marketplaces, elevates her significance in his life.

Transformation as Sociocultural Paradigm
for Political Reconstruction

With respect to Ọya, we should also consider her own mythology and apotheosis. Like Ṣàngó, Ọya is a multidimensional entity whose characteristics are human, spiritual, natural, and animalistic. She is, at once, the River Niger, the Buffalo Woman, the Tornado, and the Torrential Rains of the Western Savannah region. Her manifestations as the River Niger and Buffalo Woman link her to the regions to the north of Old Ọ̀yọ́ around Mali, Burkina Faso, and Senegal. As Buffalo Woman, she recalls the prophecy of the Buffalo Woman, the wraith of Songolon, who became Sundiata's mother in the Malian epic.[14] This *oríkì* to the buffalo from Babalola's work on *ìjálá* alludes to a Yorùbá connection to the Malian hero king.

Oríkì Ẹfọ̀n

Ẹfọ́n, ì lẹ́ o.
Labalábá inú ọ̀dàn tíí-máa-i-fò láìf'ara kan bẹẹrẹ.
Odó-ǹdo, agbégi-gbé'jù.
Ẹran tí a à fẹ́mọ lọ́wọ́ rẹ̀ tíń gb'àna lọ́wọ́ ẹni.
Òkè erin l'à i-ké
Taa ni' ó k'ókè ẹfọ̀n abeẹgunlóríwakaka.
Olóògùn àtèsín, padà lẹ́hìn ẹran.
Ẹran yó fi ṣoko jẹ
Ẹfọ̀n l'orò tíí lé ọmọ ọdẹ gun'gi wàràwàrà
Òrò t'ó l'ábẹ nígbèrì ìwo.
Ẹfọ̀n ọgbo ọmọ ukùmàrọ̀.

Salute to the Buffalo

Greetings to you, O buffalo.

Butterfly of the savannah, flying about without touching the grass.

Corpulent beast, at home both in the heavy forest and in the savannah woodland tracts.

Animal from whose hands the hunter has not received a wife,

Yet who receives self-prostration homage from the hunter.

Hunters do stand ceremonially on the head of an elephant that they have just killed.

Who would stand ceremonially on the head of a buffalo that has just been killed.

The buffalo who aggressively carries projecting bony growths upon his head.

Let the hunter whose medicinal charms are but last year's
Turn back from pursuing the buffalo.
Otherwise the beast will eat him up like grass as if by mistake.
The buffalo is the demon who frightens a young hunter,
Forcing him to climb up a thorny tree post haste.
A demonic animal who has razors at the tips of his horns.
O buffalo, ancient beast that rumbles like rain but produces no
precipitation.[15]

Several lines and images above tie Qya to Songolon, and imply a more regional historicity between the peoples of Òyọ́ and Mali, and between trade and expansion in the savannah and forests. I am not suggesting a direct link between them as much as a regional association among them. For example, the following four lines reflect the praise names for both mythico-historical women.

Butterfly of the savannah, flying about without touching the grass.
    Corpulent beast, at home both in the heavy forest and in the savan-
nah woodland tracts.
    Animal from whose hands the hunter has not received a wife,
    Yet who receives self-prostration homage from the hunter.

The buffalo's comfort in the forest (Òyọ́) and the savannah woodland (Nupe/Mali) traces its movement across the region into those territories. The reference to the hunter who has not received a wife alludes to the wraith of Songolon, the mother of Sundiata, and her mythical royalty as the estranged daughter of an earlier Soso king. The appearance of the wraith embodies ancestry and metamorphosis, both of which underlie Òyọ́'s mythical images in the Yorùbá texts. The hunter dare not stand on the head of a royal woman, lest he lose his own.

In the following *oríkì*, Qya's dominion and power to influence Ṣàngó on behalf of petitioners is well established. Those who seek her must do so with reverence lest they incur the wrath of Ṣàngó. The mutual respect and reciprocity between Qya and Ṣàngó models the significance of gender balance in the social and cultural order, a pairing that is symbolized in the *Ẹdan Òṣùgbó* or *Ògbóni* staff of authority.[16] Ṣàngó's dominion over Òyọ́ and her environs again are reinforced by allusions to Qya as one with fire in her eyes and fire in her mouth. In the last line, the chanter begs Qya not to fight her/him, especially in the dry season, when the land is vulnerable to droughts and soil erosion, the antithesis to the Yorùbá concept of fecundity and longevity:

Oríkì Ọya

Èèyàn tí ò bá ti b'Ọya ṣe
Ṣàngó ò bá a ṣe!
Arugbá-àáyán[17] wò-bí-òdòdó;
Mo b'Ọya ṣe, Ṣàngó sì bá n ṣe.

Arugbáayán wò-bí-òdòdó,
È r'Ọyaà mi, à b'ẹ ò rí i?
Ìkọ́làbà, àjà tíí jí,
Tíí t'ọkọ ẹ lẹ́hín!
Ajogún-joóje

Ọya tíí ya wó pani bíí Poolo!
Poolo tíí p'orí èké mọ́!
Ọya ò kúkú ṣeé f'ọ̀rọ̀ ìjà bi!
Iná l'ójú, iná ní ẹnu!
Aṣípọ̀nǹlá-borí-èké.

Òya ò kuku ṣeé f'ọ́rọ́ ìjà bi!
Ọya o! Òríírì!
Ẹkùn aṣèké!
Aṣípónnlá-borí-èké.
Ọya má bá n jà lẹ́ẹ̀kan!

Aṣípọ̀nǹlá-borí-èké.
Ọya má bá n jù lẹ́ẹ̀run gangan-an-gan![18]

Praise Song for Ọya: English Translation

People who have no dealing with Ọya,
Ṣàngó has no dealing with them.
She who carries a calabash of pounded yam like a flower.
I deal with Ọya, and Ṣàngó deals with me.

She who carries a calabash of pounded yam like a flower.
So you see that Ọya is [working] for me, or do you not?
Ìkọ́làbà,[19] the dog that wakes up,
The one that very closely follows her husband.
Ajogún-joóje[20]

Ọya who swiftly kills like Poolo![21]
Poolo who chops off the heads of the deceitful.
Ọya is certainly not the one to be challenged to a fight!
She with fire in the eyes, with fire in the mouth!
Aṣípọ̀nńlá[22] who overcomes the dishonest.
Ọya is certainly not the one to be challenged to a fight!
She with fire in her eyes, with fire in her mouth!
Aṣípọ́nńlá who overcomes the dishonest.
Ọya is certainly not the one to be challenged to a fight!
Ọya o! Oríírì![23]

The terror of the dishonest.
Ọya, please fight not with me anytime.
Aṣípónnlá-borí-èké.[24]
Ọya, please fight not with me in severe dry season![25]

Among its tightly woven lines, we find Ọya, the fierce woman, carrying Ṣàngó's favorite food, *àmàlà,* gently like a flower in order to serve him. Except for its references to Ṣàngó, this *oríkì Ọya* is itself fierce, and its images connote strength and awesome power. Ọya, it claims, is not one to challenge to a fight. In fact, her closeness to her husband is reiterated when she is described as one with fire in her eyes and her mouth. Like Ṣàngó, she too is a warrior, albeit one who seeks justice, as suggested by the references to her distaste for dishonest people. Her justice is swift like Poolo, the executioner, and yet she protects those who worship her and her husband. In spite of her prowess, Ọya walks quickly behind Ṣàngó when in his court, not out of subservience but out of respect and deference to his role as the "King of the Mightiest King." As will become clearer in the following praise poem from the Ọ̀ṣun shrine in Ọ̀ṣogbo,[26] the imagery of Ṣàngó and that of Ọya are inextricably intertwined, suggesting a gendered model of social discourse and harmony.

Gender as a Function of Cultural Political Development and Yorùbá Historicism

The subtleties of Yorùbá praise poetry are well illustrated in the *oríkì Ṣàngó ọkọ Ọya* which follows. The title of the poem itself indicates that Ṣàngó and Ọya are defined in temporal and metaphysical terms. References to towns where Ṣàngó and Ọya are most notably present map the bend of the Niger river in such places as Kòso and Òwu, mentioned

above. Many of their images are woven throughout the fabric of the
oríkì, with frequent evocations to "my husband/my lord" as remind-
ers of Ṣàngó's familial and empirical roles. Coupled with their domestic
roles, the chanter invokes the image of camaraderie, marital companion-
ship, and a fusion of their more bellicose tendencies. Together, Ṣàngó
and Ọya symbolize the spiritual and political warriors of Ọ̀yọ́, with Ọya
sometimes depicted as wearing a beard, an image which sharply contra-
dicts her purported gentleness with her husband, Ṣàngó. In some ways,
the poem codifies the ways in which Ọya reinforces Ṣàngó's image by
placing him within a husbandly as well as kingly context. Indeed, because
of her loyalty, we are apt to be more sympathetic to Ṣàngó's demise than
we may have been toward a more virulent and singular warrior such as
Ògún.

From a literary perspective, the praise poem itself reflects the undu-
lating flow of Ọ̀ṣun's watery sway punctuated by the repetition of key
images and praise names. It is chanted a cappella by Mrs. Ṣàngótúndùn
Àṣàbí, a trained praise singer in Òṣogbo, who embodies both her devotion to Ọ̀ṣun and her relationship to Ṣàngó as intimated by her given
name, Ṣàngótúndùn. Its highly stylized tonal and melodic rhythms mime
the vacillation between the awesome silence that precedes Ṣàngó's lightning bursts and his terrifying claps of thunder. Its poetic language produces the sweet sounds found in its alliteration, excerpted below, that
speak to the poetic sophistication and literary artistry of Yoruba *oríkì.*
The repetition of certain lines reinforces Ṣàngó's repudiated fierce and
cavalier manner. Here, his spiritual authority is unquestionable, and his
presence is potentially fatal whether he resides in the heavens or on earth.
His spoken words appear as hail and his look is as powerful as death, we
are told. In fact, even Death runs in order not to confront him.

> *Iná lójú, iná lẹ́nu*
>> *Ọkọ̀ọ̀ mi, òrò ìjàkadì létè!*
>> *Mònàmónà ṣojú òrun tàn-ǹ-bọnnà;-yanùn!*
>> *Ṣàngó l'èèbó òkè tíí f'ẹdùn-ún sòrò!*
>> *Ajẹbí-ojú-kú,[27] irin méjì gbèdu[28]*
>> *Ṣàngó t'ó bá baálé jiyán-àn gángán tán,*
>> *Orímóògùnjé,[29] t'ó p'ọmọ rẹ̀ sí ìloro!*
>> *Jẹ́ kó yẹ mí,[30] baba ẹni níí pé ni kó yẹni.*
>> *Ṣàngó ni ànìkànsorò*
>> *T'ó ko'kú lọ́nà tí ò yà!*
>> *Ikú l'ó kò ó ló sá,*

You, with fire in the eyes, fire in the mouth.
My Husband, with provocative words on the lips
The lighting that causes the sky to tremble and to lighten
Ṣàngó whose pugnacity is at its highest,
Who is the master of the skies,
Whose nature is hostility.
Who rebounds like the fortitude of death
(Hostility and Death resembling the hitting sticks of the *gbèdu*
drum).
Ṣàngó, who eats pounded *igángán* yam with the master of the house,
Activator and Protector,
Who kills his child on the porch!
Who shields his child in seclusion!
Protect and keep me.
Jẹ́kóyẹmí! It is one's father [ancestors] who brings good fortune.
Ṣàngó is the sole celebrant who personifies himself.
Whom Death will not confront.
Death retreats in order not to meet him![31]

Couched masterfully in hyperbole, the beauty and power of Yorùbá poetic language, nevertheless it warns us to regard seriously the threat posed by Ṣàngó's earthly ferocity as Aláàfin of Òyó. The consolidation of power under his reign partially explains this reputation, which is bolstered by his war-mongering generals.[32] His crimson gaze terrified most courtesans and commoners, who withered before him—that is, except for his generals Tìmì and Gbòǹńkà. In fact, his fierceness is mirrored in his cruelty and indifference toward his subjects, who, we are told, are simultaneously victimized by his experimentation with lightning and the unpredictability of his thunder strikes, while also being protected by his efficacious medicinal powers. These factors allude to Ṣàngó's ascension to power as exemplary of transformation in Yorùbá cultural and political historiography and praxis. For in both his manifestations, Ṣàngó's life represents a pattern of migration, resettlement, conquest, consolidation, and transformation that seems to dominate Yorùbá history and culture. His lineage, as noted previously, establishes his credentials as warrior/conqueror in the tradition of his father and grandfather, and these, in turn, dominate his narrative and shape his tragic persona.

As is characteristic of Yorùbá praise poetry, many notable predecessors are mentioned in the work, along with several cognomens for Òṣun and Oya. But therein lies a dichotomy as well; for as Òṣun rejoices at giving and seeing children, Ṣàngó, and indeed, Oya, behave most callously toward them. Where Òṣun praises and protects children, in the fierceness of their raging storms, Ọya and Ṣàngó kill and maim them. The inter-relationship between Ṣàngó, Ọya, and Òṣun poses a dilemma for Yoruba thought, which simultaneously accepts carnage in the name of conquest and longevity in the name of children. It may also explain why there are few indications of Ṣàngó producing children with Òṣun in the oral tradi-tion. This problem also exists in the references to *ẹrú*, or slaves, as well as *ẹbọ*, or sacrifice, and continues to challenge the fundamental principles of *ire* and *ìwàpẹ̀lẹ́* in Yorùbá thought until today.

Oríkì Ṣàngó ọkọ Ọya

In-In: Erínfọlámí[33] oo!

Ìwọ tún fi gbogbo ara k'ápó!

Olórọ̀ọ Kòso![34]

Èéfín l'à ń dá láyé

Ta ni ò mọ̀ pénàń bẹ lódòọ Ṣàngó?

Ọkọ Ọlógbọ́n-ńnú Ìbíyẹmí Alealeku!

Iná ń bẹ lódò ọkọọ mi.

Ìbíyẹmí,[35] ajájúmọ'ni k'ó tóó fi'ni ṣọmọ!

Ṣàngó là ń báá wí!

Aráa Moleyo![36]

Ọ̀rọ̀ Òkè,[37] ab'ónílépelá'lé-e-mo-beebee!

Kò mọmọ s'ẹni tí ò lè bà lòrì jẹ́!

Ṣàngó, mọ́mọ̀ bà mí lórí jẹ́!

Kele ò kúkú tán l'ọ́rùn-ùn mi.

Ìbíyẹmí tíí sorí burúkú d'oríire,

Ṣọ'bànújẹ́ ọmọ ẹ duyọ̀!

Ṣọ'bànújẹ́ mi dẹ̀rín, ọkọ Alógbọ́n-ńnú

O gbè fún mi

Bí ò jájẹẹ́ ó ṣọlé dayọ̀ níléẹ mi.

Ìbíyẹmí, ọmọ lójú ṣẹbọra!

Èéfín là ń dá láyé!

Ta ni ò mọ̀ bínáń bẹ l'ọ́dòọ Wòrú?

Wèrè là ń p'Ewégbèmí.

Ẹni ọlá bí!

Orí níí pé ní k'óògùn ó jẹ́!

Bẹ̀ẹ̀ ni ò tìì bu'ni jẹ!

Iná lójú, iná lẹ́nu!

Ọkọọ mi, ọ̀rọ̀ ìjàkadì létè!

Mọ̀nàmọ̀ná ṣ'ojú ọ̀run tàn-ń-bọ́nnà-yànún!

Ṣàngó l'èèbó òkè tíí f'ẹdùn-ún sọ̀rọ̀!

Ajẹ́bí-ojú-kú,[38] irin méjì gbẹ̀du
Ṣàngó tó bá baálé jiyán-àn gángán tán,
Orímóògùnjẹ́, tó p'ọmọ rẹ̀ sí ìloro!
Jẹ́ kó yẹ mí, baba ẹni níí pé ni kó yẹ'ni.
Ṣàngó ni ẹnìkàn-sọsọ
T'ó ko'kú lọ́nà tí ò yà!
Ikú l'ó kò ó ló sá,
Ọlọ́rọ̀ọ Kòso![39]
Ọkọọ̀ mi, ààrùn l'ó kò ó, ló yà.
Apa'ni má mògùnún jó,
N ló kò ó, ló kúkú dapo
Dọfà sílẹ̀, o mọ́ yáa lọ.
Erínfọlámí oo!
Àrá s'ọwọ́ọ̀jà láláálá!
Orímóògùnjẹ́,[40] níbo l'ó wà, n ò rí i!
Agbénákarí Ẹlẹ́dàá!
Ìbíyẹmí, níbo l'ó wà? N ò rí i!
Orí èlẹ̀ wọ́n ń gbé gúnyán léyàn.
Ọlọ́rọ̀ọ Kòso!
Orí èlẹ̀ wọ́n ń gbé rokà lókà.
Orí èlẹ̀ wọ́n ń gbé p'òko l'álẹ́.
Ọba Kóso, tí ò gbọdọ̀ s'òkanran,
Àní, tí ò gbọdọ̀ dojú dé!
B'ó bá dojú dé,
Ọpa ajá ọba níí pa wọ́n jẹ
Ọpa ajá ọba má mà j'árúgbó ó kú,
Ọmọ ẹlẹ́gbà,[41]
Má j'árúgbó ó kú, ẹlẹ́gbàa Kòso.
Ìwọ n mo gbójú lé, Ọlọ́rọ̀ọ Kòso!
Ọkọọ̀ mi, ìwọ n mo mọ̀ f'àyà tì.
Ìwọ n mo mọ̀ l'émi ń jíí ṣe "l'óo gbó?"
"Oo gbó" ni ń ó máa ṣe Gbólákànbí.[42]
Ìbíyẹmí tí mo gbénlá rù gẹ́gẹ́ bí ọṣẹ.
Erínfọlámí Ṣàngó, irin méjì gbẹ̀du!
Dákan-lùkan, ńnú oko aláwo.
Ọkọọ̀ mi, ọ̀rọ̀-jẹ-nǹkan-mọ̀là,
Fi-nǹkan-mọ̀là-bora-sùn!
Ṣàngó, t'ó bá baálé jiyán ìgángán tán,
Erínfọlámí o!
Ìbíyẹmí, t'ó p'ọmọ è sí'loro!
Agbàawẹ̀-má-kásámú,

Abónímàle-jẹ̀'sọnu!
Ìbíyẹmí tíí kó'yán rúgúdú bọ abẹ́ aṣọ!
Ọkọ̀ọ̀ mi, mọ̀mọ̀ gbà mí,
Abomimiwura-ní-ṣòkòtò!
Erínfọlámí, Ṣàngó, irin méjìì gbẹ̀du!
Ẹni t'ó ní kó o wáá kú
Ṣe bí Ifá fi kọ páráa rẹ̀
Ọkọ̀ọ̀ mi, mọ̀mọ̀ gbá mí,
Ọkọ̀ọ̀ mi, ọ̀pẹ̀lẹ̀ fiiri pọ̀ lójà!
Òòṣà kéékèèkéé fi í pọ̀ l'ágbẹ̀dẹ[43]
Alọ-ikú-lọọ-gborí, ọmọọ Yemọja
Odù-mi-ò-lówó, ò ṣeé rò, o ò lówó o ó jogbó.

The Praise Name Of Ṣàngó, Husband of Ọya

The gargantuan one who is above reproach!
You who uses your whole body to destroy.
Grand Patron of Kòso town!
It is mere smoke we are making on earth.
Who does not know that the real fire is with Ṣàngó
The Very Clever Husband of Royal Birth,
Whose hostility confronts even to death's end!
Yes, fire is my husband's name!
Ìbíyẹmí, your hostility is meant to call us to love you
Before you take us as your children.
It is Ṣàngó we are talking about!
Native of Mọlẹyọ̀!
We crave your attention Ṣàngó.
King of the Sky who spears no landlord,
I beseech you and adore you
Because there is definitely no one he cannot ruin.
Ṣàngó! Please do not ruin my future,
For reverence is my constant demeanor toward you.
Ìbíyẹmí, whose ferocity has turned my misfortune
Into prosperity.
Please turn my sadness to joy, My Very Clever Husband.
Don't be unhappy, one with joyful thoughts.
Who will be unhappy when fortitude remains
Even while wisdom is failing.
Ìbíyẹmí, whose ferocity stopped the witches from being
Victorious in my home.
Ferocious and Mysterious One!

It is your praises that we are singing
Who doesn't know that fire
Is beneath your intense heat.
Yet we regard Ewégbèmí as a lunatic,
One of Royal Birth!
It is one's goodwill that dictates the efficacy of medicine.
You, with fire in the eyes, fire in the mouth.
My Husband, with provocative words on the lips.
The lighting that causes the sky to tremble and to lighten.
Ṣàngó whose pugnacity is at its highest,
Who is the master of the skies,
Whose nature is hostility.
Who rebounds like the fortitude of death
(Hostility and Death resembling the hitting sticks of the gbèdu
drum).
Ṣàngó, who eats pounded ìgángán yam with the master of the house,
Activator and Protector,
Who kills his child on the porch,
Who shields his child in seclusion!
Protect and keep me.
Jékóyẹmí! It is one's father [ancestors] who brings one good fortune.
Ṣàngó is the sole celebrant who personifies himself always.
Who death will not confront.
Death retreats in order not to meet him!
Grand Patron of Kòso town!
My lord, as you met me, my sickness disappears.
If you don't meet him [properly], would you too not retreat?
He who kills without medicine is the one who is dancing.
If you are going to the farm, be prepared,
Put down your weapons and go with Ọya [Ṣàngó's wife].
O king of all the mightiest gargantuan kings!
Thunder strikes and all fall in respect!
He who determines everything, where is He I do not see Him!
O king of all the mightiest gargantuan kings!
Where is He I do not see him! Where will he go unnoticed?
A big gourd sits on the wine tapers head!
Ìbíyẹmí! Where is He I do not see Him!
Unique one! Where would you go and be unnoticed?
Grand Patron of Kòso town!
It is inside the mortar that pounded yam is pounded and pounded,
It is inside of the cooking pot that mixes are mixed,

It is inside of the mixer that they turn corn gruel every night.

Yes, King of Kòso who must never waver!

He who must never fall.

If he falls,

The roofs will collapse and kill many,

Let the roofs not fall and kill the Elderly.

You, son of the mighty Savior!

Do not let the Elderly die, the savior at Kòso!

It is you I look up to, my lord; grand patron of Kòso town!

My Husband, you are my lasting hope.

It is your confidence,

That strengthens my resolve unto the end.

It is the Elderly who always know the start of things.

Mightiest One who cleanses the world like soap,

O King of the mightiest gargantuan Kings,

Ṣàngó, Doubly Strengthened with your thunderous sounds like the *gbèdu* drum,

Stumbling and Falling is what makes the farm rows,

My Husband shower prosperity on me,

And remain prosperous till my old age, until death.

Ṣàngó, who had lunch with the master of the house,

Eating his specially prepared pounded yam.

You, King of the Mightiest Kings!

Unique one who grants protection to his children.

One who causes us to miss meals without proper prayers.

Only to eat his meals after sunset [like fasting Muslims].

Special one whose pounded yam is always wrapped.

My Husband, please grant my wishes, deliver me,

The one who carries the shower of blessings in his pants.

King of the Mightiest Kings, Ṣàngó

Doubly Strengthened with your thunderous sounds like the *gbèdu* drum,

Anyone who confronts him seeks his/her own death.

Everyone knows that adding palm-oil to Ifá is for Peace,

My Husband, please grant my requests, deliver me!

My Husband, whose call to the house upsets the market!

Let the lesser gods give respect to blacksmithing!

Sudden appearance of Death kills,

Child of Yemoja!

My *odù* is not one of poverty,

That will be adjusted from above for my own good![44]

A Few Final Thoughts

More than for the other male òrìṣà, Ṣàngó's mythology and histori-cism live at the dynamic epicenter of Yorùbá transformation in cultural and mythical ideology. The evocation to powerful Ṣàngó priests and the allusion to both Ọya and Ọ̀ṣun in his praise poem confront us with the image of a very powerful ruler whose awe-inspiring ferocity embraces the challenges and dynamics of changing political realities. The domi-nance of his wives in his mythology suggests his concurrence with the Ẹdan Ọ̀ṣùgbó, which represents the necessity for balance and coordi-nation between the genders for the purpose of sustaining the human community and the very essence of life itself. Their conflicting personas acknowledge the objective realities of human contradiction, which for the Yorùbá is oftentimes the quintessential àṣẹ of existence. Moreover, the oral narratives intimate that, despite the presence of his wives, his generals, his advisors, and his royal lineage, Ṣàngó, after all, reflects man himself. Ṣàngó is, nonetheless, susceptible to the foibles of humankind and is mirrored by the divine, beloved only to those who believed in him. It is for this reason that his apotheosis is heralded by chanting, Ọba Kò so! Truly, the King did not hang.

NOTES

1. Isaiah O. Adegbile, *Yorùbá Names and Their Meanings plus Proverbs with English Translations* (Ibadan, Nigeria: Taa Printing and Publishing Co., 1999), 10.

2. Duro Ladipo, *Ọba Kòso (The King Did Not Hang)* (Ibadan, Nigeria: Insti-tute of African Studies at the University of Ibadan, 1972).

3. Diedre Badejo, "Methodologies in Yorùbá Oral Historiographies and Aes-thetics," in *Writing African History*, ed. John Edward Phillips (Rochester, N.Y.: University of Rochester Press, 2004).

4. Wole Soyinka, *Myth, Literature and the African World* (London: Cam-bridge University Press, 1976), 1–60.

5. E. Bolaji Idowu, *Olódùmarè: God in Yorùbá Belief* (London: Longmans, 1962), 92.

6. Christopher Ehret, *The Civilizations of Africa: A History of 1800* (Char-lottesville: University Press of Virginia, 2002). See also I. A. Akinjogbin, "The Expansion of Ọ̀yọ́ and the Rise of Dahomey, 1600–1800," in *The History of West Africa*, vol. 1 (New York: Columbia University Press, 1972), and J. A. Atanda, *An Introduction to Yorùbá History* (Ibadan, Nigeria: Ibadan University Press, 1980).

7. S. A. Babalola, *Content and Form of Yorùbá Ìjálá* (London: Oxford Uni-versity Press, 1966), 222–23.

8. Diedre L. Badejo, Field Notes, 1982.

9. Babalola, *Content and Form,* 222–23.

10. Jacob Olupona, *Kingship, Religion, and Rituals in a Nigerian Community: A Phenomenological Study of Oǹdó Yorùbá Festivals* (Stockholm, Sweden: Almqvist and Wiksell International, 1991), 3.

11. Babalola, *Content and Form,* 222–23.

12. Atanda, *An Introduction to Yorùbá History,* 9–12.

13. Robin Law, *The Ọ̀yọ́ Empire, c 1600–1836: A West African Imperialism in the Era of the Atlantic Slave Trade* (Oxford: Clarendon Press, 1977), 41–71.

14. D. T. Niane, *Sundiata: An Epic of Old Mali* (London: Longman Group, 1965), 4–12. See also John William Johnson and Fa-Digi Sisoko, *Son-Jara: The Mande Epic* (Bloomington: Indiana University Press, 2003), 3–62.

15. Babalola, *Content and Form,* 104–105.

16. Henry John Drewal, John Pemberton, and Rowland Abiodun, "The Yorùbá World," in *Yorùbá: Nine Centuries of African Art and Thought* (New York: Center for African Art in association with Harry Abrams, 1989), 13–42.

17. *Arugbá-àáyán* can be translated as "The sacrifice of the *àáyán* tree." It refers to the fact that Ṣàngó hung himself on the *àáyán* tree, which is now sacred to him.

18. Badejo, Field Notes, 1982.

19. A title, probably from the Ìjẹ̀bú area. Chief Jàkúta states that Ìkólàbà is one of the titled houses where Ṣàngó chiefs are trained and selected, but it is not the title of the chief priest of Ṣàngó. See also R. C. Abrahams, *Dictionary of Modern Yorùbá* (London: Hodder and Stoughton, 1962), 498.

20. Although it is unclear, the term possibly refers to a gathering of malevolent forces against whom the petitioner seeks the protection of Ọya and Ṣàngó as warriors.

21. Abrahams, *Dictionary,* 498. Abrahams defines Poolo as an executioner of the guilty, who lives in a cave. He also notes that there is a relationship between Poolo and Òrìṣà Oko, the deity of the farm.

22. According to Chief Jàkúta of Ọ̀yọ́, *asípónnlá* was a Ṣàngó priest as well as an Ifá diviner. Personal correspondence, 1982.

23. Òríírì refers to Ọya's great powers in bending tree and their branches when she is annoyed.

24. According to Chief Jàkúta, this praise name means one who covers the head of a liar with Ifá tray, indicating that he is offended by the person being a liar. This also means that he was a great diviner who knew many Ifá verses.

25. Transcription and translation by Professor Yíwọ́lá Awóyalé.

26. Badejo, Field Notes, 1982.

27. Ajẹbí-ojú-kú is one who acts like he has a blind eye.

28. According to Akin Euba, *gbẹ̀du* belongs to the family of *dùndún* drums, which are associated with royalty. Euba argues that the *dùndún* ensemble probably migrated to Ọ̀yọ́ around the fifteenth century from Hausaland, and *gbẹ̀du* itself is often referred to as *gbẹ̀du* Mecca, or royal drums of Mecca. He notes that

gbèdu denotes "single-headed, fixed-pitched pedestal drums of the *igbìn* type," which most certainly predate the *dùndún*. See Akin Euba, *Yorùbá Drumming: The Dùndún Tradition* (Bayreuth, Germany: African Studies Series, 1990), 37–60.

29. Orímóògùnjẹ́ is a powerful Ṣàngó priest. His name literally means "It's the head that makes medicine strong." Field notes, 1982.

30. Jẹ́kóyẹmí is a much loved and handsome Ṣàngó priest. (See ibid.)

31. Ibid. Transcription and translation with assistance from Professor Yíwọ́lá Awóyalé and Apènà Táíyéwò Ògúnadé.

32. Atanda, *An Introduction*, 9–18.

33. A notable Ṣàngó priest who came from Ọ̀yọ́-Ilé (Old Ọ̀yọ́), according to Chief Jàkúta. (See Badejo, Field Notes, 1982.)

34. The hot-tempered, much feared one from Kòso, according to Chief Jàkúta.

35. Ìbíyẹmí, meaning a befitting birth, refers to the status of the lineage to which a child is born. Peter Badejo, Personal Communication, 2004.

36. Moleyo, according to Chief Jàkúta, refers to "one who sees children and becomes happy; that is, Ọ̀ṣun." (See Badejo, Field Notes, 1982.)

37. Ọ̀rọ̀ Òkè refers to the *òrìṣà* of the hills.

38. Ajẹ́bí-ojú-kú is one who acts like he has a blind eye.

39. The hot-tempered, much feared one from Kòso, according to Jàkúta, a reference to Ṣàngó and his birthplace. Badejo, Field Notes, 1982.

40. Orímóògùnjẹ́ is another very powerful Ṣàngó priest, whose name means "It is the head (destiny) that makes medicine to be effective." Ibid.

41. Chief Jàkúta states that Ọmọ Ẹlégba is one of the great sons of one of the chief priests of Ṣàngó at Ọ̀yọ́.

42. Chief Jàkúta notes that Gbọ́lákanbi belonged to the Mọgbà ruling house, which was very well-known for its peace and gentility.

43. The line refers to the little *òrìṣà* who are left at the blacksmith's forge, the site of Ògún.

44. Badejo, Field notes, 1982. Transcription and translation with the assistance of Professor Yíwọ́lá Awóyalé and Apènà Táíyéwò Ògúnadé.

CHAPTER SEVEN

Reconfiguration of Ṣàngó on the Screen

DÚRÓTOYÈ A. ADÉLÉKÈ

With the unalloyed support and assistance of Ulli Beier, who made Samuel Johnson's *The History of the Yorùbás* available to him, Dúró Ládipọ̀ was able to put *Ọba Kòso* on the stage in 1963 to mark the first anniversary of Mbárí-Mbáyọ̀ at Òṣogbo.[1] Notwithstanding the flaws in this premiere as reflected in the simple costumes donned by the actors/actresses and the poor craftsmanship on the stage, *Ọba Kòso,* in Beier's words, "had the impact of an explosion," so receptive was the audience. Ever since, Dúró Ládipọ̀ not only has been linked to the god of thunder, he is also synonymous with Ṣàngó, as he was able to popularize and configure the awesome figure of Ṣàngó on the stage within and outside Nigeria. His constant production of *Ọba Kòso* provided an avalanche of materials which many scholars have since utilized for critical works. One then begins to wonder what more is to be written or discussed on Ṣàngó. On a long look, one discovers that Dúró Ládipọ̀'s production largely focuses on intrigues between Ṣàngó and his warlords, and his eventual apotheosis. Besides, Dúró Ládipọ̀ was unable to have a film production of the play before his demise in 1978. Perhaps in order not to create a vacuum, some film producers fashioned their production along the lines of Dúró Ládipọ̀'s, while some alluded to Ṣàngó's conflict with other gods. In sum, Yorùbá videographers have been able to touch on more aspects of Ṣàngó's life, ranging from mundane to sacred motifs. His spirit is visible in the worldview of the Yorùbá. This chapter therefore attempts to give a general overview of the portrait of Ṣàngó and the belief held by his acolytes and the general members of the public, using semiotics and

135

mediumship as our analytical tools. It becomes apparent that Ṣàngó has become a living character in Yorùbáland, and despite the seeming explosion of the two major religions, Islam and Christianity, some people still find solace in Ṣàngó, while others are caught in religious conflicts.

More often than not a number of works find their ancestry in an earlier one. This is why any dramatic piece on Ṣàngó always finds its antecedent in Dúró Ládipọ̀'s *Ọba Kòso,* a play which brought both national and international recognition to the Duro Ladipo Theatre Troupe.[2] After the premiere on stage in March 1963 to mark the first anniversary of Mbárí-Mbáyọ̀ at the Yorùbá city of Òṣogbo in Nigeria, the play became the most dominant production in Dúró Ládipọ̀'s theater repertory since it "had the impact of an explosion" that constantly put the ecstatic audience on the edge wishing for a repeat performance.[3] This constant production of the play shaped and fine-tuned the various dramatic elements—the actors and the actresses, the costumes, the craftsmanship on stage—to the extent that the new production was always a better one than the previous. Until Dúró Ládipọ̀'s demise, the play kept evolving on stage. This means that *Ọba Kòso* evolved for a good fifteen years. Yemi Ogunbiyi claims that the play had been performed more than two thousand times before Dúró Ládipọ̀ died.[4] Thus Dúró Ládipọ̀, who played the role of Ṣàngó, was venerated as the god of thunder while his wife, Abiodun Ladipo, who took on the role of Ọya, was, and remains, synonymous with Ọya, the goddess of the Niger river. As a result of "Duro's towering stage presence"[5] and the indelible footprints he had left on the sands of time, several other actors who attempted to revive the role of Ṣàngó in the theater world "had neither the commanding stature nor the imposing stage presence of the late Duro Ladipo."[6] Yemi Ogunbiyi blamed the failure of Dúró Ládipọ̀'s successors as Ṣàngó's icon on the inability to possess that "tremendous and awe-inspiring power,"[7] which could enable them to display what Robert Armstrong calls *brio ad éclat* that was inherent in Dúró Ládipọ̀'s performance.[8] In other words, theater practitioners, artists, critics and theater-goers have used, and continue to use, Dúró Ládipọ̀'s *Ọba Kòso* to judge other productions featuring a Ṣàngó character. Thus, Dúró Ládipọ̀, as the icon of Ṣàngó on stage, has therefore become the standard barometer to measure other performances.

Though there were several stage performances both at home and abroad, it was unfortunate that *Ọba Kòso* could not be filmed before Dúró Ládipọ̀'s death. Before his demise a plan was in the making to have the play as an optical film, as Yemi Ogunbiyi was "convinced more than ever, of the need to document Dúró Ládipọ̀'s works on film."[9] It is important to say that he had had a stint with mass media, whether it be print or electronic. For instance, he had had Ọba Kòso both as atọ́ka (a Yorùbá photo play) and as a textbook—published by Macmillan Nigeria. Also with regard to the electronic media, Dúró Ládipọ̀ had excerpts from Ọba Kòso and Ẹ̀dá on discography in 1965. The complete editions of the discs being shipped from the United States to Nigeria were lost in transit, and Curt Wittig had to do a new recording at Òṣogbo on reel-to-reel tape.[10] At the instance of Ulli Beier, Ọba Kòso was recorded on two Nagra tape recorders by Curt Wittig of Washington, D. C., then a worker at the Institute of African Studies at the University of Ibadan. Decca (Nigeria Ltd.) published Ọba Kòso as Nigerian Cultural Records NCR 1/2 as recorded by the Institute of African Studies, Ibadan. Apart from the discography, there are excerpts of the play in motion pictures. Armstrong observes that a part of Ọba Kòso is on at least one color film: *New Images' Documentary of Òṣogbo,* made by Frank Speed and Ulli Beier in 1964. The scene of Tìmì's appearance at Ẹdẹ is on the clips.[11] That aside, Dúró Ládipọ̀ was one of the theater practitioners to appear in the first Yorùbá feature film, *Àjàní Ògún,* by Ola Balogun, in 1976. He later took part in another film, *Ìjà Òmìnira,* produced by Adeyemi Afolayan (aka Ade Love); he plays the role of Olúmokò, the feudal monarch of Ọ̀yọ́. Being one of the pioneering actors in the Yorùbá film industry, Dúró Ládipọ̀ could have been desirous to have his Ọba Kòso on film as he had warmed himself to the heart of his various audiences drawn from far and near. But this he could not do, thereby creating a vacuum for some of his contemporaries: Hubert Ogunde, Moses Olaiya Adejumo (aka Bàbáa Sàlá), Adeyemi Afolayan, and Akin Ogungbe, who were able to put some of their stage plays on film. Others, such as Oyin Adejobi, who could not afford the financial outlay of celluloid, had to make do with video. By the mid-1980s, the reality of economic recession dawned on the Nigerian film producers, and they could not afford to produce celluloid films. Since then, the video culture has been thriving and flourishing in Yorùbá society, where today the video industry churns out well over ten video films daily. This enormous production has given rise to low quality in its totality—themes, costume, dialogue, choreography, and other aspects.

Nevertheless, the Yorùbá videographers attempt to cover different aspects of Yorùbá life and culture in their video productions. They therefore allow their artistic lens to catch different aspects of the mythical and historical Ṣàngó. Thus, unlike Dúró Ládipọ̀, who dwells on the motifs of intrigues, stubbornness, impatience, and apotheosis, the video filmmakers are able to extend their coverage of Ṣàngó's life—ranging from mundane to sacred themes. Our data therefore derive from different Yorùbá video films but largely from Wálé Ògúnyẹmí's *Ṣàngó*, Afọlábí Adésànyà's *Osé(e) Ṣàngó*, Adebimpe Adekola's *Ìbínú Olúkòso*, and Lérè Pàímọ́'s *Lákáayé*. These four films serve as our primary sources, while other films where allusion is made to Ṣàngó's name or spirit make up our secondary sources. Different written texts and documents also fall under our secondary sources.

It is important to place on record that there are copious critical materials on *Ọba Kòso*. Philip A. Ogundeji's 1988 doctoral thesis, at the University of Ibadan, is on Dúró Ládipọ̀'s mythico-historical plays, while Ulli Beier, Dúró Ládipọ̀'s mentor, also has a text titled *The Return of Shàngó: The Theatre of Duro Ladipo*. There exist so many other articles, reviews, and notes—within and outside our reach—on Ṣàngó that one begins to wonder what else one can say on him that all these scholars, critics, reviewers, and writers have not already written or discussed. For instance, Ogundeji takes a global look at Ṣàngó's image in three plays of Dúró Ládipọ̀: *Ọba Kòso, Ọbàtálá*, and *Òṣun àti Ọbà*. In these three plays, Ṣàngó assumes the position of a king, or Aláàfin. Ogundeji, having considered his behavioral pattern, then concludes that Ṣàngó's personality verges between femininity and masculinity, that is, "weakling" and "warlikeness."[12] Ulli Beier's text dwells on the growth and development of Dúró Ládipọ̀'s theater. He then gives a synopsis of the play before presenting an English version of *Ọba Kòso* and *Mọrèmi*. Yemi Ogunbiyi's tribute to Dúró Ládipọ̀ also sums up Dúró's theater career, and he includes a resume of *Ọba Kòso*. He does not forget to include the idea being nursed of having *Ọba Kòso* on celluloid. Robert Armstrong gives an insight with regard to different unsuccessful attempts made to have *Ọba Kòso* on the electronic media, considering the inherent problems associated with translation from one language to another, with special reference to the poetry. Oludare Olajubu, in his own contribution, draws attention to various sources from which Dúró Ládipọ̀ must have drawn his materials for *Ọba Kòso*. He mentions Samuel Johnson's *The History of the Yorùbás*, A. L. Hethersett's *Ìwé Kíkà Ẹ̀kẹrin Li Èdè Yorùbá*, and Olunlade's *Ẹdẹ: A Short History*. However, Olu Obafemi sees Dúró Ládipọ̀'s *Ọba Kòso* as a text that aims at fostering social harmony after the turbulence. I have gone this far so as to make it abundantly clear that much has been written on Ṣàngó in writing on Dúró Ládipọ̀.

Semiotics and Mediumship

To facilitate my discussion on the image of Ṣàngó on screen, I hinge it on semiotics (like Ogundeji) and mediumship, as this seems to be the preoccupation of two films, *Osé(e) Ṣàngó* and *Ìbínú Olúkòso*. As observed by Ogundeji, any actor who plays the role of Ṣàngó is Ṣàngó's icon on stage. And Ṣàngó is frequently iconized at different levels and phases. Aside from human iconization, Ṣàngó may be iconized through his paraphernalia, which Ogundeji calls identificatory features. The list includes: *osù* (Ṣàngó's tuft), *yẹrì* (skirt), *òjáa wàbì* (girdle flaps of leather stuff), *osé* (wand), *ìrùkẹ̀rẹ̀* (whisk), *gbérí* (vest), *iná* (fire), and *aṣọ pupa* (red attire). Sometimes he may be emotionally iconized, and this Ogundeji refers to as behavioral features, which include humility, love, consideration, weakness, power, and irascibility. In fact, the Yorùbá videographers iconize Ṣàngó in both identificatory and behavioral ways, as will be highlighted below.

With regard to trance, it borders on spirit possession or spirit mediumship.[13] It is a common religious institution and is not exclusive to Yorùbá society. The *bori* spirit mediumship in Hausaland is another good example, which Horn has written on. The gods usually enter their mediums and acolytes when performing private or public ritual; and more importantly, spirit possession cuts across the gender divide.[14] It is through possession by the deity that the deity himself or herself becomes anthropomorphized; hence the saying: *òòṣàá gùn ún* ("the spirit mounts the person," or "the person mounts the spirit")[15] or *ẹ̀mí òòṣà* ("animating spirit of the deity").[16] Such an individual possessed with the spirit of the deity is normally imbued with the powers of such a deity. Hence Horn affirms: "The medium has now become the spirit which has mounted her and is treated as the spirit, not as herself, her own familiar personality suspended for the duration of the trance."[17]

Mediumship provides ample opportunity for human beings to relate with the spirit, thereby establishing communicative relationships with the spirit, which is possible only through what Horn calls "multiple personality."[18] It is through trance or mediumship that the existence of a permanent dualism in the human being—that is, the power of being oneself and the spirit at one and the same time—is brought to the fore. The spiritual communion is thus achieved in trance, as the entranced person, who has been imbued with "an extra-human entity," now provides a direct link between the terrestrial world and the ethereal world. And, in actual fact, Ṣàngó does constantly ride his mediums and acolytes, as it will be shortly explicated below.

Ṣàngó Persona

It is necessary to give a précis of the different films that present the character of Ṣàngó and his mediums, or "containers" as Drewal calls them.[19] It is in *Ṣàngó* and *Lákáayé* that Ṣàngó is physically iconized on the screen. The film titled *Ṣàngó*, to a very large extent, corresponds with Dúró Ládipọ̀'s *Ọba Kòso*, but it goes a little farther than Dúró Ládipọ̀'s themes.

In Wálé Ògúnyẹmí's *Ṣàngó*, Prince Ṣàngó has to come all the way from Nupeland to ransom Aláàfin Àjàká from the Olówu's bondage, at the instance of the Ọ̀yọ́mèsì. As the Ọ̀yọ́mèsì can no longer tolerate a weakling who allows the Aláàfinate's status to be challenged by the vassal towns, they ask Aláàfin Àjàká to be in exile at Ìgbòho. Thereafter, Prince Ṣàngó, whose blue blood runs through his veins from both the maternal and paternal sides, is recalled and made the next Aláàfin. As part of his character to always challenge any Aláàfin, the Olówu challenges Aláàfin Ṣàngó for not according him due respect and honor by extending an invitation to him during his coronation. Aláàfin Ṣàngó, who has been imbued with mystic power at Nupeland, and coupled with the support of his were-animal wife, Ọya Òrírì, is able to rout and subdue Òwu's war and constant aggression. However, his two warlords, Ẹlírí and Olúǹdẹ, are poised for more wars. The yearning and urge for more wars triggers an uprising in Ọ̀yọ́, especially among the widows and orphans. The people are of the opinion that the leadership seems to "abandon the hope, or stop making the effort to grow and improve the quality of life of the people."[20] Aláàfin Ṣàngó's attempts to call his two warlords to order degenerates into a series of conflicts—conflicts between Aláàfin Ṣàngó and the two warlords, between Aláàfin Ṣàngó and the Ọ̀yọ́mèsì, and between Olúǹdẹ and Ẹlírí. There seems to be a "moral crisis" as every citizen and denizen has realized that "[t]here is in fact, a feeling of moral chaos, of total loss of values and lack of respect for human life."[21] The dominant themes in Wálé Ògúnyẹmí's *Ṣàngó* are intra-class and inter-class struggles. The uprising from the townspeople who are tired of war is an example of inter-class struggle between the ruler and the ruled. Olówu's invasion is precipitated as a form of inter-class struggle, while the conflicts between Aláàfin and the Ọ̀yọ́mèsì and Ẹlírí and Olúǹdẹ fall under intra-class struggle. Having discovered the Alaafin's sinister game plan to eliminate him, Ẹlírí, who now considers himself too powerful to curtail, asks Aláàfin Ṣàngó to abdicate the throne if he does not want to be shamed. In his anger Aláàfin Ṣàngó utilizes his emotive charm, which he thought was no longer potent, while facing his palace from the hilltop overshadowing it. This results in a conflagration that eventually consumes lives and property. Having lost wives, children, and other personal effects, he then and there decides to go back to his maternal home in Tapaland. This conforms to the Yorùbá expression that "[t]here is no god like mother" (*òrìṣà bí ìyá kò sí*). On being confronted on a desolate road by Ẹlírí, he transmogrifies and then consumes Gbọ̀nńkà and his flutist with fire ignited from lightning. He then promises to bless those who honor him in spirit and to provide energy for the good of mankind.

It is important that I quickly draw the parallels and dissimilarities between Wálé Ògúnyẹmí and Dúró Ládipọ̀. Other films which make allusion to Ṣàngó's spirit tend to draw from *Ọba Kòso's* text, hence the valid basis for this comparison. In Wálé Ògúnyẹmí's *Ṣàngó*, the producer seems to have the English audience in mind because of the use of bilingualism. But more dialogue is in English than in Yorùbá. Yorùbá is employed by the characters when greetings are being exchanged or incantations or native airs are rendered. Dialogue dominates, unlike the operatic form which permeates Dúró Ládipọ̀'s *Ọba Kòso,* produced in elegant and rich Yorùbá. This accounts for the reason why the film producer has to draw most of his cast from the veterans of English drama productions, such as Wálé Ògúnyẹmí himself, Jìmí Sólànké, Ayọ̀ Akínwálé, Láídé Adéwálé, Wálé Adébáyọ, Peter Fátómilọlá, Kọlá Ọ̀yéwọ, Jídé Ògúngbádé, Rachael Oniga, Rẹmí Abíọlá, Albert Aka-Eze, and many others.[22] One can observe that the nonverbal code also features in *Ṣàngó,* especially with regard to telegraphic code. The drummers in the film freely pass messages to the Aláàfin, the chiefs, and the townspeople, while the flutist announces the coming of Gbọ̀nńkà. This must have been borrowed from Dúró Ládipọ̀'s piece.

The casting and the use of bilingualism, with special reference to Albert Aka-Eze as Ẹlírí, demean the quality of the production, as he is unable to render any memorable incantations. He is no match for Dúró Ládipọ̀'s Gbọ̀nńkà (Adémọ́lá Oníbọn-Òkúta, later played by Abídoyè Òjó). Even his charm vest is not dreadful, either. The same thing goes for Wálé Adébáyọ, who plays the role of Ṣàngó; he fails to attract or iconize the awesomeness of Ṣàngó as Dúró Ládipọ̀ did on the stage. His paraphernalia has scanty cowries sewn on them. He wears common dress and sometimes a tie wrapper when in the inner chamber with Ọya. Wálé Ògúnyẹmí's Ṣàngó exhibits masculinity and hot-temperedness from the beginning of the film till the end. There is no inkling of being a weakling as such. He constantly destroys and kills known and unknown enemies with his magical charms. He, however, crosses the border by having the ṣùkú hairstyle plaited on his head by Ọya instead of using the carved agògo as the iconization of Ṣàngó's hairdo as in Ọba Kòso. This can be taken as a symbol of his femininity, showing love and affection for Ọya, his wife who has been supportive in his prosecution of wars. We notice further that Aláàfin Ṣàngó dons the ceremonial crown, which is the symbol of power and authority—that is, the iconization of his political power. His chiefs, the Ọyọ́mèsì, were properly clad in well-embroidered agbádá, gbáríyè, and dàńdógó, made from traditional aṣọ̀ òkè stuff, with different caps either of abetí ajá, or kọrí style.[23] The chiefs in Òwu put on outfits similar to the Ọyọ́mèsì, and they wear beads round their necks and wrists to symbolize their political authority.

As noted above, Ṣàngó is more loaded in terms of content, setting, and characterization than Ọba Kòso. Just as the indebtedness of Ọba Kòso to Hethersett's Ìwé Kíkà Ẹ̀kẹrin Lí Èdè Yorùbá is very high, so too is Ṣàngó's indebtedness to Samuel Johnson's The History of the Yorùbás. The content in Ṣàngó covers: Aláàfin Àjàká's reign, Olówu of Òwu, Prince Ṣàngó in his maternal home (Nupeland), the domestic life of Ṣàngó—as husband of Ọbà, Ọ̀sun, and later Ọya, Ọya's mythology as a were-animal—oracular consultations on different occasions by the Ọyọ́mèsì and Aláàfin Ṣàngó, the prosecution of wars in the open fields and between the hills, the protest by the townspeople, Olúńdẹ's appearance at Ẹdẹ, the rituals performed by the Olówu of Òwu and Òwu's warriors, rituals performed for Prince Ṣàngó including his coronation as the Aláàfin of Ọ̀yọ́, the fights between Ẹlíri and Olúńdẹ, the inadvertent destruction of the palace with the emotive charm, and his final transfiguration on his way to Tapaland. But Ọba Kòso focuses on Ṣàngó as the Aláàfin, the ruler of Ọ̀yọ́, Ọya and other unnamed wives, the Ọyọ́mèsì as the chiefs-in-council, Tìmì's appearance at Ẹdẹ, the fights between Tìmì and Gbọ̀nńkà, the consultation with the witches in the forest, and Ṣàngó and Ọya in the open field on their way to Ṣàngó's maternal home. Though my explication of the two texts, Ṣàngó and Ọba Kòso, touches more on the settings of the film and the stage play, a close look at the macro settings reveals that Wálé Ògúnyẹmí's production has Old Ọ̀yọ́, Ọ̀yọ́ Koro, Òwu, Ilé-Ifẹ̀, Ẹdẹ, and Nupeland, whereas Dúró Ládipọ̀'s production has just Ọ̀yọ́ and Ẹdẹ. The film production is able to establish the extended kin group of Ṣàngó. We are able to know that Olówu and Aláàfin are cross-cousins. According to Ogunmola, "The Olówu was a descendant of Akèsán, the grand-daughter of Dàda, who reigned before and after Ṣàngó; . . . This was about 1669."[24] Perhaps Olówu's insurgence is aimed at challenging the patrilineal culture that gives exclusive rights of paternal children to the institution of Aláàfin, while maternal children of Aláàfin are denied the same rights. This is taken as part of the social discriminations and injustice in gender issues. The consanguine and affined kins of different categories are also established through these macro and micro settings. The film brings to the fore that Ṣàngó and Dàda Àjàká are brothers, and this is firmly established in one Yorùbá proverb: *Dàda kò lè jà, ṣùgbọ́n ó ní àbúrò tí ó gbójú* ("Dada might not be able to fight, but he had a brave younger brother").[25] This is an allusion to Ṣàngó's valor in ransoming Àjàká from Olówu's claws. Ọba Eléṅpe of Nupeland is Ṣàngó's maternal uncle, hence Ṣàngó is venerated as *Ṣàngó ọmọ Eléṅpe* (Ṣàngó offspring of Eléṅpe). The Ifẹ̀ trip to the grave of Ọ̀rànmíyàn, his father, by Ṣàngó, only confirms the omnipresence of the dead among the living and the willingness of the ancestral spirit to render support. This extended kinship firmly confirms him as a true heir to the stool of Aláàfin. The movement to Ọ̀yọ́ Koro depicts Ṣàngó as a trickster who guiles the Ọba of Ọ̀yọ́ Koro, the royal princes, and the chiefs of Ọ̀yọ́ to have Èyọ̀ marks cut all over their bodies. While these people are in pain, Ṣàngó and his subjects move in and seize the palace of Ọ̀yọ́ Koro. Some people may see this trickery as a kind of war strategy, thereby calling him a "war strategist."

At the level of characterization, we have six kings: Aláàfin Àjàká, Olówu of Òwu, Aláàfin Ṣàngó, Ọba Eléṅpe of Nupeland, Ọba of Ọ̀yọ́ Koro, and Tìmì of Ẹdẹ (that is, Olúṅdẹ, who has been installed as a king) in the film, while we have just two kings, Aláàfin Ṣàngó and Tìmì of Ẹdẹ, in the stage production. Dúró Ládipọ̀ can lay claim to Ọya and other unnamed wives of Ṣàngó; Wálé Ògúnyẹmí categorically mentions Ọbà, Ọ̀ṣun, and Ọya as the Aláàfin Ṣàngó's wives, thereby establishing the affined kinship between Ṣàngó and these three women as husband and wives and as co-wives. Ṣàngó, however, takes Ọya as his favorite for the obvious reason that she complements his magical powers. Ọya evokes the rain, which in turn enhances the switch movement of the lightning and thunder, which he controls. He is so immersed in his love for Ọya that he allows Ọya to touch his head, thus permitting Ọya to commit an abominable offence. Both Ọbà and Ọ̀ṣun, who are senior to Ọya, are bewildered that the Aláàfin's head is being touched. Their astonishment may have even been more premised on co-wife envy rather than genuine concern for the tradition. He is thus portrayed as a partial husband, for he even sends away Ọbà and Ọ̀ṣun on account of their having quarreled with Ọya. This co-wife rivalry has since precipitated this saying:

Ọ̀ṣun gba ìyàwó
Ó gba lékelèke
Ó gba Ọya tí ń yọni lẹ́nu
Ó gba Ọbà tí ń báni mọ́lẹ́

Ọ̀ṣun has co-wives
She has oppressors
She has Ọya who troubles one
She also has Ọba, who torments one[26]

Co-wife rivalry is a common phenomenon in Yorùbá society, and a good husband does not take sides. Besides, the husband will endeavor as much as possible to rotate bed-sharing as appropriate and adequate among the number of women in his harem. Ṣàngó is unable to do this in Wálé Ògúnyẹmí's film.

Furthermore, unlike Dúró Ládipọ̀'s production, where all Ọ̀yọ́mèsì are lumped together, Wálé Ògúnyẹmí's text identifies the Ọ̀yọ́mèsì by their traditional titles, such as Baṣọ̀run, Alápiínni, Sàmu, and Àgbàakin. Instead of adopting the title name of the one warlord, the Gọ̀nǹkà, Wálé Ògúnyẹmí settles for Ẹlírí, as contained in Samuel Johnson; he cuts off part of the compound name.[27] The full name is Ẹlírí-Onígbànjo, the Gbọ̀nǹkà. Rather than use Tìmì as Dúró Ládipọ̀ had, Wálé Ògúnyẹmí opts for Olúnde and only refers to Olúnde as the Tìmì after he has been installed as the Ọba of Ẹdẹ.

Wálé Ògúnyẹmí portrays Ṣàngó as a being obsessed with magic powers. He is immersed in metaphysics right from his prime age and has supernatural support from his maternal community, Tapaland. Even when he is installed as the Aláàfin, the ghost of his father, Ọ̀rànmíyàn, acknowledges the magical prowess of the Nupe people. This is why he directs Ṣàngó to Tapaland. He obtains his *osé* (axe wand) and *ẹdùn àrá* (thunderbolt) from Nupe. The Tapa subtly fosters the theory of binary complementarity by encouraging Ṣàngó to work with Ọya if he wants his metaphysics to be emotively potent, because Ọya herself is also a numinous being. It is through Ọya's support that the Òwu warriors are subdued. Ọya stirs the storm while Ṣàngó sends the lightning and thunder. He has implicit faith in oracular consultations; hence he frequents the Ifá priest to seek direction from Ifá on major issues, such as ransoming Aláàfin Àjàká and prosecuting the Òwu war. He has a strong belief in ancestor worship, as demonstrated in his visit to his father's grave. More importantly, he takes along the Egúngún to prosecute the Òwu war. This is the metaphor of the "dead" supporting the living. It equally confirms the dependence of the living on the dead. His earlier exposure and constant renewal of his metaphysical charms appears to prepare him for his imminent transmogrification, instead of hanging as concluded in Dúró Ládipọ̀'s text. It is also evident that Ṣàngó utilizes his metaphysical powers for both positive and negative ends. Ṣàngó consumes all the enemies of Ọ̀yọ́, and his own enemies, such as Tàmẹ̀dù, an assassin (role played by Kayode Odumosu), and Gbọ̀nńkà, but in his anger he destroys his own home. Thus in the film, Ṣàngó symbolizes power, authority, violence, and destruction. The film audience may not be wrong then to conclude or infer, "that things go bad for anyone who cannot master his bad temper, and that magic should not be used for negative ends. Temper as well as evil magic must be balanced . . . a certain morality must be pursued."[28]

Before I draw curtains on Wálé Ògúnyẹmí's *Ṣàngó,* a passing comment is necessary on the narrator used. The film makes use of a narrator, who gives brief information to a particular scene. You may wish to liken it to the stage direction in a written text. For instance, when the film is about to begin after the usual preliminaries—listing of film title, the production studio, casts and characters, writer, director, and other production crews—the film narrator says, "Long time ago around fifteenth century, the old Ọ̀yọ́ empire of the Yorùbá was faced with crises and wars." Thereafter, the warriors appear on screen chanting war songs:

Ojú ogun là ń lọ
Ìba ẹni la pè, igba ẹni ló jẹ́.

To the battlefield we march
Few were invited and many responded.

Though his information may be effective and appropriate, sometimes it sounds absurd for the information to be presented by voice-over when it has already been captured by the lens of the camera. The director or producer has forgotten that the film medium has its own language and grammar. The film medium relies heavily on images and symbols, not too many words. The narration almost mars the film. The film could still have been enjoyed without the voice-over from the narrator. The narrator at one level, therefore, constitutes a noise.

Ṣàngó in Wálé Ògúnyẹmí and Dúró Ládipọ̀'s text is the historical Ṣàngó, the fourth Aláàfin of Ọ̀yọ́.[29] Lérè Pàímọ́, a former prominent member in the Dúró Ládipọ̀'s theater troupe, presents Ṣàngó as a deity in his film *Lákáayé.* In this film Lérè Pàímọ́ highlights the feud between

That we all deities relied on in paving way to the terrestrial plane.
You own the cutlass
You own the gun
Have you forgotten? I'm your superior.

He then emits fire before they both clash. Furthermore, *Lákáayé* offers us another myth as to how Ọya became Ṣàngó's wife. In Wálé Ògúnyẹmí's *Ṣàngó,* Ọya is a were-animal whom Ṣàngó has to chase into her abode in the wild forest. Having seized her slough, Ṣàngó is able to enter Ọya with his magic charms, and Ọya becomes his wife. A significant incident worthy of note that occurs during this encounter is the curse uttered by Ọya in nudity that whosoever has seized her animal should have "a tragic end." In Yorùbá mythology, it is always dangerous for one to be cursed by someone nude,[31] especially by a woman, as it is believed that the curse will come to pass. Though Ọya retracts the curse after having been commanded by Ṣàngó to do so, it is rather belated as the curse eventually materializes in Ṣàngó's life. The bottom line in the two films is that Ọya was Ṣàngó's wife, hence Ṣàngó is praised in Wálé Ògúnyẹmí's film as:

Ṣàngó ooo
  Olúrèkú
  Arèkújayé
  À-kò-tagìrì ọkùnrin
  A-jẹ́-líle
  A-fa-líle
  A kù wẹri
  A-rìn-gìà-gìà wọjà
  Olówó-orí Ọya
  Ọba kò sooo

Ṣàngó ooo
  He-who-puts-on the mantle
  He-who masks-for-pleasure
  The awesome man that gives jitters
  He-who-thunders
  He-who-compounds [troubles]
  He-who-swiftly-plunges
  He-who-hastily-enters the marketplace
  Husband of Ọya
  The king does not hang.

This song seems to sum up the personality of Ṣàngó in its totality as explicated above.

Myths and Myth Making

There are other myths pertaining to Ṣàngó apart from the earlier ones highlighted. It is the Ṣàngó in *Lákáayé* who once more offers us an explanation of why he takes *orógbó* (bitter kola), and not *obì* (kola nut). He explains to Ọya that he, Ṣàngó, was born under the kola nut tree. He therefore believes that he would be an ingrate to consume kola nuts, the fruits of the protective tree at his birth. It may not be out of place to regard it as the "Ṣàngó manger tree." With regard to the bitter kola, it helps to pacify him when enraged. Hence, I term it the "antidotal nut." His devotees render in their chants:

> *Orógbó ni ẹ mú wá o*
> *Ṣàngó ì í jobì o*

> Bitter kola should be offered
> Ṣàngó does not chew kola nut

We also notice that Ṣàngó can decide to pick on a non-initiate as his plenipotentiary. This is the lot of Chief Ìbíyẹmí Adélékè, who is entranced by the *osé* in the film titled *Osé(e) Ṣàngó*. He is enthralled in merely seeing it:

> *Osé(e) Ṣàngó rè é!*
> *Olúbánbí*
> *Arígba-ọta ṣégun*
> *Ò làgiri-kàkà*
> *Ọkùnrin alágbara inú afẹ́fẹ̀*
> *Tíí tibi gegele bókè jà*
> *Ṣàngó ì í jobì*
> *Orógbó ni fi í dánu.*

> Here is the Ṣàngó's wand!
> Olúbánbí
> He-who-possesses-enough bullets to rout enemies
> He-who-splits the wall open
> An awesome man in the wind
> That goes to the high riff to attack the hills

Ṣàngó does not chew kola nut
It is the bitter kola he takes for his refreshment.

His wife, who is bewildered by this empathy, asks him why he wants to turn to an *abòrìṣà* ("paganism"). In *Osé(e) Ṣàngó,* by Afọlábí Adésànyà, the iconization of Ṣàngó through human agency and symbolic objects dominates the motif of the film. Chief Ìbíyẹmí Adéléké (played by Kọlá Òyéwọ), a lover of culture, stumbles on *osée Ṣàngó* while purchasing other artifacts in Òyó—incidentally the ancient city of the historical Aláàfin Ṣàngó—on his way to Lagos. Unknown to Chief Adeleke, Ọya has transformed herself to an ordinary human being (perhaps an allusion to her anthropomorphic nature earlier captured by Wálé Ògúnyẹmí's *Ṣàngó*), who now sells the *osé* to him, which is already imbued with Ṣàngó's spirit. Chief Adeleke is able to realize this during his encounter with the traffic wardens, who wanted to check his vehicle. In his anger at being insulted, he curses them, by saying, "*Ṣàngó ní ó pa yín*" (Ṣàngó will strike you down dead). Almost immediately, the two wardens and his driver are struck by lightning. Chief Adeleke is able to revive his driver by the spiritual powers already bestowed on him as Ṣàngó's empathizer. It then dawns on him that he is a Ṣàngó novitiate. He now begins to use the wand to settle scores with anybody. Even the members of Ṣàngó cultic group are not spared (perhaps an allusion to Ṣàngó's own self-destruction of his home). While testifying in a murder case against Chief Adeleke, a non-initiate, the Ṣàngó worshippers say he is a parasite. The cultic head of Ṣàngó, known as Baba Mọgbà, sets in motion various machineries to dispossess Chief Adeleke of the *osé,* yet is unable to achieve his aim. Later, Chief Adeleke is reluctantly and formally initiated into Ṣàngó cultic group. The conflict between Baba Mọgbà and Chief Adeleke persists, and in their physical combat Chief Adeleke is able to eliminate Baba Mọgbà. He also dies in his house, where he asks his wife to take proper care of the newborn baby boy Ṣàngó-wá-n-wá, and ensure that he is not as irascible in his actions. Chief Adeleke's and Baba Mọgbà's behaviors confirm what Canizares aptly observed: "Ṣàngó-type persons may exhibit quick tempers, over-indulgent appetites, sexual promiscuity, abuse charisma."[32]

The film *Osé(e) Ṣàngó* highlights a number of mysteries which defied any scientific explanation. One astonishing incident is that Chief Adeleke's newborn baby has the *osé* mark on his left hand. This is a rare honor from Ṣàngó, whose spirit has been constantly hovering around Chief Adeleke's house. Chief Adeleke therefore names the baby Ṣàngó-wá-n-wá (Ṣàngó-has-come-to-me) to reciprocate the honor his patron god has given him.[33] By implication, the boy has become Ṣàngó's icon from his birth. He might have to face trouble if later in life he decides not to be one of Ṣàngó's votaries. In fact, it is Ṣàngó-wá-n-wá's birth that aggravates the existing feud between the mọgbà and Chief Adeleke. Some of the symbol-objects of Ṣàngó are used for healing sickness or other ailments. An impostor who is not entranced by the spirit medium is often punished, like Aláràn-án, who is struck by lightning. He goes blind after stealing Ṣàngó's magical wand of Chief Adeleke when disguised as a priest. The thunderbolt or stone (ẹdùn àrá) is searched for in his house. He is able to regain his sight after the mọgbà has immersed the thunderbolt in the water. The role of the mọgbà in appeasing on behalf of the offended is also highlighted. Anywhere Ṣàngó strikes, it is his priests who propitiate.

The mystery behind Ṣàngó's lightning power still defies any scientific proof. When Chief Adeleke is accused of murder with his osé, the laboratory test carried out by the nuclear physicist at the university fails to confirm the electric energy in the axe wand. Chief Adeleke is then discharged and acquitted of murder, as the wand has been taken as mere decorative wood. We may need to refresh our memory that Aláàfin Ṣàngó in Wálé Ògúnyẹmí's production kills many Òwu warriors with his magical wand. In other words, one of the symbol-objects of Ṣàngó is employed for malefic ends by his votaries.

Ìbínú Olúkòso, by the late Adebimpe Adekola (aka Ìrètí), highlights the issues of "possession" or "mediumship" and the dilemma of a votary in the face of strong proselytizing through the new religion of Christianity. Kẹ́mi (Ṣàngókẹ̀mi) was born after her parents had offered prayer to Ṣàngó. The mọgbà instructed the parents that Kẹ́mi must always come back home to participate in the annual Ṣàngó ritual festival. The mother, who is now a Christian, sees it as a fetish act. Since Kẹ́mi happens to be the alter-ego of the god Ṣàngó, anytime she is provoked she becomes possessed. Her incessant trances are taken as a fit, which explains why she did not have a steady suitor. Nevertheless, she is able to build up a relationship with Tìmíléyìn, an indigent car-wash boy, who is honest enough to return the expensive trinkets she had forgotten at the car wash. Her father, who normally revives her with red palm oil whenever entranced, is now worried. He has to tongue-lash his wife, who is a Christian fanatic, when she will not agree that Kẹ́mi should appear at the Ṣàngó festival:

> *Ìyá Kẹ́mi: Daddy, ẹ ò nígbàgbọ́ nínú Ọlọ́run rárá o!*
> *Bàbá Kẹ́mi: Má daddy mi,*
> *Má daddy mi.*

Èyin yìí lè gba wèrè mésìn.
Ẹ ti sọ Jésù di nǹkan mìíràn.
Kí àwọn great-grandfather rẹ
Kí wọn tó délé ayé yìí
Nǹkankan ni wọ́n ń sìn o
Nígbà tí kírísítẹ̀nì dé
Kiriyó, ẹ sì gba gbogbo rẹ̀ sódì

Kémi's Mother: Daddy, you do not have faith in God at all
Kémi's Father: Don't daddy me at all
Don't daddy me
You have combined malady with religion
You have turned faith in Jesus into something else
Before your great-grandfather existed
Before they appeared in this world
They were worshipping something
When Christianity emerged
"Kiriyó,"[34] you now misconceived everything.

Thereafter, Kémi is taken to her country home to perform the necessary ritual at the Ṣàngó shrine. The *mọgbà* tells her that she will have to be in religious sanctuary for few days. Before her returns, her spouse, Tìmílẹ́ yìn, and Tọ́lá, who is one of her bosom friends, have already eloped. On returning to Lagos, they now poison her and dump her body into the bush, where she is rescued by a Christian brother named Káyòdé. Her parents then take her back to the Ṣàngó shrine, where she is re-imbued with Ṣàngó's metaphysical power. As a plenipotentiary of Ṣàngó, she kills Tìmíléyìn and Tọ́lá with lightning. She is eventually married to the Christian brother (Káyòdé), who now delivers her from being the medium of Ṣàngó. The iconization of the god of thunder enables her to exhibit some of the personality traits of Ṣàngó, such as hot-temperedness and the metaphysical entrancement of enemies. The final entrancement of Kémi by the new religion, Christianity, seems to validate that only the spirit can confront the spirit. Man cannot subdue the metaphysical realm with mere mortal powers. The Christian brother has also become the icon of Jesus, and therefore he is able to dispossess her of Ṣàngó's spirit.

This issue of entrancement by Ṣàngó still exists, as highlighted in passing in a number of Yorùbá films. Olajubu is right to say Ṣàngó is "a living character among the Ọ̀yọ́ Yorùbá," as his spirit and name are constantly invoked to either punish or discipline evil-doers.[35] For instance, Oleyo, a minor character in *Lákáayé,* invokes the spirit of Ṣàngó to punish him if he has the coral beads he is handing over to his wife. He is flung outside and struck down by the lightning and the stolen beads are placed on his chest as an exhibit of the offense committed. This incident proves that Ṣàngó does not condone liars who engage in false swearing. Also in *Àfọ̀ njá*, the spirit of Ṣàngó is invoked by Aláàfin Aólẹ̀ to fish out the Holy Qur'an forcefully seized by the Baṣọ̀run's bodyguards. Instantly there is thunder and lightning, and the Qur'an is fished out. This incident is not a figment of imagination of the film producer, as it actually occurred during the reign of Aláàfin Aólẹ̀ and Baṣọ̀run Àṣàmú Arógangan (1789–96). Ogunmola records:

> The Empire was experiencing a lot of stress from its burden of social disorders like slavery, tyranny, lawlessness and the excesses of princes and chiefs. *On the issue of a Koran (Muslim Holy Book) lost by an Hausa man, a quarrel started between the Aláàfin and Baṣọ̀run Àṣàmú. Ṣàngó was therefore invoked to punish Àṣàmú through a lightning incident that struck his property.* (Italics mine)[36]

This incident corroborates Olajubu's claim that Ṣàngó is "the patron god of the Aláàfin of Ọ̀yọ́." It also supports the praise name Akunlépolè (He-who-raises-the building-into-ashes-to-smite-the-thief) given to Ṣàngó.[37]

It equally confirms that Ṣàngó is an embodiment of justice. Ṣàngó serves as patron to other lesser gods. Some of these lesser gods fortify and enhance their powers with the symbol-objects of Ṣàngó such as ẹdùn àrá (thunder stone). An example that readily comes to mind is the empowerment of Òòṣà ṣoore-ṣìkà in Iganmó in the film *A Pón Bépo Ré*, or that of Òòṣà Àkábá in *Àkábá Ìdènà*. As earlier stated, ẹdùn àrá possesses mystical power which is tapped for curative measures. This is also highlighted in the film, where Bewaji's snake bite is cured with this symbol-object of Ṣàngó. The priests of other gods cash in on the fact that Ṣàngó is "the agency of lightning, and lightning in turn being the cosmic instrument of a swift retributive justice," by exploiting and exploring it to deal with criminals in their community.[38] In *Erinlòòṣà*, the two youths who are about to poison the village stream are struck by lightning.

In sum, the awesome essence of Ṣàngó as principle of justice is highly visible among the Ọ̀yọ́ Yorùbá. Lightning is thus among the iconography of Ṣàngó. Ṣàngó is also venerated as the god of war; the Ìbàdàn warriors consult Ṣàngó before embarking on war with the Èkìtì as exemplified in *Ògèdèǹgbé*. Chief Àdùbí also evokes the spirit of Ṣàngó before confronting the enemies as highlighted in the video *Àdùbí*. This confirms Drewal's submission that Ṣàngó is a "male warrior deity."[39]

The children also feel the impact of Ṣàngó. It is noticed that some parents when scolding do curse their children and wards by using Ṣàngó's name. Òkò Ìrèsé does this in the Òkèrè film. It is brought to the fore too that the remnants of the feud between Ṣàngó and Gbònńkà still linger on unabated among the descendants of Oníṣàngó and Gbònńkà. It is taboo or sacrilege for any child from "Ṣàngó lineage" to marry someone from "Gbònńkà lineage." If the lovers contravene the taboo and go ahead with the marriage, it is believed that the wife would always have stillbirths. This is strongly demonstrated in the video Òkèrè, where Baba Mọgbà refuses her daughter permission to marry her heartthrob from Gbònńkà's household.

Conclusion

Yorùbá videographers acknowledge Ṣàngó's temperament, fieriness, awesomeness, and metaphysics in their productions. They equally present the duality of his being as an embodiment of beneficence and destruction, healing power, and justice. His portrait on the screen confirms him as the provider of synergy for other lesser gods. The principle of communality and essence of binary complementarity in Yorùbá thought are strengthened in his configuration. He is configured as both the historical-hero and a sacred figure. Despite the explosive expansion of the foreign religions, Ṣàngó's spirit still has a strong hold on his followers, to at least a certain extent. Though his arrogance stemming from primeval mystical power intoxication is highly visible in his alter-ego, the hold may be on the wane as the urban-bred followers are now being entranced by another, if not more powerful, spirit. His mystical power that entrances or electrifies, which his acolytes often misuse in settling scores with their enemies, is still beyond the knowledge of scientists. Notwithstanding this numinous nature, Ṣàngó still remains a living deity, especially among the Ọ̀yọ́ Yorùbá who frequently consult him for quick justice dispensation. The Yorùbá videographers give Ṣàngó a better and more honorable place on the screen than the ignominious existence given him on the stage.

NOTES

1. The Mbárí-Mbáyọ̀ Club, at Ibadan, served as a theater club, and Dúró Ládípọ̀ had the opportunity of performing there. He asked Ulli Beier to assist in establishing one at Oṣogbo; thus the Popular Bar owned by him was converted to Mbárí-Mbáyọ̀. The word mbárí is an Igbo word signifying "creation" but eventually turned into a Yorùbá expression, "When we see it, we'll be happy."

See Ulli Beier, *The Return of Shàngó: The Theatre of Duro Ladipo* (Bayreuth, Germany: University of Bayreuth Press, 1994), 15–21.

2. It might be plausible that Dúró Ládipọ̀'s *Ọba Kòso* also find its ancestry in the Ṣàngó sketch of the Apidán Theatre repertoire. Citing the example of the Ayélabọ́lá performance of Ṣàngó drama, Gotrick writes: "[A]n adult entered, dressed like the Ṣàngó. On his head he had a wooden hair-do; a red cloth mask covered his face. He was dressed in a brown vest with cowries attached to it and a 'skirt made of strips.'"

For a comprehensive explanation, see Kacke Gotrick, *Apidán Theatre and Modern Drama* (Stockholm: Almovist and Wiskell International, 1984), 53, 96–99.

3. Beier, *The Return of Shàngó*, 26.

4. Yemi Ogunbiyi, *Drama and Theatre in Nigeria: A Critical Source Book* (Lagos: Nigeria Magazine, 1981), 345.

5. Beier, *The Return of Shàngó*, 23.

6. Beier, ibid., 70. See also Oludare Olajubu, "The Sources of Duro Ladipo's *Ọba Kòso*," *Research in African Literatures* 9, no. 3 (Winter 1978): 327–62; Philip Adedotun Ogundeji, "The Image of Ṣàngó in Duro Ladipo's Plays," *Research in African Literatures* 29, no. 2 (Summer 1998): 57–75; and Philip Adedotun Ogundeji, "A Semiotic Study of Duro Ladipo's Mythico-Historical Plays" (Ph.D. diss., University of Ibadan, 1988).

7. Ogunbiyi, *Drama and Theatre*, 345.

8. Robert Armstrong, "Traditional Poetry in Ladipo's Opera *Ọba Kòso*," *Research in African Literatures* 9, no. 3 (Winter 1978): 366–67.

9. Ogunbiyi, *Drama and Theatre*, 333.

10. Beier, *The Return of Shàngó*, 221.

11. Ìwàlẹwà-Haus, Bayreuth University, Bayreuth, Germany has in its possession at least a copy (if not more) of Dúró Ládipọ̀'s *Ọba Kòso* film clips. In 1967, there was a film made by America Educational Television in the series *Creative Person*. The film highlights the Duro Ladipo Company on tour. The film also contains an "interview with Duro Ladipo and excerpts from performances including one, that was held in the palace of Ọ̀yọ́ in the presence of the Aláàfin and Tìmì Laoye of Ẹdẹ" (Beier, ibid. 222). Western Nigeria Television (WNTV), later the Nigeria Television Authority (NTA), had a complete production of *Ọba Kòso*. I am uncertain if the copy still survives, for the Nigeria Television Authority has no durable storage facility as such. Besides, they often wipe off programs from tapes so as to make use of such tapes for other programs. All these productions, print and electronic, might have not been able to match the quality of *Ọba Kòso* had it been put on celluloid before Lapido's death in 1978. Who could have known?

12. Ogundeji, "Image of Ṣàngó," 69.

13. Andrew Horn, "Ritual, Drama and the Theatrical: The Case of Bori Spirit Medium," in *Drama and Theatre in Nigeria: A Critical Source Book*, ed. Yemi Ogunbiyi (Lagos: Nigeria Magazine, 1981), 181–202. See also Margret

Thompson Drewal, *Yorùbá Ritual: Performers, Play, Agency* (Bloomington: Indiana University Press, 1992).

14. Drewal, *Yorùbá Ritual*, 180–90. See also Oyeronke Oyewumi, *The Invention of Women* (Minneapolis: University of Minnesota Press, 1997), 100.

15. Dapo Adelugba, "Trance and Theatre: The Nigerian Experience," in Ogunbiyi, 203–18.

16. Drewal, *Yorùbá Ritual*, 100.

17. Horn, "Ritual," 190.

18. Ibid., 187.

19. Drewal, *Yorùbá Ritual*, 180.

20. J. F. Ade Ajayi, "Development Is about People," in *Humanity in Context*, ed. Ayo Banjo (Ibadan, Nigeria: Nigerian Academy of Letters, 2000), 24.

21. Ibid., 24.

22. We are referring to the Nigerian theater artists who perform in English mainly for the literate members of the public. They are usually university based or standing artists for different electronic media, especially television stations.

23. All these clothes are traditional outfits of the Yorùbá. *Agbádá* is a voluminous outfit like *dàǹdógó*. *Gbáríyè* is not as voluminous as either the *agbádá* or *dàǹdógó*.

24. M. O. Ogunmola, *A New Perspective to Òyó Empire History: 1530–1944* (Ibadan, Nigeria: Vantage Publishers, 1985), 5.

25. Ibid., 65.

26. Ibid., 66.

27. Samuel Johnson, *The History of the Yorùbás* (Lagos: CSS Ltd., 1921), 157.

28. Gotrick, *Apidán Theatre*, 84.

29. There seems to be a contradiction as to whether he was the fourth Aláàfin or not. The narrator in the film said Ṣàngó was the fourth Aláàfin, but Gotrick, *Apidán Theatre*, 93, says that Ṣàngó was the third Aláàfin and not the fourth as claimed by Johnson in *The History*, 149. This is always the problem with oral history. Historians need to resolve this contradiction as there seems to be a gap. In Johnson's account—Òrànmíyàn's rule was followed by that of Àjàká and then by Ṣàngó. However, Chief Moses Oyedele Ogunmola, who doubles as the Aṣíwájú and Òtún of Òyó, provides a seeming solution in his text, *A New Perspective*, 165–66: Appendix III, List of Aláàfins and Baṣòruns of Òyó (Showing Dates of Advent or Succession)

Alaafin	Baṣòrun
1. Odùduwà, AD 782	Olórun-fún-mi
2. Òràn-án-yàn, AD 892	Èfúùfù kò-fé-orí
3. Àjàká Dàda, AD 1042	Èrìndínlógún-Agbòn
4. Ṣàngó (Àfònjá), 1077	Sale-ku-odi
5. Àjàká Dàda, 1137	Sale-ku-odi
6. Aganjú, 1137	Banija

His list ends on the reign of Aláàfin Bello Gbádégẹsin Ọládígbòlù II, 1956–68, most likely the 43rd Aláàfin. In this same text he says: "Traditionally, the Aláàfin was the head of Ṣàngó worship. Ṣàngó was the third Aláàfin in Odùduwà dynasty. The list reveals that the first Aláàfin was, Òràn-án-yàn the Great, then Dàda Àjàká Àjùwọn and Ṣàngó, King Ṣàngó also had the appellation of Olúfinràn."

30. Baba R. Canizares, *Shàngó: Santeria and the Òrìshà of Thunder* (Plainview, N.Y.: Original Productions, 2000), 18.

31. In most Yorùbá communities, when people are fed up with the reign of a particular monarch, women are sometimes to parade the whole town in nude to symbolize rejection of that king. The king may abdicate the throne or go into exile or he may commit suicide.

32. Canizares, *Shàngó,* 18.

33. It is a commonplace tradition among the different African traditional religious devotees to name their children after their patron gods or goddesses. For instance, the Ifá worshippers name their children as Fálétí, Fágbèmí, etc. The Egúngún devotees call their children Eégúnrántí, Òjéníyì, etc.

34. *Kiriyó* is a corrupt name for the Christians by the non-Christians, who believed that the Christians moved from one house to another to feast at any Christian festival—Christmas, Easter, and the Harvest season.

35. Olajubu, "The Sources," 354.

36. Ogunmola, *A New Perspective,* 20.

37. Olajubu, "The Sources," 358, and Akinwumi Isola, "Orin Etíyẹrí" (unpublished paper), 2.

38. Wole Soyinka, *Myth, Literature, and the African World* (Cambridge: Cambridge University Press, 1976), 8.

39. Drewal, *Yorùbá Ritual,* 99.

CHAPTER EIGHT

Art in the Service of Ṣàngó

STEPHEN FỌLÁRÀNMÍ

Ṣàngó, the deified king of ancient Ọ̀yọ́, is one of the fearsome, malevolent òrìṣà among the Yorùbá. Ṣàngó's devotees and worship, however,
extend beyond the Yorùbá of Nigeria, and can also be found in Benin
Republic, Brazil, Cuba, Haiti, Mexico, and Trinidad and Tobago.

The role of art in the devotion, religious rites, and worship of the
hundreds of òrìṣà among the Yorùbá has been severally identified. It will
therefore not be out of place to find numerous images and art forms as
religious paraphernalia in the service and decoration of Ṣàngó shrines
all over the world. This study identifies the varieties of art objects, their
uses, and their importance as it relates to Ṣàngó worship. It also examines
the uses of these art forms and motifs in contemporary times, be it for
decoration, identification, or veneration of the òrìṣà. It is very interesting
to experience contemporary paintings or other art forms, especially that
of Adémọ́lá Olúgébéfọlá, where icons and images are used as codified
forms to represent the forces and powers of Ṣàngó as a revered, deified
king of Ọ̀yọ́. Series of visual signs and signifiers are also used to elucidate
the concept of Ṣàngó. Representations such as these are similar to the
numerous shrine paintings in Yorùbáland, where emblems and symbols
are used to represent the deity.

Ṣàngó is one of the most colorful personalities of the Yorùbá pantheon. It may have been that an earlier form of thunder worship was
once known in the Yorùbá country, but in Ọ̀yọ́ the worship of thunder
soon became associated with Ṣàngó.[1] Ṣàngó's cult played an important
role in securing the people's loyalty to the Aláàfin in the days of the Ọ̀yọ́

Empire. In many Yorùbá towns, most especially in Ọ̀yọ́, Ìbàdàn, and Ẹdẹ, the worship of Ṣàngó is a principal festival which lasts for as long as seven days, the end of which marks the annual circle of festivals. The fierceness of Ṣàngó and his volatile nature put him in the "exalted position to be so identified with the Yorùbá conception of the manifestation of the wrath of Olódùmarè."[2] Rev. Samuel Johnson, Bolaji Idowu, Owosade Awolalu, N. A. Fadipe, and Ulli Beier all gave both historical and legendary versions of how Ṣàngó became a deified king and hero among his people.[3] History has it that Ṣàngó ruled over the Yorùbá, including Benin, the Popos, and Dahomey, and his worship continues in all these places to this day. Ṣàngó was a strong man, a powerful hunter, and was very skilled in the use of various magical arts. Obstinate, cruel, and oppressive, he ruled with an iron hand and sought to keep everybody under his thumb. Ṣàngó fought and won many battles with many surrounding settlements and neighboring towns. He was said to have established the supremacy of Ọ̀yọ́ over many other groups by defeating the mighty town of Òwu.[4] His reign was restless and warlike. When the people of Ọ̀yọ́ became tired of continuous warfare, they entreated him to cease fighting: "[W]e have suffered much and our sons have died in great numbers and the farms are neglected."[5] Ṣàngó thus accepted their plea after much consideration; he left the town for exile, where he was believed to have hung himself. Another version had it that his authority was threatened by the popularity of two of his courtiers (Tìmì and Gbò nńkà). Being weary of this, Ṣàngó craftily set these courtiers against each other, and one of them (Tìmì) was killed in the process. The surviving one (Gbònńkà), realizing Ṣàngó's tricks, went after him. Overcome with grief, Ṣàngó found the only way left was to "play the man" by hanging himself.[6]

Worship of Ṣàngó

In spite of his tempestuous and cruel character, Ṣàngó commanded the loyalty of many friends. It was therefore not too long after he disappeared or died (whichever version of the story we choose to believe) that his friends repaired the site of his supposed suicide, and there originated his worship. They then returned to the city proclaiming, *ọba kò so, ọba kò so,* meaning, "the king did not hang, the king did not hang." Their implication in saying this was that Ṣàngó was not dead but was still alive and now possessed supernatural divine powers to take vengeance on his enemies. Whenever a man is struck dead or a house is struck and damaged by lightning and thunder, it is generally believed to be the visitation of the wrath of Ṣàngó on the residents. A house struck by lightning and thunder can therefore not be used until the necessary propitiation sacrifice has been offered.[7] To appease Ṣàngó, an act of confession and submission, the payment of propitiation fines in the form of rams, sheep, fowls, kola nuts, and palm oil soon followed. Later a shrine was erected, and after that a temple, for the purpose of the worship of Ṣàngó at the site where he was believed to have hung himself, which was renamed Kòso.[8]

Those who had originated the worship of Ṣàngó became the first priests of Ṣàngó; they held the exalted positions of the *mọgbá* (advocates of Ṣàngó). More typical of the nature of Ṣàngó are the *adósù*. They were the ones that the *òrìṣà* had personally chosen to join or be initiated into the cult. They were often recognized by their large protruding eyes and, irrespective of their sex, their hair that was elaborately plaited and decorated, especially during festivals, as a mark of identification of their *òrìṣà*. The *adósù* also had their own hierarchy; the senior chief among them being the *Baálẹ̀ Ṣàngó,* usually followed by *Jagun Ṣàngó;* the most important among them being the *ẹlẹ́gùn,*[9] specially trained dancers of the *Làánkù* dance.[10] In full performance at festivals times, they chanted,

FIGURE 8.1. Baba Sàngólere holding *osée Ṣàngó,* in a ritual dance. Photo courtesy of Department of Fine Arts, Ọbáfẹ́mi Awólọ́wọ̀ University, Ilé-Ifẹ̀. 2005.

sang, and danced, and became possessed by Ṣàngó by displaying some magical feats.

With the evolving worship of Ṣàngó and the setting up of a shrine, objects of worship, identification, and decoration of Ṣàngó shrines were also created. From these beginnings the worship of Ṣàngó spread all over Yorùbáland and beyond.[11]

Shrines of Ṣàngó still abound in many Yorùbá towns and villages. At one such shrine one can find images of a man (representing Ṣàngó) surrounded by three smaller figures probably representing his wives Ọya, Ọ̀sun, and Ọbà; the image of a man holding a ram's head and horns and the handle of the double-headed axe (osé), which is the most significant symbol and identification of Ṣàngó (osée Ṣàngó). Other common material symbols of Ṣàngó include: gourd rattle (ṣẹ́ẹ́rẹ́ Ṣàngó), inverted mortar used as pedestals, a big pot used as a receptacle for thunder celts, and in some cases a tray or bowl holding celts and polished stones believed to have been hurled by Ṣàngó. Apart from these, other items used in worship also included animals such as ram (àgbò), tortoise (ìjàpá), snail

FIGURE 8.2. Ṣàngó altar pieces and làbà (Ṣàngó bag) hung on the wall at Akuru compound, Agbeni Ìbàdàn. Photo courtesy of Department of Fine Arts, Ọbáfẹ́mi Awólọ́wọ̀ University, Ilé-Ifẹ̀. 1990.

FIGURE 8.3. Carved and brightly painted veranda posts. Ṣàngó shrine
at Akuru compound, Agbeni Ìbàdàn. Photo courtesy of
Department of Fine Arts, Ọbáfẹ́mi Awólọ́wọ̀ University, Ilé-Ifẹ̀. 1990.

(*ìgbín*), water bird (*ọsìn*), red tail of parrot, shea butter (*òrí*), guinea fowl
(*awó*), *tẹ̀tẹ̀* (*Amaranthus hybridus*), *pèrègún* leaves (*Dracaena manni*),
abẹ ẹ̀sù (devil's razor), and heads of cowries.[12]
   This dedication to the power over life and death and creativity is
reflected in Ṣàngó's shrines, such as the one found at the compound
of Baálẹ̀ Kòsu in Ọ̀yọ́, which overflows with carvings, pots, and other
artworks. A well-carved mortar, ritual container, figure, or dance staff
(osé) is believed to be able to better focus the worshipper's attention on
the important attributes of the god and to better lure the spirit to the
shrine.[13] A shrine of Ṣàngó is usually referred to as *gbòngàn* with the altar
being an upturned mortar *(odó),* often carved in high relief, supporting
a wooden tray of thunderbolts (stone celts or erosion-weathered pebbles
[*ẹdùn àrá*]). The mortar may be decorated with votive carvings on a
great variety of themes, such as worshiping women, or priests in their
regalia mounted on horses. The shrines contain ritual pots decorated
with moldings in high relief; hanging on the wall is a leather bag (*làbà*)
carried by the priest when visiting a place where lightning has struck. It
is in this bag that stone celts/thunderbolts and other ritual objects are
kept. The rattles (*ṣẹ́ẹ́rẹ́*) are shaken to accompany worshippers in rituals
and in the praise song of Ṣàngó.[14] All the aforementioned items are specifically required during the processes of initiation and worship of Ṣàngó,
and thus form the core materials for appeasing Ṣàngó's wrath. In 1910,
when Leo Frobenius took a photograph of an interior of a Ṣàngó shrine

in Ibadan, he wrote that "a lofty, long and very deep recess made a gap in the row of fantastically carved and brightly painted columns. These were sculptured with horsemen, men climbing trees, monkeys, women, gods and all sorts of mythological carved work. The dark chamber behind revealed a gorgeous red ceiling, pedestals with stone axes on them, wooden figures, cowrie-shell hangings."[15] This account by Frobenius is a testimony to the presence of several art objects used in the service and decoration of Ṣàngó shrines. This remains true all over the world, as Ṣàngó has a strong following beyond the shores of Yorùbáland.[16]

Yorùbá Figurative Sculpture

Among African art forms, Yorùbá wooden figurative sculpture has received a great deal of attention from Western cultures. Wood is the material typically used throughout sub-Saharan Africa because it is practical and available. The human figure is most commonly represented in sculptural form. Animals, such as birds, antelopes, monkeys, and leopards, are also depicted. Figures are represented standing with bent knees or seated on a circular stool. Few sculptures depict figures in movement. Yorùbá sculpture is very balanced and symmetrical. A common device used to create a sense of balance is the repetition of shapes within different parts of the body. While a sculpture is meant to be understood from a continuous view, by walking around it, most African sculpture does not have a predetermined direction for viewing; some figures were never intended for display, and therefore will not stand on their own. Usually being modest in size, the sculptures are made to be portable and easily handled, while figures may be made for various purposes. In giving a graphic representation of these sculptures, Leuzinger wrote:

> In spite of the multitude of themes and form of the carvers' art, it must be affirmed that the style of carving has maintained an astonishingly unified character down the centuries, so that a Yorùbá work can usually be easily recognised. Its characteristics are a naturalistic human round style, a heavy head with massive coiffure, horizontal full lip, and cut off vertically at the sides, large bulbous eyes and eye brows marked in a fleshy nose, heavy hanging breast and dazzling color.[17]

Some figures represent a deceased twin, carved upon its death. The mother would then care for the twin figure (*ìbejì*) as though it were her child, washing and feeding it, to ensure the health of the surviving twin.

FIGURE 8.4. *Ere ìbejì*. Collection of the Department of Fine Arts, Ọbáfẹ́mi Awólọ́wọ̀ University, Ilé-Ifẹ̀. Photo by Stephen Fọláránmí. 2004.

The wood surface of the figures often shows wear from the constant rubbing and use.

Figurative sculpture is widely used in divination practices. Many of the diviner's instruments are elaborately carved with heads, faces, and figures. There exist other paraphernalia which are associated with Ṣàngó worship and devotion. Some of these art objects have been intricately created by artists over centuries, while others have been created in recent times, not for use by Ṣàngó devotees, but as a means of decoration or documentation of one of the most feared of Yorùbá kings. They have been made not just for religious use but as objects of beauty to be admired and revered. We have earlier mentioned the widespread worship of Ṣàngó all over the Yorùbá country and beyond. Large varieties in the objects of worship of Ṣàngó are in evidence throughout these many regions.

Osée Ṣàngó

Osée Ṣàngó is Ṣàngó's most pervasive symbol; it is so distinguished by the double-headed axe motif, a stylized reference to the thunder celts believed to have been hurled by Ṣàngó during thunderstorms or lightning and unearthed by his worshipers. It is the primary symbol of Ṣàngó's presence and power. The double axe-head is said to also signify "my strength cuts both ways," meaning that no one, even the most distant citizens of Ọ̀yọ́, was beyond the reach of Ṣàngó's authority or immune to punishments for misdeeds.[18] This double-axe motif is the most important element associated with Ṣàngó. It represents Ṣàngó's destructive side and his ability to hurl thunder celts into the residences of his enemies and those who incur his wrath. Staffs are carried, and danced with, by the priestesses and priests in the Ṣàngó cult. It is also used as a badge of membership in the cult. The Yorùbá carvers have created many pieces of this single symbol of Ṣàngó; it is thus held in high esteem. The wand is fashioned in several varieties, and the style of design varies more than any other Ṣàngó art object. Some of these have in fact been classified into certain localities and schools, identifying them with those who carve them or with important Yorùbá towns. It is also said that the amount paid a carver for an object like this will determine how elaborate or intricate the design and emblems on the object will be. Ṣàngó wands have been carved in many simple forms: smooth-surfaced representations of the axe with the lightly decorated handle and markings, as to be able to serve its primary functions.

Others have been elaborately carved, revealing a great deal of skill and humanistic tendencies. These staffs most often depict a single female figure, whose head, carved in elaborate coiffure, supports a double axe.

There are also examples of metal Ṣàngó wands; these are not as elaborate as the more common carved wooden wands. An exhibition of Yorùbá art in 1980 at the High Museum of Art in Atlanta revealed a great deal of these varieties. According to Henry Drewal, some of the wands on display were identified with the Bamgboye school style, some of which may have been carved by the master's hand in the 1920s or 1930s. Characteristics include deeply cut eyebrow, broad nostrils, long nose, low position of the mouth, and long sharp jaw line.

Some are described as having a heavy textured headdress, large starred eyes, and stylized celts surrounding the stem of the wands. This was identified as a wand possibly carved by Toibo from the Maku School in Ọ̀yọ́.

Leo Frobenius was said to have collected some wands in Ìbàdàn around 1912, and some of these were identified as having been carved by an Ìbàdàn artist, Àmọ̀ó Láfíà, of Ìdí Aró, who was said to be about age twenty in 1912.[19] The Ìbàdàn style is characterized by a long slender shape of the double-blade axe and incised designs of alternating zigzag and straight lines on the shaft and base.

From the Ìgbómìnà region comes a distinctive rendering of the *osée Ṣàngó,* a Janus composition, which when viewed in profile surmounts a frontal head and translates as the double-axe form.

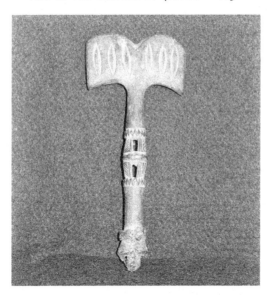

FIGURE 8.5. Simple and less decorated *osée Ṣàngó* without any image.
Collection of the Department of Fine Arts,
Ọbáfẹ́mi Awólọ́wọ̀ University, Ilé-Ifẹ̀. Photo by Stephen Fọlárànmí.

FIGURE 8.6. A breastfeeding woman. Surmounting her coiffure
is a stylized double axe. By Lamidi Fakeye. Photo by Dele Fakeye.

FIGURE 8.7A. Wood, pigment, 26 ¹/₄ inches high: Ekiti, Odo Owa, Bamgboye school. Illustration by author.

FIGURE 8.7B. Wood, 15 ¹/₄ inches high: Òyó, Erin, Maku school, possibly Toibo (?). This wand is similar to work attributed to Toibo (cf. Beier 1957: pl. 3). Illustration by author.

FIGURE 8.7C. Wood, 8 ³/₄ inches high. Òyó: Idi Aro quarter Ìbàdàn (?), possibly by Amos Lafia. They may date to the late 19th or early 20th century, for Frobenius collected four in an identical style in 1912 (cf. Krieger 1956). Illustration by author.

FIGURE FIGURE 8.7D. Wood, pigment, 16 ¹/₂ inches high. Ìgbómìnà, Oro area. A Janus composition, viewed in profile, surmounts a frontal head and translates as the double-axe form. De Havenon collection (Museum of African Art 1971: pl. 157). Illustration by author.

It must be mentioned that the Janus-styled wand has been carved in recent years by a renowned Yorùbá traditional carver, Lamidi Fakeye.

Some of these also show fine horizontal striations across the brows, on the wands, and on the faces of the figures. (Striations, or facial marks, are a form of facial decoration or identification. They are also a means of distinguishing the various Yorùbá families and towns.[20] This tradition is now only minimally practiced in some rural Yorùbá towns.)

The Èkìtì-style wands have more cubistic handling of planes and angles in the double blade, shoulders, and breasts, which also suggest affinity with other traditional carvings from Èkìtì.[21]

A common feature found in many *osée Ṣàngó* is the representation of a regal female figure holding a bowl, probably a receptacle of celts. The woman may also represent a worshiper of Ṣàngó. Many wands done in this particular style are very large, suggesting they may have been used as altar pieces and decoration and not as part of the dancing paraphernalia during festivals.

FIGURE 8.8. *Osée Ṣàngó* by Lamidi Fakeye, 1987. Here the thunderbolt appears as human faces in Janus composition. Photo by Lamidi Fakeye.

FIGURE 8.9A. Wood, 14 inches high. Èkìtì. Fine horizontal striations suggest Ìgbómìnà, but the entire composition reflects Èkìtì. Illustration by author.

FIGURE 8.9B. Wood, 14 ³/₄ inches high, Èkìtì: eyelids, ears, and cubist planes and angles on shoulder, breast suggests affinities with some Èkìtì work. Illustration by author.

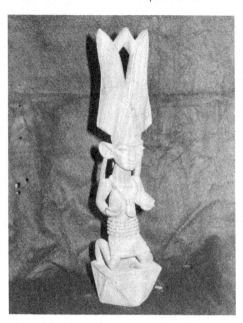

FIGURE 8.10. *Osée Ṣàngó* by Lamidi Fakeye. Photo by Lamidi Fakeye.

Some varieties of *osée Ṣàngó* also show kneeling women holding their breasts in respect, offering a bowl in thanks, or holding a bowl filled with kola nuts, all popular subjects in Yorùbá art. Figures in this pose are known as *olúmẹ̀yẹ,* meaning "one who knows honor."[22] They are found on the altars of many Yorùbá deities, with hair elaborately dressed in a traditional crested style called *agògo,* strands of waist beads signifying virginity. In this respect, the *osée Ṣàngó* can be said to be similar to the *ìrọ́kẹ́ ifá* divining tapper in its iconography. Both are important objects in invoking Ṣàngó and Ọ̀rúnmìlà respectively. The *ìrọ́kẹ́* is the divining tapper with the clapper, used to invoke Ọ̀rúnmìlà during divination by gently striking the pointed end against the *ọpọ́n ifá.* A long slim form, usually carved in ivory, ranges from twenty to sixty centimeters in length, and is a combination of three parts. But unlike the *osé,* the topmost part, which is very important, is without decorations.[23] Its similarity with Ṣàngó's wand is most vivid in the middle section, which is most commonly a human head or a kneeling half-nude woman figure holding her breast. Here again we notice that humanity is represented by the female figure because of her effectiveness in the act of honoring and saluting the gods, who all possess the surname *àkúnlẹ̀bọ* (the-one-who-must-be-worshipped-kneeling-down). This is the greatest reverence that can be shown to any *òrìṣà* in the Yorùbá tradition.[24] As a decorative support at the entrance to a Ṣàngó shrine, the female may be depicted as a priestess wearing beaded dance panels (*làbàa Ṣàngó*).[25] There is little suggestion of movement or activity, other than being reflective of intense concentration, and perhaps energy. Judging from its indispensability and the frequency of its use in the service of Ṣàngó, *osée Ṣàngó* would appear to be the most important of all the items or objects used by Ṣàngó devotees. *Osée Ṣàngó* is carried, cradled, waved, and thrust by devotees during dances in honor of Ṣàngó. Once the carved object leaves the artist's workshop, it ceases to be ordinary wood; it has become the earthly physical symbol of Ṣàngó's existence and presence since he "departed to the heavens."

Ṣàngó Ritual Pots

The design of a pot is generally determined by the purpose it is to serve. Function is taken into account when the potter makes his or her pots. Unlike utilitarian pots, whose surfaces are usually not decorated, Yorùbá ritual and ceremonial pots are easily identified by their decorative motifs. Pots are important items in any Yorùbá shrine, where they are used as containers for storing water and pebbles and other ritual materials. In some cases they serve as musical instruments or as containers for storing a medicinal or magical preparation.[26] There are pots used in purely commemorative ceremonies connected to rites of passage. Sites of shrines have often been revealed by the presence of a pot placed under a tree, or as part of altar items, as in the case of Ṣàngó shrines. Ritual pots are characteristically decorated with anthropomorphic symbols as well as other instruments and emblems of traditional worship.[27]

There are several varieties of Ṣàngó pots that vary in size and decoration, but all are put to the same uses. The majority of Ṣàngó pots are elaborately designed in very high relief, showing emblems of Ṣàngó mingled with those of other deities.

Aawè Ṣàngó is a shallow cylindrical pot with flat bottom and a ring for base. It is used for the storage of water at a Ṣàngó shrine in Ṣakí town. Another *aawè* pot from Òkèihò depicts emblems and symbols of Ṣàngó, including snakes, bitter kola (*orógbó*), gourd rattles (*sééré*), *Ifá* divination tappers (*ìróké*), and divination chains (*òpèlè*). Although made for Ṣàngó worship, it is also used in the veneration of other deities, hence the variety of designs. The mingling of symbols of various deities on one pot exemplifies their mutual interdependent relationship. In Abéòkúta, during Ṣàngó festivals, female worshippers dance around the town singing and dancing to Ṣàngó's honor. They carry with them pots containing Ṣàngó emblems, including ones with phallic symbols called *okóo Ṣàngó*.[28]

FIGURE 8.11. Ṣàngó pot showing a stylized *osé*. Ifẹ̀ Museum of Antiquities. Photo by Stephen Fọlárànmí. 2004.

FIGURE 8.12. Ṣàngó pot with high relief mould of a Y-shaped *osé*, flanked by rattles and other ritual apparatus. Ifẹ̀ Museum of Antiquities. Photo by Stephen Fọlárànmí. 2004.

FIGURE 8.13. Ṣàngó pot with images of snake, tortoise, and rattles. Ifẹ̀ Museum of Antiquities. Photo by Stephen Fọlárànmí. 2004.

FIGURE 8.14. Sacrificial urns similar to the ones also used in Erinlẹ̀ cult. Ifẹ̀ Museum of Antiquities. Photo by Stephen Fọlárànmí. 2004.

FIGURE 8.15. Ṣàngó pot with four pairs of breast in high relief mold. Collection of the Department of Fine Arts, Ọbáfẹ́mi Awólọ́wọ̀ University, Ilé-Ifẹ̀. Photo by Stephen Fọlárànmí. 2004.

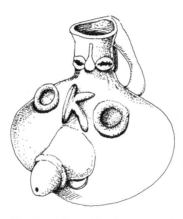

FIGURE 8.16. *Oko Ṣàngó* from Abeokuta—southwest Nigeria. Illustration by author.

Pots dedicated to Erinlẹ̀ are similar to the Ṣàngó pot in the lid structure; the strap-like forms that serve as the body can be perceived as a crown, referring to the royal status of Ṣàngó (see Figure 8.16).[29]

Ère Ìbejì (Twin Figures)

Twins (*ère ìbejì*) are sometimes called "children of thunder" and are thus consecrated to Ṣàngó. Twin figures are likely to be found in many Ṣàngó shrines, as legend states that Ṣàngó was himself a twin. Figures are created to venerate the spirit of deceased twins, and carved for the home. The Yorùbá perceive them as spirited, unpredictable, and fearless, much like their patron *òrìṣà* (Ṣàngó). Seen as spirit beings with exceptional abilities, they bring affluence and well-being to those who respect them, and their lives are filled with sacred acts.[30] The Yorùbá twin cult is only indirectly concerned with the cult of the *òrìṣà*, yet it forms an important element in Yorùbá cosmology. They are likened to the *àbíkú* spirits who lure children from their parents because they have the propensity toward dying (*àbíkú* means "born to die"). *Ìbejì* usually forms part of a domestic cult, limited to the immediate family, and is connected to the well-being of a limited number of persons. The great majority of the *ìbejì* are standing nude figures; some, however, do have apron-type garments. The head is usually large in proportion to the body, with an oval face containing prominent eyeballs, lips, and broad nose. Male and female genitals are carved well developed, and the general proportion is bigger than that of an infant. *Ìbejì* figurines have different scarification marks and a great variety of hair styles (see figure 8.4).[31]

Mortars (*Odó Ṣàngó*)

Mortars, known as *odó Ṣàngó,* are placed on altars dedicated to Ṣàngó. These carved inverted objects are decorated with relief carvings of Ṣàngó rattle, thunder stones, or rams, which are his favorite sacrificial animal. Other noticeable emblems are Ṣàngó's dance wand, lizard, or crocodile. These two animals are said to attract thunder. In other words, according to Nasiru,[32] they are provoking agents behind the anger of Ṣàngó. There are several varieties of these objects, and are all extremely heavy, of very dense wood, only slightly hollowed out on the bottom. *Odó Ṣàngó* are said to be repositories of Ṣàngó's *àṣẹ,* or spiritual powers.

In some Ṣàngó shrines, *arugbá* (calabash carrier)[33] takes the place of the upturned mortar typically found in shrines in central and western Yorùbáland. An example of an *Arugbáa Ṣàngó* was documented and photographed in 1964 by John Picton at Òkè-Onígbìín. It was reported as the centerpiece of a shrine to Ṣàngó belonging to Ṣàngódìran, the Balógun of Ọyátẹ̀dó, an Ìgbómìnà village in the Òrò Àgọ́ district of Ilorin Emirate.

The *arugbá* is among the furniture of a Ṣàngó shrine characteristic of the Ìgbómìnà region and eastward. The name, according to Picton, denotes a role for virgins, who in some cults (though not specifically Ṣàngó) carry a calabash containing sacred emblems and may experience possession by the deity. (In Ọ̀ṣun worship, the role of the *arugbá* is very vital during the annual Ọ̀ṣun festival). In this example, the *ẹdùn àrá,* the axes/thunderbolts, were kept in the bowl (carved with a leopard in the relief upon its lid) placed upon the *arugbá.*[34]

FIGURE 8.17. *Odo Ṣàngó* from Ẹdẹ. Collection of the Department of Fine Arts, Ọbáfẹ́mi Awólọ́wọ̀ University, Ilé-Ifẹ̀. Photo by Stephen Fọlárànmí.

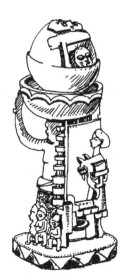

FIGURE **8.18A.** *Arugbáa Ṣàngó:* carrier of Ṣàngó's calabash, illustrated altarpieces from a shrine of Ṣàngó belonging to Ṣàngódìran, Balógun (war chief) of Ọyátẹ̀dó, an Ìgbómìnà village near Òrò Àgọ́.
From a photo by John Picton, 1964. Illustration by author.

FIGURE **8.18B.** *Ṣẹ́ẹ́rẹ́ Ṣàngó* (gourd rattles). Illustration by author.

FIGURE **8.18C.** *Làbà Ṣàngó:* Ṣàngó leather bag. Illustration by author.

Sẹ́ẹ̀rẹ̀ Ṣàngó

The Ṣàngó gourd rattle (sẹ́ẹ̀rẹ̀) is frequently decorated with incised designs or covered with leather and is shaken when prayers are being made or offered to Ṣàngó. The rattle is used to call the attention of the òrìṣà to the supplication of his devotees.[35] In his 1912 expedition, Leo Frobenius also recorded metal gourd rattles, which may have been made of brass.

Ṣàngó Costumes

Ṣàngó initiates adorn costumes complete with red and white beads; red (pupa) or maroon is the special color of Ṣàngó. A warm color speaks of Ṣàngó's malevolence (as it does with other Yorùbá gods with that attribute), volatility, and vengeful spirit.[36] The costumes are usually worn during Ṣàngó festivals and are decorated with cowry shells, miniature gourds (àdó), and many other Ṣàngó emblems. The costume may also include a Ṣàngó "royal crown," referred to as priest's tiara. The tiara is a semblance of a king's crown, alluding to Ṣàngó's reign as a king. The tiara is made of leather and cloth and elaborately embroidered with cowry shells, which are symbols of wealth and well-being. The Ṣàngó costume is also not complete without the priest or priestess carrying the làbà Ṣàngó. Ṣàngó priests' apparel whirls out from the waist when they dance. These brightly colored, fringed leather bags hang from the rear wall of Ṣàngó shrines. They bear four appliqué panels with the images of Èṣù and are used by priests to transport thunderbolts from a site visited by Ṣàngó's wrath to the altar of Ṣàngó.

Ṣàngó Shrine Painting

Shrine painting among the Yorùbá people is very widespread; however, it is almost limited to certain deities whose shrines have a long history of wall decoration, such as Ọbàtálá and Olúorogbo. Ulli Beier[37] did the pioneer study of these in 1960 and brought out the artistic beauty found in the tradition of shrine painting in Yorùbáland. Since then a good amount of writing and research has been done on shrine painting.[38] Yorùbá wall paintings are mainly restricted to ilé òrìṣà (shrines), and they usually adorn the walls to the entrance. Such shrines are dotted all over Yorùbáland, but are mostly situated in secluded areas, and are not specifically in the public arena.

Campbell wrote that "Yorùbá religious belief system produces in its wake a plethora of richly decorated histographs known as shrine paintings."[39] Although almost on the verge of decline, the art of shrine painting is still practiced in Ògbómòṣó, Ilé-Ifè, Òṣogbo, Iléṣà, Òfà, Ìbàdàn, Òyó, and various parts of Lagos. The art of shrine painting is traditionally the exclusive preserve of women in Yorùbáland, and this tradition is still well kept by the Òrìṣà Ìkirè painting school in Ilé-Ifè and Ògbómòṣó.

It is not very common to see painting in the shrines of Ṣàngó in Yorùbáland. The walls may be painted in flat red and white spotted colors, but not with any other imaging. However in Èdè, the first Ṣàngó shrine painting was commissioned in 1990 by the Ṣàngó Festival Committee under the auspices of Tìmì of Èdè[40] (the King of Èdè), born out of the desire for deep spirituality. The images are representations of Ṣàngó worshippers and devotees. The aged priestess described the images as those who have been visited by the wrath of Ṣàngó, while the artists express a contrary view. This situation is common and due to the interpretation of the artists, who may not necessarily be worshippers of Ṣàngó.

The importance of this painting is like other Yorùbá shrine paintings; they are more than mere decorations. They are intended to "create an atmosphere, a feeling of heightened reality which is conducive to worship, they assist the worshipper to achieve the state of concentration and the condition of receptiveness that is necessary if the òrìṣà is to manifest himself during the ceremony." They also mark out the shrine as a sacred place meant to be respected and revered.

The following factors are identified as the reasons for this new innovation of the mural painting on a Ṣàngó shrine. First, according to the Ṣàngó priestess in Èdè, is Tìmì of Èdè's exposure to other towns, cultural settings, and Yorùbá shrines with mural decorations (Òrìṣà Pópó, Òrìṣàlkirè, Olúorogbo shrines). The young artists Olaniran Teslim, Olániran Ahmed, and Olálékan Òṣúnsoko, who executed the paintings, said they were influenced by the decoration of the Òṣun grove in neighboring Òṣogbo, where the shrine grove has been transformed with extensive and exotic artistic designs with the assistance of Suzanne Wenger (Àdùnní Olórìṣà). The inventive endeavor was supported by the supervisor of the painting, Òṣúnsoko Olábíran. A talented artist who received art training up to college level, Òṣúnsoko was in his late sixties when the painting was executed in 1990. The attendants in the palace of Tìmì and other worshippers view the painting as a materialization of the deities' inspiration and presence among his people.[41] This painting was done on the eve of the Ṣàngó Festival in 1990 in a bid to add color to the festival unlike that of all other Yorùbá shrines.

The painting was executed in enamel paints, which is a medium now

FIGURE 8.19. Young painters of Ṣàngó shrine in Ẹdẹ. Photo courtesy Department of Fine Arts, Ọbáfẹ́mi Awólọ́wọ̀ University, Ilé-Ifẹ̀. 1990.

FIGURE 8.20. A section of Ṣàngó shrine painting in Ẹdẹ depicting priests, devotees, and other dignitaries of Ṣàngó worship. Photo courtesy Department of Fine Arts, Ọbáfẹ́mi Awólọ́wọ̀ University, Ilé-Ifẹ̀. 1990.

being used in the decoration of some shrines in Yorùbáland (such as in the Ògbóni Repository in Iléṣà). The images to be painted were dictated by the worshippers while the painters served only as a tool in the execution.[42] These images include leaders of the cult of Ṣàngó, *arugbá olóòdò* (Ṣàngó calabash bearer), *agbájere* (*ajere* carrier), *aṅdù* (royal masquerade), Ìyá Ọ̀ṣun (Ọ̀ṣun priestess), and Ẹlẹ́gùn Ṣàngó. These are all represented along with the composition of the legend about Ṣàngó.

The Colors of Ṣàngó

Red (*pupa*), a color of great modulation, is a sign of war and revolution. It symbolizes love and danger at the same time. Used along with black, its dominant tendencies become erratic. *Pupa* in Yorùbá cosmology is mostly used in relation to Ògún and Ṣàngó. Among Ṣàngó worshippers, *pupa* represents fire. Fire for them can be domesticated so it can destroy. *Pupa* to the Yorùbá is masculine in nature; it represents boldness, bloodshed, nobility, and dignity.[43] The Yorùbá have a polychromatic sensibility to color revolving around red-*pupa,* black-*dúdú,* and white-*funfun.*[44] *Pupa* is the most inviting color of the three and is very symbolic of Ṣàngó attributes.

Funfun (white) is another color symbolic of Ṣàngó, though not as prominently used as *pupa*. It is the color of Ọbàtálá (Yorùbá god of Creation) and can be found on Ṣàngó objects. The images and painting symbolize his good pride because he is a provider of children to his devotees. This goodness and significance of *funfun,* however minute, is represented by the pigeons that are common to Ṣàngó shrines.[45] In addition, in a line of one of the numerous Ṣàngó praise names, Ṣàngó is referred to as:

ṣẹ́ẹ́rẹ́ jobi, ọkọ̀ mi
ọmọ olómi tíí jẹ́ Yemọja

(*ṣẹ́ẹ́rẹ́ jobì,* my lord
Son of the water goddess, called Yemọja)[46]

One may then identify the *funfun* in Ṣàngó shrines as a relationship with his supposed mother. Yemọja's color is symbolically white.

Ṣàngó Art in the Diaspora and Contemporary Times

The fact that Yorùbá culture is rich in the arts cannot be overemphasized. This is evident in their sculpture in different media, which has been an inexhaustibly fertile ground for academic research. With a rich cultural background and highly developed skill in sculpture, the Yorùbá trace their ancestral origin to Odùduwà and regard Ilé-Ifẹ̀ as their spiritual or ancestral home.[47] It is believed that there are many *òrìṣà* to which the Yorùbá people hold their allegiance, worship, pray, and make sacrifices of appeasement. However, the introduction of the two major religions (Christianity and Islam) among the Yorùbá came with several changes. While some changes were positive, such as in the area of education and the development of a modern environment, others were very destabilizing, especially in the area of the rich artistic tradition. Many art pieces were destroyed by overzealous devotees. The religious landscape has changed so much, it is having effects on the continuation of many of these rich artistic traditions. Despite the different religious affiliations of the contemporary artists (whether Christian or Muslim), they are still able to produce art works that reveal their traditional beliefs, past religious systems, and societal values. In contemporary times both academic and traditional artists have used religious themes in their artistic production; these are done either for the service of the *òrìṣà* or as mere expressions of their religious heritage. They use their art to tell stories and tales of Yorùbá gods and heroes, and in some cases the art pieces are acquired by those who still have strong affiliations to a Yorùbá god.

One of the best examples of these are fantastic traditional wood carvings from a great Yorùbá master carver, Lamidi Fakeye, a fifth-generation Yorùbá wood carver from the northeastern Yorùbá city of Ìlá Ọ̀ràngún. His middle name, Ọlọ́nàdé, means "the carver has come," signifying that he hails from a family of carvers. His father and great-grandfather were both carvers. Lamidi, however, got his full training under George Bámidélé Ar'owóòg'un at the Roman Catholic workshop organized by Father Kevin Carroll in Ọyẹ́ Èkìtì. It was there that Lamidi first came to the wider public eye.[48] Fakeye joined the services of the University of Ifẹ̀, now Obafemi Awolowo University Ilé-Ifẹ̀, in 1978, where he taught traditional carving. Fakeye, who retired from the department in late 2002, lives presently in Ilé-Ifẹ̀. He is now an associate researcher in the Institute of Cultural Studies of the same university. His carvings in relief (doors and panels) and three-dimensional figures (veranda posts and figures) illustrate Muslim and Christian themes, as well as traditional Yorùbá religious and secular themes. A significant portion of Fakeye's works is derived from the canon of traditional imagery, while others reflect a cultural heritage of ritual usage, with their iconography stemming from both religious and societal roots. This is reflected in objects such as the doors and veranda posts, which are both decorative and utilitarian.[49] Being a Muslim has not in any way deterred Lamidi from carving objects that are related to *òrìṣà* worship; it is therefore not strange to find such objects as the examples we have here in his numerous carvings (see figures 8.6 and 8.8).

The infusion of cultural forms and ideas in Nigerian art began with many of the students trained by Kenneth C. Murray.[50] The most prolific of these artists was Professor Benedict Enwonwu (1921–94). Enwonwu experimented by transforming traditional African forms with the aid of Western training. The result of such synthesis evolved into a personal style in which Enwonwu worked throughout his artistic career.[51] Although

FIGURE 8.21. "Ṣàngó." Larger-than-life bronze statue of Ṣàngó at the
headquarters of the National Electric Power Authority (NEPA) in Lagos.
Photo by Stephen Fọláránmí.

Enwonwu came from an Igbo background (Onitsha, Anambra state), he
explored artistic traditions, themes, and ideas from other ethnic groups
in Nigeria. It was perhaps for this reason that he was commissioned to
sculpt a statue titled Ṣàngó to be erected at the new office of the National
Electric Power Authority (NEPA) in Lagos. NEPA must have recognized
Ṣàngó's affinity with lightning and thunder in addition to the exalted
position and reverence which is accorded him by the Yorùbá.

In this larger than life bronze sculpture, the *osé* double axe wand was
chosen as the central symbol, held in the hand of the monumental sculpture. According to Kojo Fosu the facial features of the muscular male statue
bear the expressive influence of the classical Ifẹ̀ style.[52] The right hand
holding the double-axe emblem is slightly overstretched to emphasize the
symbolic strength of Ṣàngó's power. Through this sculpture Enwonwu
reflects the traditional implication of Ṣàngó, the Yorùbá god of thunder
and lightning, and by its undercurrent of scientific truth, the Ṣàngó wand
becomes an appropriate modern adaptation for the energy supply.

Another artist who has drawn so significantly from the rich Yorùbá
cultural background is Tunde Nasiru, an academic artist, and a Christian,

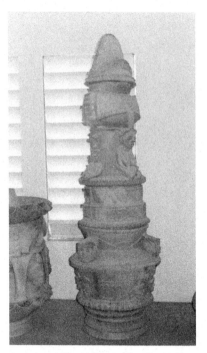

FIGURE 8.22. Giant Ṣàngó pot by Tunde Nasiru—a six-step assemblage pot. Collection of the Department of Fine Arts, Ọbáfẹ́mi Awólọ́wọ̀ University, Ilé-Ifẹ̀. Photo by Stephen Fọláránmí. 2004.

FIGURE 8.23. "Romance of the Gods" (1994) by Stephen Fọláránmí. Oil on canvas (61 x 122cm).

whose father happens to be a pastor. In 1989 he produced two nine-foot (six-step) assemblage Ṣàngó pots, probably the largest and tallest pots ever seen in this part of the world, and a high-relief plaque. These pots and plaque are elaborately decorated in high relief with Ṣàngó's symbols and emblems. Nasiru had been a student of Raphael Ibigbami, a former lecturer at the Department of Fine Arts, Obafemi Awolowo University Ilé-Ifẹ̀. Ibigbami's interest in the areas of traditional pottery in Yorùbá-land generated very fruitful ideas as a result of the several workshops on traditional pottery he organized in the late 1970s and the early 1980s.

In the area of painting, the study of Yorùbá mural painting has a high influence in my own works; I share the same ideology as the *Ọnà* group of artists in Ilé-Ifẹ̀. The artistic philosophy of representing in modern materials and forms the rich tradition and culture of the Yorùbá peo-ple, and embellishing the surfaces and the entire content of the artistic expression with rich symbolic motifs and symbols, takes a prominent place with these artists. The Yorùbá believe in the supremacy of the almighty God, Olódùmarè, who is the creator of all. He is accompanied by lesser gods, *òrìṣà*, in the work of the creation and administration of the earth. They act as intermediaries between man and almighty God. In their roles in the lives of men, they interact and work together (like Èṣù and Ọ̀rúnmìlà). This whole phenomenon becomes the subject matter in the oil on canvas, "Romance of the Gods":

> Mythical stories become symbolic representations. The chain and calabash represent the Yorùbá creation myth, the *osée Ṣàngó* and thunder represent Ṣàngó, while the divination tray, *opọ́n Ifá* with *odù* markings, represents the oracle of Ifá. The water and soil in the lower part of the painting represent the earth, where all is taking place. Therefore, my "Romance of the Gods" is a pictorial symbolic representation of the traditional religion of the Yorùbá and a testimony to the importance and position of Ṣàngó in the pantheon of the Yorùbá gods.

The Fon in the neighboring country of Benin Republic used art to praise and reinforce royal authority and to address superhuman forces. Artists were organized into palace guilds and were responsible for the decoration and production of material for state use and religious

FIGURE 8.24. "Obas Court" (1999) by Stephen Fọlárànmí. An adaptation of the symbolic images on the walls of the Aláàfin's palace in Oyo, showing the dominant *osée Ṣàngó*. Oil and tempera on canvas (92 x 102cm). Photo by Stephen Fọlárànmí. 2004.

FIGURE 8.25. Abomey clay relief, Republic of Benin. Illustration by author.

activities. For example, the exterior walls of the palace were ornamented with painted clay relief that heralded the exploits of the king and referred to the pantheon of the gods, many of them shared with the Yorùbá. Historically the kingdom of Old Ọ̀yọ́, where Ṣàngó once reigned as the supreme king, extended as far as Dahomey in the country we now know as the Republic of Benin, the influence of which is still much felt and practiced, as evidenced in figure 8.25, which depicts a ram-headed figure with a double-headed axe issuing from its mouth, an image that portrays the Fon god of thunder, Heroics.

The two double-axe forms in the background are reminiscent of the dance wands used by the worshipers of the Yorùbá thunder god Ṣàngó.

Apart from the neighboring West African countries of Nigeria, Togo, and Benin, the worship of Ṣàngó transcends the African shores into the Americas. Africans, especially from West Africa, were taken into slavery and shipped across the Atlantic from early in the sixteenth century until the second half of the nineteenth century. Seventeen million Africans survived the Atlantic crossing, and though they left their material culture behind, they carried with them the various ways of approaching and interpreting life. Therefore, in their new homes, they formed new communities reminiscent of their African origin. Those who spoke the same languages were sometimes kept on the same plantations, especially in the Caribbean and Brazil. There they revived their traditional practices, religious beliefs, and value systems.[53] It has been proven beyond reasonable doubt that culture is dynamic; new circumstances and outside forces have an effect upon artistic expressions and all other cultural practices. It is therefore not strange to find shrines and altar places dedicated to Yorùbá gods in several places in the New World. Here the African ways of doing things was combined with European or Native American ideas and practices, which automatically led to new expressions. Practices such as placing broken pottery as a mark of respect and identification on grave sites show African customs adapted to the new setting. The Yorùbá *òrìṣà* are among the most popularly revered and worshipped deities in the Diaspora. There are variations in the emblems, content, and art objects, and the shrines in the new homes wear new looks, beautiful to behold, with sparkling floors and walls. There, the significant emblem of Ṣàngó (*osée Ṣàngó*) takes its pride of place in the worship of the *òrìṣà*.

The twentieth century witnessed the development of several talented African American artists, creating memorable works of art using the forms, materials, and aesthetic tradition of European Americans. One of the early artists to explore the ideas behind African forms was Adémọ́lá Olúgébéfọl'a. He was born in the Virgin Islands and was a member of a group of artists in New York called *Weusi*, a Swahili word for blackness. In Olúgébéfọlá's painting, Ṣàngó is evoked as the deity of thunder, represented by the exciting color of red. He included cowry shells, a traditional element of monetary exchange in West Africa, in various sections of the painting, alluding to sacrificial offerings made to deities. The axe form is surrounded by a rich blue field, suggesting that Ṣàngó is a deity associated with sky forces, but the lower portion of the figure shows roots reaching toward some deep subterranean fire. As with most African art, the deity is not imagined naturalistically Instead, a series of visual signs and signifiers elucidate the concept of Ṣàngó.[54]

Conclusion

The Yorùbá people have been described as the largest producers of art in Africa. Their sculpture is better known than other artistic endeavors such as pottery, woven fabric, and wall paintings. In Bascom's words, "most African art appears to have been associated with religion."[55] This statement is not farfetched; the hundreds of divinities to which the Yorùbá people hold their allegiance facilitated the large production of these numerous artworks and objects used in the service of the various *òrìṣà*. Some deities are not represented by any art objects, but have enjoyed more patronage in the decoration of their shrines. In some cases the objects are found overflowing from the altar of such an *òrìṣà*. Ṣàngó, the Yorùbá god of thunder and lighting and the deified king of Ọ̀yọ́, falls within the ranks of such deities; his shrines are filled with numerous worship and sacrificial items in his honor and employed for his service. He has been so honored and respected in death probably because he ruled with an iron hand as the king in Old Ọ̀yọ́. The fact that his emblems, symbols, and art forms are still being used in contemporary art production, not in any way connected to the ritual services, testifies to Sàngó's importance and position whether in Yorùbáland or in the African Diaspora.

NOTES

All the photographs of pots were taken personally by the writer with special permission granted by the curator of the Ifẹ̀ Museum of Antiquities, Mr. Bode Adesina. This gesture is deeply appreciated.

1. Ulli Beier, "A Year of Sacred Festivals in One Yorùbá Town (ẸDẸ)," *Nigerian Magazine* (Special Production), 3rd ed. (1959): 72.

2. Bolaji Idowu, *Olódùmarè: God in Yorùbá Belief,* rev. and enlarged ed. (London: Longman, 1996), 88.

3. Samuel Johnson, *The History of the Yorùbás* (Lagos: CSS Bookshop, 1976), 33; Idowu, *Olódùmarè;* J. O. Awolalu, *Yorùbá Belief and Sacrificial Rites* (London: Longman Group, 1979); and many other authors have documented several versions of the stories and myths surrounding the deification of Ṣàngó.

4. Beier, "A Year of Sacred Festival," 72.

5. Ibid.

6. Idowu, *Olódùmarè,* 88.

7. Awolalu, *Yorùbá Belief,* 36.

8. Ibid., 36–37.

9. Beier, "A Year of Sacred Festival," 72.

10. Wande Abimbola, "Introduction," in *Yorùbá Oral Tradition, Poetry in Music, Dance and Drama,* ed. Wande Abimbola (Ilé-Ifẹ̀, Nigeria: Department of African Languages and Literature, University of Ifẹ̀, 1975), 65–66.

11. Idowu, *Olódùmarè,* 88.

12. Johnson, *History of the Yorùbás,* 33.

13. John Pemberton gave an account of the shrine when he visited and took the picture of the shrine in 1971.

14. J. R. O. Ojo, *A Short Illustrated Guide of the Museum of The Institute of African Studies* (Ilé-Ifẹ̀, Nigeria: University of Ifẹ̀, 1969), 9.

15. See L. Frobenius, *The Voice of Africa: An Account of the Travels of the German Inner African Exploration Expedition in the Year 1910–1912,* vol. 1, trans. Rudolf Blind (London: Hutchinson, 1913).

16. See also M. B. Visona (with introduction and preface by Rowland Abiodun and Suzanne Blier), *The History of Art in Africa* (New York: Hany Abram, 2000), 254, for the same account by Frobenius.

17. E. Leuzinger, *The Art of Black Africa* (London: Cassel and Collier Macmillan Publishers, 1976), 174.

18. Harold Courlander, *Tales of Yorùbá Gods and Heroes: Myths, Legend and Heroic Tales of the Yorùbá People of West Africa* (New York: Crown Publishers, 1973), 79.

19. Frobenius, *The Voice of Africa.*

20. Johnson, *History of the Yorùbás,* 106.

21. H. Drewal, *African Artistry: Technique and Aesthetics in Yorùbá Sculpture* (Atlanta: High Museum of Art, 1980), 29–31.

22. K. Carroll, foreword by William Fagg *Yorùbá Religious Carving: Pagan and Christian Sculpture in Nigeria and Dahomey* (London: Geoffrey Chapman, 1967), 32.

23. R. Abiodun, "Ifa Art Objects: An Interpretation Based on Oral Tradition," in *Yorùbá Oral Tradition: Poetry in Music, Dance and Drama,* ed. Wande Abimbola (Ilé-Ifẹ̀, Nigeria: Department of African Languages and Literature, University of Ifẹ, 1975), 438.

24. Ibid., 446.

25. L. Fakeye, M. Bruce, and H. David, *Lamidi Olonode Fakeye: A Retrospective Exhibition and Autobiography* (Holland, Mich.: De Pree Art Center and Gallery, 1996), 8, 17.

26. Ibid.

27. A. K. Fatunsin, *Yoruba Pottery* (Lagos: National Commission for Museums and Monuments, 1992), 43.

28. Ibid., 57.

29. Visona, *History of Art in Africa,* 252.

30. Ibid., 255.

31. R. Brain, *Art and Society in Africa* (New York: Longman Group, 1980), 204.

32. B. Nasiru, "Ṣàngó Ritual Pots," unpublished M.F.A. thesis, Department of Fine Arts, Obafemi Awolowo University, Ilé-Ifẹ̀, 1989, 177.

33. *Arugbáa Ṣàngó* (calabash carrier) is a figural representation of a maiden with a calabash containing objects of sacrifice. In Ṣàngó shrines, these images with a calabash holds the thunder celts and other important items of Ṣàngó worship.

34. J. Picton, "The Horse and Rider in Yorùbá Art: Image of Conquest and Possession," *Nigerian Field* 67, no. 2 (Oct. 2002): 132.

35. W. Bascom, *African Art in Cultural Perspective: An Introduction* (New York: W. W. Norton & Co., 1973), 88.

36. Awolalu, *Yorùbá Belief,* 36–37.

37. Ulli Beier, "Yorùbá Wall Paintings," *ODU: Journal of Yoruba and Edo Related Studies* 8 (1960): 36–39.

38. See Moyo Okediji, "Òrìṣà Ìkirè Painting School," *Kurio Africana: Journal of Art and Criticism* 1, no. 2 (1989): 116–26; Moyo Okediji, "Yorùbá Paint Making Tradition," *Nigerian Magazine* 54, no. 2 (1986): 19–26; S. Adebisi, "Shrine Painting in Ile-Ife," unpublished B.A. long essay,: Obafemi Awolalu University, Ilé-Ifẹ̀, 1986; V. B. Campbell, "Comparative Study of Selected Shrine Paintings in Ilé-Ifẹ̀ and Ilésà," unpublished M.F.A. thesis, Obafemi Awolowo University, Ilé-Ifẹ̀, 1989); V. B. Campbell, "Continuity and Change in Yorùbá

Shrine Painting Tradition," in *Kurio Africana: Journal of Art and Criticism* 1, no. 2 (1992); V. B. Campbell, "Images and Power in Sixteen Yorùbá Sacred Paintings," in *Ifẹ̀: Annals of the Institute of Cultural Studies* 6 (1995): 25–38; S. Folaranmi, "Òrìṣà Pópó Shrine Painting in Ògbómọ̀ṣọ́," unpublished B.A. long essay, Obafemi Awolowo University, Ilé-Ifẹ̀, 1995; S. Folaranmi, "Ọ̀yọ́ Palace Mural," unpublished M.F.A. thesis, Obafemi Awolowo University, Ilé-Ifẹ̀, 2000; S. Folaranmi, "Ọ̀yọ́ Palace Mural, A Symbolic Communication with Symbols," in *Journal of Art and Ideas* 4 (2002): 93–105; and S. Folaranmi, "The Importance of Oríkì In Yorùbá Mural Art," *Ijele: Art e-journal of the African World* 2, no. 4, available at www.africaresource.com.

39. Campbell, "Images and Power," 27.

40. P. A. Ladipo, "Ṣàngó Shrine Painting in Ẹdẹ," unpublished B. A. long essay, Obafemi Awolowo University, Ilé-Ifẹ̀, 1992, 20.

41. Ibid.

42. Ibid., 22.

43. O. O. Addie, "Colour Symbolism, with Special Reference to Ṣàngó Shrine in Ibadan," unpublished B. A. long essay, Obafemi Awolowo University, Ilé-Ifẹ̀, 1990), 8–9.

44. Okediji, "Òrìṣà Ìkirẹ̀ Painting School," 122.

45. Addie, "Colour Symbolism," 23.

46. A. Isola, "The Rhythm of Ṣàngó Pipè," in *Yorùbá Oral Tradition: Poetry in Music, Dance and Drama,* ed. Wande Abimbola (Ilé-Ifẹ̀, Nigeria: Department of African Languages and Literature, University of Ifẹ̀, 1975), 792–93.

47. C. A. Alade, "Aspects of Yorùbá Culture in the Diaspora," in *Culture and Society in Yorùbáland,* ed. Deji Ogunremi and Biodun Adediran (Ibadan, Nigeria: Rex Charles Publication and Connel Publication, 1998), 203.

48. Fakeye, Bruce, and David, *Lamidi Olonade Fakeye,* 3.

49. Ibid., 8.

50. Kenneth C. Murray was a colonial education officer who had a very great impact on the development of style in Nigeria art. Kenneth arrived in Nigeria in 1927 and later became an art teacher of contemporary art and taught many students. Because he was an ardent believer in the preservation of Nigerian culture through art, he encouraged his students to learn from traditional artists, and in addition to draw their inspiration from their culture. Furthermore, Murray's philosophy that modern art should of necessity be based on traditional art puts him at the threshold of the modernist movement in Nigeria.

51. D. Osa Egonwa, "Patterns and Trends of Stylistic Development in Contemporary Nigerian Art," *Kurio Africana: Journal of Art and Criticism* 2, no. 1 (1995), 6.

52. K. Fosu, *20th Century Art of Africa,* vol. 1 (Zaria, Nigeria: Gaskiya Corporation, 1986), 29.

53. Visona, *History of Art,* 500.

54. Ibid., 514–15.

55. Bascom, *African Art.*

CHAPTER NINE

The Ambivalent Representations of Ṣàngó in Yorùbá Literature

AKÍNTÚNDÉ AKÍNYẸMÍ

Ṣàngó is the most popularized Yorùbá hero-deity in literary forms. Apart from his representation in the corpus of oral praise poetry known as *Ṣàngó pípè* (intoning Ṣàngó), salient information about the deity's personality is well preserved in several verses of Yorùbá divination poetry (*odù ifá*). Various myths and stories associated with the deity have also inspired the creation of a number of literary works, such as Dúró Ládipọ̀'s trilogy, (*Ọba Kòso, Ọbàtálá,* and *Ọ̀ṣun àti Ọbà*), Ọládẹjọ Òkédìjí's *Ṣàngó,* and five movies: Wálé Ògúnyẹmí's *Ṣàngó,* Afọlábí Adésànyà's *Osé(e) Ṣàngó,* Adébímpé Adékọlá's *Ìhínú Olúkòso,* Ajíléyẹ's *Igbá(a) Ṣàngó,* and Lérè Pàímọ̀'s *Lakáayé.*

Contrary to Ògúndèjì's assertion that there are three types of distinct and yet overlapping Ṣàngó—the mythical, the historically deified, and the literary Ṣàngó—my position in this chapter is that the dialectical relationship between the three is enough to prove that there is just one Ṣàngó.[1] Therefore, the premise on which I will argue is that the unpredictable, violent, and tyrannical nature and pattern of life of the mythical Ṣàngó influenced his historical and literary representation. For instance, there is little or nothing to differentiate Dúró Ládipọ̀ and Ọládẹjọ Òkédìjí's representation of literary Ṣàngó from Hethersett's version of historical Ṣàngó. As Ògúndèjì himself rightly observes, Dúró Ládipọ̀ created his literary Ṣàngó out of the written and unwritten sources available to him about the mythical and historical Ṣàngó. I intend to use the ambivalent character of the mythical Ṣàngó to prove the inseparability of mythical Ṣàngó from historical Ṣàngó. I also intend to show that the ambivalent representations of Ṣàngó in Yorùbá oral tradition symbolize the universal contradiction of human nature in general.

The present observation on the multidimensional representation of Ṣàngó is not completely new in Yorùbá scholarship. It was Leo Frobenius, a German ethnologist, who first called attention to it when he was unable to reconcile the ambivalent attributes of Ṣàngó as a reckless and cruel ruler and a loving and just divinity.[2] Frobenius attributed the disparity to the representation of two different deities with the same name among two of the Old Ọ̀yọ́ northern neighbors—the Nupe and the Borgu peoples of central Nigeria. Writing much later, Bolaji Idowu agrees with the suggestion of Frobenius on the probability of two different deities sharing a common name, but disagrees with the idea of ascribing the variation to two different sources—the Nupe and the Borgu.[3] Rather, he postulates that in all probability, Jàkúta, the Yorùbá mythical divinity associated with lightning and thunder, is the one represented as the just and loving Ṣàngó. Using historical information provided by Johnson and Hethersett as a basis, Idowu argues further that, much later, an Aláàfin of Old Ọ̀yọ́ and a devoted worshipper of Jàkúta adopted the attributes and names of the divinity during his reign. Both Johnson and Hethersett claimed that although this tyrannical and cruel Aláàfin later hanged himself, his supporters successfully deified him and popularized his ambivalent attributes. Thus, they created a historical Ṣàngó as opposed to Jàkúta, the mythical Ṣàngó. To Idowu, therefore, it is the adoption of the attributes of a loving and just divinity by a cruel and reckless ruler that can account for the contradictory representations of Ṣàngó in Yorùbá literature.

C. L. Adéoyè later identifies the name of the Aláàfin who usurped the attributes of Ṣàngó as Sálù Babáyẹmí Ìtíolú. According to him, this Ṣàngó was the son of Ọ̀rányàn (also known in oral tradition as Ọdẹ́dẹ́ or Jẹ̀gbẹ̀), the founder of Old Ọ̀yọ́ and the first Aláàfin. There are two versions of the story of this historical Ṣàngó. Although both agree that Aláàfin Ṣàngó hanged himself as a result of some form of shame and frustration, and that his supporters later deified him, each version gives different reasons for the king's decision to hang himself. There are actually no other points of similarity between the two apart from the deification of the king after the purported suicide.

In his own version of the story, Johnson describes Aláàfin Ṣàngó as "of a very wild disposition, fiery temper, and skilful in sleight of hand tricks."[4] Johnson also records that "that particular Aláàfin had the habit of emitting fire and smoke out of his mouth, by which he greatly increased the dread his subjects had for him." Johnson recalls that one day Aláàfin Ṣàngó decided to try out his newly acquired charm that could attract lightning and fire at Òkè Àjàká, the hill at the bottom of which the Aláàfin's palace was built. The story claims that the Aláàfin's assumption was that the preparation was useless and ineffective. Therefore, he directed the experiment toward his palace. Unfortunately for him, the preparation took effect and lightning struck the palace, killing most of his wives and children. King Ṣàngó became distressed and dismayed at what happened, and therefore he decided to voluntarily abdicate his throne and return to the court of his maternal grandfather, Elénpe of Nupe kingdom. The Aláàfin had expected that his chiefs, slaves, friends, and supporters would follow him. Consequently, he decided to wait for them outside the city. But, contrary to his expectation, no one followed him. Even those few slaves who had earlier followed him later returned to the city of Òyó. Deserted by all, Johnson records, Ṣàngó became frustrated and decided to commit suicide. He climbed a shea butter tree and hanged himself. The story concludes that on hearing of the tragic death of the Aláàfin, his supporters hurriedly buried his remains under the tree where he committed suicide and deified him afterward.

The second version of the story of deification of Aláàfin Ṣàngó is credited to Hethersett.[5] According to him, Ṣàngó came from Ìgbétì hill in Òyó country to found the city of Old Òyó. He had two courtiers who were very strong in might and in the use of charms. The first courtier, Tìmì Àgbàlé, had a special arrow that, whenever it was shot, caused fire on the body of whomever it hit. As for Gbònńkà Èbìrì, he was versed in charms and there was nothing anybody could do to hurt him. In fact, this historical account claims that the two of them were already terrors to the community in general and the Aláàfin in particular. Therefore, the Aláàfin and his chiefs decided to set the two warlords against each other. When Gbònńkà eventually killed Tìmì, he accused Aláàfin Ṣàngó of supporting Tìmì during their fight. The powerful Gbònńkà therefore mandated Ṣàngó to leave the city of Òyó within five days. The story concludes that Aláàfin Ṣàngó quietly left the city of Òyó for his mother's town in Nupeland.

At the outskirts of the city of Òyó, the Aláàfin observed that only Oya (his favorite wife) and few of his slaves were with him. Therefore, he decided to wait at Ìpèsì for his friends and supporters who had promised to follow him. When no one was forthcoming, Oya and the few slaves who were with Ṣàngó also deserted him. Hethersett claims that out of frustration, Aláàfin Ṣàngó then decided to hang himself on a shea butter tree located at Kòso. When the news of the tragedy got to the supporters of the Aláàfin that *ọba so ní Kòso* ("the king hanged himself at Kòso") they were ashamed of themselves for not following him. Therefore, they decided to deify the dead king after he was hurriedly buried at Kòso, where he hanged himself, and subsequently they changed the phrase "the king hanged himself at Kòso" to "the king did not hang" (*ọba Kò so*). According to Hethersett, supporters of the Aláàfin later decided to redeem their patron's image by causing lightning and thunder to strike through evocation of mysterious powers, leaving the houses of the enemies of the Aláàfin devastated.

These stories look very much like deliberate propaganda by early Christian missionaries to discredit Yoruba indigenous religious practice. We would remember that both Johnson and Hethersett were ordained ministers of the Church Missionary Society in Yorùbáland. One finds it illogical that the followers of the Aláàfin would deify him as Ṣàngó only after the king hanged himself. The truth of the matter is that in Òyọ́ tradition every Aláàfin must be deified at death. But to be eligible for deification, a dead Aláàfin must be buried at the *Barà,* the royal mausoleum.[6] Babayemi, who was fortunate to have witnessed the rituals that accompanied the burial of the late Aláàfin Gbádégẹsin Ládùgbòlù in 1968, writes that

> when an Aláàfin died in the present Òyọ́ . . . [t]he *Ònà-oníṣẹ̀-awo,* the *Babaàyajì* and the eunuchs did the necessary rituals to the corpse. They then planned for the symbolic burial at the dead of the night. This symbolic burial is what the people of Òyọ́ believe to be the actual burial. . . . On the night that the ritual burying of the late *ọba* was to be done, none of the Aláàfin's sons or closest relatives were to be around while the dressing of the supposed corpse took place. The coffin was to be borne by the rank and file of the *Alárè* family. Sons and relatives of the Aláàfin who were brave enough were to follow at a distance. Rituals were performed at stopping places (on their way from the palace to where *Barà* is located) until they got to *òkìtì jẹ́njù* (*jẹ́njù* mound) in front of the *Alápìnnì*'s house (mid-way between the palace and *Barà*). Here, everybody had to retreat. . . . By this symbolic burial, the spirit of the dead Aláàfin was believed to have been removed from the palace and made to join the other royal ancestors. The spirit had thus become deified, and could be invoked.[7]

The fact that, as both Johnson and Hethersett claimed, Aláàfin Ṣàngó was buried at the spot where he hanged himself and not at Barà is enough to disqualify him from becoming a hero-deity by the tradition of Òyọ́.

Secondly, the story itself seems unreal for a culture that forbids the termination of one's life by hanging.[8] While it is not unusual for a tyrannical or wicked Aláàfin to commit suicide in Ọ̀yọ́ tradition, such suicide is almost always by self-inflicted poison and not by hanging. For instance, once the council of chiefs decides to remove an Aláàfin, their leader, the Baṣọ̀run, would pronounce the following formal statement of rejection: *àwọn òòṣà kọ̀ ọ́, ìlú kọ̀ ọ́, àwọn ayé kọ̀ ọ́* (The gods have rejected you, the people have rejected you, the witches have also rejected you). This, in essence, is a euphemistic call on the erring Aláàfin to commit suicide. All the nine Aláàfin who reigned between 1658 and 1754 were rejected in this way. According to Samuel Johnson, the cause of the rejection was said to be tyranny, immorality, or both on the part of individual Aláàfin.[9] A more specific case is that of Aláàfin Jáyin, who committed suicide by poison when he was implicated in the death of his own son (Olúsì), who had apparently become too popular for the Aláàfin's comfort.[10] It is therefore very unlikely that a society such as Ọ̀yọ́, which considers suicide by hanging as a serious offense, would permit the deification of a king who hanged himself, no matter how powerful he might have been. Yorùbá custom stipulates that the remains of a person who hanged himself or herself must not be buried decently at home but at the spot where she/he hanged, in order to prevent a reoccurrence of such an incident. Moreover, the dead body may not be removed from its dangling position until after certain rituals have been performed to ward off evil spirits associated with the incident.[11]

Akínwùmí Ìṣọlá has also called attention to the inconsistencies in the historical accounts presented by Johnson and Hethersett and the misrepresentation of the title of the Aláàfin in question by Hethersett.[12] Ìṣọlá argues that the activities of Tìmì and Gbọ̀nńkà, which Hethersett associated with the reign of the Aláàfin who adopted Ṣàngó's attributes, actually happened much later in the history of Ọ̀yọ́, precisely during the reign of Aláàfin Kọ̀rí.[13] According to Johnson's historical account, after the death of the Aláàfin who adopted the attributes of Ṣàngó, Aláàfin Àjùwọ̀n Àjàká was installed. It was after his demise that Aláàfin Kọ̀rí reigned. Ìṣọlá also observes that the phrase *ọbaa Kòso* (the king who reigned at Kòso), used for Aláàfin Ṣàngó, has been translated wrongly by Hethersett to be "the king did not hang." He stated further that if the word "Kòso" is broken down into two separate syllables, then it will be correct to translate the phrase *Ọba Kò So* etymologically as "the king did not hang." But why would Hethersett intentionally distort historical facts? Akínwùmí Ìṣọlá thinks that Hethersett might have thought that the

popularization of a degrading myth about Ṣàngó would do enough dam-
age to the image of the hero-deity to cause a decline in adherence.[14] One
may conclude, therefore, that it is very unlikely that the word "Kòso"
has anything to do with the hanging of an Aláàfin. Rather, I see Kòso as
the name of the place where an Aláàfin who adopted the attributes of the
deity Ṣàngó reigned. To further support the royal majesty of that Aláàfin
as the king who reigned at Kòso, he is also addressed as *Olúkòso* (the lord
at Kòso). I should also mention that the incumbent chief priest of Ṣàngó
(*Baba mọgbà*) lives in Kòso quarters in present day Ọ̀yọ́ and that the bulk
of the high-ranking priests and priestesses of Ṣàngó still reside at Kòso.

The mythico-historical representation of Ṣàngó in oral tradition has
thus created a problem of identity for the deity. This prompted Adéoyè
to conduct further research into the subject matter. The result of that
research led him to identify eight features that differentiate the mythical Ṣàngó—Jàkúta—from the historical Ṣàngó-Aláàfin Sálù Babayẹmí
Ìtíolú.[15]

Apart from the mythico-historical representation of Ṣàngó discussed
above, Ògúndèjì has recently identified the third representation of Ṣàngó,
which he describes as "the literary Ṣàngó."[16] According to him, this
Ṣàngó was popularized by the late Dúró Ládipọ̀, one of the first generation of Nigerian professional dramatists, through three of his plays, *Oba
Kò So*, *Ọ̀sun*, and *Ọbàtálá*, of which *Oba Kò So* is the most successful.
Oba Kò So, was very popular in and out of Nigeria in the 1960s. It was
successfully staged in different parts of Africa, Europe, the Middle East,
and the Americas. The international recognition won by this play led to
its performance at the International Theater Competition in Berlin, Germany, in 1965, and at the Commonwealth Arts Festival in London in the
United Kingdom the following year. Ògúndèjì observes that the ambivalence of Dúró Ládipọ̀'s presentation of literary Ṣàngó "is deeply rooted
in deliberate juxtaposition of the historical and mythical Ṣàngó."[17]

The plot of *Oba Kò So* is based largely on Hethersett's account, with
minor alterations by Dúró Ládipọ̀. In the play, Dúró Ládipọ̀ presents the
partly historical and partly mythological Ṣàngó as a fire-spitting, tactless,
hot-tempered, and weak ruler who cannot control two of his war generals, Tìmì and Gbọ̀nńkà. Therefore, he consults with his council of chiefs
on the best way to get rid of one or both of them. On the advice of the
council and that of his wife, the king sends one of the war generals, Tìmì,
to Èdẹ to check the incessant raids on the area by the Ìjẹ̀sà, a mission that
they think will lead to Tìmì's death. Contrary to their calculation, Tìmì is
made the king of Èdẹ in recognition of his military might and metaphysical power. This prompts the Aláàfin and his council of chiefs to order

Sàngó (Irúnmọlẹ̀)	Sàngó (Ọba Aláàfin)

Ó rò láti òde òrun sí òde ayé ni bíi ti àwọn Irúnmọlẹ̀ ẹgbẹ́ rẹ̀ yòókù.

Èyí kò rò láti òde òrun, Ọdẹ́dẹ́, (ọmọ Ọkànbí) tí àdàpè rẹ̀ ǹ jẹ́ Ọ̀rányàn ni ó bí i. Òrìsá àkúnlẹ̀bọ àdáyéyàn ni.

Sàngó Ayílẹ́gbẹ̀ẹ́-ọ̀run àti Odùduà jọ lo ìgbà lóde ayé ni.

Ní àsìkò yìi, Odùduà kò tíì bí Ọ̀kànbí ẹni tí ó bí Ọdẹ́dẹ́, bàbáa Sàngó.

Irúnmọlẹ̀ ni Sàngó yìí, ó ju ọba lọ, gẹ̀gẹ̀ bí iṣọ̀ọ̀rọ̀ pé "ọba ni ó ni ayé, òrìṣà ni ó sì ni ọba."

Ọba ni Sàngó yìí, kì í ṣe irúnmọlẹ̀. Lẹ̀yìn tí ó pa ara rẹ̀ tán ní Kòso ni ó di òrìsà Àdáyéyàn.

Sàngó Irúnmọlẹ̀ yìí ni àwọn ẹgbẹ́ rẹ̀ fi ojọ́ Jàkúta dá lọ́lá ni Ifẹ̀ Oòyè.

Sángó yìí kò gbé Ifẹ́ Oòyè rí. Ahoro Òkò ni ó gbé.

Sàngó yìí ni ó gba Oya lọ́wọ́ Ògún, tí ó fi ṣe ìyàwó. Òun kan náà ni ó tún gba Ọ̀sun, ìyàwó Ọ̀rúnmìlà.

Sángó yìí kò tíì dé ilé ayé ní àsìkò tí Ọya àti Ọ̀sun rò sóde ayé. Ọmọ bíbí inú àwọn irúnmọ̀lé méjèèjì yìí ju Sàngó yìí lọ lójọ́ orí.

Ayílẹ́gbẹ̀ẹ́-ọ̀run ni orúkọ irúnmọlẹ̀ yìí, àbúrò ni ó jẹ́ fún Baáyànnì lóde ọ̀run.

Ìtíolú ni orúkọ Sàngó yìí, kò gbónjú mọ Baáyànnì bẹ́ẹ ni kò sì bá a tan rárá.

Sàngó yìí gba ọ̀nà Àtìbà jáde kúrò ní Ifẹ̀-Oòyè, ó sì wọ ilẹ̀ lọ ni, kò kú.

Sàngó yìí pokùn-so ni, ní ìlú kékeré kan ní iwájú Ìgbétì lọ́nà Ọ̀yó-Ilé. Ìlú náà ni wọ́n ǹ pè ní Kòso

Odù tí Sàngó yìí bá rò láti òde òrun sí ilé ayé ni Ọ̀yẹkú-Méjì.

Sàngó yìí kò rò, ṣùgbọ́n Odù ìṣẹ̀dáyé rẹ̀ ni Ọ̀kànràn-Méjì.

The Mythical Ṣàngó (the divinity)	The Historical Ṣàngó (the Aláàfin)

He descended like other divinities to the terrestrial plane.

He did not descend from heaven. He was the child of Ọdẹ́dẹ́ (or grandchild of Ọ̀kànbí). He was only deified.

This Ṣàngó (also known as Ayílẹ́gbẹ̀ẹ́-Ọ̀run) and Odùduwà grew up together.

Odùduwà had not given birth to Ọ̀kànbí, grandfather of Ṣàngó, by then.

This divinity is greater than a king. Hence, the saying "the king owns the world, but the divinity owns the king."

This Ṣàngó only reigned as a king; he was never a divinity. He was deified after he hanged himself at Kòso.

This Ṣàngó was honored with the *Jàkúta* day by other divinities in Ifẹ̀-Oòyè.

This Ṣàngó never lived in Ifẹ̀ Oòyè. He lived in Òkò village.

It was this Ṣàngó who deprived both Ògún and Ọ̀rúnmìlà of their respective wives (Ọya and Ọ̀sun).

This Ṣàngó was not alive when Ọya and Ọ̀sun descended to the earth. The children of both deities were older than this Ṣàngó.

The other name of this Ṣàngó is Ayílé gbẹ̀ẹ́-Ọ̀run. He was the younger sibling of Baáyànnì.

The name of this Ṣàngó is Ìtíolú. He never got to know Baáyánní. They were not related at all.

This Ṣàngó was never reported dead. He disappeared in Ifẹ̀-Oòyè en route to Àtìbà.

This Ṣàngó hanged himself at Kòso near Ìgbé tì in Old Ọ̀yó. The town is known as Kòso.

The odù (Ifá corpus) *Ọ̀yẹkú-Méjì* talks about how this Ṣàngó descended.

This Ṣàngó did not descend. His deification is recorded in the odù (Ifá corpus) *Ọ̀kànràn Méjì*.

the second war general, Gbọ̀nńkà, to go down to Ẹdẹ to arrest Tìmì, in the hope that one of them will die in the process. To their dismay, rather than killing Tìmì, whom he has mesmerized with charms, Gbọ̀ nńkà brings him as captive to the Aláàfin at Ọ̀yọ́. Still bent on getting rid of one of the two warlords, the Aláàfin orders a repeat of the fight in his presence at Ọ̀yọ́. Gbọ̀nńkà cuts off Tìmì's head during the rescheduled fight and orders the Aláàfin to vacate the throne within four days. Having been deserted by his friends, chiefs, and trusted wife, the Aláàfin decides to hang himself. When the news of his hanging reaches his friends and chiefs at Ọ̀yọ́, they are ashamed and sad. They then decide to deify him to remove the stigma that the incident has put on the name of Ṣàngó and the office of the Aláàfin. The play ends when the voice of Ṣàngó is heard from heaven assuring his people of his eternal vigilance over them.

Writing under the title "The Sources of Duro Ladipo's *Ọba Kò So,*" Oludare Olajubu gives a catalog of thirty-four episodes of similarities in Dúró Ládipọ̀'s literary creation of Ṣàngó and Hethersett's account of historical Ṣàngó before he concludes that

> of the 8 acts in *Ọba Kò So,* approximately 7, or 51 pages out of 61, are based on the first part of Hethersett's story, which covers about 4 pages of prose writing of about 1,200 words. Duro Ladipo follows Hethersett rather faithfully for a large portion of the play. He seems to depart from him only in Act(s) 2 . . . and . . . 6. These 2 acts do not advance the story—they only show what has been reported. . . . Ladipo makes a number of minor alterations even in parts where he is following Hethersett's story. For instance, the advice to send Tìmì to Ẹdẹ, which Hethersett attributed to the Ọ̀yọ́-Mìsì is attributed to Oya by Ladipo. And, in the closing parts of the story, where Ṣàngó hanged himself, Hethersett says that Oya deserted Ṣàngó leaving Beri, his trusted eunuch, behind and that it was Beri who was with Ṣàngó till the end. Ladipo makes Oya decide to leave and she is actually on her way, but not too far away to prevent her from hearing her husband and king declare: "Ah! I will hang myself!" to which she shouted entreatingly:
>
> Ṣàngó, don't hang! . . .
> How will it sound to hear
> That Ṣàngó hanged at Kòso.[18]

My concern in the remaining part of this chapter is to reconstruct the history of mythico-historical Ṣàngó with the hope of showing its ambivalent representations in Yoruba oral poetry. The desire of the Yorùbá people to find a mythical origin for their religious beliefs and the existence of the òrìṣàs encouraged them to formulate different kinds of myths, legends, and stories around the origin, the superhuman nature, and the extraordinary powers of their objects of worship. All the Yorùbá òrìṣàs are said to have been either divinities that descended from heaven and lived like human beings or famous individuals deified as gods or goddesses after their death in recognition of their supernatural deeds, outstanding wisdom, and perseverance. All Yorùbá devotees attribute the same qualities of generosity, life-giving power, destructive power, and personal magnificence to their òrìṣàs. Karin Barber argues that while the beneficent power of the òrìṣàs gives children, wealth, health, and peace to the devotees, their destructive power protects devotees from the attacks of enemies.[19] She also observes that, although not all the deities have these qualities in the same proportions, the qualities ascribed to them by their devotees when praising them are much the same for all of them.

This study will benefit tremendously from odù ifá divination poetry and Ṣàngó pípè, the praise poetry (oríkì) normally rendered in honor of Ṣàngó. The relevance of the Ifá divination poetry to this work rests on Iṣọlá's observation that "any myth of a Yorùbá deity that cannot be found in eṣe ifá is not authentic."[20] To buttress Iṣọlá's claim, odù Òṣẹ́ tùúrá discusses how Ṣàngó descended to the planetary earth with some fifteen other divinities, Òyẹ̀kú Méjì tells of the source of the deity's supernatural power, Òkànràn Méjì talks about how Ṣàngó acquired the habit of spitting smoke and fire from his mouth, Òtúá Oríkò sheds lights on the story of Ṣàngó's initiation into divination, and Ogbètúrá documents his movement from Ifẹ̀ to Òyọ́-Ilé (Old Òyọ́).

My decision to use oríkì as the second resource material in this work is hinged on the fact that each Yorùbá divinity has its own origin, personality, special attributes, taboos, and observances, which are preserved in the form of oríkì. Oríkì are attributive epithets that are equivalent to names. Because they are name-like in form and vocative in address, oríkì are seen as being in some way the key to a subject's essential nature. Karin Barber argues that by uttering a subject's oríkì, one is calling upon or unlocking hidden powers; the activity of naming is thought of as being effectual.[21] Human subjects react to the utterance of their oríkì with deep gratification and with an enhancement of their aura, which is sometimes actually visible in their physical behavior.[22]

The Yorùbá recognize the fact that oríkì can be used as a vehicle of communication between man and these deities, as Barber observes:

[I]t is in *òrìṣà pípè* that the relationship between devotee and *òrìṣà* is established. *Oríkì* are the means of communications through which the relationship, which is the essence of the religion is kept alive . . . in *òrìṣà pípè*, as in all *oríkì*, the subject is always paramount and the relationship between addresser and addressee is more important than the subject's place in overall historical, genealogical or cosmological scheme of things.[23]

Barber argues further that the overwhelming importance of the *òrìṣà*-devotee bond of mutual benefit is demonstrated in two aspects of the use of *oríkì* in Yorùbá traditional religious literature. First is that the devotee can be saluted through the *oríkì* of his or her *òrìṣà*, and secondly, that the *òrìṣà* can also be saluted through the *oríkì* of his or her devotee. By so doing, the devotee is identified with her/his *òrìṣà* and she/he gains status from her/his association with the *òrìṣà*, while the *òrìṣà* is thought of as belonging to certain devotees. Therefore, it is in the religious poetry that a relationship is established between the devotee and her/his *òrìṣà*. The relationship is further demonstrated when the devotee is acclaimed the "offspring" of the *òrìṣà* that she/he worships:

> *Eégún ilé Àjàní,*
> > *Má jẹ́ wọ́n ó gbàṣeè rẹ ṣe.*
> > *Òjíṣẹ́ ayé babaa Déòtí,*
> > *N ó máa júbàa babaà mi ni;*
> > *Àdúṣe nii hunmọ̀, ìbà ò leè hùnmọ.*
> > *Òkánlàwọ́n la rí la dáṣàa Ṣàngó.*
> > *Bí Ṣàngó ò tètè jà,*
> > *Ọdẹ́jìn a kó Ṣàngó ẹ̀ lọ́wọ́.*
> > *Amúnúọláńlé, babaa Lágánnre;*
> > *Òmùmù gbé wọ̀rọ̀kọ̀,*
> > *Babaa Ṣàngowèádé.*
> > *OníṢàngó Ìpo, oníṢàngó Òfà,*
> > *Ọdẹ́jìn tó papọ̀ mọ́ t'Òró.*

> The ancestral spirit in the home of Àjàní,
> > Do not allow them to take over your responsibility.
> > Representative of his own people, father of Déòtí,
> > I will continuously pay homage to my father;
> > Lack of homage hurts, but homage does not.
> > We all copy Òkánlàwọ́n in the worship of Ṣàngó.
> > If Ṣàngó fails to act in good time,

Ọdéjìn will refuse to worship his Ṣàngó.
He-who-shares-out-part-of-the-family-wealth, father of Lágánnre;
One who is not predictable,
Father of Ṣàngówèádé.
The Ṣàngó worshippers of Ìpo and Òfà,
Ọdéjìn who combines his Ṣàngó with that of Òró.

Attributes as such associate the devotee with her/his *òrìṣà,* and the devotee benefits from that association. One may conclude therefore that, since a reasonable portion of *Ṣàngó pípè* is made up of the *oríkì* of the deity Ṣàngó and those of his devotees, the constant juxtaposition of the attributes of the mythical Ṣàngó and those of the former Aláàfin, an adherent of the deity who was later deified as historical Ṣàngó in recognition of his devotion to the *òrìṣà,* is equally inevitable.

An Ifá myth presents Ṣàngó as one of the most powerful spirits of the Yorùbá pantheon. *Odù ifá Òṣétùúrá* claims that Ṣàngó was as powerful as the other primordial deities such as Odùduwà, Òrúnmìlà, Ògún, Ọbàtálá, Èṣù, and Òṣun, and that they all worked together at the founding of the world. The corpus recalls how Olódùmarè (the Creator God) sent sixteen *òrìṣà* from his abode in Òde Ìsálórun (the primordial heaven) to establish Òde Ìsálayé (the primordial earth) for human habitation, with specific instruction on what they should do as soon as they arrived the earth in order to make the young earth a pleasant place to live:

Kómú-n-kórò,
    Awo Èwí nílé Adó;
Òrun-mù-dèdè-kanlè,
    Awo òde Ìjèsà;
Alákàn-ní-ń-bẹ-lódò,
    Tí-ń-tẹlẹ̀-tútù-rin-rin-rin;
A díá fẹ̀ẹrìndínlógún irúnmọlẹ̀;
Wọ́n ń tìkòlé òrun rò wá sí tayé.
Wọ́n délé ayé,
Wọ́n yẹgbó Orò;
Wọ́n yẹgbó Ọpa.
Wọ́n gbìmọ̀ wọ́n ò fi t'Òṣun ṣe.

The-one-who-gathers-women-and-wealth,
    The diviner of Èwí in the town of Adó;
The-sky-is-overcast (as of the threatening of rain),
    Their diviner in Ìjèsàland;

The-crab-is-in-the-river,
And-crawls-on-an-extremely-cold-ground;
They all made divination for the sixteen Divinities;
They were descending from heaven to earth.
When they arrived in the world,
They cleared Orò grove;
They cleared Ọpa grove.
They planned and never consulted with Ọ̀ṣun.[24]

Although the *Odù Ọ̀ṣẹ́tùúrá* did not specifically mention the names of the male divinities that descended to the planetary earth at the time of creation, another *odù ifá* verse, however, claims that Ọ̀ṣun, the only female divinity at creation, married Ṣàngó at a point. *Odù Ogbèsá* tells us that Ọ̀ṣun first got married to Ọ̀rúnmìlà before she divorced him to marry Ṣàngó. The *odù* records that in one of the regular visits of the *òrìṣàs* to Olódùmarè, they encountered a group of wicked cannibals in heaven who started to kill and eat up the *òrìṣàs* one after the other. But Ọ̀ṣun miraculously saved Ọ̀rúnmìlà by hiding him from the cannibals, and substituting goat meat for his flesh, which the cannibals had planned to eat that very day. The story concludes that Ọ̀rúnmìlà later decided to marry Ọ̀ṣun in appreciation of what she did for him:

> *Báyìí ni Ọ̀rúnmìlà òun Ọ̀ṣun bá sún mọ́ra.*
> *Ọ̀rúnmìlà ní irú oore tó ṣe fún mi níjelòó,*
> *Kò sírú oore kan tó tún lè tó èyíun mọ́.*
> *O wá ro ohun tó lè ṣe fún un . . .*
> *Ni Ọ̀rúnmìlà bá fẹ́ Ọ̀ṣun níyàwó*
> *Nifá bá di ọkọ Ọ̀ṣun.*

This was how Ọ̀rúnmìlà and Ọ̀ṣun became close.
Ọ̀rúnmìlà said that the good turn which she did for him,
Was an exceptional one.
He wondered what he should do in turn for her . . .
Ọ̀rúnmìlà then got married to Ọ̀ṣun
That was how Ifá became Ọ̀ṣun's Husband.[25]

Another story narrated by Adéoyè reveals that Ọ̀ṣun eventually divorced Ọ̀rúnmìlà to marry Ṣàngó much later. The following excerpt of the *oríkì* of Ọ̀ṣun attests to the fact that Ọ̀ṣun was the favorite wife of Ṣàngó:

Òòṣà mẹ́rìndínlógún ni ń bẹ lóòdẹẹ Ṣàngó;
  Ibi ká sánpá, ká sántan l'Òṣun fi gbọkọ
    lọ́wọọ́ gbogboo wọn.
Àáyòo Ṣàngó, baraá gbosùn bí oge.
Ìyá, a-bóbìnrin-gbàtọ̀;
Ládékojú, abọ́kùnrin gbàṣẹ.

There were sixteen goddesses [wives] under Ṣàngó's roof;
  Òṣun became their husband's favorite
    as a result of her majestic walk.
The favorite wife of Ṣàngó, who is adorned with camwood.
Mother who helps women to collect Semen;
Wearer of a veiled crown, who helps men to collect menstrual flow.[26]

The fact that Òṣun, Ṣàngó, and Òrúnmìlà lived about the same time, and that they even intermarried, should prove to us that the deification of Ṣàngó as a Yorùbá divinity predates the demise of the fourth Aláàfin, whom some scholars claim is the deified Ṣàngó. If we want to demystify this story, we may argue that Òṣun, Ṣàngó, and Òrúnmìlà were among the first set of extraordinarily powerful human beings, to be deified after their death in Ilé-Ifẹ̀, where they once lived. I will be discussing the connection of the mythical Ṣàngó to Òyó royalty later. But for the moment, I need to discuss the picture of Ṣàngó as painted in his *oríkì*.

The behavioral nature of mythical Ṣàngó is well represented in his *oríkì* preserved in *Ṣàngó pípè*. Of particular importance is the ability of Ṣàngó to regularly spit out smoke and fire from his mouth. This probably stems from his herbal and metaphysical knowledge, which enables him to strike his enemies with thunderbolts. Ṣàngó's magical power and association with fire is very well encapsulated in the following lines of his *oríkì*:

Iná lójú, iná lẹ́nu;
  A-gbéná-jó,
  A-gbéná-yan;
  Kèù bí iná jò láàrò.
  Èéfìn là ń dá láyé,
  Iná ń bẹ lọ́dọ̀ ọkọọ̀ mi lọ́run.
  Fẹrẹ-bí-iná-jò-láàlà.
  Ako-iná-tíí-bódòó-rìn-pọ̀.
  N ò mohun tí fíí jókòó,
  Bí iyùn bíi sègi;

Bí esóró, bí erépe;
Àkààki òòṣà tíí fawọ kaninkanin jókòó.
Olóògùn-un dànìdànì lápò.

He who spits out fire in his mouth and eyes;
    He who dangles a touch of fire while dancing,
    He who also dangles a touch of fire while walking leisurely;
    One who sets himself ablaze like fire in the hearth.
    It is mere smoke that we ignite in this world,
    Real fire abides with my lord in heaven.
    Swiftly spread like a glowing fire.
    The tough fire that burns in the river.
    I cannot explain what his seat is made of,
    It looks like a combination of the coral beads and the blue tubular
beads;
    It is equally sharp and deadly;
    The mighty deity whose seat is made of fly-Skin.
    One who has dangerous charms in his pouch.

The representation of the behavior of Ṣàngó in his *oríkì* goes beyond his magical power, to include his irrational and violent nature, his toughness, his restlessness, and his unpredictability. The way this aspect of Ṣàngó's nature has been presented in his *oríkì* makes him look more like a tyrant than a culture-hero. Indeed, *Ṣàngó pípè* aims at projecting Ṣàngó as an extraordinary superhuman; and this the poets achieve mainly through their artistic use of language. To enhance the superhuman nature of Ṣàngó, the poets sometimes present him as a controversial deity. An enigma of some sort is thus brought to the fore; and the audience becomes unsure as to whether the results of the actions attributed to him are beneficial or rather detrimental. The excerpt below helps to clarify the point I am making:

A-bọ́-lumọ-bí owú.
    Fàìbá wọn jà kọni lóminú.
A-kòbọ́-kòbọ́ọ̀-jà.
A-yánni-lọ́wọ́-bí-omi-gbígbóná;
A-múrin-jẹ-lójú-onírin;
Ò-bùrìn-jẹnu-òbẹ-yàngì.
Akọ-àparò-tíí-ké-tìjàtìjà.
Kò mọ onílé, bẹ́ẹ ni kò mọ àlejò.
Òkun ò ṣeé kojúùjà sí.

Baálèè mi, ta ló lè ko Ṣàngó lójú?
Èmi ò níí kò ọ́ lójú,
Agbadagbúdù odò tíí gbónígèrè tẹjatẹja.
A-lémọ̀-rẹrẹ-bí eégún;
A-gbọ́mọ-lójú-yọkun-nímú;
A-bínú-falágbèdè-bọ̀gún;
A-bínú-bàràbà-wó, ọbaa Kòso.
A-bínú-fàrókò-tu
A-bínú-tọmọ-owú-fọ́.
Kò mọraa rẹ̀ nígbà ìbínú bá dé.
A-pa-wọ́n-jẹ-bí-ẹranko;
Òfìkì-damọ-nù-tẹrùtẹrù.
Bínú bá ti bí Ṣàngó, ọbaa Kòso,
A sú kanlẹ̀ sú kànrun.
Mọ̀nàmọ́ná sojú ọ̀run yẹrìyẹrì.
Èlùbọ́ ẹ̀ ló dànù tó fi pẹgbèje èèyàn.

One-who-falls-on-a-child-as-the-blacksmith's-hammer.
    One-who-nurses-no-grudge with them and still instills fears.
    One whose fight is deadly.
    One-who-burns-like-boiling-water;
    One-who-destroys-metal-in-the-presence-of-its-owner;
    He-also-devastates-the-knife-violently-as-he-walks.
    The-male-bush-fowl-that-cries-belligerently.
    He cares for neither residents nor visitors.
    The ocean that cannot be confronted.
    My lord, who can confront Ṣàngó?
    I will not confront you,
    Mighty river that sweeps off the fisherman and his catch.
    He-who-pursues-a-child-like-the masqueraders;
    He-who-slaps-child's-face-as-to-force-out-mucus;
    He-who-in-rage-sacrifices-the-blacksmith-to-the-deity-Ògún;
    The king at Kòso, who falls the white silk cotton tree out of annoyance.
    He also uprooted the African teak in annoyance
    He-who-in-rage-destroys-the-blacksmith's-hammer-by-stepping-on-it.
    He has no control over his annoyance.
    He devours people like ordinary animals;
    The river whose wave is enough to sink a canoe.
    Whenever Ṣàngó, the king of Kòso, is annoyed,

He makes the cloud to cover the sky.
Accompanied with constant lightning.
He ended up killing fourteen hundred people
Just because his yam flour trickled away.

Ṣàngó is presented in the above excerpt as a tactless and highly impatient person. For instance, his irrational behavior is presented figuratively in his decision to kill as many as fourteen hundred people because of his yam flour that had poured away. His violent attitude is also encapsulated in the analogy of the mighty river that sweeps off the fisherman and his catch and the shout of the male bush-fowl. Furthermore, the fact that Ṣàngó is highly impatient is reflected in the description that "he has no control over his annoyance." However, despite the poets' frightening presentation of Ṣàngó, the implication that the deity is at the same time magnetically attractive to his devotees is reflected in other sections of the same corpus of the *oríkì*, where the devotees are pleading for Ṣàngó's protection:

Ṣàngó, bóo bá doyin, mọ́ ta mi.
Bóo bá dàlàpà, má yà lù mí.
Bóo bá dodò, mọ́mọ̀ gbé mi lọ.
Má fọrẹ́ àbo nà mí,
Má fọrẹ́ àbo namọọ̀ mi.
Ṣàngó, dákun má fi jìnnì-jìnnì kàn mí;
Má gbá mi létí àgbámógiri.
Ṣàngó, dákun má pa mí nípa o pa
  Kúmọ́lá Olúogbó;
Ṣàngó, dákun má pa mí nípa o p'Àṣàbí
  Olúmọ̀gùn.
Má fàgbàná runwóo tìyáà mi.
A-sọkùnrin-dàbí-ìyàwó.

Ṣàngó, when you turn into a bee, please do not sting me.
Whenever you become a dilapidated building, please do not fall on me.
When you become a river, please do not drown me.
Do not chastise me,
Do not chastise my child.
Ṣàngó, please do not frighten me;
Do not strike me with your lightning.
Ṣàngó, please do not kill me as you have killed
  Kúmọ́lá Olúogbó;

Ṣàngó, please do not kill me as you have killed
   Àṣàbí Olúmọ̀gùn.
Do not hypnotize my mother to squander her Money.
He who though man but looks like a bride.

Can one be secure in a relationship with such a deity then? Will it not be more difficult to approach him since one can never be too sure when one will incur his annoyance? The violent character and the unpredictability of Ṣàngó should not be taken to mean wickedness at all. Rather, it is a conscious attempt to lift the deity onto a realm where he will be different from mere mortals. He is presented as a deity that is so strong and powerful that no one can share in his privileges. It is a calculated attempt to make his superhuman nature more complex. Ṣàngó thus becomes all the more extraordinary when his actions remain unpredictable.

If we relate the picture of Ṣàngó painted in the above excerpt to Johnson's historical account mentioned earlier, one may be tempted to ascribe the violent aspect of the *oríkì* to the Aláàfin who, Johnson claimed, had the habit of emitting fire and smoke out of his mouth. That same Aláàfin was also said to have mistakenly burned down his palace while testing his newly acquired charm that could attract lightning and fire. But what the *odù ifá* corpus records on the source of Ṣàngó's metaphysical power and his knowledge of herbal medicine invalidates that line of thinking, since the mythical Ṣàngó himself was equally violent and knowledgeable in herbal medicine. For instance, the *Odù ifá Òyèkú Méjì* claims that before the divinities that created the planetary earth left Òde Ìsálórun for Òde Ìsálayé, they consulted Ifá oracle individually to know what the journey had in stock for them. When divination was made for Ṣàngó, Ifá instructed that he should offer sacrifice of pieces of dilapidated mud-wall, a sheep, and two thousand cowries, to prevent death. Ṣàngó complied, and in return, Òrúnmìlà gave him some quantity of mud powder already empowered metaphysically to rub on his entire body. The *odù* concludes that, after that, Ṣàngó started to spit smoke from his mouth.

   Kí a ká wọn rígídí,
     Kí a fibọn tì wọn,
     A dífá fún Ayílégbèé-ọ̀run (Ṣàngó)—
     Tí yóò fi àlàpà ṣégun ọ̀tá è;
     Nígbà tí Ṣàngó ń bẹ láàrin ọ̀tá;
     Nígbà tí òsììrì ọ̀tá kojú sí i.
     Òrúnmìlà ní bí ikú bá ń sa egbé rè pa,
     Òtò ni Òyèkú yóò máa yẹ ẹ sí.

Bí àrùn bá ń ṣẹgbéẹ rẹ̀,
Ọ̀tọ̀ ni Ọ̀yẹ̀kú yóò máa yẹ ẹ́ sí.
Gbogbo àlàwẹ́ obi ni ikú ń pa,
Ọ̀tọ̀ ni Ọ̀yẹ̀kú yẹ oófúà obì sí.
Ifá ní pé Ọ̀yẹ̀kú, ikú yẹ̀ lórí rẹ̀

Fold them firmly,
 And put a gun by their side,
 Divination was made for Ayílẹ́gbẹ̀ẹ́-ọ̀run (Ṣàngó)—
 Who will defeat his enemies with dilapidated mud-wall;
 When Ṣàngó was surrounded by enemies;
 When several enemies confronted him.
 Ọ̀rúnmìlà assured him that even when his mates are being killed.
 Ọ̀yẹ̀kú will keep him safe from death.
 When his mates are being inflicted by infirmity,
 Ọ̀yẹ̀kú will keep him safe from illness.
 There is no segment of kola nut that cannot be killed,
 Except the *oófúà* which Ọ̀yẹ̀kú will keep him safe from death.
 Ifá says that with Ọ̀yẹ̀kú, you will not die.

Although Ṣàngó was very popular among his contemporaries, *Odù Ifá Ọ̀kànràn Méjì* recalls that he was still looking for extra sources of supernatural power in order to be more famous. Therefore, he decided to consult Ifá, once again, for assistance:

Oríkì olóríkì kì í gbasán;
 Bí wọn ti ń pariwo rẹ̀ nílé,
 Bẹ́ẹ̀ ni wọn ń pariwo rẹ̀ lógun;
 A dífá fún Òbìlàjà Ṣàngó,
 Tó ní òun kò ní òkìkí.
 Ó ní ṣé òun lè níyì?
 Ọ̀rúnmìlà ní ó lè níyì,
 Bí ó bá tójú òrúkọ méjì
 Pẹ̀lú ìsaasùn tuntun ;
 Tí ó sì tójú ewé Ifá.

You don't acclaim another person's *oríkì* in vain;
 Just as they acclaim him at home,
 They also acclaim him in war;
 Divination was made for Òbìlàjà Ṣàngó,
 Who was complaining of not having enough fame.

He wanted to know if he could be famous?
Ọ̀rúnmìlà said that he could be famous,
If only he can provide two he-goats
With a new clay pot;
And some Ifá herbs.

Ṣàngó provided the ritual elements prescribed by Ọ̀rúnmìlà, and he was given a specially prepared meal to eat, after which he started to spit out smoke and fire from his mouth. Ṣàngó's ability to emit smoke and fire out of his mouth simultaneously increased his fame greatly, a fact attested to in this excerpt of his *oríkì:*

Ẹni à á fibòòsí ṣe lálejò bọ́rún bá dé;
    Ìwọ lo mẹ̀dàá ibòòsí wáyé;
    N ó kébòòsíì rẹ.
    Dájọ́-kunlé, ọmọọ Yemọja.
    Bó bá ti dé nìlúú hó ṣọ́ ṣọ́ ṣọ́,
    Ariwo rọ̀rọ̀ níjọ́ a gbéyàwó;
    Ariwo ní mọsàn ní mòro.
    A-wọ̀lú-tìlù-tariwo;
    A-dé-kógun-ó-ró;
    Ọ̀wàrà-òjò-tí-sú-pẹgbèje-èèyàn.

One who is dignified with thunderous praises every four days;
    That is because you love to be proclaimed;
    And I will proclaim you.
    He who pre-announces the setting of a house on fire, child of Yemọja.
    His arrival in the city is announced with uproar,
    The wailing cries that follow the wedding (the striking of the thunder);
    One who causes wailing cries all over the city.
    One whose arrival in the city is accompanied with blast;
    One whose arrival sends warriors packing;
    The mighty rain that can soak thirteen hundred people.

From the foregoing, therefore, it will not be entirely correct to associate the fame of Ṣàngó and the source of his metaphysical power solely with the fourth Aláàfin of Ọ̀yọ́, as Johnson and Ògúndèjì would want us to believe, but with the mythical Ṣàngó himself. The various verses of *odù ifá* and excerpts of Ṣàngó's *oríkì* already cited have shown the possibility of Ṣàngó existing at Ilé-Ifẹ̀ long before the founding of Old Ọ̀yọ́.

Ògún Lákáayé (the god of iron) and Ṣàngó (the god of thunder), the role of Èṣù (the trickster god or god of fate) in fanning the embers of that conflict, and the mediating role of Òrúnmìlà. Ọya is Ògún's wife, but Ṣàngó (played by Tunji Ojeyemi) snatches Ọya away (a part iconized by Abiola Paimo). Ògún (iconized by Lérè Pàímọ́ himself) is worried, and Èṣù (played by Hammed Oduola, aka Deinto) reveals to Ògún that Ọya is in Ṣàngó's home and that Ṣàngó is boasting that Ògún cannot do anything about it. This report infuriates Ògún, and it leads to a great clash between Ògún and Ṣàngó in the open field. Òrúnmìlà then has to intervene by asking the combatants to go to the gateway to heaven and propitiate. Ṣàngó, a resilient character, is able to perform the sacrifice, while Ògún fails. Thematically, love, which seems minor in Wálé Ògúnyẹ mí's production, is accentuated in *Lákáayé*. In fact, it precipitates the conflict between Ṣàngó and Ògún. In this film, Ṣàngó is portrayed as a wife snatcher and a promiscuous man. Just like Wálé Ògúnyẹmí, Lérè Pàímọ́ presents to us an energetic Ṣàngó who is "the epitome of masculine beauty and a male of gargantuan appetites, both gastronomical and sexual."[30] Aside from exhibition of quick tempers, promiscuity, and abuse of charisma, Pàímọ́'s Ṣàngó is a great dancer. It is at one of his dancing sessions that he sights Ọya as a good dancer; and there and then he becomes entranced by her dancing steps. Ṣàngó is also iconized as a cocky and proud god who ceaselessly boasts about his primeval power when he is confronted in the open field by Ògún:

> *Ògún: Àyánrán-iná?*
>   *O gbà mí lóbìnin!*
> *Ṣàngó: Èmi ni mo lẹtù*
>   *Èmi ni mo lọta*
>   *Èmi ni mo ni iná*
>   *Lóòótọ́, ìwọ lo làdá*
>   *Táwa Irúnmọlẹ̀ fi wá sáyé*
>   *Ìwọ lo làdá*
>   *Ìwọ lo nìbọn*
>   *O gbàgbé? Mo jù ọ́ lọ.*

> Ògún: Àyánrán-iná?
>   You snatch my wife!
> Ṣàngó: I own the firearms
>   I own the bullets
>   I own the fire
>   Though you own the cutlass

Although it is also possible that an Aláàfin who was a strong adherent of Ṣàngó followed the footsteps of the deity by acquiring charms that also made him emit fire and smoke out of his mouth during his reign.

What then is the relationship between Ṣàngó and the fourth Aláàfin of Ọ̀yọ́? When, how, and why did Ṣàngó move out of Ifẹ̀ Oòdáyé to Ọ̀yọ́? How did the Aláàfin become an adherent of Ṣàngó? Why is it so difficult to separate the story of the deification of Ṣàngó from that of the death of the fourth Aláàfin of Ọ̀yọ́? I intend to rely on another verse of *Odù ifá Ogbètúrá* to provide answers to these questions:

> *Igi ńlá níí dúró nínú igbó;*
> *A nàgò fànfà sílẹ̀ nítorí ifànfà ojúgun;*
> *A díá fún Jẹ̀gbẹ̀;*
> *Tí ń lọ oko ọdẹ*

The mighty tree that stands straight in the Forest;
   Which has a protruding root that people must watch out for because of their shin;
   They made divination for Jẹ̀gbẹ̀;
   Who is going on a hunting expedition.

The story recalls how a prince of Ilé-Ifẹ̀ moved out of his father's domain to found a new city at Ọ̀yọ́-Ilé (Old Ọ̀yọ́), and how the prince took with him symbols of Ṣàngó, his guiding deity on his departure. According to the story, the rite of passage into adulthood in Ilé-Ifẹ̀ of old demanded that the king, Odùduwà, must give necessary tools to every prince or princess to establish a trade or chosen profession. Jẹ̀gbẹ̀, one of the princes, wanted to be a hunter; therefore, his father gave him guns and gunpowder. Unfortunately, Jẹ̀gbẹ̀ experienced some difficulties in his numerous hunting expeditions, and his father lost faith in his ability to excel in his chosen profession. Out of confusion and frustration, Jẹ̀gbẹ̀ consulted Ifá oracle for guidance, and he was instructed to make a sacrifice of burnt offering in the heart of the forest, which he did. Incidentally, the smoke of his burnt offering attracted the attention of a group of kings and warlords who had gone to war but were lost in the forest with their spoils of war. They eventually traced their way to where Jẹ̀gbẹ̀ was and requested his assistance. Jẹ̀gbẹ̀ led the people to the city and reported the incident to his father. The king, who could not easily believe the story of Jẹ̀gbẹ̀, asked him to lead the people to wherever he wanted and be their king. But before sending Jẹ̀gbẹ̀ out of Ilé-Ifẹ̀, the story concludes, the king gave the thunderbolt, the symbol of Ṣàngó, to Jẹ̀gbẹ̀ as representative of his guiding deity. Jẹ̀gbẹ̀ thereafter led the people to establish the city that later became Ọ̀yọ́-Ilé (Old Ọ̀yọ́).

This Ifá story is similar to the most popular oral tradition of the origin of Old Ọ̀yọ́, which associates it with a warlord, Ọ̀rányàn, who was believed to be either the son or the grandson of Odùduwà, the hero-progenitor of the Yorùbá people. That tradition states that Ọ̀yọ́, like every other Yorùbá town, came into being as a result of the legendary dispersal of people from Ilé-Ifẹ̀. To fully establish the Aláàfin dynasty in and around Ọ̀yọ́-Ilé, Ọ̀rányàn fought and conquered various neighboring communities. Oral tradition also states that Ọ̀rányàn, as the first king in Ọ̀yọ́, fully integrated the worship of Ṣàngó into his new government and made it the state religion, with himself being the chief celebrant and Ṣàngó incarnate. Even in present day Ọ̀yọ́, the relevance of Ṣàngó to the success of the Aláàfin's administration cannot be overlooked. Apart from the Aláàfin's daily worship of Ṣàngó, he also visits the shrine of the deity during the annual Ṣàngó festival to pay homage. There, the Aláàfin "prostrates before the god Ṣàngó and before those possessed with the deity, calling them father."[27] The importance of the deity in the sociopolitical setup of Ọ̀yọ́ necessitates that the Aláàfin keep priestesses and priests of Ṣàngó in his palace even till today.

During installation, it is also mandatory for a new Aláàfin to visit the shrine of Ṣàngó that is located at Kòso quarters for official crowning. At Kòso, the *ọ̀tún ẹ̀fà*, the *baálẹ̀* (chief) of Kòso, the *ọmọ-ní-nárìs*, and the *ìṣọ̀nàs* would attend to the new king. There, the *ìyákere* would place the great crown on the head of the new Aláàfin, while the *ọ̀tún ẹ̀fà* would put the royal robes and *ẹjigba* beads on him. Babayemi gives a precise account of what happened during the coronation of the incumbent Aláàfin in 1971:

> One saw in the new Aláàfin a changed person after he stood at the *Èṣù* mound before he entered the *Kòso* shrine. He was blindfolded and led to where he sat until his face was ritually washed. He was then asked to face the objects of *Ṣàngó*. Before the ceremony, a statue of the new Aláàfin was carved by the royal carvers. The black dress the Aláàfin wore to the shrine, his cap, his upper garment (*agbádá*), and his sandals were removed and put on the statue. The Aláàfin was then dressed in white *sányán*, white beaded sandals, white beads and a white crown. By the time the Aláàfin was being dressed everybody avoided his direct gaze. By design, the fringes of the crown veiled his face. He was then led to the waiting crowd who burst into thunderous *Kábíyèsí* at his appearance.[28]

Thus, the wearing of the beaded crown by the new Aláàfin at the Kòso shrine of Ṣàngó, which emphasized the eternal divinity of the new king, may be said to have depersonalized him in human terms. For instance, it is believed in the society that the Aláàfin assumed the power and magic of Ṣàngó by wearing the crown of the turbulent deity at Kòso. In other words, the Kòso ritual was expected to transfer to the new Aláàfin the supernatural and superhuman power of the deity Ṣàngó. This fact comes out clearly in Babayemi's accounts when the Aláàfin transferred what was temporal in him—his dress—to the statue, to put on what was regarded as an eternal "garment"—the crown—that belongs to Ṣàngó. This procedure is what Thompson describes as "a synthesis of the world of the dead and the world of the living [depicting . . .] the king as a living ancestor."[29] Consequently, Ṣàngó, the Aláàfin in heaven, and the new Aláàfin on earth are now one. The new Aláàfin is believed to assume the power and magic of the turbulent deity, which he derives from the wearing of the crown.

This view is meant to enhance the command of the king, his power of authority, and his royal majesty. This explains why contemporary Ọ̀yọ́ royal bards would acclaim the incumbent Aláàfin as *ọmọ Ṣàngó* (offspring of Ṣàngó) and adopt for him *aròjò-múná-lọ́wọ́* (One-whose-rain-is-accompanied-by-fire), one of the attributes and praise names of Ṣàngó. The association originates from the choice of Ṣàngó as the state religion of Ọ̀yọ́ and the guiding deity of the Aláàfin, evidently shown in the elaborate religious rituals surrounding the installation of a new Aláàfin. If it is true that the first Aláàfin had the symbol of Ṣàngó with him at the foundation of Ọ̀yọ́, then it will be difficult to accept the theory of Johnson and Hethersett associating the origin of the deity to the fourth Aláàfin of Ọ̀yọ́.

This chapter has reviewed the multidimensional representation of Ṣàngó in Yorùbá literature with a view of reconstructing the history of the deity. In the course of this study, I have discussed the two levels at which previous scholars have explained the origins of Ṣàngó: the supernatural and the human. But this work has shown that the two types of traditions—mythological and historical—can be collapsed into one. While the supernatural aspect of Ṣàngó brings protection, peace, and prosperity to his devotees, his human nature authenticates and legitimizes the authority of every Aláàfin who has to adopt Ṣàngó as his patron deity. As a result, every Aláàfin incarnates Ṣàngó on accession to the throne, and when dead, he is deified and he becomes Ṣàngó. This practice has no doubt brought about the proliferation of Ṣàngó worship in Yorùbá society, most especially in Ọ̀yọ́ town, where we have "different

Ṣàngós" named after different Aláàfin. For instance, we have Ṣàngó Àtìbà and Ṣàngó Aganjú, both named after two of the past Aláàfin of Ọ̀yọ́. We also have Ṣàngó Àfọ̀njá, named after the chief of army staff of Aláàfin Olúewu; and Ṣàngó Tìmì, named after one of the warlords of Aláàfin Kọ̀rí, who was later enthroned as a king at Ẹdẹ. The creation of literary works around the personality of Ṣàngó has further complicated the ambivalent representations of the deity rather than helped in resolving it.

By Ọ̀yọ́ tradition, every Aláàfin must be deified at death. However, because at one time Aláàfin was committed to Ṣàngó to the extent that he adopted Ṣàngó's names and attributes, his deification tends to be generally confused with the mythical Ṣàngó. Unfortunately, it is the story of the historical Ṣàngó that creative writers have adopted as the basis for their literary depiction of Ṣàngó. With the exception of Lérè Pàímọ̀, who focused on mythical Ṣàngó in his movie, other literary works are based on the story of the historical Ṣàngó as presented by either Johnson or Hethersett. Although writers occasionally superimpose some aspects of the nature of the mythical Ṣàngó on their literary creation of historical Ṣàngó, neither the literary nor the historical representation of Ṣàngó must be confused with the mythical Ṣàngó, which we have shown in this chapter to have been in existence before the establishment of the institution of the Aláàfinate at Ọ̀yọ́.

NOTES

1. Philip A. Ogundeji, "The Image of Ṣàngo in Duro Ladipọ's Plays," *Research in African Literatures* 29, no. 2 (Summer 1998): 57–75.

2. Leo Frobenius, *The Voice of Africa*, vol. 1 (London: Hutchinson, 1913).

3. Bolaji Idowu, *Olódùmarè: God in Yorùbá Belief* (London: Longman, 1962).

4. Samuel Johnson, *The History of the Yorùbás* (Lagos: C.S.S. Bookshops, 1921; reprint, 1960), 149.

5. A. L. Hethersett, "Ìtàn Ṣàngó," in *Ìwé Kíkà Ẹ̀kẹrin Lí Èdè Yorùbá*, ed. A. L. Hethersett (Lagos: CMS, 1941), 50–56.

6. Johnson, *History of the Yorùbás*, 54–57.

7. Samuel Babayemi, "The Fall and Rise of Ọ̀yọ́ c. 1760–1905" (Ph.D. diss., University of Birmingham, 1979), 178–79.

8. C. Laogun Adeoye, *Àṣà àti Ìṣe Yorùbá* (Oxford: Oxford University Press, 1979), 324–25.

9. Johnson, *History of the Yorùbás*, 69–77.

10. Ibid., 170–72.

11. Adeoye, *Àṣà àti Ìṣe Yorùbá*, 342–45.

12. Akinwumi Isola, "Religious Politics and the Myth of Ṣango," in *African Traditional Religion in Contemporary Society,* ed. Jacob K. Olupona (New York: Paragon, 1991), 93–99.

13. Johnson, *History of the Yorùbás,* 156–58.

14. Isola, "Religious Politics," 95.

15. C. Laogun Adeoye, *Ìgbàgbọ́ àti Ẹ̀sìn Yorùbá* (Ibadan, Nigeria: Evans Brothers, 1985), 287–88.

16. Ogundeji, "The Image of Ṣàngó," 63–4.

17. Ibid., 64.

18. Oludare Olajubu, "The Sources of Duro Ladipo's *Ọba Kò So*," *Research in African Literature* 9, no. 3 (1978): 350–51.

19. Karin Barber, "How Man Makes God in West Africa: Yorùbá Attitudes towards the Òrìsà," *Africa* 51, no. 3 (1981): 735.

20. Isola, "Religious Politics," 95.

21. Karin Barber, "Yorùbá *Oríkì* and Deconstructive Criticism," *Research in African Literature* 15, no. 4 (1984): 503–505.

22. Adeboye Babalola, *The Content and Form of Yorùbá Ìjálá* (London: Oxford University Press, 1966), 24.

23. Karin Barber, "Oríkì in Òkukù: Relationships between Verbal and Social Structures" (Ph.D. diss., University of Ifẹ̀, 1979), 351.

24. David O. Ogungbile, "Ẹẹ̀rìndínlógún: The Seeing Eyes of Sacred Shells and Stones," in *Òsun across the Waters: A Yorùbá Goddess in Africa and the Americas,* ed. Joseph M. Murphy and Mei-Mei Sanford (Bloomington: Indiana University Press, 1998), 191–93.

25. Wande Abimbola, "The Bag of Wisdom: Òṣun and the Origins of the Ifá Divination," in *Òsun across the Waters: A Yorùbá Goddess in Africa and the Americas,* ed. Joseph M. Murphy and Mei-Mei Sanford (Bloomington: Indiana University Press, 1998), 142.

26. Adeoye, *Ìgbàgbọ́ àti Ẹ̀sìn Yorùbá,* 287.

27. Johnson, *History of the Yorùbás,* 65.

28. Babayemi, "The Fall and Rise," 179.

29. R. F. Thompson, "The Sign of the Divine King: An Essay on Yorùbá Beaded-Embroidered Crowns with Veil and Bird Decorations," *African Arts* 113 (1970): 10.

PART THREE

Ṣàngó in the African Diaspora

CHAPTER TEN

The Cultural Aesthetics of Ṣàngó Africanization

KAMARI MAXINE CLARKE

This chapter outlines a theory of contemporary religious revivalism that makes explicit the relevance of globalization in the resurgence of African religious occult movements outside Africa. I demonstrate that what we are witnessing are shifting conceptualizations of national belonging through which new forms of legitimacy of Yorùbá belonging are conceptually possible through a de-territorialized notion of spiritual linkage. To understand the particularities of change in Yorùbá òrìṣà revivalism in this regard, and to make sense of these growing forms of de-territorialized and denationalized institutions of knowledge developing in the West, this chapter explores how meanings of ritual iconography reflect historically constituted ways that people see linkages and reflect the order of particular modernities of late capitalism, in which the globalization of òrìṣà practices is leading to increased social autonomy by which new interpretations and ritual practices are becoming widely institutionalized. In this regard, this chapter is about the making of a new authorial imaginary of personhood within particular fields of historical power. By charting the uses of divination in the globalization of an òrìṣà economy and the contestations over the representation of Ṣàngó and that òrìṣà's various divinatory interpretations, I demonstrate how the black Atlantic world is providing alternate models of òrìṣà translations, formations, representations, and meanings. These highlight the nodes, assemblages, and range of domains from which formations about Yorùbá òrìṣà imagery have taken shape.

One of the primary locations for this inquiry, Òyótúnjí Village, is neither a local West African village, a neighborhood of a larger community, nor a homogenized population that can be reduced to a single location. It represents a regionally diverse transnational network of people and practices within and outside the nation. Indeed, Ọ̀yọ́túnjí is a small rural community that the sociological literature often refers to as an "intentional community," describing an intended creation of a separate domestic arena. However, it is as much ideological as it is geographic. It is a reconstructed Yorùbá village in the rural region of Beaufort, South Carolina, that operates within a de-territorialized network of Yorùbá occult revivalists throughout the United States who are committed to the re-Africanization of Yorùbá traditional practices that were transformed by enslaved Africans transported to the Americas during the transatlantic slave trade.[1]

The Yorùbá people of southwestern Nigeria were popularly classified as an ethnic group by twentieth-century sociologists and anthropologists. Described as having established their roots in West Africa, where they developed deeply complex òrìṣà veneration and communication practices between God, known as Olódùmarè, and humans, Africanist scholars continue to highlight West Africa as the "originary" home of the Yorùbá people. Yet, though òrìṣà practices were historically entrenched in the former Ọ̀yọ́ Empire and with the language became standardized in the making of the modern Nigerian state, major changes in the spread and reformulation of òrìṣà practices have taken place over the past centuries. With the history of the Yorùbá kingdom and the encroachment of the Ọ̀yọ́ Empire onto other West African regions as well as the dispersal of enslaved captives across the Atlantic throughout the sixteenth to nineteenth centuries, groupings of Lukumi/Yorùbá and Bantu speakers inside and outside the African continent contributed to the standardization and spread of varieties of Yorùbá òrìṣà practices.

As African religions moved with the spread of African captives into transatlantic slavery, there developed a repressive sphere of plantation slavery that led to the transformation of òrìṣà ritual practices in the Americas. These vast numbers of practitioners, who trace their lineage to predecessors in West and Central Africa, were transported as captives to the Caribbean and North and South America, where they participated in the transformation of ritual and religious practices that have endured over centuries. These changes have led to the reconfiguration of òrìṣà ritual practices, including the reconfiguration of ways that the òrìṣà were represented. In Brazil, the spaces of interpretive production led to the development of a variation that became Candomblé; in Cuba, it became Santería; in Trinidad and Tobago it became Ṣàngó; and in the United States, among black American cultural nationalists interested in

Africanizing òrìṣà practices, it became òrìṣà-voodoo or a return to the Yorùbá òrìṣà. These variations reflect the encounter between the West and the non-West in the making of the modern world;[2] and increasing numbers of these òrìṣà adherents are contributing to the growth of multiple networks of òrìṣà knowledge outside of the African continent.

The late twentieth- and twenty-first-century proliferation of groups of òrìṣà practitioners outside of West Africa continues to be expansive, ranging in the millions of adherents of òrìṣà-voodoo, Santería, and Candomblé religious practices. And today, practitioners in the Caribbean and South America are increasingly in conversation with practitioners from the West. Now, more than ever, vast numbers of Americans in the United States are reclaiming or converting to Yorùbá religious practices and playing central roles in reshaping how òrìṣà traditions are to be practiced.

The widening constituencies of changing Yorùbá òrìṣà practitioners, though not mutually exclusive, can be classified in four significant groups. The first are the òrìṣà practitioners, principally in Nigeria and Benin as well as various surrounding West African countries; they tend not to be educated in the West, have limited financial resources, and claim òrìṣà worship as their religious faith. The second are Òrìṣà/Santería/Lukumi practitioners in the Americas, who constitute the largest group of religious worshippers and in varying degrees tend to accept the hybridization of òrìṣà practices. Practitioners in this group span regions throughout Cuba, Haiti, Trinidad, Puerto Rico, Brazil, and the United States. The third are òrìṣà worshippers and Yorùbá or òrìṣà revivalists, who are part of a relatively new (post-1960s) òrìṣà economy of practitioners who are interested in the return to a more orthodox traditional practice. This return sometimes includes the purging of whiteness, but, more fundamentally, it is manifest through the reconfiguration of changes to the religion that were important because of the criminalization of the religion during conditions of enslavement. The fourth, òrìṣà modernists, are a relatively new (post-1980s) group of initiates, led by predominantly white American and European practitioners, who are part of a growing movement interested in the transcendence of racial membership through the emphasis of ancestral lineage. These four groups constitute multiple networks of òrìṣà practitioners that have produced òrìṣà institutional practices throughout the Americas and reflect, to a greater or lesser extent, the African origins of òrìṣà practices. Nevertheless, these relations are neither equal in impact, influence, and prestige, nor evenly distributed. Though the roots of Yorùbá traditions are seen as emerging from West Africa, Nigerian òrìṣà practitioners are, in comparison, few in number. As interest in the practice and acquisition of lifelong

apprenticeships declines, New World practitioners' de-territorial participation in òrìṣà rituals, the emergent group of Western practitioners, continues to outnumber those self-professed traditionalists in various West
African regions. The disproportionality of claims to ongoing òrìṣà practices reflects the prominence of the globalization of Yorùbá religion and
the de-territorialization of òrìṣà practices in the West. And these numbers
are growing as a result of the electronic circulation of divinatory knowledge, in which new technologies are leading to the transmission of a
plethora of interpretations and representations.

As Ọlabiyi Yai has argued, in an attempt to describe how local practices are becoming increasingly transnational, the "òrìṣà tradition has its
foot in Africa and its head in the Americas."[3] The same Yorùbá practitioners who hold the symbolic roots of Yorùbá practices are becoming
marginal to the production of new standards of practice in the global
age. This has led to particular asymmetries in which West African òrìṣà
practitioners, who have limited access to electronic technology and forms
of mobility, are having declining significance in their social worlds, which
are increasingly dominated by the popularity of Christian Pentecostalism
and Islamic brotherhoods. This is unlike earlier periods in the 1960s and
'70s, when West African òrìṣà traditionalists dominated the production
of Africanized interpretations of divinatory meanings, in which numbers
of Nigerian Yorùbá were successful in procuring clients from the Americas and extolling the symbolic capital of the origins of òrìṣà worship.
Today, West African òrìṣà practitioners are becoming increasingly limited
in their ability to directly influence the revitalization and interpretation
of òrìṣà divinatory practices in the Americas.

This chapter, then, is an attempt to explore one interpretive practice,
known as divination, which operates within particular Yorùbá cosmol-
ogies and forms of logic. I explore how new knowledge technologies
are building on old ideological divisions in worship and producing new
spaces for the development of òrìṣà expansion. Through divinatory production and the invention and reinvention of the verses of the divinatory corpus, òrìṣà practices are becoming increasingly autonomous from
West Africa and becoming re-inscribed into new nodes of knowledge.
By focusing on the recent revival of African occult practices and heritage
identities in the West, I demonstrate that these forms of spiritual awak-
enings produce linkages that are relying less on physical birthplace as
the domain of interpretive authority and more on ancestry as a form of
spiritual authority. And though race in such occult imaginaries continues to be a metaphor for expressions of Africanness, it becomes manifest
only through alternate spatial and temporal articulations of descent that

foreground the centrality of ancestry in the development of what Jean and John Comaroff refer to as an "occult economy."[4]

By exploring how the globalization of divinatory ritual is leading to disparate authoritative domains in which new representations are taking shape, I focus on one *òrìṣà*, that is Ṣàngó, as a metaphor for the transformation of Yorùbá-Lucumí practices. I will explore the ways that divinatory ritual established in three contexts—one in West Africa, one among one strand of Santería practitioners, and one among black religious nationalists—produces varying interpretations and representations of the *òrìṣà* Ṣàngó. As I will demonstrate, variation in what constitutes the terms of meaning linked with different historical particularities around the production of religious belonging shapes different rules that govern how we understand the iconic meaning of Ṣàngó masculinity and racial politics. For, unlike earlier periods, in which *òrìṣà* practices were imported from the former Ọ̀yọ́ Empire (which fell in the 1830s with the encroachment of British colonial governance, which in 1914 would become modern Nigeria), the forms of religious resurgence that we are seeing today are fundamentally connected to a new heritage-based economy in which the globalization of religious practices is leading to new domains of interpretive power. Such uses of particular *òrìṣà* mythologies in transnational domains highlight the inter-relationship between religious revivalism, innovative technologies of knowledge and transmission, and new occult economies.

Information Networks and Transnational Linkages

In 2002 a keyword search on the Internet using "*òrìṣà* practitioners," "Santería," "Yorùbá," and "divination" yielded over seven thousand web sites. Such a vast index reflects the range of transnational *òrìṣà* institutions that could be called upon for obtaining online divinatory readings, information about the history and culture of Yorùbá practices, and adaptations of *òrìṣà* rituals by Africans in the Americas. They provide organizational missions and divinatory services, packages of divinatory knowledge, forms of redemption, and individual and community empowerment through which iconic representations and meanings of membership are shaped. Practitioners in these religious networks limit themselves to neither one school or affiliation nor one territory of influence. Instead, these various packages of knowledge operate within an "occult economy." In the context of the globalization of an *òrìṣà* occult economy, new variations of *òrìṣà* practices and meanings are being increasingly supported by more books, videos, and packages of ancestral validation produced for mass conversion and religious reproduction. As they engage in the consumption of òrìṣà practices, participants reformulate òrìṣà-based religious practices along racial imaginaries, where òrìṣà practices are being distinguished by crosscutting forms of social distinction such as lineage, race, and forms of aesthetic and ritual practice. Characteristic of the globalization of divinatory practices are the ways in which transnationally relevant events are invoked to make sense of modern problems. This, the modernity of the occult is a critical feature of contemporary religious revivalism. New divinatory mechanisms, such as "readings" of the year, readings conducted annually on January 1, are posted online by large numbers of òrìṣà organizations in the United States. Once posted over the Internet, they are available for public consumption and provide modern mechanisms for the circulation and rethinking of older versions of òrìṣà practices and representation.[5] The challenge, however, is that as centrally interpreted in locally demarcated spheres of power, the meanings vary from region to region, and alliances are shaped within particular historical nodes of influence. And because there are fundamental differences in how different groups represent various mythic, spiritual, and historical aspects of òrìṣà, divinatory representations and interpretations are sites of tremendous contestation over spiritual signs and their meanings. As a result, new forms of affiliation, knowledge networks, and membership categories are being transformed by varied categories of ancestry legitimated through ritual practices. And membership in varied religious networks is often understood in relation to packages of ancestral knowledge that crosscut national belonging.

Differences in Ṣàngó Interpretations

In West African contexts, historical depictions of Ṣàngó in ancient Yorùbáland often represent him as a heroic man who reigned in the late 1700s as the fourth Aláàfin of Òyó and was immortalized after his death. Mythic narratives describe his central prominence at the height of the Òyó Empire until lightening descended on his palace and destroyed it and his family. So horrified was he that, as a symbol of manliness, he hanged himself. The second narrative describes Ṣàngó with spiritual powers, in which he was magically inclined and able to breathe fire and smoke through his nostrils. However, according to the mythology, his wives were so quarrelsome, and he so angered by this, that one day he angrily mounted his horse and threatened them, and others who were embattled, with thunder, lightening, and destruction. Ultimately, both narratives reflect a description of Ṣàngó that highlight his historical leadership, virility, and

FIGURE 10.1. "Chango drawing." Public domain.

bravery. Although he was feared for his tyranny, after his deification the renditions of historical Ṣàngó represent him as revered for his bravery and fairness and his tremendous powers to "call lightning from heaven."[6] And thus, after his death, when thunder and lightning struck, people called out, *"Kábíyèsí!"* (as if to hail his majesty) in order to recognize his ongoing thunderous presence in their lives.

In Ọ̀yọ́ contexts, Ṣàngó is often presented as wearing a cotton red top with many cowry shells, charms and symbols of Ṣàngó, and carrying a double axe. The representations of *bàtá* drums, singing, and drumming are ways that devotees revere the deity. The nobility of the historical Ṣàngó as a symbol of the prestige of the Ọ̀yọ́ Empire is fundamentally embedded in the revitalizations of Ṣàngó imagery by black American revivalists making claims to the authenticity of Ṣàngó and Ṣàngó as the king of kings.

In contrast, however, Ṣàngó in Santería mythology, referred to as Chàngó, is popularly represented as a virile, stealthy, sexual, and promiscuous man with three wives: "Ọya, who is represented as having stolen Ṣàngó's secrets of magic; Ọchun, the river goddess represented as Ṣàngó's favorite; and Ọbà, who tried to win his love by making the ultimate sacrifice—offering her ear to him to eat." These mythic representations of Ṣàngó are coupled with the imagery of him as the God of thunder, lighting, and fire.

On Cuban plantations, the flow of ideas about civilization and purity, racial hierarchies, and legitimate ritual practices pushed underground the worship of Ṣàngó, and more generally, African-based religious practices. Alongside the criminalization of African religions was the crime of miscegenation, in which inter-mixing between whites and blacks was outlawed. This led to increasing regimentation of race relations and the introduction of various forms of Christianity in the iconic representation of òrìṣà practices. The word, "Santería," for example, was derived from the Spanish *santo*, or saint, and means the worship of saints—as in Catholic saints and in the history of the formation of Santería. Yoruba òrìṣàs, once outlawed on plantations in Cuba, led to the production of two stages in the development of òrìṣà transformation. The first stage, the establishment of the *regla de ocha*, occurred during the first generation of African slaves in Cuba, when the Spanish colonial government encouraged enslaved Africans to create mutual aid societies.[7] The second critical moment took place during the second and third generations of enslaved Africans, who adapted òrìṣà practices based on their social circumstances, producing new hybrid representations of òrìṣà icons in which Catholic symbols came to stand in for them in *Santería*, as a reflection of Afro-Cubanness.

In relation to Ọ̀yọ́-Ṣàngó's parallel, therefore, it is the Catholic icon Saint Barbara that became the point of departure for understanding the mythic power of Ṣàngó. The legend popularly represented and, of late, reproduced throughout the Internet describes Saint Barbara as the "extremely beautiful daughter of a wealthy heathen named Dioscorus, who lived near Nicomedia in Asia Minor." Because of her beauty, and fearful that she would marry and leave him, he jealously locked her in a tower to protect her from the outside world. Shortly before embarking on a journey, he commissioned a bathhouse to be built for her. During the building, Barbara heard of the teachings of Christ, and while her father was away she looked out upon the surrounding countryside and marveled at the growing things; the trees, the animals, and the people. She contemplated their beauty and decided that all these must be part of a master plan, and that the idols of wood and stone worshipped by her parents must be condemned as false. Gradually she rejected the occult and accepted the Christian faith.

As her belief became firm, she directed that the builders redesign the bathhouse her father had planned, adding another window so that the three windows might symbolize the Holy Trinity. When her father returned, he was enraged at the changes and infuriated when Barbara acknowledged that she was a Christian. He dragged her before the prefect of the province, who decreed that she be tortured and put to death by decapitation. Dioscorus himself carried out the death sentence, and on his way home he was struck by lightning and his body consumed by the electric fields. This legend of the lightning bolt which struck down Saint Barbara's persecutor caused her to be regarded as the patron saint to be called upon in times of danger from thunderstorms, earthquakes, fires, and sudden death.

Nevertheless, this memory of Ṣàngó-like features in the imagery of saints is being undermined by African-centered movements, which are interested in eradicating the memory of slave adaptations and reclaiming and returning Santería to its òrìṣà roots. And although at various times Santería leaders have been allied with òrìṣà-voodoo practitioners, there is a growing divide between those practitioners who use the Catholic imagery that constituted Santería as a Cuban religion and Ọ̀yọ́túnjí òrìṣà-voodoo orthodoxy. In the context of the Africanization of òrìṣà icons, the imagery and meaning of Ṣàngó represents the disaggregating of Christian influences from òrìṣà iconography and a return to the grandeur of the historical Ṣàngó.

Given these histories of both grandeur and regulation of African practices, the development of òrìṣà-voodoo Yorùbá revivalism was self-consciously driven by the growing tide of black nationalism in the 1960s, in which black Americans reconceptualized Santería in order to disentangle it from its Spanish and Christian influences. Ultimately, these changes meant symbolically "blackening" Santería and referentially indexing the West African empires and kingdoms that preceded the colonization of Nigeria by the British Empire. Ọ̀yọ́túnjí Village practitioners are one such example of practitioners interested in Africanizing Christian influences of Santería iconic meanings, thus returning Ṣàngó imagery to its historical and mythic origins.

The Africanization of Ṣàngó in Ọ̀yọ́túnjí Village Networks

Ọ̀yọ́túnjí revivalists often highlight the bringing of òrìṣà-voodoo to the United States as the event in which Afro-Cubans were called on by the gods to give their secrets back to black people. They often recall it through the following narrative told to me by the leader of Ọ̀yọ́túnjí, known as the ọba (or king). This took place in 1959, when the soon-to-be-founder of Ọ̀yọ́túnjí Village, then named Serge King, and his friend, a Cuban American man named Chris Oliana, were the first two U.S. Americans to be initiated into the Afro-Cuban priesthood cult of Ṣàngó in Matanzas, Cuba. This ritual moment is seen as critical because the diviner identified King as being protected by the patron òrìṣà Ọbàtálá but, in a negative configuration, (Ọ̀ṣẹ́ Méjì in osóbà). He told King that he should not assume positions of leadership. So rather than initiating King into the Ọbàtálá cult, the diviner initiated him into the Ṣàngó secret society and warned that he was to be careful to not share the secrets of Africa's gods with others.

Relegating the divinatory interpretation of the *odù* to white Cuban racism, King noted that white Cubans are afraid that black Americans would enter the Santería priesthood and Africanize it. He disagreed that Ṣàngó powers were uncontrollable and instead wanted to interpret the powers of Ṣàngó as fundamentally about royal grandeur, manly governance, and responsibility. As explained to me by King, now *ọba* (king) of Ọ̀yọ́túnjí, the central reason he entered the Santería priesthood was so that he could gain the necessary ritual training in order to return Santería practices to their "purest African form." King began his loyal collaborations with his Santería alliances in New York City and tried to abide by the basic cultural and political rules of secrecy and discretion—central legacies from the disguising of Yorùbá religion during conditions of slavery.[8] King and Oliana together established an *òrìṣà* religious organization and named it the Ṣàngó Temple. During this period, increasing numbers of Santería networks began to proliferate. They ranged from ritual products—thousands of saint candles, and packaged herbs and remedies—to *òrìṣà* objects, witchcraft protection, and good luck charms. However, by the mid-1960s, King had incorporated into his practice the fundamental principles of Black Nationalism that had been circulating within artistic and political circles of the time. He renamed his new version of Santería *òrìṣà*-voodoo, naming the new temple the "Yorùbá Temple," emphasizing the African origins of Santería and not the conditions of slavery that led to the creation of Santería from Yorùbá-*òrìṣà* practices.[9]

In an attempt to symbolically Africanize what is popularly referred to as the European features of Catholic saints, they substituted the white faces of the saints with brown faces, painted pictures that emphasized thick lips and broad noses, and changed the spelling of Spanish/Lucumí ritual words as well as the pronunciation of ritual objects, creating a landscape that referenced the symbolic prestige of precolonial *òrìṣà* life. The imagery of Ṣàngó was transformed from that which emphasized his sexual cunning to that which foregrounded his extravagant rule.

On a basic level of signification, therefore, Ọ̀yọ́túnjí practitioners argued for the need of re-Africanizing Santería as fundamentally Yorùbá and visibly "African." Therefore, in order to "purify" Santería from what they saw as its problematic psychology of slavery and residual colonial hegemony, Yorùbá revivalists engaged in actively re-signifying Santería within racial discourses of African origins. Spurred by ideological clashes over the "whitening" of Yorùbá ritual practices in Cuba, and the incorporation of Catholic saints, Yorùbá revivalists in the U.S—black American nationalists—renamed their version of Yorùbá-Santería "*òrìṣà*-voodoo," substituting Spanish-language words and pronunciations with African words. Using representations that incorporated the mythic visual imagery of the old empire from which Yorùbá people are known to have descended, the founders created landscapes that resembled Nigerian Yorùbá religious and political institutions thought to be more "authentically" African. They substituted their Anglophone names with Yorùbá names, producing performance cartographies of Yorùbá membership. For example, Serge King, the *ọba,* changed his family name to Adéfúnmi.

Through routine practices that emphasized the African origins of Yorùbá practices—from Africa to the Americas—Yorùbá revivalists recast Santería through the signs of African grandeur and performed nobility. Adéfúnmi and other prominent *òrìṣà*-voodoo leaders changed the Santería saint-like representations of deities, replacing them with symbolic objects from the earth. The membership officially adopted the principles of Black Nationalism and began wearing West African *dàñṣíkí*s and *bùbá*s, with afros, and adopting what they saw as either African names in general or Yorùbá names in particular. Arguing that such Eurocentric vestiges needed to be shed, he emphasized the aesthetic return to African forms, even while he emphasized the need to pursue such goals in the Americas. These aesthetic interventions into religious representation were embedded in values connected to differences between whiteness and blackness, Christianity and Santería-based practices, and reflected King's attempts to re-signify the meaning of Santería through a temporal return to a precolonial period and in referentially African spatial and aesthetic terms. These reformulations of Africanness not only declared a narrative of race as the modality through which new authorial conceptions of Yorùbá belonging were lived, it also established the realm of spiritual ancestry, and not simply biological birthplace, as the basis for black American claims to a precolonial African past, yet a heritage traceable with the phenotypic establishment of racial belonging.

How *òrìṣà* practitioners make and remake the imaginary within particular boundaries of hegemonic conceptions of reality is deeply embedded in the institutionalization of what is "authentically African." In the case of Yorùbá revivalism, the sign of Ṣàngó as a metaphor of particular forms of manhood represents struggles over religious meanings and their histories of power. The ideological domain of de-territorialized Yorùbá aesthetics is embedded in the production of particular relations of value. And the relations of value to which I am referring are influenced by particular racial hierarchies in which the historical meaning of the black body became the basis for the development of racial discourses concerning the degeneration of African peoples in the making of the modern world.[10] Therefore, how the racial body is read and transformed into a sign of membership and how it is connected through the historical production of modern subjectivities is as much about the institutional representation of racial belonging as it is about the historical, mythical, and spiritual roots that constitute their differences in interpretations. However, it is also linked to new chronotopic logics of transmission and authority, in which spiritual means are temporally and spatially reconceptualized in the archaic precolonial past and the physicality of geography rendered secondary. Here, we see that the imaginaries and domains of authority in which interpretations of Ṣàngó are rendered legitimate are shaped by institutional ideologies that legitimatize Africanness in particular ways.

Understanding ritual and representational transformations means understanding the workings of power and agency in the making of new interpretive meanings. Michel Foucault, in an attempt to understand the conditions of arranging social life so that agents create domains of knowledge which are ordered in relation to hegemonic power, emphasized that though state regulations work to shape the structure of order, it is conceptual ordering through particular institutions and ultimately through individual participation that leads to the reproduction and cultivation of particular types of subjects.[11] Seen thus, the force of state governmental power is its ability to influence meaning and order, not so much through overt force, but through understanding the effects of the state (Cuban criminalization of Santería, or U.S. Jim Crow regulations, for example); it is the "governmentality" of power, the regimes of knowledge, and forms of ordering that are embodiments of the institutional effects of new classifications of modern knowledge. Following this roadmap for thinking about the apparatuses of regulation and the historical and contemporary politics through which practitioners participate in the regulation of meanings, it is critical to approach the making of the Yorùbá-Ṣàngó imaginary in terms that call on the recognition of various techniques of knowledge that are used to re-narrate belonging, to create distinctive spaces, values, and practices within it.

The production of specific meanings from which to read landmarks does not just represent the making of signifiers of Africanness in and of themselves; they become signs of territorial attachment, and their meanings are produced in ways that differentiate between state citizenship and new domains of authority in which alternate innovations for understanding belonging are possible. Therefore, representations of Ṣàngó in relation to African origins, Cuban transformations, or nonracial but spiritual lineage highlight how various practices are ultimately about how sites, people, things are imbued with particular ideological meanings. As such, iconic representations and the practices inhabited by them are shaped by ideological units from which people produce boundaries, enact social distinctions, and call on institutions to derive the authority from which to rearticulate meaning. As we shall see, new domains of legitimatizing Yorùbá belonging through ritual made possible spiritual linkages to West Africa and led to new ways of configuring belonging as a result of de-territorialized spiritual connections.

Back to Africa: Re-Africanization and the Spiritual Making of Ọ̀yọ́túnjí

By the early to mid-1970s, the development of Yorùbá revivalism benefited from both the rising tide of black history institutions in the United States and the development of different urban networks from which to disseminate knowledge of Yorùbá cultural history.[12] And by the late 1970s, the membership of the growing Yorùbá movement, an outgrowth of Santería, comprised hundreds of U.S. voodoo practitioners spread throughout the United States and Canada. This form of Yorùbá transnational religious nationalism, as well as the proliferation of Afrocentricity and African American cultural movements, can also be seen as a sort of culture industry, in which the production of local aesthetic forms is today part of the globalization process;[13] as such, it is within particular nodes that we need to understand the channels and circuits for the global circulation of òrìṣà aesthetics of various kinds,[14] as well as the ways that particular events contribute to particular imprints.[15]

Combined with attention to the need to obtain and read African-centered textbooks, Ọ̀yọ́túnjí Yorùbá revivalists, in establishing the fundamental mission of Yorùbá revivalism, focused on the educational and ritual development of Ọ̀yọ́túnjí's Archministry. With the task of recasting Santería as not sufficiently African and recreating a social organization that would resemble their African-centered alliances, the formation of Yorùbá traditionalism, a new intentional community in the bushes of South Carolina—absent of lived or historical knowledge about the particularities of Yorùbá cultural practices—had a difficult institutional beginning.

As a result of increasing transnational travel made possible by the increasing affordability of travel for middle-class Americans interested in experiencing life elsewhere, thousands of black nationalists embarked on pilgrimages to the Middle East and heritage tours to various parts of Africa. To strengthen their ties to Nigerian Yorùbá clan groups and to gain the ritual legitimacy of Nigerian rituals, in 1972 Adéfúnmi joined many of those voyagers by traveling to Nigeria. While there, he embarked on a ritual initiation and returned to South Carolina with the symbolic power of having undergone West African rituals. With the goal of studying and learning about Yorùbá ritual processes, Adéfúnmi lived among families for a four-month period and learned the Yorùbá language in order to study the organization and history of Nigerian Yorùbá practices. There he was initiated into the cult of Ifá (a ritual cult group) in Abòkú-ta—which provided him with the legitimacy that he sought.

The ritual process clarified for him the 1959 Santería interpretation of his initiation *odù*, Ọṣẹ́ Méjì. In responding to his request that they clarify the symbolic meaning of Ọṣẹ́ Méjì in *osóbà*, his new Nigerian advisors told him that his configuration of Ọṣẹ́ Méjì did not represent someone who would be a dangerous leader. Rather, the Abẹ́òkúta-based Yorùbá priest who initiated him explained that the divinatory *odù* represented a highly powerful leader who would do many things that could have honorable consequences for his family. Herein was reinstated a predominantly Ọ̀yọ́ interpretation of Ṣàngó as leader, as responsible monarch.

In *òrìṣà* spheres of practice there are both divinatory rules produced for personal purposes and sociopolitical rules for civic purposes. The primary source of Yorùbá religious rules is derived from verses from the divinatory corpus, and the application is based on the diviner's interpretation of the verses (*odù*) to give personal advice or to explain issues of larger social relevance. It is believed that the divinatory sources—the stories of ritual knowledge—are sacred because they were communicated in the form of stories/verses (*ẹsẹ*) from Olódùmarè (the Yorùbá god) through intermediaries known as *òrìṣà*. These stories, manifest in proverbs and songs, represent characterizations of *òrìṣà* believed to have once been kings, heroes, and soldiers with human imperfections. Upon death, these figures are believed to have transformed themselves and reentered the human world in the form of the sky, sea, and earth. In their symbolic form they are represented by various colors, environmental conditions, and personality characteristics. Today, those who follow the teachings of Olódùmarè do so by interpreting verses through various divinatory oracles, such as Ifá. These forms of divinatory teachings are constituted in the verses of the Ifá oracle and describe the life-worlds of the *òrìṣà*, seen as Olódùmarè's messages to his sons and daughters and therefore timeless and a reflection of Olódùmarè's divinity. Ultimately, divinatory knowledge is the gateway into the cosmic world, and it is through such forms of ritual that narratives of ancestry are concretized. Diviners are critical, thus, for not only are they key intellectual producers, but they possess the power of interpretation, thereby producing knowledge about the past, present, and future (destiny) and, in so doing, using divinatory sources to shape, enforce, and rethink social rules in everyday life.

Nevertheless, differences in the interpretation of the divinatory corpus reflect differences in the field of cultural production within which practitioners are situated. For when, at the end of 1972, Adéfúnmi completed his travels, he returned to Ọ̀yọ́túnjí, where his constituency crowned him as *ọba* (their king), endowing him with the official Yorùbá title *kábíyèsí*. *Kábíyèsí,* often translated to mean "Long Live the King" or "Your/His Royal Highness," a marker of a leader—an *ọba* or king— signaled the temporal and spatial power of Yorùbá governance, establishing symbolic codes which set the terms of particular social relations. Since his ascent to the throne, Kábíyèsí became the leader of Ọ̀yọ́túnjí, a democratic dictatorship governing Yorùbá revivalists in the United States. With symbolic as well as ultimate power, his leadership set the terms for particular assertions of Yorùbá social memory which worked within the historical workings of race.

As community leaders established political structures,[16] legal codes, Yorùbá language training, and the physical spatial design in a way that represented Yorùbá social life, members interested in developing religious and ancestral and *òrìṣà* worship organized social and religious cult groups and constructed a physical plant that was organized around a large palace courtyard called the Aàfin (palace) in order to replicate images of African kingdoms. Unlike the social organization of Santería as a covert practice that incorporated the structure of paternal and maternal descent (*madrino* and *padrino*) in relation to "houses," and that initiated neophytes into a multiplicity of *òrìṣà* domains, the founders of Ọ̀yọ́túnjí attempted to re-Africanize *òrìṣà* worship by creating a structure of *òrìṣà* cults in their own towns with chieftaincy structures and by initiating neophytes into only one *òrìṣà* domain. In the case of the making of distinct Yorùbáland towns, this created a public sphere in which the Africanization of *òrìṣà*s such as Ṣàngó could be revered as an extension of the modernity of African membership. The transformation of multiple *òrìṣà* initiations is believed to have transformed with the multiplicity of enslaved Africans in highly concentrated areas and, therefore, the need to equip practitioners with the skills to work with a more diverse array of *òrìṣà* practitioners.

However, with the 1990s' proliferation of the *òrìṣà* commodities on the Internet, the commodification of spirituality and the availability of religious packages of *òrìṣà* knowledge became controversial. What was new in the 1990s was the contestation over the explanations for ritual policies and differences in the representation of the *òrìṣà* and *òrìṣà* life. Electronic technologies such as the Internet and mass technologies of knowledge circulation are providing the engines by which religious inter- pretive meanings are being played out. And if technology is providing the engine, then what is particular about the global revival of these forms of autochthonous religious claims to homelands is that the domains of authorial determination are becoming increasingly autonomous and reproducing spheres of logic that produce particular ideological invest- ments. With such cultural underpinnings, Yorùbá religious revivalism is being transformed by a modernity of religious heritage in which we are seeing the innovation of cultural meanings that are being called on to address social exclusions and institutional failures. And as a result, capi- talist modernity reflects corporate climates in which corporations today are increasingly transnational and less loyal to nationalist projects. Today, capitalism of the early twenty-first century is centrally allied with new heritage claims and working alongside rights and democratization move- ments toward the circulation of new transnational imaginaries. Charting these linkages enables us to recognize that the new cultural politics—as it's being played out in religious terms—must be understood in relation to particular modernities of interpretive power which are complexly his- torical and produced within contexts of difference.

In the end, the modernity of Ṣàngó revivalism, in this age in which new technologies are used to publicize particular renditions of Ṣàngó worship, continues to employ the logics of various divinatory interpreta- tions in order to explain new forms of inequalities. Using varied forms of modernity for understanding the processes of reinterpreting how signs— racial, national, regional, spiritual, mythic—are constituted through the simultaneous conjunctures of institutions of power, new global markets, and the precariousness by which people participate in the reproduction of norms allows us to detail various regulatory orders and the contexts in which they become manifest.

Conclusion: The Realm of the Transnational

As new forms of social organization are negotiated between religious houses, credentialing institutions, and market pressures, we see that how *òrìṣà*s are represented or their mythology translated is an attempt both to rectify social inequalities and to become a discourse on power that gives local meaning to the functioning of power in the nation, transnational spheres, and the world. In understanding these processes of producing meanings, meanings of the iconic signs of Ṣàngó, it is not just the regulatory power of the state, its laws, or its codes of subjugation that are at play. The role of agents and their moral imaginaries coupled with the globalization of a new industry—that of occult markets spread through a heritage and culture industry—that enable practitioners to re-signify meanings according to historically constituted modernities of power. For in ritual arenas, spaces of occult transformation exist within the vestiges of hegemonic order. These seemingly contradictory connections between Christianity, Spanish and British cultural hegemonies, and colonial laws in the expression of Yorùbá revivalist religious practices are fundamental to the reformulation of Yorùbá revivalism in Ọ̀yọ́túnjí. They are part of the encounter with European colonial pasts, American expansionism, and the demise of the West African empires and must be understood in relation to contemporary modernities of subjecthood.

NOTES

This chapter originally appeared in Kamari Maxine Clarke, *Mapping Yoruba Networks: Power and Agency in the Making of Transnational Communities* (Durham, N.C.: Duke University Press, 2004).

1. I neither locate it as only a physical place or a marginal site, which relies on black-white dichotomies, nor take its unit of analysis as a demographically small community as the end of the story. Rather, I treat it as the middle of an ongoing story about the cultural production in which religious interpretations are struggled over, contested, and produced in particular regional zones.

2. Ultimately, there is no clear separation between the religious ritual system that shapes Yorùbá knowledge and the customary rules that frame which practices are acceptable. They operate in overlapping institutions of knowledge and vary in hierarchy of sources. The differences in application lie in three domains: the interpretive authority of particular divinatory forms that shape the legitimacy of *òrìṣà* logic, the recognition of those forms of logic by others, and the methodologies by which practitioners achieve such logic.

3. Ọlabiyi Babalola Yai, "Yorùbá Religion and Globalization: Some Reflections," *Cuadernos Digitales* 15 (Oct. 2001): 1–21.

4. Jean Comaroff and John L. Comaroff, "Millennial Capitalism: First Thoughts on a Second Coming," in *Millennial Capitalism and the Culture of Neoliberalism,* ed. Jean Comaroff and John L. Comaroff, 1–56 (Durham, N.C.: Duke University Press, 2001).

5. Take, for example, this reading of the year for Year 2004, in which Ṣàngó is centrally figured in a Santería reading: Governing Mpungo/Òrìshà this Coming Year 2004:

SHANGO—*Siete Rayos.* Path: War, Disrespect, Tragedy, Financial Recovery and Prosperity. Flag: Red with Yellow or Gold Border. To be placed at the

Highest Point in Your Home, or behind front door. *Bandera* / Flag for the Year 2004—Marks War and Chàngó get Involved!

1. Avoid conflicts between Elders and Juniors. Prepare for continued battles and war.

  • As the past few years have indicated, war continues. This year Shàngó get involved. Shàngó comes to help "his people."

  • Avoid any and all battles and wars between Elder and Junior.

  • Junior members must act with total respect towards their Elders.

  • Elders must not give away their work for free this year. Junior members must pay all "*derechos*" complete and placed at the foot of Muerto/ Eggun or Òrìsà, or as described by Elder.

  • Elders must take their responsibility seriously and stand firm this year with their godchildren and other junior members, although the Elder must continue to be compassionate and understanding.

  • Avoid unnecessary battles and wars (conflicts) be it, in the work place, social gatherings, religious gatherings, in family matters and in the home. Show respect to others.

  • Clarify misunderstandings by demonstrating patience and respect for one another.

  • Continue to be a person of Good and Morale Character.

  • Do not drink alcohol this coming year.

2. In this year's reading there is contradiction.

  • Prosperity comes but war continues.

  • Receive and follow advice from one source this coming year to avoid confusion.

  • There will be grave consequences in places where there is uncertainty.

  • Avoid traveling abroad to preserve your safety. Stay close to home and stay close to your family.

  **• Shàngó comes this year to take over the disarray of worldly matters that plagues us.

  • Elders should dress up Shàngó with as much red fabric as possible or place him in an altar. He must be located near the front door of the home or facing the front door for everyone to see. Do not hide Shàngó this year. Reveal him to the World.

  • If you are a *palero* and not crowned in Ocha, dress up your *prendas* with red colored fabric or place red fabric around the *prenda*.

  ***• Shàngó must not eat separately this year. Whenever Shàngó gets fed, Eggun must eat with him.

  • Shango and Eggun must be fed White Roosters this Year, and every three months.

  • Eggun can be fed separately all year long, but when Shàngó eats, Eggun eats. Note: Shàngó can be fed rooster alongside any *prenda*.

  ****• This year give Òchun offerings of very sweet pastries along side of Eggun.

- Do not disperse of Ọ̀chun's and Eggun's offerings at the river this year.
- Do not ask for favors of Ọ̀chun this year. Give Ọ̀chun thanks for your blessings once this coming year and that's it.
- Avoid going to the river this coming year to prevent accidents, drowning, misfortune, and other problems occurring there. Do not give any offerings at the river this year.

3. Personal Prosperity etc.

- Make every effort to progress this year in business and other employment.
- Do not reveal your secrets or knowledge to friends, family or co-workers.
- Keep all your private matters, private. Keep all business matters private as well.
- Try to learn as much as possible from others this coming year and use to your advantage in business or other employment. Be subtle.
- This year give an offering after every blessing received, to seal the blessing and protect it. The process is: first an offering, then a blessing, then an offering again. If you receive more blessings after the last offering, give another offering again to bless it and protect it.
- Do not lend out money and do not give money away. Keep all your blessings for you and your immediate family (if married). However, pay all your debts and properly maintain your finances.

*• For those who have been advised to receive their warriors this year must do so within the first three months of the year.

- The reception of *resguardos,* other objects and *àddìmú òrìṣà* that has been previously divined must be completed as soon as possible.

4. Shàngó says that this year there is not sitting on the fence!

- This year is a decisive year. Those who have received blessings from Ocha must at least receive their warriors and *elekes*. There is no sitting on the fence. You must decide whether or not you want to adhere to the "*reglas*" (laws) that govern our way of life or move on with your life. This applies to all ways of life, including Palo and Ifá.
- Elders must take a stand this year and demand compliance with all *reglas* of our way of life.
- Junior members must continue respecting their Elders in every facet of our culture.

6. J. Omosade Awolalu. *Yorùbá Beliefs and Sacrificial Rites* (Brooklyn: Athelia Henrietta Press, 1979), 34.

7. It is believed that the *regla de ocha* was encouraged in order to avoid slave uprisings.

8. Santería regulations required that ritual initiations had to be presided over by Babaláwos (the highest ranking priest—that of the Ifá *òrìṣà*), and as a young priest without a congregation of qualified African-centered priests, it was difficult for the king to function in Santería religious circles without their support.

9. The consequence of developing an African-centric orientation was that over time he lost his constituency and therefore potential economic power when most of the Santería consultants refused to support his increasingly race-centered approach and Oliana severed ties with him.

10. Robert J. C. Young, *Colonial Desire: Hybridity in Theory, Culture and Race* (London: Routledge, 1995), 4.

11. Michel Foucault, "Governmentality," in *The Foucault Effect: Studies in Governmentality,* ed. G. Burchell, C. Gordon, and P. Miller (London: Harvester Wheatsheaf, 1991).

12. By 1970, five families moved with Adéfúnmi to Beaufort, South Carolina, some sixty miles southwest of Charleston, with the goal of establishing a black separatist community in the bushes of South Carolina. The members decided that Adéfúnmi, as the former spiritual leader of the Yorùbá temple, should become the leader of the entire Òyótúnjí establishment. The significant years of formulating the structure and layout of Òyótúnjí Village began after their second move in 1972, when they were forced to relocate from their initial rented site on Brays Island Road to the new ten-acre site on Route 17, which they purchased collectively. Nevertheless, constructing a community that undermined Santero racism, yet had minimal access to Nigerian Yorùbá traditionalists, meant that practitioners had to depend on the scant publications about Yorùbá religious practices available to them. Unlike the intergenerational training of Santería, deeply entrenched in the social memory of families, the *òrìsà*-voodoo movement drew its strength from the deployment of educational institutional knowledge.

13. Michael Hardt and Antonio Negri, *Empire* (Cambridge, Mass.: Harvard University Press, 2000).

14. Ariana Hernandez-Reguant, "Radio Taino and the Globalization of the Cuban Culture Industries," Ph.D. diss., University of Chicago, 2002.

15. Anna Tsing, "The Global Situation," *Cultural Anthropology* 15, no. 3 (2000): 327–60.

16. Joined by the arrival of over a hundred residents throughout 1974 and 1975, the growing members of Òyótúnjí had to contend with implementing their visions of Yorùbá social organization. They set up a traditional decision-making council, referred to in Yorùbá as the Ògbóni society, a council of landholders and chiefs. With the Ògbóni, designed to replicate the organization of Yorùbá customary towns, establishing continuities in ancestral governance and contemporary governance, village leaders were able to implement practical decision-making rules and procedures.

CHAPTER ELEVEN

Wither Ṣàngó?

An Inquiry into Ṣàngó's "Authenticity" and Prominence in the Caribbean

STEPHEN D. GLAZIER

Many twentieth-century studies of African religions in the Caribbean focused on correspondences between members of the Yorùbá pantheon and Catholic saints. On Trinidad, Grenada, and St. Vincent the major associations are between Ṣàngó and Saint John. In Cuba, however, the main correspondence is said to be between Ṣàngó and Saint Barbara. This contrasts with other Caribbean islands (notably Haiti and Dominica) and Brazil, where major associations are between Ṣàngó and Saint Michael, Saint Jerome, and/or Saint Peter.

Associations with Catholic saints are widely known, and informants—if asked—are both able and willing to provide detailed information on the topic. But judging from the tone of their responses, such correspondences seem to have been a major focus for earlier generations of researchers, but are not a major concern for believers. Devotees are increasingly concerned about personality traits and relationships between various members of the *òrìṣà* pantheon; especially in terms of hierarchies and "family" relationships. The most exhaustive compilation of *òrìṣà*-saint correspondences is provided by William Bascom.[1] *Òrìṣà* devotees found Bascom's chart—borrowing a phrase from nineteenth-century existential theologian Søren Kierkegaard—"interesting but not edifying." Nevertheless, the comprehensive and elaborate nature of these correspondences bespeaks an urgently felt need on the part of those who created them.

With respect to Ṣàngó shrines in the English-speaking Caribbean, Melville J. Herskovits, George Eaton Simpson, William Bascom, and

Frances Henry documented extensive Ṣàngó devotion, especially on the island of Trinidad, where all forms of Yorùbá religion were reported as "Ṣàngó worship." Bascom reports only two Caribbean islands—Trinidad and Grenada—where Ṣàngó is the name of the cult and òrìṣà worship is identified primarily with Ṣàngó.[2]

Recently, leaders within various African religious communities in Trinidad have attempted to deemphasize the significance of Ṣàngó, labeling all African-derived religions as "Òrìṣà work." At the Ninth International Òrìṣà conference, which was held in Port-of-Spain in 1999, Ṣàngó was not featured even by his own priests and priestesses. For example, in the address given by Ṣàngó priestess Patrica McLeod—Ìyá Ṣàngó Wùmí— the òrìṣà religion was treated in general, but she did not deal with Ṣàngó in particular. Nevertheless, a recent survey of Ṣàngó shrines indicates a resurgence of Ṣàngó. Ṣàngó stools are well maintained, there is evidence of fresh sacrifices, and Ṣàngó appears to have attracted a new generation of devotees in Trinidad—both male and female. It is of interest that among new devotees, Ṣàngó is increasingly identified with Saint Barbara.

In *The Encyclopedia of Contemporary Latin American and Caribbean Cultures,* a brief unsigned entry on "Ṣàngó" states: "According to historians, Ṣàngó in Trinidad acquired its name from the observation of some European, who mistakenly attributed one òrìṣa's name to an entire religious system. In the late twentieth century, many practitioners promoted the use of the more accurate term '*òrìṣà*' worship, but the term Ṣàngó remains in common usage."[3]

The actual situation, of course, is much more complex. The term "Ṣàngó" was not introduced by "some European" but by four prominent American anthropologists: Melville J. Herskovits, Francis Henry, William Bascom, and George Eaton Simpson. And it was not a mistake. Herskovits, Henry, Bascom, and Simpson dealt with informants who saw themselves primarily as followers of Ṣàngó. While many of their informants' public rituals were open to other members of the òrìṣà pantheon, their personal (house) altars were dedicated solely to Ṣàngó.

Researchers never deal with religions in the abstract. They come to understand religions as mediated through a number of key informants. George Eaton Simpson's description of Ṣàngó as "mild, calm, understated, and sympathetic" is more in keeping with the personality of his major informant, Fitzroy Small, than it is of traditional descriptions of Ṣàngó. As the Yoruba god of thunder, Ṣàngó is often described as quick to anger and is seldom portrayed as "mild and understated." Fitzroy Small, who served as Simpson's introduction to Ṣàngó, worked as a doorman at

the Trinidad Hilton. Small took Simpson to òrìṣà ceremonies in Laven-
tille (the same neighborhood fictionalized in Earl Lovelace's 1972 novel,
Dragon Can't Dance). Fitzroy's soft-spoken congeniality—along with his
ability to function as a culture broker and ambassador of Ṣàngó—made
him an ideal informant. He was also host to William and Bertha Bascom
during their time in Trinidad. Small died in 1982. He took me to feasts at
his *palais* during the summers of 1978 and 1979. To his dying day, Fitzroy thought of his religion as "Ṣàngó" and identified himself as a "Ṣàngó
Baptist." This was not merely a label imposed by outsiders. It was the way
a prominent and knowledgeable believer articulated his faith.

According to Tracey E. Hucks, òrìṣà worship in Trinidad is divided
into two main groups: "Ọpa Òrìṣà" (Ṣàngó) and "the Òrìṣà Movement."[4]
But there are other important distinctions. A small number of "Ọpa
Òrìṣà" followers identify exclusively with Ṣàngó. While other òrìṣà may
be present at their feasts, they personally are possessed only by Ṣàngó.
Some Ṣàngó devotees claim to have no connections with Catholicism at
all, while others emphasize primary ties with a number of òrìṣà (Ògún,
Èṣù, and so on) and with Roman Catholicism. These devotees consider
themselves primarily Catholics who are also involved in òrìṣà work. Such
distinctions, of course, are largely matters of personal choice and self-
definition.

A large percentage of òrìṣà devotees maintain secondary ties with the
Spiritual Baptist faith, while others ("Ṣàngó Baptists") see themselves primarily as Spiritual Baptists who also attend òrìṣà feasts. Since òrìṣà feasts
are held only once or twice a year and Baptist services are held at least
twice a week, Baptist churches provide the major organizational nexus
for Ṣàngó Baptists. In addition, some òrìṣà devotees and Spiritual Baptists sponsor yearly "banquets" in the Kabala tradition.[5] But Ṣàngó devotees who claim no connections to Christianity seldom sponsor Kabala
"banquets."

My own experiences with Fitzroy Small contrast markedly with Frances Henry's encounter with her chief informant, Pa Neezer—also a devotee of Ṣàngó. Henry portrays Ṣàngó as "irascible and unpredictable."
Her depiction is more consistent with Yorùbá mythology and the literature surrounding Ṣàngó. But it is also more consistent with Pa Neezer's
reputation. Neezer was both feared and revered.

Early in their research, Melville and Frances Herskovits incorrectly
believed that the "purest" and most "authentic" forms of African religion were to be found away from major urban areas. This proved unfortunate, because Yorùbá religion in the New World is primarily an urban
phenomenon. As William Bascom points out, the Yorùbá have a long

tradition of urban life in Africa, and "more knowledgeable priests may have moved to urban areas in order to attract a larger and wealthier clientele."[6] In addition, rural-urban distinctions do not mean as much in the Caribbean as in Africa, especially on islands such as Trinidad, where one can get almost anywhere within a day.

The Herskovitses ended up in the remote Trinidad village of Toco, where, to their great disappointment, they found no evidence of Ṣàngó religion at all. Contemporary residents of Toco emphasize that Ṣàngó was indeed present during the Herskovitses' fieldwork, but somehow the followers of Ṣàngó managed to elude the Herskovitses. Melville and Frances ended up studying Toco's Spiritual Baptists instead.

Even today, Toco remains an isolated community. One does not just end up in Toco, one has to want to get there. But as Kevin Birth points out in *Any Time Is Trinidad Time*, "the poor quality of the roads discourages outsiders from coming, but the roads do not discourage residents from leaving."[7] There is considerable outmigration. For example, Toco's Ṣàngó Baptists regularly hold joint worship services (known as "pilgrimages") with other Ṣàngó Baptist and Spiritual Baptist churches throughout the island.

The Herskovitses (and later George Eaton Simpson) also worked with King Ford, a prominent Ṣàngó leader in Tunapuna, Trinidad, a suburb of Port-of-Spain. Ford was a devotee of Ògún, but his center was frequented by followers of Ṣàngó. While Ford remained a forceful, disciplined, and proud devotee of Ògún, it was Ṣàngó—and not Ògún—who dominated his center.

These early ethnographic studies are of greater than passing interest. From these studies, one gets a feel for the growth of the *òrìṣà* movement over time. Contemporary followers of *òrìṣà*—such as Rawle Gibbons—consult these and other anthropological texts.[8] In addition, Simpson and Bascom are highly reliable and refreshingly candid about the limitations of their research. Both attempt to separate descriptions from their interpretations, which makes many of their observations useful—even when they are based on theoretical assumptions that are incorrect or out of fashion.

All researchers, of course, bring their personal agendas, shortcomings, and perspectives into their research. Melville Herskovits and William Bascom, for example, did their initial fieldwork in Africa and later went to the Caribbean. This colored their impressions of Trinidadian Ṣàngó. George Eaton Simpson went to Africa long after completing his Caribbean fieldwork, and Frances Henry has examined the *òrìṣà* movement only in Canada and the Caribbean.

African languages constitute a major barrier for some researchers and some informants. Many difficulties Simpson encountered while compiling a list of òrìṣà in Trinidad stem from his lack of familiarity with the Yorùbá language. In reproducing a list of òrìṣàs, for example, Simpson names "Adoweh?," "Ahmeeoh?," "Aireeahsan?," and "Aireelay?"[9] He cautions the reader that he is unsure if these names represent a single òrìṣà or four separate òrìṣàs. Only recently have scholars begun to utilize linguistic analyses to document the religious significance of Yorùbá retentions in the Caribbean.[10]

At the time Herskovits, Bascom, Simpson, and Henry conducted their research, religious knowledge was transmitted orally. Past generations of òrìṣà leaders in Trinidad (e.g., Fitzroy Small and King Ford) knew little Yorùbá aside from the opening songs they had learned by rote. Ford provided me with rough English translations of some songs. Small knew the African names of only six or seven òrìṣàs and referred to other òrìṣàs exclusively by their saint names. This contrasts with contemporary òrìṣà leaders—such as Rawle Gibbons and Patrica McLeod (Ìyá Ṣàngó Wùmí)—who have formally studied Yorùbá.

Of earlier researchers, only Frances Henry gives much attention to personal relationships between individual òrìṣàs and their followers. Earlier research focused on public feasts to the exclusion of private (household) rituals. This may have skewed perceptions of the religion. Public ceremonies are held infrequently, but private rituals are an everyday occurrence. Followers of Ṣàngó, for example, maintain personal altars to Ṣàngó in their homes, and the òrìṣàs play pivotal roles in all family, financial, and community interactions.

Many of the shrines mentioned by Simpson, Bascom, and Henry are still in operation, and most are in their original locations. Even when a property has changed hands and/or has been purchased by someone who is not a follower of the òrìṣàs, new owners have allowed ceremonies to continue. This is seen as a way to gain the favor and protection of the òrìṣàs.

Rawle Gibbons—who is both a follower of the òrìṣàs and one of the leading scholars of the movement—claims that there are now over eighty active shrines in Trinidad.[11] James Houk estimated that there are about seventy-five shrines.[12] Houk also estimated that the òrìṣà movement has between eight thousand and fifty thousand adherents in Trinidad. My own survey suggests that a more accurate number may be between forty and sixty shrines. One reason for discrepancies is that a number of shrines are used by multiple sponsors at different times. Often, ceremonial sites are given different names depending on who is utilizing them. Even my lower figure represents a substantial increase in activity. Between forty and sixty shrines is nearly twice the number of shrines reported by the Herskovitses.[13]

European historians usually trace the beginnings of the òrìṣà movement in Trinidad to the arrival of free African Americans following Emancipation in 1838.[14] But this ignores over three hundred years of Spanish rule. Eighteenth-century Spanish immigration policies had a tremendous impact on the development of African religions in Trinidad. In 1776 the Spanish Crown opened Trinidad to settlement by French Catholics from other Caribbean islands. As a result, between 1777 and 1797 the population of Trinidad increased from about three thousand to seventeen thousand—a majority of immigrants arriving from the islands of Martinique, Dominica, and Grenada.[15] Under the "Cedula for the Population of Trinidad of 1783," the Spanish Crown extended generous land grants to planters from other Caribbean islands, and, in 1793, a contingent of French plantation owners (and their slaves) migrated to Trinidad from Santo Domingo. A large percentage of Santo Domingo slaves were of Fon origin, which may, in part, account for the prominence and persistence of Ṣàngó in Trinidad as well as for differences between Ṣàngó veneration in Trinidad and elsewhere in the English-speaking Caribbean, especially in Grenada.

Connections to Santo Domingo continue to influence the spread of Ṣàngó; for example, the presence of Haitian cane workers in nineteenth- and twentieth-century Cuba influenced spread of Ṣàngó traditions in Cuban Santería, and subsequently, the spread of Ṣàngó traditions in the United States and Canada. Similar migration patterns—or lack of migration—may account for some places in the Americas where no Ṣàngó traditions have been identified; examples include: Jamaica, Guyana, Paraguay, Bolivia, Uruguay, Chile, Peru, Colombia, French Guiana, the Bahamas, and Bermuda.[16]

Much early research addressed the concept of syncretism, which was first introduced into anthropology in 1947 by Melville J. Herskovits.[17] This was the same year that Herskovits also published *Trinidad Village*. Syncretism is an attempt to merge religious traditions and/or establish analogies between originally discrete religious and/or mythological traditions. At various times and places, religions have embraced syncretism, while at other times these same religions have rejected the practice as lacking in "authenticity."[18] Syncretism is sometimes seen as a devaluation of real, salient religious distinctions.

A number of conceptual shortcomings have been identified in Herskovits's original formulation.[19] Nevertheless, most contemporary anthropologists agree that it may be more valid to look at syncretism in terms of power relations. With respect to Ṣàngó, it may be more useful to examine syncretism from the perspectives of the "syncretizers." When seen from the perspectives of syncretizers, syncretism appears as a series of individual acts rather than as an abstract and impersonal process.

Central to this discussion is the perceived relationship between African-derived religions and Roman Catholicism. It has been suggested that Catholic elements within the òrìṣà movement were brought in to mask or hide African forms of worship under the cloak of Christianity. This explanation is not altogether satisfactory. As David Trotman astutely observed, if early followers of the òrìṣà wanted to disguise their religion by incorporating elements of Roman Catholicism, it would not have been a very good disguise because no one could have confused òrìṣà and Catholic rituals. Trotman also correctly contended that if devotees identified Catholic saints and Yorùbá deities in attempting to disguise the latter, any saint would have provided an equally good disguise.[20] But such was never the case. Only *some* saints became identified with a limited number of òrìṣà, and many Catholic saints were neglected altogether. Ultimately, Trotman concluded that in the case of Trinidad it is most likely that the òrìṣà religion and the veneration of the Catholic saints evolved together.

No one suggests that syncretism does not exist. Obviously, cultures that come into contact influence one another. But the term "syncretism," as it has been applied to the òrìṣà movement, assumes too much passivity on the part of slave populations. As Morton Klass opined:

> [I]n a universe where gods can do anything, theological studies are manifestly more important and interesting than the study of history, biology, geology, and astronomy put together. It follows that if a god is alleged to create the entire universe in the blink of an eye and knows all that has happened, is happening, and will happen—any inkling of that god's plans, whims, or preferences are of the utmost concern to humans.[21]

Caribbean slaves had more than a passing interest in the religion of their masters. They had an urgent need to incorporate European gods (and the powers of those gods) into their own lives. This urgent need, too, is perhaps at the root of perceived correspondences between Ṣàngó, Saint John, Saint Jerome, Saint Peter, and Saint Barbara.

Some contemporary followers of the òrìṣà have expressed a desire to "liberate" the òrìṣà from Catholicism and to reassert what they see as its fundamental Yorùbá elements. They seek to emphasize Yorùbá elements at shrines and expunge Catholic ones. As I have noted elsewhere, such attempts on the part of African American religious leaders have met with varying degrees of success elsewhere in the New World.[22]

Funso Aiyejina and Rawle Gibbons underscore a major difference between òrìṣà ceremonies held in Africa and òrìṣà ceremonies held in the New World: "Among the Yorùbá of Nigeria, each individual/family/community is associated with a particular òrìṣà. . . . In Trinidad, all or as many of the òrìṣà as possible are represented in the yard."[23] Aiyejina and Gibbons interpret this as the "unification of òrìṣà under one roof." This may be an oversimplification, but it is nonetheless an important distinction. Òrìṣà feasts in the Caribbean tend to be inclusive rather than exclusive.[24]

Ṣàngó feasts in Trinidad tend to attract participants from within extended families and neighborhoods. Trinidad devotees sponsor feasts once or twice a year. Feasts can last from a week to two nights. Cost is a major consideration since a well-attended feast costs their sponsors as much as 1200 TT (about $400 US) each day. In 1986, I attended a feast in Tunapuna that lasted for six consecutive days and nights. This is uncommon. A majority of feasts last for three days and four nights, with the highest attendance and most major rituals occurring at night. Most frequently, ceremonial spirit possession and major sacrifices happen in the early morning and after midnight. As in all ritual, researchers need to document daylight activities in order to get a better sense of the preparations and expenses involved.[25] I have witnessed occasional daytime possessions and observed numerous private sacrifices during daylight hours. These, too, are an integral part of the ceremony.

Feasts begin with a flag raising (red and white for Ṣàngó). Christian prayers are usually part of the preparations. Again, if Catholic elements were intended only as disguise for òrìṣà worship, they would occur throughout the feast and not merely at the beginning, when few participants are in attendance.

The most important element of any feast is the drumming. Drummers are almost always followers of the òrìṣà, but, unlike other attendees, they are usually paid for their services. One of the most difficult responsibilities of feast sponsors is to secure enough drummers for the duration of a ceremony.[26]

Following songs to Èṣù (who opens the gate for the other òrìṣà), Ṣàngó, Oya, Ògún, Òṣun, and other major òrìṣàs possess their devotees. A typical one-night ceremony consists of eight to ten concurrent possessions. On the other hand, often many hours pass before the òrìṣàs arrive. I have attended feasts in which there is no spirit possession on the first night. Sometimes, this pattern continues for the first two nights of the ceremony, but there is almost always possession by the third night.

As noted, most spirits arrive well after midnight. This underscores devotees' lack of control over the òrìṣàs. Sponsors do not direct the òrìṣàs. The òrìṣàs come and go according to their own whims. As Fitzroy Small pointed out, individuals cannot choose to follow a particular òrìṣà. It is always the òrìṣàs who choose their followers and not vice versa.

In some respects, feasts are highly organized. Yet in other respects, they lack centralized authority. Individual sponsors determine the times and the dates; they are responsible for all preparations. Sometimes sponsors obtain help from others; other times, they do everything themselves. Attendance varies. Feasts attract devotees and onlookers from nearby, but also attract followers from other parts of the island who may have experienced their first possession at that shrine or know the feast's sponsor through Spiritual Baptist or other religious connections.

According to Henry, some active Ṣàngóists attend twenty to thirty major feasts a year.[27] This, too, assures high attendance. In addition, each ceremony attracts a large number of onlookers. The number of onlookers is important for sponsors because they are required to provide food and beverages to all who are present.

A notable trend is for fewer and fewer different òrìṣàs to be represented within any given feast. Simpson[28] lists over forty òrìṣàs and suggests that his list be compared to the lists of Herskovits and Herskovits[29] and Mischel.[30] In my experience, however, only eight or nine different òrìṣàs manifest within a typical ceremony. Among the most popular are: Emanjah, Ògún, Ọṣun, Ọya, Ọbàtálá, Ṣànkpàná, and Ṣàngó. A number of òrìṣàs listed by Simpson, Herskovits, Bascom, and Henry are no longer represented at all. In Trinidad, as in Haiti,[31] the Yorùbá pantheon is shrinking. For example, different aspects of Ṣàngó are combined with traits once associated with other òrìṣà. Ṣàngó is sometimes merged with other òrìṣàs (e.g., Ṣàngó/Ọbàtálá; Ṣàngó/Ṣànkpàná; Ṣàngó/Èṣù). According to followers, this is to be expected since each òrìṣà possesses multiple personalities and attributes, only some of which are manifested at any given time. The merging of Ṣàngó/Ṣànkpàná, for example, gives Ṣàngó an opportunity to display aspects of his/her personality that are usually associated with Ṣànkpàná. From an organizational standpoint, it is politically advantageous for would-be leaders in the movement to be associated with the most powerful members of the pantheon. For example, individuals possessed by Ṣànkpàná alone are accorded lower status than one who follows Ṣàngó/Ṣànkpàná or Ògún/Ṣànkpàná.

Contemporary Ṣàngó yards look very similar to the yards described by Herskovits, Bascom, Simpson, and Henry. A typical yard consists of two major areas, the *palais* (an open-aired area with cement or packed earth floor and an aluminum or *tapia* roof; this is where drumming and ceremonial possession takes place) and the *chapelle* (an enclosed building where ritual implements are stored and three to four altars to the saints are maintained). In addition, each center has between five and twenty stools devoted to individual *òrìṣàs*. Each yard is presided over by an *iyá* (female leader) and/or a *mọgbà* (a male leader). It is of interest that the words for buildings continue to be referred to in French, while leadership titles are expressed in African terms.

Female leaders (*iyá*) have always existed within the *òrìṣà* movement. Earlier researchers, who were predominantly male, did not seek them out. Today, a majority of the Trinidadian leadership is female. Rawle Gibbons estimates that over 50 percent of *òrìṣà* shrines are owned by women.[32] Tracey Hucks claims that female members are among the most prominent, for example, "Ma Diamond" and "Mother Gerrald" (a Ṣàngó Baptist).[33] Hucks points out that the head of the *òrìṣà* movement in Trinidad and Tobago is also a female, Melvina Rodney. Rodney is a Catholic, but her first husband was a prominent Ṣàngó Baptist leader.

The status of women in Afro-Caribbean religions is changing rapidly. In exploring gender roles, it is important to keep in mind the contributions of John K. Thornton, J. Lorand Matory, and Ruth Landes. Thornton, in *The Kingdom of Kongo: Civil War and Transition, 1641–1718,* underscores the changing nature of African politics and religion at the height of the slave trade.[34] It has been common for scholars to focus on syncretism in the formation of New World societies but to lose sight of the fact that such syncretism and a great deal of religious change was going on in Africa at the same time. Many of the same forces that led to the formation and expansion of *vodun* in Haiti were also at work in the Kongo.

In *Sex and the Empire That Is No More,* J. Lorand Matory takes this argument one step further.[35] Matory not only underscores syncretic and innovative aspects of Ọ̀yọ́ religion, but emphasizes the general malleability of sex roles and religious leadership in African society and religion.

Ruth Landes's *City of Women*—based on fieldwork conducted in northern Brazil during the late 1930s—challenged prevailing notions of Afro-Brazilian religious leadership as well as shedding light on the roles of women in these organizations.[36] Her work was first published in 1947. Both the work and its author were largely ignored and never entered into the mainstream of Afro-Brazilian studies then dominated by Melville Herskovits, Pierre Verger, and Roger Bastide. Some critiques of Landes's book took the form of personal attack.[37] She was accused of going to Bahia primarily "to have sex with the natives." The charges against her were unfounded since the focus of her research was on celibate, female religious orders.

Treatment of Landes's work has been redressed, at least in part, by the reissue of *City of Women* by the University of New Mexico Press, with a new introduction that gives a history of the anthropological reception to the work. In 1947, Ruth Landes established once and for all the malleability of sex roles and leadership in Afro-Brazilian religious organizations, and—by implication—in Caribbean religions as well. But it has taken scholars fifty years to recognize her role.

Malleability of sex roles is apparent in New World religions such as Ṣàngó. In Cuba, and now in Trinidad, Ṣàngó has become increasingly identified with Saint Barbara. In attempting to account for Ṣàngó's identification with Saint Barbara, Ṣàngó leaders (both male and female) emphasize that òrìṣàs are not limited by human categories and attributes All òrìṣàs have the potential to be male and female; black and white; and young and old. In Trinidad, for example, Ṣàngó is often depicted as a mulatto. Trinidadian followers of Ṣàngó, like Ṣàngó devotees in Cuba,[38] argue that Ṣàngó may wear the clothes of a woman, but he is the epitome of maleness because of his many wives and love affairs. It is emphasized that Ṣàngó has many names because he used different names as he went from town to town seeking out amorous adventures. Erika Bourguignon, herself a student of Melville Herskovits, suggested to me that Herskovits did not foreground transvestitism and homosexuality in his depictions of African and African American rituals because he believed it would be detrimental to the cause of blacks in the United States.[39]

Landes concluded *City of Women* by noting that women occupy dominant positions within supposedly patriarchal structures. Her findings for Bahia indicate that surface male authority hid real female authority. But it is not an either/or situation. Males and females have different conceptions of power and authority. Is power centered on getting one's own way (as Thomas Hobbs conceived it) or in re-creating and/or re-defining one's situation (as Nietzsche conceived it)? Few followers of African American religions enjoy power in the Hobbsian sense.

The real question is whether or not scholars have grasped the true nature of female religious authority in the Caribbean. Women constitute the overwhelming majority of adherents in all of these faiths. The anthropological literature characterizes these religions—following Vittorio Lanternari[40] and I. M. Lewis[41]—as "peripheral" cults. But what is meant by "peripheral?" Are these religions considered "peripheral" because they are predominantly composed of females (which is Lanternari's assertion), or are females attracted to these religions because they are seen by women as providing an alternative source of power (which is Lewis's argument)? The relationship between gender, power, and authority is always complex. I. M. Lewis's original research on spirit possession and gender wars in Somalia concluded that spirit possession provides a mechanism by which the weak can appropriate symbols of power. But as Erika Bourguignon has pointed out, Lewis's theory is predicated on a shared understanding and acceptance of how the world works.[42]

Unlike many issues in the academic study of religion, debates about gender and authority can be resolved empirically, with attention to denominational structures and the place of women within these structures. For more than twenty years, I have examined the position of women among Trinidad's Ṣàngó Baptists. The results are clear. Women constitute the overwhelming majority of participants in all Ṣàngó Baptist ritual, and women own the vast majority of Ṣàngó Baptist religious structures (Baptist churches, *palais,* and *chapelles*). How could this not affect the status of Ṣàngó Baptist women? It should be emphasized that while women may own the buildings outright, they do not always own the land upon which these structures rest. But even if we do not count cases where men actually own the land, women still own over 58 percent of the buildings (28 out of 46 in my sample of Ṣàngó structures in Trinidad), and they sponsor more than half the feasts.

Previous generations of researchers looked for male dominance within Ṣàngó Baptist organizations, and they found it. The trappings are there. Almost all paramount leaders and bishops are male. Only males are allowed to perform the Baptist sacraments; only males are allowed to preach from a raised pulpit in the front of the church; only males are allowed to "line out" hymns and direct readings from the Bible; and only males can initiate prayer. In a number of Ṣàngó Baptist churches, participants are segregated according to sex (males sit on the right, females sit on the left). On the other hand, males are usually *invited* (by females) to officiate at religious ceremonies. They do not own the churches. They are guests. And if the predominantly female congregation is not pleased, they will not be invited back. This suggests that power relations between males and females are not what they at first appear to be.

Contrary to the desires of some leaders within the òrìṣà movement, Ṣàngó's popularity and prominence may be on the rise. A number of Trinidadian informants have expressed preference for Ṣàngó over Ògún (who is generally thought to be more powerful within the Yoruba pantheon). In a multiracial society like Trinidad, one factor may be that Ṣàngó is frequently depicted as a mulatto, while Ògún is invariably portrayed as black. Another explanation may be that Ṣàngó is perceived as being much "easier" on his followers. Followers assert that Ṣàngó is "more approachable." He understands human limitations and is acquainted with sorrow.

Ṣàngó was once a king, but he lost his kingdom. His magic failed him; and he was betrayed by those he trusted. While Ògún (and his consort Òṣun) demand absolute obedience and military precision from devotees in all areas of life, Ṣàngó is said to be slightly more flexible. Ṣàngó is unpredictable and quick to anger, but is believed not to hold a grudge. Sometimes, he does not punish as severely as Ògún/Òṣun or even Ṣàngó's loyal wife, Ọya. "Thunder gets your attention, but lightening and wind kills." Moreover, there are strong associations between Ṣàngó and electronics. Many of Ṣàngó's devotees work in electronics and computers, and Ṣàngó's websites are among the most frequented in the Caribbean.[43]

Frances Henry, who has conducted research on Ṣàngó for nearly fifty years, concluded her entry to *The Encyclopedia of African and African-American Religions* by noting that contemporary leaders in the *òrìṣà* movement are attempting to create centralized structures along denominational lines (e.g., to establish an "Òrìṣà Council of Elders").[44] Adherents want the *òrìṣà* movement to be recognized as a "legitimate" religion by the Trinidadian government so that their *iyá* and *mọgbà* can officiate at weddings and funerals. Henry also documented a concerted effort to "Africanize" *òrìṣà* rituals.[45] While scholarly debates surrounding the origins and authenticity of New World African ritual are far from new,[46] current debates are more significant because the major participants are themselves members of the religions in question. This establishes a different tone to the debate, and there is greater perceived urgency. Another major change is that the forum of debate has shifted. Debate is no longer carried out exclusively within the domain of books, conferences, and paper presentations. It occurs in heated arguments taking place within the context of worship itself.

NOTES

1. William Bascom, *Shàngó in the New World* (Austin: African and Afro-American Research Institute, University of Texas at Austin, 1972), 16–17.

2. Ibid., 16.

3. The same encyclopedia has an entry on "Shouter Baptists," without acknowledging that members of the group prefer to be called "Spiritual Baptists" and that many adherents find the term "Shouter" derogatory.

4. Tracey E. Hucks, "Trinidad, African-Derived Religions," in *Encyclopedia of African and African-American Religions,* ed. Stephen D. Glazier (New York: Routledge, 2001), 342.

5. See James T. Houk, *Spirits, Blood, and Drums: The Òrìṣà Religion in Trinidad* (Philadelphia: Temple University Press, 1995); Kenneth Lum, *Praising His Name in the Dance: Spirit Possession in the Spiritual Baptist Faith and*

Òrìshà Work in Trinidad, West Indies (Amsterdam: Harwood Academic Publishers, 2000); and Stephen D. Glazier, ed. Encyclopedia of African and African-American Religions (New York: Routledge, 2001).

6. Bascom, Shàngó in the New World, 19.

7. Kevin Birth, Any Time Is Trinidad Time: Social Meanings and Temporal Consciousness (Gainesville: University Press of Florida, 1999), 6.

8. See Stephen D. Glazier, "Responding to the Anthropologist: When the Spiritual Baptists of Trinidad Read What I Write about Them," in When They Read What We Write: The Politics of Ethnography, ed. Caroline B. Brettell (Westport, Conn.: Bergin and Garvey, 1993), 37–48.

9. George Eaton Simpson, Religious Cults of the Caribbean: Trinidad, Jamaica, and Haiti (Rio Pedras: Institute of Caribbean Studies, University of Puerto Rico, 1980), 17.

10. See Maureen Warner-Lewis, Trinidad Yorùbá: From Mother Tongue to Memory (Tuscaloosa: University of Alabama Press, 1996), and David B. Welch, Voice of Thunder, Eyes of Fire: In Search of Shàngó in the African Diaspora (Pittsburgh: Dorrance Publishing, 2001).

11. Rawle Gibbons, "Introduction and Welcome," paper presented at the Ninth International Òrìsà Congress, Port of Spain, Trinidad, 1999.

12. Houk, Sprits, Blood, and Drums, 223.

13. Melville J. Herskovits and Frances Herskovits, Trinidad Village (New York: Alfred A. Knopf, 1947).

14. See Donald Wood, Trinidad in Transition: The Years after Slavery (New York: Oxford University Press, 1968), and Bridget Brereton, Race Relations in Colonial Trinidad, 1870–1900 (New York: Cambridge University Press, 1979).

15. Linda A. Newson, Aboriginal and Spanish Colonial Trinidad: A Study in Culture Contact (New York: Academic Press, 1976), 184.

16. Bascom, Shàngó in the New World, 19.

17. Melville J. Herskovits, Culture Dynamics (New York: Alfred A. Knopf, 1947).

18. See Stephen D. Glazier, "New World African Ritual: Genuine and Spurious," Journal for the Scientific Study of Religion 35, no. 4 (1996): 420–31.

19. Sidney M. Greenfield and Andre Droogers, Reinventing Religions: Syncretism and Transformation in Africa and the Americas (New York: Rowman and Littlefield, 2002).

20. David Trotman, "The Yorùbá and Òrìshà Worship in Trinidad and British Guiana, 1938–1970," African Studies Review 19, no. 2 (1976): 1–17.

21. Morton Klass, "When God Can Do Anything: Belief Systems in Collision," Anthropology of Consciousness 2 (1991): 32.

22. Glazier, "New World."

23. Funso Aiyejina and Rawle Gibbons, "Òrìsà (Òrìshà) Tradition in Trinidad," paper presented at the Ninth International Òrìsà Congress, Port of Spain, Trinidad, 1999.

24. One of the more dramatic expressions of inclusiveness is to be found in the Nation Dance—one of the most studied of Caribbean rituals. See Lorna

McDaniel, *The Big Drum Ritual of Carriacou: Praisesongs in Rememory of Flight* (Gainesville: University Press of Florida, 1998).

25. Ronald Grimes, *Beginnings in Ritual Studies* (Columbia: University of South Carolina Press, 1994).

26. Stephen D. Glazier, "The Religious Mosaic: Playful Celebration in Trinidadian Shàngó," *Play and Culture* 1 (1988): 231.

27. Frances Henry, "The Òrìshà (Shàngó) Movement in Trinidad," in *Encyclopedia of African and African-American Religions*, ed. Stephen D. Glazier (New York: Routledge, 2001), 223.

28. Simpson, 17–19.

29. Herskovits and Herskovits, *Trinidad Village*, 331–33.

30. Frances (Henry) Mischel, "African Powers in Trinidad: The Shàngó Cult," *Anthropological Quarterly* 30 (1958): 53–59.

31. Elizabeth McAlister, *Rara! Vodou, Power, and Performance in Haiti and Its Diaspora* (Berkeley and Los Angeles: University of California Press, 2002).

32. Gibbons, "Introduction and Welcome," 196.

33. Hucks, *Spirits, Blood, and Drums*, 342.

34. John K. Thornton, *The Kingdom of the Kongo: Civil War and Transition, 1641–1718* (Madison: University of Wisconsin Press, 1983).

35. J. Lorand Matory, *Sex and the Empire That Is No More: Gender and the Politics of Metaphor in Òyó Yorùbá Religion* (Minneapolis: University of Minnesota Press, 1994).

36. Ruth Landes, *City of Women* (Albuquerque: University of New Mexico Press, 1994).

37. See James Walter Wafer, *The Taste of Blood: Spirit Possession in Brazilian Candomble* (Philadelphia: University of Pennsylvania Press, 1991).

38. Bascom, *Shàngó in the New World*, 14.

39. Erika Bourguignon, "Relativism and Ambivalence in the Work of M. J. Herskovits," *Ethos* 28, no. 1 (2000): 103–14. For another perspective, see Randy P. Conner and David Hatfield Sparks, *Queering Creole Spiritual Traditions: Lesbian, Gay, Bisexual, and Transgender Participation in African-Inspired Traditions in the Americas* (New York: Harrington Park Press, 2004), 22–24.

40. Vittorio Lanternari, *Religions of the Oppressed* (New York: Alfred A. Knopf, 1963).

41. I. M. Lewis, *Ecstatic Religion* (Middlesex, England: Penguin Books, 1971).

42. Bourguignon, "Relativism and Ambivalence," 103–14.

43. Nicole Castor, "Virtual Community: The Òrìsà Tradition in the New World and Cyberspace," paper presented at the Ninth International Òrìsà Conference, Port of Spain, Trinidad, 1999.

44. Henry, "Òrìsà Movement," 256–58.

45. Henry, *Reclaiming*, 108–36.

46. Glazier, "New World," 420–21.

CHAPTER TWELVE

Xangô in Afro-Brazilian Religion

"Aristocracy" and "Syncretic" Interactions

LUIS NICOLAU PARÉS

Some Preliminary Historical Antecedents

In his analysis of Church Missionary Society (CMS) records from Yorùbá-land in the second half of the nineteenth century, John Peel found that, except for Ifá, Ṣàngó "is mentioned far more often in the journals than any other orisa."[1] Similarly, in the satirical newspaper *O Alabama*, published in Salvador, Bahia, from 1863 onward, the African deity most often cited is Xangô.[2] In Recife, as in Trinidad, Xangô became the local name for the religious institution derived from African practices. The evidence suggests that the Òyó imperial thunder deity simultaneously enjoyed an equal popularity on both sides of the Atlantic. This socioreligious success may be explained in part by historical antecedents.

The existence of thunder god cults is reported with different regional variations and names in the Gulf of Benin from the late sixteenth century, and is probably far older than that.[3] In Yorùbáland, there were several thunder deities,[4] the most important of these being Ṣàngó, a deity of probable Nupe origin[5] who was appropriated by, and closely associated with, the ruling dynasties of Òyó-Ilé. Òyó was the capital of an empire that dominated most of Yorùbáland from the seventeenth century until the early decades of the nineteenth century. As Ajayi observes, the long Òyó hegemony in the region favored the expansion of the cult of Ṣàngó, which, as a centralized emblem of royal authority, became fused with Òyó's imperial administration.[6]

Controlled by a titled eunuch called ọ̀tún ìwèfà, the Ṣàngó cult, with a staff of ajẹlẹ̀ (the king's resident overlords or viceroys) and ìlàrí (the king's messengers and tax collectors), was closely involved with the empire's administration. Ṣàngó priests from the provinces traveled to the metropole for final initiation and instruction by the mọgbà priest at the royal shrine in Kòso. Thus, the dangerous cult of thunder and lightning identified with the Aláàfin's authority sanctioned the unity of the empire.[7] Curiously enough, the same dynamic was reproduced in Abomey, capital of the kingdom of Dahomey, where the thunder *vodun* Hevioso, the Adja-Fon counterpart of Ṣàngó, was also associated with royalty and the kingdom's ideology of conquest and expansion.[8]

Peel provides several further reasons for Ṣàngó's success in spreading throughout Yorùbáland, and particularly after 1820, during the period he labels the "Age of Confusion" which ultimately resulted in the fall of Òyọ́. Besides the cult's distinct organization, with its powerful leader in each town, its mọgbà (possession priests) and many active devotees of both sexes, the cult priests enjoyed important privileges, such as the right to impose heavy sanctions on any compound struck by lightning (understood as an expression of Ṣàngó's anger) and exemption from municipal toll taxes. Their public displays were spectacular, particularly such fire ordeals as the *ajere* ritual, in which they paraded around town carrying bowls of fire on their heads. As noted by Peel, "confident in the power of their fearsome god, Sangó's devotees conducted themselves in public far more assertively than any other cult," allowing them to demand heavy sacrifices from the population.[9]

During the first half of the nineteenth century, Ṣàngó worship became one of the most well organized and dominant cults in the region, especially in the western and central zones of Yorùbáland. This was also the time when the greatest number of Yorùbá-speaking slaves were shipped to Brazil, where they were known as Nagô and, from the 1820s onward, constituted the majority of the African population in Bahia. Beyond the fact that the Ṣàngó cult was spread throughout many Òyọ́ provinces, Òyọ́ slaves accounted for the largest contingent of Bahian Nagô, especially after the civil wars of the "Age of Confusion."[10] It is therefore only logical that the Xangô cult would have played a central role in the ongoing formation of Bahian Candomblé—and indeed, it was instrumental in that process. Yet, as I will argue, Xangô's Brazilian preeminence was more than a question of mere demographics.

The Foundation of the "First" Candomblés
by Xangô Priestesses

Xangô devotees figured prominently in the foundation of a number of important temples in both Bahia and Maranhão; a factor that was significant in ensuring the god's social visibility and religious centrality. The famous Axé Ilé Iyá Nassô Oká, in Salvador for example (also known as Casa Branca and Engenho Velho), is considered by both contemporary oral traditions and Afro-Brazilian studies to be "the oldest *terreiro* (Candomblé cult house) in Brazil."[11] Despite controversies over its founders and foundation process, it is widely acknowledged that one of the key figures in that process was a priestess by the name of Iyá Nassô, who after freeing herself from slavery, is said to have returned to Africa, and later back to Bahia to lead her religious congregation there.[12] As reported by Johnson, "Ìyá-Nàsó" is the title of the high priestess of the cult of Ṣàngó in Òyó, responsible for the private sanctuary of the Aláàfin. Costa Lima maintains that in nineteenth-century Bahia, with its large numbers of people from throughout Yorùbáland, including Òyó, no one would have dared use the title of Iyá Nassô were they not authorized to do so.[13]

This Òyó liturgical link poses some problems as regards the current identification of the cult house as belonging to the Kétu "nation." In a recent paper, Renato da Silveira attempts to reconcile this contradiction by suggesting that the temple was originally founded by Kétu worshippers of the hunter *òrìshà* Òsóòsì, and that only in the 1830s would Iyá Nassô have arrived to give new force to the Ṣàngó cult. According to some versions, Iyá Nassô would have been accompanied by Bamboxê (Bámgbóshé), who, as the name indicates, may himself have been a Ṣàngó priest.[14] These facts would explain why today the spiritual owner of the *terreiro* (i.e., the land) is Oxóssi, while the spiritual owner of the *barracão* (i.e., the house) is Xangô.

The critical agency of Xangô priests in the founding of Brazilian temples is echoed in São Luis in the northern state of Maranhão, where the local Afro-Brazilian religion is known as Tambor de Mina (Mina Drum). The two oldest existing cult houses there, both founded by Africans in the late 1840s, are the Casa das Minas and the Casa de Nagô. While the former is famous for the cult of royal *voduns* from the Dahomey kingdom, the latter, inspired by the Yorùbá traditions of *òrìshà* worship, became the major referent or ritual model for the organization of Tambor de Mina as a distinct religious institution.

According to its late high priestess, Mãe Dudú, the Casa de Nagô was founded by four women and a man, including the first leader, Josefa de Nagô, and Joana, who succeeded her. They were assisted by Maria Jesuína, founder of the Casa das Minas. Josefa may have been of Angola origin, yet was a devotee of Xangô or, according to another version, of Badé, a thunder *vodun* in the Jeje (i.e., Dahomeyan) tradition (see below). Joana is also said to have been a devotee of Xangô.[15] Hence, Xangô is referred to as the spiritual "owner" of the cult house, although sometimes Badé is also mentioned. We see here the tendency to install as spiritual "owners" of the temples the deities consecrated to its founders.[16]

A further sign of the Casa de Nagô's influence on other temples and of the consequent spread of Xangô's centrality is the use of the *abatá* drums, this being one of the ritual features that most distinguishes Tambor de Mina from other Afro-Brazilian religious traditions. *Abatás* are two hollowed sections of tree trunks covered with leather skins on both sides and played by hand. The term *abatá* recalls the Yoruba *bàtá*, the special Ṣàngó drum also characterized by two skins. Although the *bàtá* is smaller and is hung with a leather band around the player's neck, rather than supported on trestles like the *abatá*, the compelling phonetic similarity of the two terms and the basic structural similarity of the two instruments strongly point to a common origin.

This evidence indicates the critical role of Xangô in the early institutionalization of Afro-Brazilian religion. As noted by Karin Barber, an *òrìshà*'s life and success depend upon the active worship of his or her devotees.[17] Thus, while demographic factors may have made it more likely for Ṣàngó priests to arrive in colonial Brazil, it was the initiative and charisma of some of those priestesses and priests that underlay the Xangô cult's persistence and subsequent expansion.

Xangô's Symbolic Attributes: Justice and Royalty

It is also likely that beyond the fascination inspired by Ṣàngó's frightening natural manifestation in the form of lighting, thunder, and fire, his appeal to devotees was mainly due to his primary symbolic association with royalty and justice. To begin with the latter, we have seen that in West Africa Ṣàngó was represented as a god of justice who punished robbers and liars with lightning.[18] Like the *òrìshà* Ògún, Ṣàngó is identified as a "hot" warrior but, unlike Ògún, who is reputed to be instinctively impulsive and violent, the "judge" Ṣàngó is said to listen to all parties before acting, and to be a skilled negotiator. Yet, in accordance with the characteristic ambivalence of all *òrìshàs*, Ṣàngó can also be a fearsome and vengeful deity.

Roger Bastide maintains that the sociocultural conditions of slavery tended to emphasize and privilege those attributes of African deities that were most relevant to the slaves' situation, while ignoring those that were less so. In this light, the justice-seeking character of Xangô, with his warrior nature, would have contributed to transform him into a popular emblem of resistance and an allied spiritual force in the struggle against slavery.[19] This sociological interpretation may explain some of Xangô's appeal, but a critical role in his capturing the imagination of his devotees may also have been played by his symbolic representation as a king, and hence an icon of power, aristocracy, and leadership, capable of confronting all sorts of enemies and adversities.

After the famous double axe (*oṣé*), one of Xangô's most important emblems in Brazil is his crown. In Ilé Iyá Nassô, a huge highly decorated crown presides over the center of the dance hall in homage to him.[20] In Maranhão, he is sometimes referred as "Rei Nagô" ("King Nagô"). It is well known that representations of *òrìṣàs* and *voduns* are often inspired and shaped by images of royalty. In Candomblé, for example, a number of *orixás*, including the *iabás* (female *orixás*, such as Iemanjá, Oiá and Oxum) use the *adé* or royal beaded crown of the Aláàfin. Myths recount how some *òrìṣàs* were kings during their original human lives (Ogún, for example, was king of Ìrè). Ṣàngó, however, as symbolic king of the Òyó empire, was king par excellence, a true king of kings.

Before further exploring the implications of this royal theme, I will briefly comment on the historicity of this legend. The first author to mention Ṣàngó's human reign was Bowen, who stated in 1858 that Ṣàngó, also called *Djàkúta* ("The Stone Thrower), was king in Ikòso (or Kòso, a village near Òyó-Ilé). These same details were reproduced and expanded upon by Father Baudin and Colonel Ellis in 1884 and 1894 respectively. In 1921, Johnson conferred on the myth some historical legitimacy when he listed Ṣàngó as the fourth king of Òyó and included him among the "mythological kings and deified heroes."[21]

Baudin's version of the story, allegedly told to him by "fetich-priests," states that Ṣàngó was a cruel, wicked, tyrannical king. In order to stop his despotism, and in accordance with an old custom, the town's elders ritually invited him to commit suicide. He refused and escaped into exile in Nupe territory, his mother's homeland. Deserted by his wives and favorites, he ultimately committed suicide by hanging himself from a shea-butter tree. After the news reached Òyó, his political allies quickly installed a shrine near the tree, but there was a great controversy over whether he had transformed himself into an *òrìṣà* and descended into the earth or simply committed suicide. When a violent thunderstorm set Òyó on fire and killed many, this was interpreted as a sign of Ṣàngó's rage against those who insisted on his suicide. People began to say, "*Ọba kò so*" ("the king did not hang") and Ṣàngó's shrine, which was slowly transformed into a city, became known as "Kòso." Similarly, "Ọba Kòso" became a new title of Ṣàngó. It is worth noting that Baudin considers this legend "*of more recent date.*"[22]

Bowen had already reported that together with Ṣàngó's royal "human-ized" form, what we might call the historical Ṣàngó, there coexisted an "abstract" non-human form, what we might call the mythical Ṣàngó, in which he was the son of Yemọja and Ọrunga, and grand-son of Aganju. His brothers were Dàda and Ògún, and his wives Ọya, Ọshun, and Ọbà.[23] Baudin reproduces and expands upon this story, adding that Ọrunga was the son of Yemọja and Aganju (both children of Ọbàtálá and Odùduwà), and that he had an incestuous relation with his mother from which Ṣàngó and all the other *òrìshàs* were born. Baudin's more elaborated narrative apparently intended to promote a unified and hier-archical Yoruba pantheon. In any case, he explicitly states that the mythi-cal Ṣàngó "of the negro theogony" was more ancient than the historical Ṣàngó "that is now venerated."[24]

One may speculate that this relatively modern narrative identifying Ṣàngó as king of Ọyọ́ was elaborated during the "Age of Confusion" fol-lowing the fall of Ọyọ́, perhaps as a mythical expression of the old bond between the Ṣàngó cult and the Ọyọ́ sovereign. This may have served the Ṣàngó priests and their political allies in reaffirming their status in a time of conflict and social instability. The narrative's episode of Ṣàngó's desertion by his wives evokes the myth of Ṣàngó's marriage to the river deities Ọya, Ọshun, and Ọbà, first reported by Bowen in 1858. That myth may have resulted from the actual juxtaposition of their respective cults, a process likely to have occurred during the heterogeneous gath-erings of displaced war refugees in the 1830s and 1840s, particularly in the Yorùbáland's new southern cities, such as Abẹ́òkúta and Ìbàdàn. It was from this southern area that many Nagô people were enslaved and shipped to Brazil. The topoi of Ṣàngó and Ọya's marriage were already circulating in Bahia in the 1860s, suggesting that these interwoven nar-ratives may have been introduced in Brazil during the slave trade period prior to 1850.[25]

Regardless of this possibility, the euhemeristic interpretation (attribut-ing a human origin to deities) was one of the arguments used by Protes-tant evangelists in Yorùbáland in the second half of the nineteenth cen-tury as a strategy to discredit "pagan" myths and gain new converts. As reported by Peel, the *òrìshà* who was most conspicuously subject to this treatment was Ṣàngó.[26] The story of Ṣàngó's human existence and suicide was reproduced—with a few clerical distortions, as noted by Verger—in a Yorùbá text of the CMS entitled *Ìwé Kíkà Ẹ̀kẹrin Lí Èdè Yorùbá* (*The fourth primer in Yorùbá language*).[27]

Atlantic commerce facilitated the circulation of this didactic clerical literature and other English publications such as Yorùbá-English dictionaries. By the end of the century, Nina Rodrigues had access to the work of Alfred B. Ellis and a copy of the *Ìwé Kíkà Ẹ̀kẹrin* brought to him and translated by his informant, the *babalaô* (diviner) Martiniano Eliseu do Bomfim, who had lived in Lagos for some years. Rodrigues remarks that, in Bahia, local people of Yorùbá origin who were under the instruction of English Protestant missionaries in Lagos (most likely referring to Bomfim) criticized certain versions of myths attributing a past human life to the thunder *òrìshà* Ṣàngó.[28] Besides Rodrigues, who at that time had little direct influence on the religious community, these texts also reached a small circle of Yorùbá-Anglophone literate religious experts such as Bomfim, and through them some religious ideas were further propagated through oral transmission.

As far as we can infer from the evidence, this euhemeristic interpretation of Ṣàngó probably dates from the first half of the nineteenth century. By the end of the century however, it was filtered, disseminated, and reified, along with other myths (like that of Yemoja as mother of all other *òrìshàs*), by Christian missions into the Nagô religious circles in Bahia. Despite Bomfim's early erudite criticism, the representation of Ṣàngó as a king must have quickly spread among Candomblé devotees, and Bomfim himself used the myth some years later to justify the creation of the *Obás de Xangô* (see below). My assumption is that the royal aristocratic expression of the *òrìshà* might have engendered the imagination of a royal "court" that helped galvanize Candomblé's liturgical structure as a multi-divinity cult, while at the same time favoring on the social level the formation of a local Nagô religious elite.

Multi-Divinity Cults and the Imagery of the Royal Court

Andrew Apter argues that in Yorùbáland ritual organization co-varies with political organization. According to him, "the ritual system *in abstracto* highlights the complementary principles of Yorùbá government, which are horizontal opposition between corporate political units (*àdúgbò*) and their vertical inclusion within the kingdom (*ìlú*) at large."[29] In Ọ̀yọ́'s religious context, Ṣàngó occupied the Aláàfin's position, at the vertex of the social pyramid. Yet below him, there existed a plurality of concurrent and relatively autonomous *òrìshà* cults, which in social terms represented corporate lineage groups promoting rival interpretations of power within the kingdom. In that sense, ritual mediated between hierarchical unity and horizontal fragmentation. It is my argument that the organizational model of the Yorùbá royal court, comprising the ọba and his ìwàrèfà council of civil chiefs, was somehow replicated in Candomblé, involving a similar integration of heterogeneous and potentially conflictive multiethnic groups and their cults under the unifying leadership of a single religious congregation. Ṣàngó, with his "aristocratic" credentials and Ọ̀yọ́ connections, was particularly well positioned to play a leading role at the mythical-ritual level.

I have argued elsewhere that the religious organization of Candomblé, consisting of the worship of multiple deities within the same temple and the organization of serial forms of ritual performance allowing for several deities to dance in a single ceremony, was not necessarily a New World innovation. In West Africa, and especially in the *vodun* area of the present Republic of Benin, there were clear antecedents of such forms of multi-divinity cults that may have significantly influenced the reproduction of this model in Brazil.[30] The Nagô diasporic priests, in part inspired by the Jeje model already in place, used their own referents to organize their multi-divinity cults.[31] In the Nagô context, the "king" Xangô was one of the *orixás* best suited to gather around him a "court" of other deities—although, as we shall see, he was not the only one.[32]

As previously noted, mythical narratives dating from the mid-nineteenth century recount Ṣàngó's polygamous marriage to three wives: Ọya, Ọ̀shun, and Ọbà.[33] Present-day Bahian oral testimonies also recount that Xangô had several children with Oiá, such as Iroco and the twin Ibêjis. In some cult houses, Xangô is further associated with other deities, such as Oranyian (his father), Iamacê and Baiâni (different names for his mother), and Dadá (his older brother.)[34] On the mythological level therefore, and frequently expressed via kinship metaphors, Xangô essentially functions as a node aggregating a constellation of deities (sometimes referred to as the "royal family") and configuring a particular "ritual field"—a fact that favored the development of multi-divinity worship. The organization of multi-divinity cults may have at the same time reinforced Xangô's centrality within the new aggregates.

In the public festivals of Ilê Iyá Nassô, the *Xirê*, or opening song sequence, celebrates and summons the deities in a particular order: (1) Ogum, (2) Oxóssi, (3) Oçânhim, (4) Logunedé, (5) Oxumarê (Agué), (6) Obaluaiê, (7) Xangô (before the *iabás* or female deities), (8) Oxum, (9) Oiá (Iansã), (10) Iemanjá, (11) Nanã, (12) Obá, (13) Euá, and (14) the "Roda de Xangô" (after the *iabás*) with new songs for Xangô. The "Roda de Xangô" (the dance circle of Xangô) is the crucial moment in which the *orixás* manifest and incorporate their devotees (except for occasional devotees who cannot resist and are "possessed" earlier in the ritual).[35] Xangô thus plays a central role in presiding over and orchestrating the mediation between this world (Ayé) and the "other" world (*Òrum*), facilitating the manifestation of the deities. While in private rituals other *orixás* may figure in more prominent positions, public ceremonies, even when held in honor of other deities, fall under the "reign" of Xangô.[36]

As regards ritual calendars, a great variability is found in Candomblé, depending upon the specificities of each cult house. In the hegemonic Nagô-Kétu model begun by Ilé Iyá Nassô and followed by such *terreiros* as Gantois or Axé Opô Afonjá, whose founders had been initiated in that house, the ritual calendar opens with the feast of Oxóssi, the day of Corpus Christi, and is followed by the Xangô cycle, starting on the 29th of June (Saint Peter's Day in the Catholic calendar), and lasting for twelve days (the sacred number of Xangô). In Ilê Axé Opô Afonjá, the Xangô cycle comprises homages to Odudua, Oranyian and Iamacê during the first day—manifesting only female *orixás* in the festival—and to Baiâni on the last day. The Xangô cycle is followed by a three-month interruption of public activities until September, when the Oxalá cycle begins with the ceremonies called "Águas de Oxalá" (the waters of Òshálá). It is worth noting that the first Xangô to be celebrated on June 29 is Xangô Airá, a "quality" of Xangô who dresses in white and is associated with Oxalá (see below), and that Odudua, who is often associated with the white or *funfun orixás,* is also praised along with Xangô. Xangô also has a feast during the Oxalá cycle.[37]

Despite this interpenetration of the Xangô and the Oxalá groups of *orixás,* the structural division of the calendar between the Xangô and the Oxalá cycles is significant. This division is often referred to as the "red" and the "white" parts. While the "dynamic" Xangô is associated with red and hot attributes and receives "red" offerings of *dendẹ́* palm oil, the "static" Oxalá is associated with white and cool attributes and receives white corn meal.[38] This symbolic opposition establishes two distinct ritual fields that seem to be at the base of Candomblé's structure. Even cult houses of other nations, such as the Jeje Bogum house in Salvador, use this division of red and white ritual segments—although in this case the order is inverted and the calendar starts with the Oxalá (Lisa) part and is followed by the Xangô (Sogbo) part. It may be noted that in this house, Sogbo's thunder pantheon is considered to be the "royal" family.

The Xangô–Oxalá Polarity

In Bahia, as in Cuba, there is a myth involving both Xangô and Oxalá that has clear antecedents in West Africa, particularly in Ifẹ̀ narratives. The story goes that Oxalufã, the old Oxalá (Ọbalùfọ̀n or Ọbàtálá in Ifẹ̀), despite Ifá's negative oracle, decided to visit his friend Xangô. Ifá recommended that he endure all adversities with patience. On his way, Oxalá had three encounters with Exu (the Yorùbá trickster deity), who maliciously spilled red palm oil (and other products, according to some versions) on his white clothes. Oxalá changed them and continued without complaint. When finally reaching Xangô's kingdom, Oxalá found one of the king's horses that had escaped. Xangô's servants appeared at that moment and, thinking that he was attempting to steal the horse, seized him and imprisoned him for seven years. While he remained in jail the kingdom experienced all manner of misfortune, epidemic, and sickness. Women were barren, the ground was infertile, and so on. Xangô, unaware of Oxalá's imprisonment, consulted Ifá and was told that an old man was being unjustly held in his jail. He eventually found his old friend and immediately ordered his release. Ashamed of this terrible mistake, Xangô ordered his servants to wash Oxalá and dress him once again in white. He was lavished with presents and returned to his home.[39]

One noticeable aspect of this myth is that it reinforces the royal nature of Xangô. In Bahian Kétu houses, the legend is ritually evoked in the Oxalá cycle, in the "Águas de Oxalá." The cycle begins with a private ceremony performed before dawn in which the calabash containing Oxalá's *axés* (the sanctified objects imbued with the god's spiritual force) is removed from his shrine room (*peji*) and taken outside the temple into a hut made of palm-tree leaves. This symbolic displacement is supposed to represent Oxalá's trip outside his kingdom. Three times, the white-dressed devotees go in procession to a nearby fountain, where they fetch water which they carry in small vessels on their heads. With this water, they wash and purify Oxalá's *axés*, and make ritual offerings while singing praises. This ritual segment would seem to evoke Oxalá's release and the restoration of his royal dignity. In most temples Oxalá's *axés* will be restored to their original place in the *peji* only after about a week, evoking his seven years of imprisonment. This is accomplished with another solemn procession representing Oxalá's return to his kingdom. During Oxalá's public festival, there is also a dance in which Xangô Airá carries Oxalufã (the old aspect of Oxalá) on his back, reenacting the moment in which the latter was liberated from prison in a weakened condition.[40]

Apter, following Beier, has analyzed this Ṣàngó-Ọbàtálá myth in its Ifọ́n variant (in which Ọbàtálá is known as ỌbalùfỌ̀n) and in relation to a particular ritual performed in an Ọbàtálá festival in Ẹ̀dẹ, once a southern Ọ̀yọ́ military outpost. In this ritual, an Ọbàtálá priest (Ajagẹmọ) is expelled from the palace and taken prisoner by a concurrent priest (Olunwi), and finally liberated and returned to the palace by the king. Beier interprets this ritual as a "passion play," showing that "the ability to suffer and not to retaliate is one of the virtues of every Ọbàtálá."[41]

Apter proposes a more thought-provoking interpretation with historical and political implications. In analyzing the Ọ̀yọ́ founding myths and those of neighboring kingdoms, he identifies a major opposition between the official Ọ̀yọ́-centered royal genealogies and the Ifẹ̀-centered ones, the latter usually reflecting the counter-hegemonic standing of vassal kingdoms. This tension is also expressed at the mythological and ritual levels, configuring an Ọ̀yọ́-centric ritual field around the figures of Ṣàngó and Èshù and a concurrent Ifẹ̀-centric ritual field around the figures of Ọbàtálá and Ifá.[42] According to Apter, the Ẹ̀dẹ ritual evokes and preserves the myth, and the myth evokes the historical rivalry between Ọ̀yọ́ and Ifẹ̀ as well as the compromise through which Ifẹ̀, after having been politically conquered, was restored to a position of official power, but only in a sacred sense. Apter reads the myth's imprisonment of Ọbàtálá as "a euphemism of Oyo conquest," concluding that "Obatala, a paradigmatic white deity, or òrìṣà funfun, is thus the òrìṣà of political displacement: his ritual power, cool and controlled, dignifies surrendered political authority and discourages rebellion."[43]

Would these religious expressions of political tensions have been preserved in the New Word? Silveira argues that in the first half of the nineteenth century, Ilê Iyá Nassô became the center of political organization of the Bahian Nagô community, where secret societies like Ogbóni and Gèlẹ̀dẹ́ would have operated, albeit in an adapted form, in an attempt to recreate the Ọ̀yọ́ social power structure.[44] While the existence of a conscious political agenda in this sense seems doubtful, the Ọ̀yọ́-Ifẹ̀ polarity may nevertheless have reemerged in the gathering of a plurality of Yorùbá ethnic groups under the same roof; a possibility that the Xangô-Oxalá ritual division would seem to confirm. Although the "hot" warrior Xangô may have succeeded as an emblem of political authority, encouraging resistance and rebellion, Oxalá's more peaceful tactics of passive resistance also appears to have gained its supporters, and it is by now well established that in slave societies, conflict and negotiation intermingled as alternative strategies for the empowerment of Africans and their descendants.[45]

This Oxalá-Xangô equilibrium, imbued with conflictive tension, finds another ritual expression in the Olórógun festival held the first Sunday after carnival, marking the end of the annual ritual calendar. In the Olórógun, "the *court* of Oxalá and the *court* of Xangô, *fight* in the *terreiros* to the sounds of drum beating and religious songs." In other words, the devotees from one group try to capture members of the other group until one of them becomes the first to be "possessed" by the *orixás,* thus signaling the defeat of her/his group.[46] The war game ends and the *orixá,* holding his flag, gathers all devotees in a procession. It is believed that after the Olórógun the *orixás* return to Africa for the Lent period, and some say that "the *orixás* go to war."[47] Although Xangô exerted a critical ritual aggregation role, we should not forget, however, that under his unifying reign there coexisted a plurality of often contradictory and counter-hegemonic interests that somehow managed to be integrated and reconciled in the multi-divinity structure of Candomblé.

The *Obás de Xangô* and Political Aristocracy

Yet the popularity of Xangô never ceased to increase. In 1910, Eugénia Ana dos Santos, or Mãe Aninha, a Xangô devotee (*filha de Xangô*) who had been partially initiated at Ilê Iyá Nassô, founded her own *terreiro,* Ilê Axé Opô Afonjá, under the auspices of her spiritual owner (*dono de cabeça*), Xangô Afonjá. Mãe Aninha, who enjoyed wide social recognition, was one of the first high priestesses to cultivate friendships with intellectuals. In the 1930s, she hid in her *terreiro* the communist Edson Carneiro from police persecution, and in 1937 she received in her house the participants of the Second Afro-Brazilian Congress, organized by Carneiro. Mãe Aninha once expressed her dream: "I want to see my spiritual grandchildren with doctor's rings, prostrated in front of Xangô."[48] This dream began to become reality when, with the collaboration of *babalaô* Martiniano Eliseu de Bomfim, she founded, also in 1937, the institution of the *Obás de Xangô* (Ministers of Xangô). The *Obás* were a series of twelve dignitaries, six "of the right" and six "of the left," in charge of assisting the high priestess in her religious leadership.

Despite his earlier criticism of the myth of Xangô's suicide, Bomfim used this very myth to justify the new institution, identifying the *Obás* with the Ministers of Ṣàngó, the council of elders that had installed Ṣàngó's shrine in Kòso after his death.[49] As several authors have demonstrated, the institution of the *Obás de Xangô* was inspired by the political organization of the Òyó kingdom and the Yorùbá logic of left and right division.[50] In fact, the Brazilian institution of the *Obás* was a creative adaption of the Ṣàngó priesthood hierarchy in Òyó. Father Baudin, who Martiniano may have read, described it as consisting of a chief, the *magba*, attended by twelve assistants: "the first calls himself *Oton* (the right arm); the second, *Osin* (the left arm); the third, *Eketu*; the fourth, *Ekerin*, etc. The chief and his assistants live at Oyo."[51] Yet, as constituted in Bahia, the *Obás* institution was a rather original arrangement which did not find any counterpart in Yorùbáland.

Conceived as legitimating an imagined African orthodoxy, the *Obás de Xangô* could be interpreted as a self-conscious attempt to invest a "disturbed past" (as Sidney Mintz qualifies the past of any Afro-American culture) with continuity and moral significance, and, in that sense, it offers a textbook example of a Hobbsbawmian "invented tradition."[52] Ultimately, the initiative served wide political goals of black self-determination and empowerment, but also served as a marker of distinction vis-à-vis concurrent religious congregations, such as Ilê Iyá Nassô. The "ideology of prestige" founded on the conceptual triad "Africa-purity-tradition" had been promoted within Candomblé since its beginnings and was part and parcel of the institution. Direct contacts with West Africa, such as Bomfim's, provided strategic elements and additional resources in an otherwise local dynamic of legitimacy and authority.

The *Obá* titles were first granted to reputed religious experts (*ogãs*). Under the leadership of Mãe Senhora (1940–67), however, their number was increased to thirty-six (with each of the twelve original *Obás* now having his own "left" and "right" representatives) and offered to several eminent figures of Bahian intellectual society; such as writer Jorge Amado, painter Carybé, musicians Dorival Caymmi and Gilberto Gil, photographer-ethnographer Pierre Verger, sociologist Roger Bastide, and anthropologist Vivaldo da Costa Lima—many of them already Xangô devotees. As noted by Sansi, the Obás of Xangô "were people of social value, who could help build a 'court society' in the temple and increase its value and fame, the *axé*."[53]

Indeed, the royal court model was again reproduced, not on the mythical level, but on the human social level, with the high priestess—herself representative of Xangô—surrounded and supported by an entourage of ministers. Beyond increasing the *terreiro*'s social visibility and prestige, the "court" symbolic imagery further contributed—whether consciously intended or not—to the establishment of this particular religious congregation in an "aristocratic" position in relation to the wider Candomblé community.

In 1952 Pierre Verger, who was then working to reestablish the communication between Bahia and West Africa, brought from Nigeria to Mãe Senhora two central emblems of the Xangô cult, a *xeré* (Xangô's rattle) and an *ẹdùn àrá* (Xangô's sacred stone or thunderbolt supposed to be fallen from the sky), along with a letter from the king of Ọ̀yọ́ conferring upon the high priestess the title of Iyá Nassô.[54] Through these means, Xangô's ritual centrality as a hierarchical superior unifying the plural horizontal diversity became by extension an instrumental icon for the consolidation of a Nagô-Kétu religious elite in Bahian Candomblé. Herein lies what may be the true key to Xangô's political importance in twentieth-century Bahia.

In the opening ceremony of the Semana Cultural de Herança Africana na Bahia (Cultural week of the African heritage in Bahia), or Alaiandê Xirê, held in Ilê Axé Opô Afonjá in August of 2003, the new minister of culture in the Lula's government, Gilberto Gil, reminded the audience that he held the title of *Obá,* or Minister of Xangô. Accepting his new job in Brasília, he said, had been greatly facilitated by the fact that he already was a minister "at the spiritual level" long before his current position as a minister of state. In front of TV cameras and a responsive audience, he praised Xangô, that "great saint," and expressed his deepest respect and the respect of all the ministers and members of Parliament in Brasília to the high priestess Mãe Stella and to the Candomblé community. The opening of the Alaiandê Xirê ended with a presentation of "Xangô Awards" to people whose outstanding support for the community was seen as deserving of special mention.[55] The Semana proceeded with an international seminar that gathered intellectuals, artists, and cultural agents, most of them, including myself, starting their interventions by paying homage and respect to Xangô, the house spiritual leader, and patron of the event. Mãe Aninha's dream had been fulfilled.

One can perceive from the preceding discussion that the case of Xangô involves a complex set of interactions or correlations between practice and myth, and more specifically between the political and the religious spheres. In imperial Ọ̀yọ́, for example, the royal political system provided a model for the hierarchical organization of the *òrìshà* cults, while the Aláàfin inspired a particular mythological expression of Ṣàngó as a human king. It is interesting to note that Ṣàngó's "humanization" was a later process that was accreted to his existing role as thunder deity, a fact that calls into question the hypothesis according to which *òrìshàs* originate from the deification of prominent ancestors and suggests the quite contrary possibility that heroes may also be created from deities. Still other political events and social changes seem to have shaped the mythological level, such as the Ṣàngó-Òshálá narrative reflecting the Ọ̀yọ́ conquest of Ifẹ̀, or the myth of Ṣàngó's wives, which quite probably expressed the gathering of diverse cults during the "Age of Confusion."

These examples would in some sense support the Durkheimian idea that religious concepts tend to be products or expressions of social facts. Yet in the Brazilian case, one also finds the reverse process, in which symbolic or conceptual religious motives seem to have determined both ritual practice and the political sphere. Xangô's royal status and mythical position as an aggregating node, for example, seem to have favored the consolidation of multi-divinity cults and informed the development of a type of socioreligious organization with strong political connotations (i.e., the Obás de Xangô.) Such examples tend to support a more Weberian vision in which social action is oriented by religious ideas. Even in imperial Òyó, the dangerous thunder òrìshà, with his attributes of justice and strength, already served to sanction and project a public image of the Aláàfin's power. Thus we see that—as both Weber and Durkheim themselves recognized—social practice and religious ideas (including those expressed in ritual and myth) tend in practice to form a continuous feedback interaction or dialectic, making it ultimately impossible to determine the preeminence of one over the other.[56]

Xangô's Diversity and Syncretic Interactions

Up until now, I have mostly referred to Xangô as a generic category. Yet, like other orixás in Bahia, Xangô is said to have many "qualities." Some people list twelve, in accordance with the orixá's sacred number, although there is no clear consensus on this. Some of these "qualities" may have originally been distinct entities, and some of them were already worshiped in the Òyó palace as Sàngó's "siblings," such as Òrányàn (the legendary founder of Òyó and father of Sàngó), Dàda (his eldest brother), and Aganju (a later king of Òyó, considered the youngest Sàngó). Some of these "qualities" may derive from the deification of historical characters, such as Àfònjá, the rebel military dignitary of the Òyó empire. Some may have been praise titles, like Djàkúta ("the Stone Thrower") and Oba Kòso. Others may be explained as regional variants of thunder deities, such as Ogodô, reputed to be of Nupe origin, and Oloroké, probably of ÈfÒn origin. The above-mentioned Airá, is said to have three variants, Airá Intilé, Airá ÌgbÒnàn, and Airá Mofé, all quite "old" Sàngós. Some say that the Airás were originally from Sabe (a western Yorùbá kingdom), although the association with the white (funfun) òrishàs suggests they may have a more ancient eastern origin. Still other names are Oba Lúbé, Baru, and Òrunga (the "Middle of the Day," "Master of the Sun," in some myths considered the incestuous father of Sàngó). Finally, Biri, or Èshù Biri (translated by Baudin as "darkness") is one of of Ṣàngó's Èshùs, or "slaves."[57]

At the same time, Xangô finds equivalents in the pantheons of the other Candomblé "nations." In the Jeje "nation," thunder *voduns* such as Sogbo, Badé, or Akolombe, belonging to the Hevioso family, are compared with Xangô. In the Angola "nation," the *enquice* (*nkisi*) Zaze Luango is also related to Xangô. Beyond these African internal correlations there are external associations with Catholic saints. Aganju is usually praised on June 24 (Saint John's Day), St. John being represented as a child with a ram (Xangô's sacrificial animal). Afonjá is honored with the Airás on the 27th of June (Saint Peter's Day). On the Iberian Peninsula, the summer solstice feasts were celebrated with bonfires, a tradition perpetuated in colonial Brazil. The fire element would explain the association between these saints and the thunder-lightning-fire African deities. In Bahia, however, Xangô's most widespread Catholic syncretic association is with Saint Jeremy, a saint who in Catholic iconography appears beside a lion, the king of animals, just as Xangô is the king of men and gods.[58]

In Maranhão there emerges a more complex situation. Given the importance of the Jeje *voduns* in the area, Noche Sogbo, here a female deity, is identified as the patroness of Tambor de Mina and related to Saint Barbara (who in Bahia is associated with Oiá). Yet the closest association of Xangô is established with the "young" *vodun* Badé, often honored on Saint John's Day. As I have mentioned, in the Casa de Nagô, Xangô and Badé are both ambiguously identified as the spiritual owners of the cult house (*donos da casa*) and, when further queried, some devotees will even include in this role the female Sogbo.[59] These interconnections—some of which may have been already established in Africa—also suggest an early Maranhese juxtaposition of religious practices of various Nagô and Jeje groups.

Besides the proper African *voduns* (and *orixás*) in Tambor de Mina, there are a number of other categories of non-African spiritual entities, such as the *gentis* (Gentiles), representing members of the European nobility, or the *caboclos,* including the Turks and other categories of "Brazilian" entities. To further complicate the picture, some African entities may manifest as *gentiles* or *caboclos,* depending upon the "line" (*linha,* or song sequence) through which they chose to manifest themselves. In the Casa de Nagô, for example, Badé can "come down" through the Nagô "line" (as a form of Xangô), in which case he will be treated as the "owner" of the house. Yet he can also manifest through the bush "line," in which case he will merely be *caboclo* Badé. Similarly, Rei Nagô ("King Nagô") and Toi Azezinho—often referred as forms of Xangô—also manifest as *gentiles.*

There are several other *gentiles* and *caboclos* who are said to be "types" of Xangô, or "to come through the irradiation of Xangô," such as Dom Luis Rei da França. Some of these hide their "true" identity behind the Catholic name of Xangô's syncretic counterparts Saint John and Saint Peter, such as Dom João (also known as "Rei da Mina"), João Soeira, Pedro Estrela, and Pedrinho ("Little Peter"). The latter was a nickname for Xangô Ogodô, one of the main spiritual entities of Mãe Anastácia, founder of the famous Terreiro da Turquia.[60] Entities like Pedro Angaço and Toi Ajahunto, both evolutions of different "qualities" of the Dahomeyan panther *vodun* Kpo (Agassu from Abomey and Ajahuto from Allada), are also referred to as types of Xangô.[61] Finally, the *vodun* Averekete, belonging to the Hevioso family, and the *vodun cambinda* Jan de Arauna (or São Miguel de Arauna), both of whom generally "come in the front" to open the way for other deities, may also manifest as forms of Xangô.[62]

This brief overview suggests that in Afro-Brazilian religion, Xangô became something of a broad category, or an ideal-type in Weberian terms, used to describe and classify the diversity of the spiritual world. Yet different kinds of "syncretic" interactions can be distinguished. Xangô's relationship with the Jeje *voduns* was due to a great extent to previous African geographical diffusionism that resulted in a fluid continuity of correspondences of both conceptual and ritual attributes. The association with Catholic saints is of a different nature and was established through discrete symbolic elements and their correlations with the Catholic calendar (e.g., the bonfire in the June festivals) or by metaphoric analogies derived from the iconography (e.g., the lion or the ram). The associations with Catholic saints seem to be mostly formal and do not necessarily imply a deeper correspondence of qualitative values. As regards the interactions with the *gentiles* and *caboclos,* the inverse would seem to be the case. This is where Xangô may be seen to operate more clearly as a class, a label or mental image used to rationalize a wide semantic field that includes ideas of power, strength, royalty, virility, dynamism, fighting, justice and so on. The new "Brazilian" entities may share with Xangô some ritual attributes, such as colors, emblems, and food offerings. Yet what is really "translated" in calling them "Xangô" is a particular sort of qualitative character, some personality features and moral values that may more readily express in behavior. Thus, despite the great creative eclecticism of Afro-Brazilian religion, "old meanings" may be seen to have managed to replicate themselves under new forms and to be inscribed in new expressions.

I have shown how Xangô's "power," as expressed in his natural forms of thunder, lightning, and fire, and his moral attributes of justice and royalty (another of these, virility, not being discussed here), may have been decisive in the consolidation of his ritual centrality and functioning as an aggregating force in the multi-divinity dynamics of Candomblé. I have further suggested that Xangô's ritual significance expanded beyond the religious field into the wider social domain, becoming intimately interwoven with the fabrics of political power, ultimately transforming him into a central emblem of the aristocratic Nagô-Kétu religious elite. Finally, I suggest that it was precisely this socioreligious preeminence and visibility that permitted Xangô to become an ideal-type, a generic conceptual "brand" typifying a wide and diverse field of representational forms within the Afro-Brazilian spiritual universe. All this without mentioning his iconic reproduction in art and popular culture in the form of carnival groups, orchestras, T-shirts, postcards and so on. But this is already the subject for another essay.

NOTES

Following the editors' suggestion, in this essay the names of deities are spelled in Yorùbá when mentioned in relation to the West African context (i.e. Ṣàngó, òrìshà). However, when dealing with the Brazilian context the Brazilian-Portuguese spelling is used (i.e. Xangô, orixá). Similarly, for institutions and formal titles, I use the local Yorùbá or Brazilian spelling as appropriate. When quoting other sources, I observe the original spelling. I would like to thank Peter Cohen for the English revision and for his comments.

This chapter originally appeared as Luis Nicolau Parés, "Shango in Afro-Brazilian Religion: 'Aristocracy' and 'Syncretic' Interactions," *Religioni e Società Rivista de Scienze Sociali della Religione,* no. 54 (2006): 70–98.

1. John D. Y. Peel, *Religious Encounter and the Making of the Yorùbá* (Bloomington: Indiana University Press, 2000), 109.

2. Xangô is explicitly mentioned three times, and in one of them referred to as "the great Xangô" ("o grande Changó"). He is also mentioned under his Jeje (i.e., Dahomeyan) name, Sogbo. In this particular case, Oiá is identified as "the wife of the greatest saint Sogbo" (*a mulher do santo maior—Soubó*). See *O Alabama,* December 24, 1863, and May 2 and 19, 1869, 3.

3. For an overview of historical references on the thunder cults in the Gulf of Benin, see Luis Nicolau Parés, "Transformations of the Sea and Thunder Voduns in the Gbe-Speaking Area and in the Bahian Jeje Candomblé," in *Africa and the Americas: Interconnections during the Slave Trade,* ed. José C. Curto and Rene Soulodre-La France (Trenton, N.J.: Africa World Press, 2005), 69-93. Based on the work of Colonel A. B. Ellis, Nina Rodrigues, *Os Africanos no Brasil* (1906) (São Paulo, Brazil: Companhia Editora Nacional, 1977), 225, recalls that one of

Xangô's names is Dzakúta, "the thrower of stones," and refers to the deity as a lithological manifestation associated with the cult of meteocrites and stone axes, and hence dating back to the Stone Age. In colonial Brazil, there were similar Amerindian cults.

4. For example, Òràmfẹ̀ in Ifẹ̀, Àrá [Airá] in Kétu and Sábẹ̀ẹ̀. See Peel, *Religious,* 111–12.

5. Paul Baudin, *Fetichism and Fetich Worshippers* (1884) (New York: Benziger Bros., 1885), 23, followed by others, such as Samuel Johnson, *The History of the Yorùbás* (1921) (Lagos: C.S.S. Bookshops, 1976), 36, reports that the mother of Ṣàngó was from Nupe.

6. J. F. A. Ajayi, "The Aftermath of the Fall of Òyọ́." In *History of West Africa,* ed. J. F. Ade Ajayi and Michael Crowder (London: Longman, 1974), 133, writes explicitly about the dissemination of Ṣàngó's cult with the expansion of Òyọ́. Another discussion on this theme may be found in J. Lorand Matory, *Sex and the Empire That Is No More: Gender and the Politics of Metaphor in Òyọ́ Yorùbá Religion* (Minneapolis: University of Minesota Press, 1994), 13–22.

7. Andrew Apter, *Black Critics and Kings: The Hermeneutics of Power in Yorùbá Society* (Chicago: University of Chicago Press, 1992), 24–25; P. Morton Williams, "An Outline of the Cult Organization and Cosmology of Old Oyo," *Africa* 34, no. 3 (1964): 258; P. C. Lloyd, *The Political Development of Yorùbá Kingdoms in Eighteenth and Nineteenth Centuries,* Occasional Paper no. 31 (London: Royal Anthropological Institute, 1971), 10; and Johnson, *History of the Yorùbás,* 59–62. In 1885, Baudin, *Fetichism,* 25, stated that "the new sovereigns of Yorouba come to Ikoso on the day of their consecration to receive the sword of Chango, the insignia of their executive power."

8. Parés, "Transformations," 18.

9. Peel, *Religious,* 106, 112.

10. João José Reis, *Rebelião Escrava no Brasil: A história do Levante dos Malés em 1835* (São Paulo: Companhia das Letras, 2003), 336–37. Reis also holds that in 1820 and 1830 the majority of males in Bahia (responsible for the revolt of 1835) were Yorùbá Muslims from the Òyọ́ kingdom, many of them gathered in Ìlọrin.

11. The founding date of Ilê Iyá Nassô Oká is uncertain. Some authors speculate that it could be the end of the eighteenth century, while conservative hypotheses suggest the early decades of the nineteenth century. Regardless, oral tradition and Afro-Brazilian studies have regularly insisted that on the Candomblé origin myth that attributes to Ilê Iyá Nassô the privileged role of oldest *terreiro* in Brazil. For a critique of such an assumption see Luis Nicolau Parés, "The Nagôization Process in Bahian Candomblé," in *The Yorùbá Diaspora in the Atlantic World,* ed. Toyin Falola and Matt D. Child (Bloomington: Indiana University Press, 2004).

12. For different versions of the foundation process, see Edison Carneiro. *Candomblés da Bahia* (1948) (Salvador, Brazil: Ediouro, 1985), 48; Pierre Verger, *Orixás* (Salvador, Brazil: Corrupio, 1981), 28–29; and Roger Bastide, *Sociologia*

de la Religion [Les religions africaines au Brésil] (1960) (Gijón, Spain: Ediciones Jucar, 1986), 323. For a recent interpretation, see Renato da Silveira, "Jeje-Nagó, Iorubá-Tapá, Aon Efan, Ijexá: Processo de constituição do candomblé da Barroquinha—1764–1851," *Cultura Vozes 6*, no. 94 (2000): 80–100.

13. Johnson, *History of the Yorùbás*, 64, and Vivaldo da Costa Lima, *A família-de-santo nos Candomblés Jeje-Nagôs da Bahia: um estudo de relações intragrupais* (Salvador, Brazil: UFBa., 1977), 24.

14. Silveira, "Jeje-Nagô," 83–89: Bastide, *Sociologia*. 323. In a recent work, Vivaldo da Costa Lima, "Ainda sobre a nação de queto," in *Faraimará—o caçador traz alegria: Mãe Stella, 60 anos de iniciação*, ed. Cléo Martins and Raul Lody (Rio de Janeiro: Pallas, 2000), 75, suggests that Iyá Nassô may have come from a small village called Kétu near Ọ̀yọ́, rather from the more famous city of Ilé Kétu in Dahomey. The name Bamboxê or Bámgbóshé would translate as "help me to secure the *oṣé*," referring to the ceremonial double axe (*oxé* in Brazilian Portuguese) used in Ṣàngó worship: Lima, "A família," 25: Peel, *Religious*, 102.

15. Maria do Rosário Carvalho Santos, *O Caminho das Matriarcas Jeje-Nagô. Uma contribuição para a história da religião afro no Maranhão* (São Luis, Brazil: Func, 2001), 26, 48, and 87. For a slightly different version, see Maria Rosário Carvalho Santos, and Manoel Santos Neto, *Bomboromina: Terreiros de São Luis - Uma interpretação sócio cultural* (São Luis, Brazil: SECMA/SIOGE, 1989), 52. Another version would assign a Nagô-Tapa origin to Josefa and a Cabinda origin to Joana: Jorge Oliveira Itacy. *Orixás e voduns nos terreiros de Mina* (São Luis, Brazil: VCR Produções e Publicidades, 1989), 31.

16. Another example involves Mãe Anastácia L. Dos Santos (Akiciobená Obá-Delou), who founded the Terreiro Fé em Deus (Nifé Olorum), known as Terreiro da Turquia, on June 23, 1889, a year after the abolition of slavery. The spiritual "owners" of that cult house are Vô Missã (Nanã), Pedrinho (Xangô), and Navé (Oxum), while the spiritual "guide" is the *caboclo* Rei Turquia. Both Xangô (under the nickname of "Pedrinho") and Rei Turquia were the main spiritual entities of Mãe Anastácia.

17. Karin Barber, "Como o homen cria Deus na África Ocidental: atitudes dos Yoruba para com o òrìṣà," in *Meu Sinal está no teu corpo*, ed. C. E. M. Moura (São Paulo: EDICON-EDUSP, 1989), 142, 144.

18. See Rev. T. J. Bowen, *A Grammar and Dictionary of the Yorùbá Language*, (Washington, D.C.: Smithsonian Institution, 1858), 16; Pierre Verger, *Notas sobre o culto aos Orixás e Voduns na Bahia de Todos os Santos, no Brasil, e na antiga Costa dos Escravos, na África* (1957) (São Paulo, Brazil: Edusp, 1999), 343; and Johnson, *History of the Yorùbás*, 35–36. In Dahomey, see Frederick E. Forbes, *Dahomey and the Dahomeans* London: Longman, Brown, Green, and Longmans, 1851), 1:102–104, and Francesco Borghero, *Journal de Francesco Borghero, premier missionnaire du Dahomey (1861–1865)* (1865), ed. Renzo Mandirola and Yves Morel (Paris: Karthala, 1997), 129–34. The association of Ṣàngó with justice may also derive from the fact that the Ìlàrí, Ọ̀yọ́'s royal messengers, who

were often Ṣàngó priests, also acted as judges to settle legal disputes in the neighboring kingdoms: Apter, *Black Critics*, 20.

19. Bastide, *Sociologia*, 120–21. Bastide believes that in Brazil, forced labor on the plantations propitiated the disappearance of agricultural gods like (*òrìshà*) Oko, who were no longer of benefit for the slaves, while the oppressive social asymmentry of slavery favored the hegemony of justice gods like Ṣàngó, war gods like Ògún, or entities ruling the dynamics of communication like Èshù.

20. The crown is for Xangô Ogodô, the "king of the house" and its spiritual owner (*dono da casa*). Ogodô is reputed to be of Nupe origin. According to family members of Bamboxê (one of the religious experts involved in the house's foundation), Xangô Ogodô was Bamboxê's *orixá*, and he would have been responsible for the construction of the first crown (Renato da Silveira, personal communication to Luis Nicolau Parés, May 3, 2004).

21. Bowen, *A Grammar*, 16; Baudin, *Fetichism*, 20–26; Ellis, *The Yorùbá-Speaking Peoples* (London, 1894), 46; and Johnson, *History of the Yorùbás*, 34, 149–52.

22. Baudin, *Fetichism*, 20–25. For variants of the same story see Verger, *Notas*, 308.

23. Bowen, *A Grammar*, 16.

24. Baudin, *Fetichism*, 17–20 and 25–27, followed by Ellis, who also was responsible for publicizing the tale of Oya and Ṣàngó's acquisition of fire from Obàtálá (here considered Ṣàngó's father), as well as the tale of Ṣàngó's titanic fight with Huisi near Porto Novo while persecuting Oya for stealing his fire. All these myths were reproduced in Brazil by Rodrigues, *Os Africanos*, 222–25.

25. For the Oiá-Xangô (Sogbo) reference in Bahia, see note 2. It must be noted that the mythical marital relationship between Ṣàngó and Oya may date from the early period of the Òyọ́ empire, when Ṣàngó's cult expanded north toward the Niger river and Nupeland, where Oya was worshiped. My suggestion is that only the myth of Ṣàngó being married to the three river deities was a late elaboration, probably coinciding with the early nineteenth-century civil wars.

26. Peel, *Religious*, 296. Peel's evidence is in D. Williams, Journal, 29 Dec. 1878, and S. Johnson, 18 Apr. 1881.

27. Verger, *Notas*, 345–46. The stories of Xangô were published in the *Ìwé Kikà Èkẹrin* as *Ìtàn Oba Ṣàngó* by A. L. Hethersett (no date).

28. Rodrigues, *Os Africanos*, 133, 224.

29. Apter, *Black Critics*, 21.

30. Luis Nicolau Parés, *A Formação do Candomblé: História e Ritual da Nação Jeje na Bahia* (Campinas, Brazil: Editora Unicamp, 2006), and "Transformations."

31. Andrew Apter, "Notes on Orisha Cults in the Ekiti Yorùbá Highlands," *Cahiers d'Études africaines* 35, nos. 138–139 (1995): 373, 392–93, 396–97, has argued that the cult of multiple deities was also common in Yorùbáland. My view is that the cults of multiple deities in Yorùbáland became significant only after

the fall of Ọ̀yọ́ and therefore that they could have not influenced the formation of Candomblé as the older vodun cults may have.

32. Idálsio Tavares, *Xangó* (Rio de Janeiro: Pallas, 2000), 68 also maintains that "the *terreiro* flourished as a zone of aggregation, mobilization, and cohesion around the king."

33. It is worth noting that this mythical kingship configuration is unknown in Maranhão.

34. For Baàyání in West Africa, see Peel, *Religious,* 106, 343. In 1873, the goddess's "idol" is described as "a cap made of cowries, with strings of cowries hanging from the rim with a bell on the end of each one, which was also part of the Sàngó regalia." For Baiâni in Bahia, and a description of her ritual in the Axé Opô Afonjá, see Deoscóredes Maximiliano dos Santos, *História de um terreiro Nagô: crónica histórica,* (São Paulo, Brazil: Carthago and Forte, 1994), 52. Baiâni is sometimes considered the wife of Xangô Afonjá, and in other cases the mother of Xangô.

35. After the Roda de Xangô, the "possessed" (*adoxês*) are dressed in their deities' ritual clothes and return to the *barracão* for new dances. The ceremony ends with songs for Oxalá. The pattern is reproduced in most of the Nagô-Kétu *candomblés,* which "descend" from Ilê Iyá Nassô, such as Gantois, Axé Opô Afonjá, Pilão de Prata, and others. A similar pattern is found in the Casa de Nagô in São Luis and the houses that follow its model. In the Tambor de Mina the *Xirê* may be called Roda de Alauê.

36. I thank Rafael Soares, *ogan* from Ilê Iyá Nassô, for information on the Roda de Xangô.

37. Santos, *História de um terreiro,* 46–59, 63. Airá's position at the beginning of the Xangô cycle may be due to his seniority (since he is considered the eldest Xangô) but it may also indicate his founding role in the Ilé Iyá Nassô. Verger, *Orixás,* 28, 140, reports that an old name of this cult house was Iyá Omi Àṣẹ Airá Intilé. He also reports three qualities of Airá; Airá Intilé, Airá Ìgbọ̀nàn and Airá Mofẹ́ (See Verger, *Notas,* 326). Baudin, *Fetichism,* 20, refers to Àrá (thunder) as Ṣàngó's messenger "who sends forth with loud noise *manamana* (the chain of fire)."

38. Tavares, *Xangô,* 46, 121–22. For Xangô's food offerings see Raul Lody, "O rei come quiabo e a rainha come fogo. Temas da culinária sagrada no Candomblé," in *Leopardo dos Olhos de Fogo: escritos sobre a religião dos orixás VI,* ed. C. E. M. de Moura (São Paulo, Brazil: Atelié Editorial, 1998), 155–157. For a comparative study of the *orixás* attributes (colors, food offerings, sacrificial animals, etc.), see Claude Lépine, "Análise formal do panteão Nagô," in *Bandeira de Alairá: outros escritos sobre a religião dos orixás,* ed. C. E. M. de Moura (São Paulo, Brazil: Nobel, 1982), 13–70.

39. Verger, *Notas,* 428–30, reports two versions collected in Bahia. Lydia Cabrera, *El Monte* (1954) (Miami, Fla.: Ediciones Universal, 1983), 491, reports a similar story in Cuba. Another Brazilian version, by Tavares, *Xangô,* 77, reports

that Oxalá initiated his journey looking for his wife Nanã, who had been seduced and abducted by Xangô. Seu Geninho (Cachoeira, 2002) told me another version in which Oxalá starts his journey in search of his son Oxaguiã. Once he is released from prison, Xangô orders one of his generals, Airá, to accompany Oxalá forever, which would explain why Xangô Airá dresses in white. In one of Verger's stories, Airá is considered a slave rather than a general. For the West African Ifon antecedents see Apter, *Black Critics*, 28; Ulli Beier, *A Year of Sacred Festivals in One Yorùbá Town* (Lagos: Nigeria Magazine, 1959), 14; and J. A. Adedeji, "The Place of Drama in Yorùbá Religious Observance," *Odu* 3 (1966): 88–94.

40. Verger, *Notas*, 430–34. The Águas de Oxalá have a certain parallelism with the Lavagem do Bonfim, a popular feast held in January in Salvador. The stairs of the church of the Senhor do Bomfim (Jesus Christ syncretized with Oxalá) are washed by Afro-Brazilian women (*baianas*) who, as in the Candomblé ritual, bring the water on vessels on their head. As suggested by Roger Bastide, *Images du nordeste mystique en noir et blanc* (1945) (Paris: Pandora Editions, 1978), 108, "derrière la façade Catholique est bien célébrée, en réalité, une cérémonie fétichiste."

41. Beier, *A Year*, 14.

42. Apter, *Black Critics*, 25 and 15–17, convincingly demonstrates the political intent of mythical narratives. In the face of Ọ̀yọ́-centric founding myths, Ifẹ̀-centric rival traditions were restricted to esoteric ritual knowledge. By means of the hidden meaning of their symbols, rituals have the ability to "preserve" subversive founding myths in the face of coercive censorship and repression (22). The opposition Ṣàngó-Ọbàtálá is somehow confirmed by Peel's analysis of the regional distribution of the former's cults in the central-western zone of Yorùbáland, neighboring the Ifẹ̀ eastern region, where the cult is less prominent (see Peel, *Religious*, 110).

43. Apter, *Black Critics*, 30.

44. Silveira, "Jeje-Nagô," 89–93. According to Verger, *Orixás*, 73, in the *padé* ritual the founders of the Kétu *terreiros* are praised as *essá*. Verger gives the names of seven of these, including the *essá Obouro*, who, according to Silveira (93) is a devotee of Xangô Airá. For the *essá* see also Júlio Braga, *Ancestralidade Afro-Brasileira: o culto de babá egum* (Salvador, Brazil: CEAO-Ianamá, 1992), 111–12, and Juana Elbeim dos Santos and Deoscóredes Maximiliano Santos, "O culto dos ancestrais na Bahia: o culto dos eguns," in *Oloorisa: escritos sobre a religião dos orixás*, ed. C. E. M. de Moura (São Paulo, Brazil: Ágora, 1981). In Ilê Axé Opô Afonjá, the *Arafẽma* is a council of six elder men "with posts in the Oxossi house" who receive the title of *essá*: Santos, *História de um terreiro*, 46, 64, 97, and Silveira (92) claims that the *Arafẽma* was a Bahian adaptation of the Ìwàrèfà, the council of six ministers leading the Ògbóni male secret society in Ọ̀yọ́ that would have operated in Salvador since the early nineteenth century.

45. See, for example, João José Reis and Eduardo Silva, *Conflito e negociação. A resistência negra no Brasil escravista* (São Paulo, Brazil: Companhia das Letras, 1989). Reis, *Rebelião*, 100, 102 also suggests that two Bahian slave rebellions in 1826, one initiated in a *candomblé*, may have been linked to the Xangô cult.

46. "[A]s cortes de Oxalá (Senhor do Bomfim) e Xangô (São Jerónimo) lutarão nos terreiros de candomblé ao som dos atabaques e cánticos religiosos. Perderá a luta o grupo que primeiro deixar 'baixar' um orixá no terreiro." (See Francisco Viana, "Ritual da Guerra Fecha Candomblés após o Carnaval," *A Tarde*, February 17, 1973).

47. In the 1860s the Olórógun held before Lent was known as the feast of *feixar o balaio* (literally, "to close the basket," an expression alluding to sexual abstinence) and gathered big crowds: *O Alabama*, March 6, 1867, and February 16, 1869.

48. "Quero ver meus netos espirituais com anéis de doutores, aos pés de Xangô."

49. Martiniano Eliseu do Bomfim, "Os Ministros de Xangô," in *O Negro no Brazil: trabalhos apresentados ao 2° Congresso Afro-Brasileiro, Bahia 1937* (Rio de Janeiro: Civilização Brasileira, 1940), 233–36. Although published in the proceedings, the text was not presented at the Congress. A version (ed. Edson Carneiro) was first published in the local newspaper *Estado da Bahia*, on May 19, 1937: Vivaldo da Costa Lima and Liza Earl Castillo, personal communications, February 14, 2004.

50. Vivaldo da Costa Lima, "Os Obás de Xangô," *Afro-Ásia* 2–3, June–Dec. 1966: 5–36; Júlio Braga, *Na Gamela do Feitiço, Repressão e Resisténcia nos Candomblés da Bahia* (Salvador, Brazil: EDUFBa, 1995), 47–49; Stefania Capone, *La quête de l'Afrique dans le candomblé: Pouvoir et tradition au Brésil* (Paris: Karthala, 1999), 260–66.

51. Baudin, *Fetichism*, 73–74.

52. Sidney Mintz, *Caribbean Transformations* (1974) (New York: Columbia University Press, 1989), 14; Sefan Palmié. "Against Syncretism. 'Africanizing' and 'Cubanizing' Discourses in North American Òrìsà worship," *Counterworks* (1993): 93.

53. Roger Sansi, *Fetishes and Monuments: Afro-Brazilian Art and Culture in the 20th Century Bahia* (New York: Berghahn Books, 2007), 69.

54. Santos, *História de um terreiro*, 18–19. Mãe Senhora, who was consecrated to Oxum, claimed to be both a spiritual and kin descendent from the Iyá Nassô founder of Ilê Iyá Nassô.

55. This event is also commented by Mattijs van Deport, "Candomblé in Pink, Green, and Black: Re-scripting the Afro-Brazilian Religious Heritage in the Public Sphere of Salvador, Bahia", *Social Anthropology* 13 (2005), 3-26. The year 2003 was declared Xangô's year in Brazil. Besides the Alaiandê Xirê held at Ilê Axé Opô Afonjá, the "V Congresso de Umbanda e Candomblé de Diadema a Grande São Paulo" was also held in the state of São Paulo. The patron of that event was Orixá Xangô, Vodum Badé, Nkisi Zaze/Luango; among many other activities, it included the book signing for *Xangô, O Trovão*, by academic sociologist Reginaldo Prandi.

56. For an analysis of Weber and Durkheim, see Bastide, *Sociología*, 4–8.

57. For different lists of Xangô "qualities" in Bahia, see Verger, *Notas*, 326, and Tavares, *Xangô*, 81–82. For the legendary figures of Òyó, see Johnson,

History of the Yorùbás, 143–48, 155, and 189–200. For Dàda, "god of Nature and vegetables," see Baudin, *Fetichism,* 28; Rodrigues, *Os Africanos,* 222; and Peel, *Religious,* 261. For *Airá* (or Àrá), see Baudin, *Fetichism,* 20; Verger, *Notas,* 140, 326–27; and Silveira, "Jeje-Nagô," 85. For Aganju, see Verger, *Notas,* 32, and Tavares, *Xangô,* 69. For Òrunga, see Baudin, *Fetichism,* 17; Rodrigues, *Os Africanos,* 222–23; Verger, *Notas,* 343; and Tavares, *Xangô,* 76. For Biri in West Africa, see Baudin, *Fetichism,* 28. Tavares, *Xangô,* 136, mentions Yangui, the first Exu or proto-Exu, as linked to Xangô.

58. In the early 1980s, Mãe Stella, current leader of Ilê Axé Opô Afonjá, initiated an anti-syncretic movement against Catholic imagery, but in the time of Mãe Aninha, the shrine of Xangô was presided over by an image of Saint Jeremy. See Donald Pierson, *Brancos e Pretos na Bahia* (São Paulo, Brazil: Editora Nacional, 1971), 322. In Cachoeira (Bahia), although "identified" with Saint Jeremy, Xangô is also celebrated in some domestic cults together with Saint Benedict: Louis Heins Marcelin, "A Invenção da Família Afro-Americana. Familia, Parentesco e Domesticidade entre os Negros do Recôncavo da Bahia, Brasil" (Ph.D. diss., Universidade Federal do Rio de Janeiro, 1996), chap. 5. In 1904, in Rio de Janeiro, João do Rio relates Xangô with Saint Michael: Arthur Ramos, "Os mythos de Xangô e sua degradação no Brasil" in *Estudos Afro-Brasileiros: trabalhos apresentados ao 1er Congresso Afro-Brasileiro reunidos no Recife em 1934* (Rio de Janeiro: Ariel Editora, 1935), 54.

59. The Nagô identity of Badé and Sogbo may have been an influence from the Casa das Minas. It is to be remembered that Maria Jesuina, founder of the Casa das Minas, participated in the foundation of the Casa de Nagô. In the Casa das Minas, Badé and Sogbo are said to belong to the Kevioso family, which is also known as the Nagô family.

60. Pai Euclides Menezes Ferreira, interview with Luis Nicolau Parés, June 25, 2003. For more details about the Terreiro da Turquia, see note 16.

61. It is to be noted that in the Jeje *terreiros* of Bahia, Kpo, or Kposu, belongs to the Hevioso thunder pantheon and is sometimes considered the father of Sogbo.

62. The Maranhese and Bahian data about spiritual entities derives from my fieldwork in both Brazilian states between 1992 and 2003.

CHAPTER THIRTEEN

The Literary Manifestation
of Xangô in Brazil

Esmeralda Ribeiro's
"A procura de uma borboleta preta"

LAURA EDMUNDS

In 2001, Níyì Afọlábí's "Beyond the Curtains: Unveiling Afro-Brazilian Women Writers" addressed the movement in Afro-Brazilian writing that calls for a new way of seeing Brazil's racial past and present. This movement, particularly amongst Afro-Brazilian women, moves forward steadily, and its latest success is the 2005 publication of *Mulheres Escrevendo*, or in English: *Women Righting*. The collection of eight short stories by Afro-Brazilian women writers is the follow-up project to *Enfim Nós* (*Finally Us*), a collection of poetry published in 1995, and the short story collection takes the next steps in liberating and recovering identity from a literary history in which, described by Afọlábí: "dating from the era of slavery, the Afro-Brazilian woman has been portrayed as a slave, domestic servant, black mammy, and at best, a '*mulatta*,' a sexual object whose function is to satisfy the perverse pleasures of the master without any hesitation."[1] The first story in this bilingual collection is Esmeralda Ribeiro's "A procura de uma borboleta preta," or, "In Search of a Black Butterfly," a story which fulfills Afọlábí's assertion that the Afro-Brazilian woman, who is often "fulfilling the roles of mother, lover, provider, spokesperson, encourager, nourisher, . . . becomes fragmented in an effort to assert her individuality in the midst of social conventions and racial stereotypes."[2] Ribeiro's story demonstrates this fragmentation by way of a complex narrative voice. The story is told almost exclusively in dialogue by three separate narrators. The search for the butterfly is undertaken by all three narrators, and it is the primary concern of the story. The story also addresses "the metaphor of the 'absent protagonist'" expressed in Afọlábí's article, in that the "Search" becomes a literary one by way of the mystical butterflies, who ultimately are the still fleeting and unrealized authentic identities for which Afro-Brazilian women writers search. It's best though, to understand this search through a Yorùbá worldview, for a reading conducted through this particular religious and historical framework reveals the complex forces of Xangô, Yorùbá god of fire, thunder, lightning, and justice.

Reading the story in this way, and emphasizing the importance of Xangô, also addresses one of Ribeiro's major aesthetic concerns in all Afro-Brazilian writing: that women and men work together in developing and critiquing an Afro-Brazilian literary tradition.[3] The butterfly, conventionally a symbol of Yansan (Ọya), Xangô's most loyal wife and goddess of the wind that precedes Xangô's thunder and lightning, simultaneously invokes Xangô himself. Ribeiro's use of the butterfly symbol demonstrates a development in the diasporic tradition, for it invokes two Yorùbá deities, but does so in a Brazilian social context for the purpose of developing Afro-Brazilian aesthetics. Yansan (Ọya) and Xangô's unique place in the Yorùbá pantheon makes them the guiding force behind this story as well the entire collection. Xangô's justice is not always blind or democratic, and he also is a fragmented figure, having a history as both mortal and *orixá,* and manifesting a complex articulation of gender and social relations in his worship, but in Ribeiro's story, the complex and paradoxical forces associated with Xangô are community-forming and revolutionary.

The story itself covers fewer than ten pages, and the narrative is constructed in the form of a recounted telephone conversation. An operator at a crisis center overhears the pleas made by Leila to Baby, asking her to help find her black butterfly. The operator then relates the story, secretly, to the reading audience. The depth of the friendship between Leila and Baby is somewhat uncertain, as Baby tells Leila, "Friend? I've never known that much about your life."[4] Leila's pleas are the result of the loss of her black butterfly, who is described as the child Leila is carrying: "When I went to the doctor . . . found out I was carrying a butterfly inside of me. I've never told anyone although I was happy. It would be a beautiful butterfly like the boys."[5] Following the conversation, the operator and the reader learn that the butterfly was lost one night in a violent confrontation between Leila and her neighbors. After Leila was seen by a neighbor's child while she was riding a Ferris wheel with her lover, Jean, who is of French ancestry, the community suddenly appears, and both she and her lover are violently attacked. The boy is the child of one of Leila's neighbors, and he had threatened Leila previously, not liking her "foreign" lover. The neighbor is vocal about this dislike and publicly promises other neighbors to "find a way to fuck [Leila]."[6] When Leila comes down from the Ferris wheel after the child has already revealed her presence in a public place with a soldier-with-French-ancestry lover, the community begins to attack Leila and Jean, throwing rocks at the couple. Leila manages to escape, but is taken to the hospital with blood running down her legs. She is told by a doctor that her butterfly had miscarried, and he did not know where it went. Eventually the "operator" loses the connection and is no longer able to hear the conversation between Baby and Leila. Part of the operator's daily routine is to go to the amusement park every morning, following her night shift at the crisis center, but in the closing scene of the story, she tells her readers: "I've slept poorly since that day. That conversation, I don't know, moved me."[7] Her experience in the park in the mornings is forever changed by the conversation, because she observes "how many girl-butterflies there are sleeping on the rocks," and she wonders, "what kind of future they will have when they become women."[8]

There are a few clues in the story indicating that Leila was dreaming this episode. The time of the phone call is 11 PM. Baby is about to take a shower and wait for her own husband/lover/boyfriend, Tiago, to return home. Her alarm clock is playing music, and she comments on the need to turn it off: "Wait a minute, Leila, I have to turn off my radio-alarm clock. It must be broken since it only works with music."[9] All three women seem to be on the night shift, since at 11 PM, Baby's alarm clock has just sounded and the night operator has just begun her work. Leila's general disorientation and rapid narration of events throughout the story reads like she is trying to recount a dream that was so vivid she must share it with someone else in order to bring herself back to reality. Moreover, when she tells the story, the sudden appearance of the entire stone-throwing neighborhood at the amusement park also indicates a dreamlike quality. She remembers, "I closed my eyes. When I opened them, the park had been taken over by my neighbors."[10] We all know that a dream demands our interpretation. What conditions of society determine Leila's dream? What events contribute to the subconscious formation of the symbols at work in the dream and the narrative? What is the nature of the fear expressed in the dream, and what does it mean to have that fear overheard, hijacked, and relocated into storytelling by another narrative voice?

Yorùbá philosophy and oral tradition can construct a useful methodology through which to explore these questions. Though Xangô's presence is left unnamed in Ribeiro's story, it is dynamic and well documented in Brazil. However, he still emerges from the language of Leila's dream in a collection of rather ordinary symbols accumulated during the recounting of the story. These symbols, and potentially the concepts behind them, are ultimately passed to the operator, whose life is forever changed by Leila's narration. Scholars of history, religion, and art have pointed to the mobility and inclusive nature of the Yorùbá worldview as the principal characteristic that enabled it to survive and flourish through the middle passage and in the New World, but since my concern here is literary, I would simply point to Wole Soyinka, who describes this tendency toward accommodation in *Myth, Literature and the African World*. Soyinka describes how new experiences are absorbed into a deity's agency, and how their interpretation is left to intermediaries who are not bound by the dogma that constrains monotheistic religions like Christianity and Islam.

> [A]n attitude of philosophic accommodation, is constantly demonstrated in the attributes accorded most African deities, attributes which deny the existence of impurities or "foreign" matter, in the god's digestive system. Experiences which, until the event, lie outside the tribe's cognition are absorbed through the god's agency, are converted into yet another piece of the social armoury in its struggle for existence, and enter the lore of the tribe. This principle creates for society a non-doctrinaire mould of constant awareness, one which stays outside the monopolistic orbit of the priesthood, outside any claims to Gnostic secrets by special cults. Interpretation, as it does universally, rests mostly in the hands of such intermediaries, but rarely with the dogmatic finality of Christianity or Islam. The principle function is to reinforce by observances, rituals, and mytho-historical recitals the existing consciousness of cosmic entanglement in the community, and to arbitrate in the sometimes difficult application of such truths to domestic and community undertakings.[11]

It is from this kind of inclusive and accommodating perspective that I wish to approach Leila and eventually the operator in Ribeiro's story, for they are engaged in precisely the cosmic and communal entanglement mentioned above, and the outcome is still uncertain.

Generally, Xangô is easily identifiable. The Yorùbá God of thunder, lightning, fire, justice, and electricity, he is always associated with the color red, and is often portrayed wielding his double-headed axe. However, it can be more difficult to identify him in literature, as his signifiers are sometimes rather ordinary and can easily be associated with unrelated concepts. But in "A procura de uma borboleta preta," a specific set of signs limits the possibilities for interpretation. Leila's wearing of the color red and the blood flowing down her legs is combined with the subject of the butterfly, and a recurring presence of stones. When Leila describes her date with Jean, she tells Baby that she "was wearing jeans and a red blouse, red sandals with high heels, a red pocketbook, and also a red bandana to tie my braids."[12] Later, in describing the attack, Leila tells Baby, "I was taken straight to the hospital because there were clots of blood running down my legs."[13] The prominence of the color red certainly is a potential signifier for Xangô, and it is also associated exclusively with Leila.

Leila is also the character engaged in the search for the black butterfly. The butterfly is also a potential sign pointing to Xangô's presence, as his double-headed axe has a butterfly shape, as do the thunderstones used in his worship in Bahia. Robert Farris Thompson makes the connection between the *osée Ṣàngó,* a dance wand used in ritual ceremonies, in *Flash of the Spirit,* writing that

> the balancing of twin bolts of meteoric fire on the head of the devotee is also meant to convey a promise of moral vengeance. This powerful dual metaphor spread to the far corners of the Atlantic Yorùbá world. It appears with particular strength in Bahia, where in the late nineteenth century the butterflylike shape of the thunderstones balanced on the represented worshipper's head revealed influence from Ketu, where thunder axes frequently are shaped this way.[14]

The butterfly, as the main symbol of question in Ribeiro's story, can be interpreted through Yorùbá-inspired Afro-Brazilian religious art as an allusion to Xangô and therefore all the forces associated with him. Though Leila describes the butterfly as her unborn child (she is literally "pregnant" with a black butterfly), a reading assisted by a Yorùbá set of signifiers and images can begin to penetrate its function. If Leila, in her dream, subconsciously associates the butterfly with Xangô, then she has been pregnant with justice. The search for the black butterfly, then, is not a quest for a miscarried child, but for miscarried justice. Leila wears red and "loses" her black butterfly on the same evening. By alluding to Xangô and all his power, Leila's subconscious operates in an appeal to Xangô and his forces. As Soyinka explains, "in what primary sense a deity is thought upon in a community of worshippers, the affective ends towards which he is most readily invoked. In Ṣàngó's case, it is as the agency of lightning, lightning in turn being the cosmic instrument of a swift, retributive justice."[15]

Also operating in Leila's subconscious is the recurring presence of stones. Leila first encounters the stones rather unremarkably when she arrives at the amusement park and has to remove her red sandals because the "ground at the park is all gravel."[16] While Leila and Jean ride the Ferris wheel, she notices that the Ferris wheel operator is distracted by "butterflies perching on the rocks."[17] Later, when the neighbor child sees her and the community appears to judge her, Leila and Jean are assaulted with stones and are severely injured. As the operator recounts this scene, she is incredulous, but eventually she develops new way of seeing, because she goes to the park every morning following her shift at the crisis center, and after hearing Leila's story, she sits in the park, "observing how many girl-butterflies are sleeping on the rocks."[18] She develops a concern for the butterflies, wondering "what kind of future will they have when they become women."[19] This final scene is the second one in which butterflies and rocks appear together. Taken as single occurrences, none of these colors or objects would be enough to defend Xangô's presence in the story, but taken together they can only point to Xangô and all the intricacies associated with him. Given the position of this story as first in the collection and the fact that it is transparently a metafiction introducing all the stories that follow, a Yorùbá reading of this story effectively situates the Xangô/Yansan partnership as the *orixá* of the collection, and potentially of Afro-Brazilian literature and gender discourse.

If interpreting the butterfly as a signifying shape for Xangô seems to take much of a leap of faith, one can build a stronger association with him through the story by looking at his relationship to stones. This requires looking deep into Xangô's history and discovering some of the many myths that establish his divine status and explain how he came to be associated with fire, thunder, and lightning. First, how did Xangô become an *orixá*? There are too many stories associated with Xangô's deification to review here, but a popular and concise version of the myth states that one day, Xangô

> was recklessly experimenting with a leaf that had the power to bring down lightning from the skies and inadvertently caused the roof of the palace of Ọ̀yọ́ to be set afire by lightning. In the blaze his wife and children were killed. Half crazed with grief and guilt, Sango went to a spot outside his royal capital and hanged himself from the branches of an *àáyán* tree. He thus suffered the consequences of playing arrogantly with God's fire, and became lightning itself.[20]

His connection to stones derives from his somewhat esoteric relationship to Jàkúta:

Mythologically, Ṣàngó is a dynamic personality whose name is recorded in any literature concerning the Yorùbá. It is believed that Ṣàngó is not strictly of Yorùbá origin, introduced from the Niger territory north of Old Ọ̀yọ́. The derivation of the òrìṣà is obscure. Jàkúta, a common epithet, is spoken of as a separate deity by some, but this is generally not accepted. The probability is that Jàkúta is the ancient name for the Yoruba solar deity, and when Sango was deified he was identified with the òrìṣà who had been formerly called Jàkúta.[21]

Welch effectively introduces Xangô's position as outsider, and he also suggests that at some point, an ancient syncretization with another God occurred, foreshadowing Xangô's many syncretizations with Catholic saints in the New World. Welch also points out that most people consider Xangô and Jàkúta to be the same *orixá*. Strengthening this position is William Bascom, who writes:

> Shàngó lives in the sky and hurls thunderstones to the earth, killing those who offend him or setting their houses on fire. Because of this he is called Jàkúta, one who fights (*jà*) with stones (*òkúta*). His thunderstones are prehistoric stone celts, ground like those of the European Neolithic period. When farmers find these stone axes in the field they take them to Shàngó's worshippers, who keep them at his shrines as the symbols through which Shàngó is fed.[22]

Here we can begin to establish Xangô's connection to stones. They derive from the sky, and Yorùbá thought held that the stones were formed when lightning struck the earth. All "thunderstones" are sacred, but the most prized are those that resemble the doubled-headed axe form. The stones are Xangô's tools of punishment, as well as spiritual symbols used in his worship. Bascom also introduces the beginnings of Xangô's role as administrator of justice. This idea may have gained power in the New World, especially in Bahia, a possible setting for Ribeiro's story. Xangô's power is expressed in stones, as explained by Thompson:

> [T]he power of Sango streaks down in meteorites and thunderstones, stones both symbolic and real. The *àshẹ* of Shàngó is found within a stone, the flaming stone that only he and his brave followers know how to balance unsupported on their heads. Flaming stones have become a metaphoric burden . . . the balancing of twin bolts of meteoric fire on the head of the devotee is also meant to convey a promise of moral vengeance. This powerful dual metaphor spread to the far corners of

the Atlantic Yoruba world. It appears with particular strength in Bahia, where in the late nineteenth century the butterflylike shape of the thunderstones balanced on the represented worshipper's head revealed influence from Kétu, where thunder axes frequently are shaped this way.[23]

Thompson refers here to the common practice in Brazil of representing Xangô and/or his worshippers in sculpture with a butterfly-like shape atop his head. According to Thompson, this shape shows, in artistic form, the force of the stones, which are flaming, bolts, or meteoric in nature. In this way, the butterfly in "A procura de uma borboleta preta" becomes an even more powerful symbol. It embodies not only the double-headed axe of Xangô, but also the "bolts of meteoric fire." By naming this shape "butterfly," as Ribeiro does in both symbol and title in her story, she enlivens the image, making a living, breathing force. The visual qualities of the *osée Ṣàngó,* the dance staff used in worship, are creatively transposed into literature.

Yet something is out of place. Leila is nearly killed with stones. Her community appears suddenly out of shadows to exact punishment upon her. The stones they throw kill her black butterfly, and cause her to suffer. When she asks for help in searching for the butterfly, she cannot get it. Why does Xangô not protect Leila? In this scene, Ribeiro effectively invokes Xangô's passionate nature, revealing his ability to act outside of reason. This is an important departure from previous treatments of Xangô in Brazilian literature, in which well-meaning and well-informed white authors attempted to recreate Xangô as a rational figure, as in Jorge Amado's *Tent of Miracles* and Zora Seljan's *The Story of Òxálá.* If indeed Leila is relating a dream to her friend Baby, then it is likely that she expresses fear in that dream of having somehow offended Xangô and incurring his displeasure. Leila worries, as does Baby, about the relationship with the soldier with French ancestry: "We couldn't hold hands on the streets because we were afraid people would stare at us."[24] Baby also worries about appearances: "Has anyone seen you, Leila?"[25] While this is more than likely not a direct offense to Xangô, Leila's relationship is an offense to her community. In the introduction to the collection, Maria Helena Lima describes a common thread that unites all the works in the collection: "for if there is a commonality of spirit in these stories, it lies in their creation of a space in which the socially prescribed myth of a Brazilian 'racial democracy' is questioned, problematized, and subverted."[26] This is precisely the tension that Leila tries to untangle in her dream, and is explored throughout the remaining stories in the collection. Is it an offense to date a soldier with French ancestry? Does she create or undermine the ideal of racial democracy by creating mixed-race children? The community that hurls stones at Leila and Jean does enact a retributive justice, even if it is a racist retribution. The action of the community may also be merely a reflection of Leila's own worries. An effective way to interpret this story is to see the community mastering, for a moment, a morally neutral force. This force can be mastered again and employed by others who wish to exact vengeance, and it is a faithful transmission of the nature of Xangô, known in Yorùbáland as a "hothead" and a god of short temper and acts of passion. However, when read in a strictly allegorical sense, the story shows that Ribeiro is effectively killing off the literary image of the *mulatta*. Leila's child, if born, would be of a mixed-race heritage. As Afọlábí points out, the Brazilian literary tradition has for years characterized the *mulatto* woman incompletely and with racial and gender bias. Ribeiro revises the literary tradition by killing the existing literary image of mixed-race women in her own fiction.

The remastering of Xangô's force is eventually accomplished by the formation of a new community: one comprised of women, and one deeply concerned with the fate of female black butterflies. The women who take part in the telephone conversation, as speakers or listeners, are sharing a set of signifiers, even if they do not know it. These signifiers point to Xangô, but they can also be supported with an examination of the form the story takes. By situating the story as a telephone conversation, Ribeiro privileges the oral mode. The entire story is composed of dialogue, with only a few short lines that reflect the editorializing of the Operator: ". . . what an absurd story I'm thinking . . . Leila calls Baby telling her about a Black Butterfly that flew from her womb . . ." and later: "why doesn't Leila bang the phone in this bitch's face . . . great friend she is . . . if Baby really wanted to help her, she would have put her coat on and gone straight to the amusement park."[27] The Operator, however, is really in conversation with the reader, addressing him or her as "you": "You'd better call me Operator."[28] The oral mode of history and storytelling kept Xangô's stories alive for centuries before they were written first by Europeans and then by Nigerians. The oral mode also sustained Xangô and Yansan (Ọya) through the middle passage and the experience of slavery in the many countries of the New World where Yorùbá people were made to work and live.

The women also meet in Xangô's realm. As Soyinka points out, the accommodation at work in the Yorùbá worldview does not pollute the nature of the *orixá*: "[T]his accommodative nature, which does not, however, contradict or pollute their true essences, is what makes Xangô capable of extending his territory of lightning to embrace electricity in the affective consciousness of his followers."[29] To accommodate even further, one can infer that Xangô is also to be found in any force that needs wires or cables. This would make him the *orixá* of cable television, of the Internet, and also of telephones. In the Brazilian context, Ogun is more likely to be considered the *orixá* of technology, but it is Xangô's energy that provides the power to run that technology. Indeed, in emphasizing Xangô's flashing quality, Thompson writes that "the Yorùbá realize a vision of his spirit in poetry charged with flashing images" and quotes a poem collected by Pierre Verger which contains a line stating that Xangô "makes a detour in telegraphic wire."[30]

Understanding the butterfly shape at work in Ribeiro's story as a literary manifestation of the forces of Xangô also uncovers significant connections between "A procura de uma borboleta preta" and other stories in the collection. *Orixá* appear or are referred to in at least two other stories, "Foram Sete/Lucky Seven" and "Abajur/Nightlamp." In these stories, the *orixá* act as forces of justice and as protectors. The inspiration for a young woman to kill the man who molested her sister in "Lucky Seven" comes as a thunderbolt, another of Xangô's manifestations, and in "Nightlamp" the guardian is a protector of secrets, like a benevolent *orixá*. Establishing these connections reveals that Riberio's story can also be read as metafiction that introduces the stories that follow. This fleeting female community then, in both "A procura de uma borboleta preta" and the collection as a whole, is formed through Xangô, whether or not any of the community members are consciously aware of it. This process can also be seen as a possible way that African and specifically Yorùbá influences and philosophical stances become occluded in New World settings. The butterflies also become embodiments of the black female literary identities that have yet to be realized in Brazilian literature. In the final scenes of Ribeiro's story, the Operator reveals how much she has been affected because of her involvement in this conversation. She says that she has not slept well since that night, and: "I sit there, observing how many girl-butterflies there are sleeping on the rocks."[31] This observation leaves the reader with the powerful assemblage of Xangô's signifiers, and it is also something new, a sight the Operator would not have thought important or even noticed prior to her meeting Leila and Baby on the telephone. In the Operator's New World, as well as the audience's, there is an increased awareness of the fate of the butterflies, and the *orixá* are present, their forces at work, guiding a course of literary action.

NOTES

1. Niyi Afolabi, "Beyond the Curtains: Unveiling Afro-Brazilian Women Writers," *Research in African Literatures* 32 , no. 4 (Winter 2001): 117.

2. Ibid.

3. Esmeralda Ribeiro, "A escritora negra e o seu ato de escrever participando." In *Criação crioula, Nu elefante branco* (São Paulo: Impr. Oficial do Estado, 1987), 65.

4. Ibid., 29.

5. Ibid.

6. Ibid., 35.

7. Ibid., 39.

8. Ibid.

9. Ibid., 35.

10. Ibid., 33.

11. Wole Soyinka, *Myth, Literature and the African World* (Cambridge: Cambridge University Press, 1976), 54.

12. Ribeiro, "A procura de uma borboleta preta," in *Mulheres Escrevendo: Uma Antologia Bilíngüe de Escritoras Afro-Brasileiras Contemporâneas,* ed. Miriam Alves and Maria Helena Lima (London: Mango Publishing, 2005), 31.

13. Ibid., 33.

14. Robert Farris Thompson, *Flash of the Spirit* (New York: Random House, 1983), 87.

15. Soyinka, *Myth,* 8.

16. Ribeiro, "A procura," 31.

17. Ibid.

18. Ibid., 39.

19. Ibid.

20. Thompson, *Flash,* 85.

21. David B. Welch, *Voice of Thunder, Eyes of Fire: In Search of Shàngó in the African Diaspora* (Pittsburgh: Dorrance Publishing, 2001), 39.

22. William Bascom, *Shango in the New World* (Austin: African and Afro-American Research Institute, University of Texas at Austin, 1972), 4.

23. Thompson, *Flash,* 86–87.

24. Ribeiro, "A procura," 31.

25. Ibid., 33.

26. Ibid., 22.

27. Ibid., 29, 37.

28. Ibid., 27.

29. Soyinka, *Myth,* 54.

30. Thompson, *Flash,* 85.

31. Ribeiro, "A procura," 39.

CHAPTER FOURTEEN

Drums of Ṣàngó

Bàtá *Drum and the Symbolic Reestablishment of Ọ̀yọ́ in Colonial Cuba, 1817–1867*

HENRY B. LOVEJOY

Most of Yorùbá music, and perhaps the most exciting, is associated
with religion. Yorùbá secular music has been strongly influenced by
Islam, while another modern influence on secular music is that known
by the Yorùbá as "Spanish music," which is in large part Afro-Cuban.
. . . *Bàtá* are a special type of two-toned drums, believed to be found
only among the Yorùbá, and used only for religious music.[1]

This study of *bàtá* drums is specifically concerned with an examination
of Ọ̀yọ́ and the process of ethnic reconfiguration under slavery revealed
in the emergence of Lucumí culture in Cuba.[2] While Yorùbá were being
taken to Cuba before the nineteenth century, they arrived in small numbers. In the nineteenth century, large numbers of Yorùbá arrived in
Cuba, perhaps as many as 85,000 people. As is argued here, the presence
of *bàtá* drums, an important cultural icon, suggests that a large number
of these Yorùbá, and certainly an influential segment, were from Ọ̀yọ́,
which experienced internal revolt and collapse between 1817 and 1836.
Moreover, it is argued that closer attention to specific cultural features
can lead to a better understanding of the linkages across the Atlantic during the period of slavery and indeed afterward. Easily identifiable cultural
icons, such as *bàtá* drums, can reveal the conscious efforts of people to
reestablish institutions of their homeland, even if only in symbolic and
ritualized forms associated with religion, in this case *òrìṣà* worship. Furthermore, the use of *bàtá* drums reveals a vision of Ọ̀yọ́ paradigms symbolically interconnected across the Atlantic world.

The largest number of slaves of Yorùbá descent left the Bight of Benin for the Americas in the first half of the nineteenth century. David Eltis has estimated (based on an analysis of shipping records) that between 1801 and 1867, perhaps a million people from the Bight of Benin, many of them Yorùbá, were moved.[3] He has further estimated that roughly 96,200 enslaved Yoruba left the Bight of Benin for the Hispanic Caribbean, of whom probably 80–85,000 actually arrived in Cuba. Between 1801 and 1825, there were only an estimated 5,600 African departures from the Bight of Benin for the Hispanic Caribbean. Thereafter the number increased dramatically, with an estimated 65,600 Yorùbá leaving West Africa for Cuba between 1826 and 1850, which is the most important period for this chapter. From 1851 until the trade ended in 1867, another 25,000 Yorùbá are estimated to have departed. The numbers dropped steadily with the British blockade of the slave trade off the West African coast.[4]

The time frame for this study begins with the uprising at Ìlọrin in 1817, before which probably very few Ọ̀yọ́ entered the trade, and ends with the last documented slave ship unloading in Cuba in 1867. Despite British abolition in 1807, a regenerated slave trade forced the migration of Yorùbá slaves to Cuba, which overlapped with the disintegration of Ọ̀yọ́. The collapse was associated with the Muslim uprising at Ìlọrin in 1817, the Òwu War (c. 1820–25), and the declaration of Ìlọrin as an emirate within the Sokoto Caliphate (1823), and coincided with the destruction of many towns and settlements and even the abandonment of the capital district of Old Ọ̀yọ́ (c. 1836).[5] As Paul E. Lovejoy points out, the attempt to estimate how many Yorùbá were forcibly moved, including when and where they went, "raises questions of which Yorùbá are in question, and what the concept of 'Yorùbá' and related terms [such as Lucumí] may have meant."[6] The twenty years before and after the final collapse of Ọ̀yọ́ was at a peak in the slave trade; it coincided with the many wars and shifting political alliances in Yorùbáland and thereby affected the continuing movement of Yorùbá people from Africa to Cuba.

Sources and Methodology

Bàtá drums were chosen as a means of examining the process of Yorùbá migration for the following four reasons: First, they are easily identifiable in physical terms, in that there are at least three membranophones of different sizes. Second, *bàtá* drums have certain spiritual affiliations, specifically in relation to *òrìṣà* (deity) worship, and the Ṣàngó cult. It must be emphasized at this point that the Ṣàngó cult was the principal religious organization of the Ọ̀yọ́ Empire, and *bàtá* drummers occupied roles within its political administration. Third, the collapse of Ọ̀yọ́ at a peak in the transatlantic slave trade set in motion major demographic, political, and social changes affecting both West Africa and Cuban societies. And finally, the "trans-culturation" of Ọ̀yọ́ practices shaped Lucumí culture in Cuba, in which *bàtá* drums demonstrate a clear historical connection across the Atlantic world.[7]

General patterns and specific elements of data surrounding *bàtá* drums and drumming can be projected into historical interpretation. The oral sources specifically related to *bàtá* drums are extensive. One of the most accepted versions of a myth of origin is that "*bàtá* drummers once occupied the lowest status among drummers, until Ṣàngó, at a competition, selected *bàtá* as his personal ensemble."[8] Despite variations in myth, Ṣàngó was supposedly one of the earliest Aláàfin (kings) of Ọ̀yọ́ (in some traditions the third, while others say the fourth or even fifth).[9] After his death, Ṣàngó was deified, and in turn a cult developed in his honor and memory. As Robin Law has demonstrated, there is insufficient historical data to date his exact reign, which would have been before the sixteenth century.[10] Later patterns in oral traditions show that powerful and successful rulers were sometimes raised locally to the level of *òrìṣà*, so there may be elements of truth in those oral traditions. Nevertheless, oral traditions in both West Africa and Cuba have maintained that the mythical Aláàfin Ṣàngó sanctified *bàtá* drums. Whether or not Ṣàngó was actually a person, he became recognized as a powerful mythological figure that had a strong and important historical relationship with *òrìṣà* worship in Ọ̀yọ́, but also with *bàtá* drums.

The first written reference to *bàtá* drums in West Africa, albeit a brief one, appeared in the work of Reverend Samuel Johnson (d. 1901), who was originally from Ọ̀yọ́. His early life clearly exposed him to the cultural and political patterns associated with Ọ̀yọ́. Although liberated by the British Navy and taken to Sierra Leone, he was always exposed to other refugees from Ọ̀yọ́. However, when he became an Anglican missionary, he consciously identified with conversion to Christianity and rejection of religious practices associated with *òrìṣà* worship, such as the use of *bàtá* drums in ritualized settings. The references to drums and *òrìṣà* in his masterpiece, *The History of the Yorùbás,* should be understood in the context of his association with the Church Missionary Society (CMS). From 1881 he was stationed in New Ọ̀yọ́, where many refugees had settled, and it can be reasonably assumed that he regularly heard the sound of *bàtá* drums. Johnson examined and recorded political, social, and cultural traditions of his countrymen. He mapped out the political hierarchy of Ọ̀yọ́, starting with the Aláàfin (king), and also recorded aspects of ritual culture that involved royal drummers. The association of drums with the political and spiritual administration of Ọ̀yọ́ is clearly spelled out in his work.[11]

As Law demonstrated methodologically, Johnson's descriptions of Ọ̀yọ́'s political administration can be confirmed, as the observations of Hugh Clapperton (1788–1827) have shown.[12] While Clapperton never directly referred to *bàtá* drums, he correctly recognized the importance of drumming in Ọ̀yọ́ politics, society, and culture. However, there is a problem in identifying *bàtá* drums specifically with references to drumming. Methodologically, therefore, it is assumed that the interconnection between *bàtá* drums, Ọ̀yọ́ politics, and Ṣàngó has remained unchanged in the transposition from West Africa to Cuba, although the relationship to power, and the ability to implement cultural practices in a meaningful way, did change. An examination of this cultural icon supplements material derived from written records in helping to understand the nature of Yorùbá culture in Cuba in the nineteenth century. In short, it is assumed that the symbolic continuity in cultural expression in Cuba can reveal patterns of historical change.

Bàtá drums were not mentioned specifically in the documentation that has survived from the early nineteenth century in West Africa and Cuba. Clapperton and his servant Richard Lander provided, however, the earliest written record relating to drums from Ọ̀yọ́. In January 1826, Clapperton was in the capital, "Eyeo," and observed the use of drums without providing specific details of *bàtá* drums.[13] At the court, for example, "they kept drumming and singing all night." As he summiced, "the only instruments were drums and horns & whistles which were blown and beaten without intermission." Clapperton also observed, "their attendants were so numerous ['horse & foot' inserted in the margin] that every corner was filled with them and they kept drumming & singing all night." And "warriors and drummers the last well executed conveying the expression and attitude of a man vain and well pleased with his own music and wearing his head and cap on one side his eyes half cast up."[14] Later in the nineteenth century, *bàtá* drums were used at these occasions, and there is every reason to assume that Clapperton heard and saw *bàtá* drums. Clapperton's observations included *bàtá* drums because of their importance to Ṣàngó worship in Ọ̀yọ́. There is no question that *bàtá* drums existed before Johnson and Fernando Ortiz actually described them. Based on oral data, Clapperton's journal, and references to *tambor,* one can reasonably assume that *bàtá* drums were long associated with Ọ̀yọ́, and as chronicled in Johnson's work, long before 1817.

In Cuba, Fernando Ortiz (1881–1968) provided the first written reference to *bàtá* drums and those only appeared well into the twentieth century. Ortiz undertook what was the earliest and arguably the most extensive study of *bàtá* drum culture to date. Between 1952 and 1955, Ortiz published a five-volume series called *Los Instrumentos de la Música Afro-Cubana,* wherein *bàtá* drums were truly represented.[15] His conception of ethnic reconfiguration in Cuba's multiracial society was groundbreaking for the time in which he was publishing. He conducted numerous interviews of former slaves and/or their direct descendents. Based on oral sources recorded by Ortiz in Havana and Matanzas, "a Yorùbá named Añabi (son of Aña or Àyàn) was brought to Cuba who was an *oluaña* and *olósanìn* (had Aña and Òsanìn), and he consecrated the first *bata*s in 1830."[16] However, references to his oral data were often left imprecise.[17] Nevertheless, Ortiz's extensive collection of oral data related to *bàtá* drums and drumming from Cuba is extremely pertinent to this historical discussion.

Unfortunately, written documentation which specifically identifies *bàtá* drums in Cuba during the era of slavery have not been located. Written references to African drums, however, are sporadically found in eighteenth- and nineteenth-century documentation. In Spanish colonial records, for example, African drums were referred to as *tambor* (drum) and in *bailes de tambores* (dances with drums). But these references refer to any type of drum, drumming, and dancing of any African origin and do not provide detailed descriptions about actual drums and dances. The word *tambor* is referred to in colonial sources as an identifiable icon representing the quest for African autonomy and therefore implicitly the target of regulation. The term was codified into law at least as early as 1842 in Cuba. In the *Reglamento de Esclavos* (Slave Code), 3 of the 260 articles directly referred to drums or dancing, specifically in relation to an annual festival known as the Día de Reyes (Day of Kings).[18] More detailed descriptions of *bailes de tambores* on the Día de Reyes began to emerge after the middle of the nineteenth century.[19] Despite the absence of any direct mention of *bàtá* drums in the first half of the nineteenth century, Ortiz collected oral data tracing *bàtá* back to the 1830s that coincide with written references to *tambor* in colonial documentation.

It is therefore proposed that Law's methodology can also be used within the Cuban context because the earliest evidence of Changó's presence in Cuba is displayed on the Lucumí *bandera* (banner). It reads, LA SOCIEDAD DE SOCORROS MUTUOS NACION LUCUMI DE SANTA BARBARA, AÑO 1820. David H. Brown states, "Historically, *banderas* were time-honored markers of political units, institutions, and regions, as well as religious mutual aid, and occupational societies in the Iberian-Atlantic world."[20] As early as 1820, therefore, Lucumí slaves had already organized into a *cabildo* (brotherhood or mutual aid society) in Havana, which was centered on Changó. Changó is the Cuban spelling of Sàngó, and the use of Santa Barbara established that slaves of Yorùbá descent had begun to worship Changó from at least the 1820s onward. *Bàtá* drums in Cuba also have an important relationship to Changó in that they "belong" to him. Furthermore, Ortiz's work on oral traditions claims the first *bàtá* set were consecrated in the 1830s.

Nevertheless, it is impossible to ascertain exactly when the first set was consecrated in Cuba or when the first *bàtá* drummers arrived. It is argued here that sizes, shapes, and components of the *bàtá* drum genre can be documented systematically when projected backward into early-nineteenth-century references to *drum* or *tambor*. *Bàtá* drums as a model, in conjunction with this plethora of circumstantial evidence, raises many questions related to the Yorùbá in the Diaspora. Rituals and ceremonies involving *bàtá* drums enable a comparative assessment of the influence of *bàtá* drum culture in West Africa and Cuba.

Physical Complexion and Modes of Transference

In examining the influence of *bàtá* drums in the Atlantic World, four characteristics are prominent: first, the unique physical complexions and modes of transference of *bàtá* drums in West Africa and Cuba are identical; second, the relationship between *bàtá* drums and the Sàngó cult were a part of the political administration of Òyó; third, the fate of *bàtá* drummers during Òyó's collapse resulted in the transference of *bàtá* drums from West Africa to Cuba; and finally, the functions of *bàtá* drums in annual festivals are comparable in both West Africa and Cuba. A consideration of these manifestations of *bàtá* drum culture reveals a symbolic reestablishment of the spiritual and even political structure of Òyó in Cuba, while providing the illusion of "integration" or "submissive subordination" to the colonial state.

Bàtá drums have maintained identical physical characteristics in both West Africa and Cuba since the 1950s. This can be seen in a photograph of *bàtá* drums taken by William Bascom near the city of Old Òyó in 1951[21] and another taken by Fernando Ortiz in Havana about 1954.[22] Only since the mid-1980s have Cuban and Nigerian *òrìsà* devotees had any real direct contact with one another, though effectively occurring on a rather perfunctory level, save a mere handful of exceptions.[23] These two images have received much acclaim by themselves, but presented side-by-side they prove how *bàtá* drums from West Africa have a physical identity indistinguishable from *bàtá* sets from Cuba.

Darius L. Thieme's dissertation best described the physical characteristics of *bàtá* drums found in West Africa: "The *bàtá* drum family includes a homogeneous group of double membrane drums whose hollow wooden bodies are carved in the shape of a truncated cone. On each drum, membranes cover the opposite ends of the drum body, and thus each instrument has one large and one small membrane."[24] Thieme's physical description is identical to Ortiz's descriptions of what he found in Cuba. In terms of physicality, *bàtá* drums are, therefore, easily identifiable. It is argued that sizes, shapes, and components of the *bàtá* drum genre can be documented rather systematically and that their physical development has remained relatively consistent over long periods of time.

During fabrication the drums undergo a physical as well as a spiritual construction. While the drums are being fabricated, they must also be consecrated.[25] According to Pedro Pérez Sarduy, the secret of making the sacred drums of the *òrìṣà*s in Cuba is passed on from generation to generation, to our time. Juan Benkomo has inherited the secrets and is today a maker of *bàtá* drums in Matanzas, and he revealed some of those secrets to Sarduy.[26] Benkomo states, "This drum has to come into being by hand, not on a lathe. That's how it has to be. The sacred instrument has to be a hand instrument."

In terms of their construction process, the best soundbox for any drum is made from a solid piece of wood hollowed out with a hammer and chisel. Staved drums are also a possibility, as seen in Brazil, but are generally less solid and are regarded by most professional drummers as inferior in terms of sound quality. Many different types of hardwoods have been used, such as African satinwood tree, apa wood, caoba, cedar, almond, and mahogany.[27] Even today, the carving and hollowing out of a soundbox requires meticulous dedication and untiring patience. After the general shape of the body is carved, hollowed, and smoothed, there is often a process of applying and tightening the drumhead. Up to ten laces are used to fasten, stretch, and tighten the drumheads. In West Africa and Cuba, uncastrated male goats or rams provide the ideal animal membrane. In both regions bulls, cows, female goats, and sheep are generally avoided. Drumheads are also made from animal hides, such as antelope, and when necessity dictates, rope is a convenient substitute. These animals are often sacred and sacrificed to the gods and the drums.

During the spiritual construction process, ritualistic elements are literally sealed inside the chamber of the largest drum. The drums are said to "house" Àyàn, or in Cuba, Aña, a goddess of drumming. *Bàtá* drums are believed to represent the embodiment of the *òrìṣà* Àyàn, and when these drums are played her voice is heard. Because the hides used for the drumheads often come from the sacrificed animals, the spiritual connection establishes how *bàtá* drums should be thought of as religious icons embodied within the physical nature of an historical artifact.

In both West Africa and Cuba, the largest drum is considered to be female and is generally called *iyá ìlù* (mother drum) and Àyàn. The name for the ensemble is *bàtá*, and the largest drum, *iyá ìlù*, has remained constant between regions. The names for the smaller drums differ between Africa and Cuba, as well as within Africa and within Cuba. The smaller drums in any given *bàtá* ensemble have a number of names. Thieme, in accordance with Láoyè I. Tìmì of Ẹdẹ, a former Ọba (king) of Ẹdẹ, an ethnomusicologist and a drum master, "give[s] the names of the instruments as: *iyá'lù, omele akọ,* and *omele abo* or *omele kudi.*"[28] In the Republic of Benin it is also called *omele abo.*[29] In West Africa, the middle drum is also called simply the *ọmọ* or *omole.* In Cuba, the middle drum is called *okonkoló.*[30] In Havana and Matanzas the smallest drum is called *itótele,* while in Santiago de Cuba, and also Matanzas, it has been known as *secundo.*

The Tìmì of Ẹdẹ and Thieme have defined the standard ensemble size as consisting of four membranophones, whereas Ortiz states, "This orchestra is only comprised of three drums and not one instrument more or less." Bascom defined a *bàtá* ensemble as having only three drums. But debates related to *bàtá* drums of this nature are not the focus here. Besides, what does it matter if the parts of the *bàtá* genre have different names in different places or that there may be four or three membranophones in a given ensemble? Without sufficient historical evidence to date these linguistic or technical transformations, the process whereby ethnic reconfigurations occurred from one "temple-house" of Yorùbá belief to another remains unclear.

The names of the individual drums have comparable meanings related to their physical size and gender—small (male or female), medium (male), and large (mother drum). What remains important in these examples of linguistic deviation is not the change of oral expression, but the incorporation of new languages, such as Spanish, into the continuance of traditions conveyed through a trend in meaning. For the purpose of this paper, *bàtá* drums are only to be considered at the very least as a drum trio of membranophones. In circumstances when other percussion instruments join in, the added instruments should be considered as a separate liturgy, even though they may be played in unison.[31]

An examination of the form and physical complexion of *bàtá* drums only goes to demonstrate that these drums must not be confused with other drums found in Yoruba culture. In discussing the complexity of categorizing drum genres in Yorùbáland, the Tìmì of Ẹdẹ has observed that "the drums that the Yorùbá use are not completely exclusive. Many [drums] have equivalents between other tribes from the Nigerian occidental region. Possibly they have a common historical origin. Each tribe has its own traditional genre of drums, which look like one to the other in their form, in the manner of their fabrication and in the style of playing."[32] Contemporary musicologists and anthropologists have agreed that *bàtá* and *dùndún* drums share qualities in their physical structure because they are both membranophones of approximately the same size, shaped like an hourglass or a truncated cone. They are also both used in various forms of *òrìṣà* worship.

Furthermore, both *bàtá* and *dùndún* drums are classified as "talking drums" because they encode structural properties of Yoruba speech. As Bascom has observed, "there is a true drum language and the drums actually 'talk,' reproducing the melody and the rhythm of the sentence, and approximating the quality of consonants and vowels by fingering the head with the left hand."[33] Johnson described the duties of a royal drummer in New Ọ̀yọ́:

> The *Aludùndún* or the Dùndún drummer knows the names, praises and attributes of every family of note, and they are experts in eulogizing and enlarging the praises of any one they wish to honour, *speaking* it with their drums. If for one instance a white man enters the palace, the drummer would strike up: "Ọ̀yìnbó, Ọ̀yìnbó, afi òkun ṣe ọ̀nà" (the white man, the white man who makes of the ocean a highway).[34]

Yorùbá is a tonal language, in which tone or pitch is used to distinguish words which otherwise share the same consonants and vowels. Johnson continued, "[H]aving learnt how to make their instruments, they then begin to learn how to *speak* with them, an operation to which the Yorùbá language readily lends itself, as it consists chiefly in modulation of the voice; this the instrument tries to imitate." When played, complex polyrhythms are said to reconstruct basic phrases, proverbs, metaphors and/or religious praises. However, to understand this drum language invariably requires prolonged study of Yorùbá language and frequent exposure to this form of drum culture.

Bàtá drums differ from their *dùndún* cousins when examined in more detail. The *dùndún* construction is far more complex than *bàtá* drums because it can change pitch when the drum is squeezed with the elbow. Quite possibly, the earliest written reference to *dùndún* drums can be dated back to 1875, based on a description by John Whitford, a British merchant in Lagos. He witnessed the use of *dùndún* drums in a procession held for King Docemo (1853–72): "Their principal musical instrument consists of a half-bagpipe, half-drum—a cylinder eighteen inches long and five inches in diameter, covered at the ends with skin stretched tightly. It is placed underneath the left arm, whilst the performer, with the right hand, strikes it with a curved drum-stick, at the same time squeezing the sides to modulate the sound."[35] *Dùndún* drums can have ninety to one hundred tensioning thongs attached to each drumhead, thereby providing a greater number of tones and a larger vocabulary per drum when compared with the drums of a *bàtá* set.

Bàtá drums, in contrast to *dùndún,* sit directly on the lap or hang in front of the abdomen from an ornamental strap. Both drumheads are generally struck with open hands, and sometimes a flat leather strap is used as a drumstick, but that can vary, once again, from region to region. For example, leather straps are sometimes used as drumsticks in parts of Benin and Nigeria, but other times they are not, while they are frequently used in Matanzas, but rarely in Havana. *Bàtá* are said to "talk" only when the ensemble plays together. The complex polyrhythms made by at least six hands upon six drumheads of different sizes can recreate certain tones comparable to similar sounds in Yorùbá and Yorùbá derived languages. Classifying *bàtá* and *dùndún* drums as "talking" has many implications in association with oral sources because music and drums are mnemonic devices.

Spiritual Similarities

In order to isolate *bàtá* drums further from other drum ensembles in Yorùbáland and Cuba, specific aspects about their spiritual properties must be examined in more detail. As it has been established, *bàtá* drums have remained relatively consistent—symbolically, culturally, and iconographically—over extended periods of time. In terms of cultural traits, the *bàtá* and *dùndún* drumming genres differ because *bàtá* drums are said to have a stronger religious affiliation to Ṣàngó. Bascom stated, "*Bata* drums are regarded as sacred to the deity Shàngó, and to his wife, Ọya; but other drums may be used for these deities, and *bàtá* may be played for some other deities as well."[36] While Yorùbá religious culture differs from territory to territory and over time, the physical evidence of *bàtá* drums in similar religious contexts across the Atlantic reinforces the assumption that transformations in their physical shape and material culture developed at a relatively slow rate over long periods of time.

The mere presence of *bàtá* drums in different historical contexts across the Atlantic reveals the diffusion of widespread and diversified cultural systems of Yorùbá belief. *Bàtá* drums in both West Africa and Cuba possess spiritual associations that have nearly identical cultural tendencies. A number of Yorùbá religious practices from West Africa and Cuba involve *bàtá* drumming. They are represented in initiation rituals, consecrations, coronations, annual festivals, and Egúngún (ancestral spirits) ceremonies—all of which center upon the worship of *òrìsà*s. The importance of *bàtá* drums in Şàngó and Changó worship, therefore, is an additional key element to their unique identity.

Bàtá drums can be further distinguished from the numerous drum genres found in West Africa because they are associated with specific cultural connections to the *òrìsà*s Àyàn and Şàngó. The *bàtá* drums are sacred objects with spiritual potency. The drums are said to "house" Àyàn, a goddess of drumming, embodied by the ritualistic materials (*àṣẹ*) sealed inside the *iyá ìlù*. Àyàn is the *òrìsà* portrayed as the female patron deity of drumming and also associated with *bàtá* drums. Àyàn's symbol is a drum, which serves as both a repository of divine power and literally as a vehicle to give a voice to god. In *òrìsà* worship, drums "with" Àyàn are consecrated in a series of rituals and considered to be sacred objects. In West Africa and Cuba, there are many different types of percussion instruments, ranging in size and shape from the maracas to larger drums, as well as the *bàtá*, capable of encapsulating Àyàn. These rituals and ceremonies involve prayer, preparations of special herbs, and the sacrifice of animals, much as the Cuban *bàtá* maker, Benkomo, has described. In Cuba, *bàtá* drum masters, such as the *olúbàtá*, possess Aña and are the only ones qualified to place the spirit of Aña inside the chamber.

In Yorùbá culture, specific drum genres are associated with the worship of particular *òrìsà*s.[37] *Bàtá* drums are religious icons and sacred objects said to "belong" to Şàngó, god of war, thunder, lightning, and drumming. Leo Frobenius wrote in 1913, "A special drum, the Bàttá, is beaten. The Shàngó dances are not, however, ordinary amusements, but sacrosanct and profoundly significant ceremonial. Shàngó descends on some man or woman dancer's head."[38] Şàngó devotees and *bàtá* drummers played active roles in the Şàngó cult, which was directly tied to Òyọ́'s political administration.

The Şàngó cult, much like other Yorùbá cults, is remarkable for its elaborate ritual and abundance of symbols, which had specific functions in the kingdom. *Bàtá* drums are also a spiritual and cultural symbol of Şàngó. The cult was certainly an important prop of royal power in Òyọ́. As a sign of acceptance into the Şàngó cult in West Africa, a priest, for example, is required to have a *làbà* (beaded bag). The *làbà* is worn when the priest travels to officiate at some rite away from his shrine. According to descriptions related to the function of the *làbà*, "[t]he bag itself is used to contain ritual objects, and is carried by the priests when purifying a spot where lightning has struck and, also, when in full panoply they join the procession of the priesthood at the main annual rite of the god."[39] It is never worn when the priest is in a state of possession. Ṣàngó priests, adorned with a red and white *làbà,* would have been easily recognized as coming from Ọ̀yọ́ in past historical contexts. The Ṣàngó cult had centralized organization most likely modeled after Ọ̀yọ́'s political structure. As Law argues, "[t]he *Ṣàngó* cult played an important role in securing the loyalty of the provinces of the *Aláàfin.* . . . The organization of the *Ṣàngó* cult in the provincial towns was controlled from the capital, and *Ṣàngó* priests in the provinces had to travel to Ọ̀yọ́ to receive instruction and initiation from the *Mọgbà,* the *Ṣàngó* priest of the royal shrine."[40] Since Ọ̀yọ́ was under the rule of the Aláàfin, the Ṣàngó cult consciously promoted Ọ̀yọ́ culture and political policy.[41] A unit of *bàtá* drummers in nineteenth-century West Africa would have been identified as having direct ties to Ọ̀yọ́.

The most important figure in the political system of Ọ̀yọ́ was the Aláàfin. According to oral tradition, the Aláàfin has sometimes been portrayed as a "divine king." Frobenius argued that the Aláàfin was regarded specifically as the incarnation of Ṣàngó, and one of the "earliest" Aláàfin. But there is no evidence that the Aláàfin was ever worshipped as an *òrìṣà.* According to Law, "[the Aláàfin's] power was limited by the need to retain public confidence, and in particular he was expected to take account of the advice of the *Baṣọ̀run* and the other Ọ̀yọ́ *Mèsì.*" They were a council advisory to the Aláàfin composed of free-Ọ̀yọ́ and nonroyal lineages. Still, many important officers of this political administration were members of high-ranking Ọ̀yọ́ lineages,[42] which would have required devotion to Ṣàngó.

Ọ̀yọ́'s political organization centered on the town (*ìlú*). Ọ̀yọ́ city was where the Aláàfin resided and ruled over a federation of lineages. According to Law, "the empire over which the *Aláàfin* rules was comprised of territories which were subjected to Ọ̀yọ́ control in different ways and to varying degrees."[43] Peel states:

> In the center of every town was the *àfin* (palace). An *ìlú* was both
> "town" and "polity," with typically the latter named after the former.
> The political field of Yorùbáland, though involving territories and border posts and "sub-tribal" identities, should still be conceived as a

system of relations between *ilú* as point sources of power, like a galaxy of stars of greater or lesser magnitude with shifting fields of gravitational pull between them.[44]

The largest towns, such as Ìbàdàn or Abẹ́òkúta, which began to grow exponentially in the years after Ọ̀yọ́'s collapse, were estimated to have had populations of up to 100,000 by the mid-nineteenth century. These towns were recent products of the wars, and most *ilú* were much smaller, in the 5,000–20,000 range. The total area of the Ọ̀yọ́ kingdom at its greatest extent cannot be calculated with any precision, but must have been something on the order of 18,000 square miles.[45]

The Aláàfin controlled a large administration which carried out political and ceremonial tasks connected to the city of Ọ̀yọ́. In all probability, palace slaves numbered several thousand. The three principal royal slaves were eunuchs called the *ọtun iwẹ̀fà* (eunuch of the right), the *ọnà iwẹ̀-fà* (eunuch of the middle), and the *òsì iwẹ̀fà* (eunuch of the left). These three were in charge respectively of religious, judicial, and administrative matters. Furthermore, the Aláàfin's principal officers included the master of the horse, his *mọgbà* (Ṣàngó chief priest or chief diviner), various lieutenants, youth leaders and the *isùgbín*s. The *isùgbín*s were members of the palace orchestra and numbered "about 210 persons." *Bàtá* drums were more than likely represented here because they "belong" to Ṣàngó.

Although *bàtá* drummers played an important role in the political administration of the Ọ̀yọ́ Empire, they were quite separate from most official or political matters. In terms of a hierarchy with the Aláàfin sitting on top, *bàtá* drummers and common priests would have ranked fairly low in the overall structure, and most likely did not have direct interaction with the Aláàfin. The drummers would travel away from the city center, accompanied by priests, in order to promote Ṣàngó. As Law's work demonstrates, based in large part on Johnson, the decline of Ọ̀yọ́ after 1817 inevitably affected the royal cult of Ṣàngó, and therefore *bàtá* drummers and their knowledge were brought over with them to Cuba.

Transference of *Bàtá* Drums to Cuba

As Law's work demonstrates, based in large part on Johnson, the decline of Ọ̀yọ́ after 1817, inevitably affected the royal cult of Ṣàngó. Being reminded of Ọ̀yọ́'s collapse at a regenerated peak in the slave trade suggests the spread of the Ṣàngó cult accelerated in the Diaspora through the 1830s. The resulting migrations and displacement that occurred with the decline and destruction of Ọ̀yọ́ in the first third of the nineteenth century continued to mix up the Yoruba population. Àfọ̀njá, the *ààrẹ-ọ̀ nà-kakaǹfò*, or commander of the military, though not a Muslim himself, decided to enhance his support by calling up the growing Muslim interest. He invited to Ìlọrin an influential Fulani cleric, known to the Yorùbá as Alímì (Uthman dan Fodio), who soon proclaimed *jihad* against "pagan" Ọ̀yọ́. The Muslim uprising won widespread support among Muslims in Ọ̀yọ́, provoking revolt among Ọ̀yọ́'s cavalry and slaves of northern origin. Àfọ̀njá's war-bands, known as *jama'a,* spread further and deeper into the Ọ̀yọ́ kingdom. The displacement of Ọ̀yọ́ southward pressured by the Fulani-led *jihad* meant that "pagans" of Ọ̀yọ́ decent were more than likely targets for enslavement.

According to Peel, around 1823 Àfọ̀njá was killed and Alímì's son Abudusalami took charge of Ìlọrin, declaring his allegiance to the Sokoto Caliphate.[46] By this time, Ọ̀yọ́'s eastern provinces had fallen apart. Refugees migrated east and south beyond the borders of the old kingdom. In 1831–33, a last attempt to throw off the Fulani failed when the Aláàfin Oluewu was killed and Ọ̀yọ́'s remaining habitants fled further south (c. 1836). The Fulani of Ìlọrin finally overran nearly all the provincial towns in the north and west and reduced Ọ̀yọ́ to tributary status.

Bolanle Awe acknowledges that many Ọ̀yọ́ citizens who were unwilling to submit to Fulani rule, in consequence of the *jihad*, fled southward and

> joined in a fray involving the three powerful kingdoms in the south—Ifẹ̀ and Ìjẹ̀bú on one side, and Òwu on the other. Òwu and its Ẹ̀gbá neighbours were destroyed, and the Ọ̀yọ́-Yorùbá refugees and some of their Ìjẹ̀bú and Ifẹ̀ allies took over their homes; by the 1830s they founded new settlements for themselves at Ìbàdàn, Ìjàyè, and modern Ọ̀yọ́; most of the Òwu and the Ẹ̈gbá at the same time created a new settlement for themselves in the southeast, at Abẹ́òkúta.[47]

A son of Aláàfin Abiọ́dún named Àtìbà, who had once professed Islam at Ìlọrin, secured enough support from Ọ̀yọ́'s surviving senior chiefs and warriors to be recognized as Aláàfin and established himself well to the south at a place called Àgọ́ Ọ̀jà, commonly known as New Ọ̀yọ́. Here he and his successors recreated as much as they could of the Old Ọ̀yọ́. But in the face of threat from Ìlọrin, practical measures were also needed, and Ìbàdàn exemplified Yorùbá militarism during this period. Astutely recognizing the new centers of power, Àtìbà conferred high Ọ̀yọ́ titles on the principal warlords: Olúyọ̀lé of Ìbàdàn was made Baṣọ̀run, and Kúrunmí of Ìjàyè was made Ààrẹ̀-Ọ̀nà-Kakaǹfò.[48] According to Awe, "the slaves who stayed around the compound served as messengers, drummers and praise singers."[49]

In the 1840s, the politics of Yorùbáland faced a radically new agenda. In the post-*jihad* and the establishment of an emirate at Ìlọrin, Christianity appeared to the Yorùbá as the epitome of modernity. The vacuum left by Old Ọ̀yọ́'s collapse provided plenty of internal political struggles.[50] Ìbàdàn was the main producing power of the interior because it was also the main military power. It was community of a very different social character, which sought to establish regional hegemony. Mainly derived from Ọ̀yọ́ traditions and political administrations, it came to control the savanna/forest divide, but it did not have access to the coast. Ọ̀yọ́'s coastward rivals, Abẹ́òkúta and Ìjẹ̀bú, often cut trade routes between the coast and the interior, causing additional problems. Ọ̀yọ́ continued southeastward, radically affecting their ethnic balance and consequently their religious and cultural complexions. After the British annexed Lagos in 1861, Yorùbá politics eventually had to respond to the end of the slave trade.

Yorùbáland in the first half of the nineteenth century was a "triangular encounter of religions." Islam and "traditional" religion had been in contact with one another long before the arrival of Christian missionaries in the 1840s.[51] It is assumed that *jihad* principles would have sought to destroy non-Islamic religious practices and male lineages. Peel argues that "Islam moves through a trajectory of three stages: quarantine, mixing, and reform. These stages are not rigid, and one society might yield examples of all three orientations at the time. The Yorùbá Islam encountered by the missions was overwhelmingly and conspicuously of the "mixing" kind, with "reform" only at its edges."[52] *Jihad* would be an extreme example of reform. As male-cultural icons, a *bàtá* trio, or priests with *làbà* bags, were easy targets for cultural suppression because they *were* identifiable.

Jihad principles would have sought to destroy non-Islamic religious practices and male lineages. Lovejoy argues, "Generally the [slave] trade involved more males and especially more boys."[53] In most Yorùbá-based societies, drumming was a male-dominated institution. Music was not only a pastime, but also an occupation for many men and boys. Based on contemporary observations of Yorùbá drum families, the teaching process consisted of a mentor/apprentice relationship, often father/son. Moreover, professional drummers in Yorùbá culture, whether in Africa or the Americas, typically formed patriarchal guilds or complex social performance groups. Drummers had to learn how to manufacture their instruments, so that each drummer could repair damaged drums.[54]

Drumming guilds often identified themselves by adding prefixes to their surnames, such as Aludùndún or Alukósó, as recorded by Johnson.[55] According to the research of Ortiz, "the high *bàtá* masters have the rank known as *olú bàtá*, a status that many excellent percussionists do not attain. The repertoire was learned through years of hard study, which was achieved through living in the environment of the religion."[56] Yorùbá drummers, starting at very young ages, dedicated their lives to learning the art, history, and religious philosophy associated with every aspect of the musical instrument.

Documents from the Mixed Commission in Havana recorded that the Cuban slave ship *Ingadadora* was "bound from the River Lagos on the Coast of Africa to the Island of Cuba."[57] The British Schooner *Speedwell* caught the notorious slave ship off the Isle of Pines on July 23, 1832. According to Mixed Commission reports, the notorious slave ship had made an average of two crossings a year to Lagos since 1827.[58] According to a registry of all items on board, Commander Don Bartolomé Alemány of the *Ingadadora* had on board at the time of her detention 22 men as crew, and 134 "Negroes" as cargo. Out of the 134 Negroes, 109 were men, 12 were women, and 19 were boys, nearly all of whom were classified as "*nación Lucumí Oyllo*."[59] In Cuba, slaves of Yorùbá origin were generally identified as Lucumís, but also it was also common to use distortions of Ọ̀yọ́ (*Ayllo* or *Eyó*). The example of the *Ingadadora* also reinforces the likelihood that men and small boys from Ọ̀yọ́ were targeted for enslavement. It is argued here, speculatively, that *bàtá* drummers were among those who were targeted.

Bàtá drummers and their instruments were an easily identifiable cultural representation of Ṣàngó worship and hence loyalty to "pagan" Ọ̀yọ́. As Ṣàngó is a god of war, *bàtá* drums were most likely involved in warfare to mobilize troops on the battlefield and provide morale.

The "Trans-culturation" of Ọ̀yọ́ in Cuba

By focusing on the term *tambor* as it appears in colonial documentation, one can examine colonial attitudes toward African drumming in Cuban slave society. These drums have been described in colonial documentation as "*tambores* made out of hollowed tree trunks and covered on one end by a patch of ox-hide tempered by fire."[60] We now know that this reference does not refer to *bàtá* drums because this does not conform to the type of hide used in the "proper" consecration of a *bàtá* set. As a means of identification, a drum's physical complexion is a viable cultural indicator of African ethnicity. It is clear that in the decades after the Ọ̀yọ́

Yorùbá began to arrive in Cuba, enslaved Yorùbá had little, if anything, to do with Christianity. The nominal commitment of Cuban officials and church authorities was conversion by baptism. By 1846, Regino Martin, a Cuban official, noted that "it is not necessary to have lived very long in our countryside to know that with few, but very honorable exceptions, the slaves have hardly more religion than the stupid idolatry which they brought from their country of birth."[61] That "idolatry" would have involved drumming.

In 1827, one of the earliest known references to the term *tambor* appeared in the colonial countryside. On January 7 of that year, Juan Martínez wrote to D. Cicilio Ayllón, governor of Matanzas, that nine *negros* from a group of thirteen *cimarrones* (runaways) had been captured. They were accused of uniting with the *dotación* (plantation) of Francisco Prieto and making a lot of noise, "with the beating of three *tambores,* that was heard over a wide region."[62] According to the first section of *penal del reglamento de la finca rural,* a fine of twenty-five pesos was imposed on the owner.

The evidence described how *tres tambores* were used that night. Although *bàtá* drums can be a trio, this document does not specifically indicate what type of drums they were, nor does it specify from which *nación* those slaves came. In Cuba, there were other genres of drum trios, which may or may not have been membranophones, such as *tambores bembé* or *gangá*. Although this document appears in a paper about *bàtá* trios, it cannot be used to establish, on its own, what type of drums were used that night. However, what is most important to note is the date on the letter. It was written the day after the Día de Reyes.

This document proves that African slaves had already begun to take advantage of the relative freedom associated with this colonial festival as early as 1827. Initially, the Día de Reyes owed its inspiration to Catholic Corpus Christi processions, certainly brought over to Cuba by the Spanish. According to Brown, "Epiphany marked the moment on the Catholic sacred calendar when the Three Magi, or Kings, traveled to present gifts to the baby Jesus."[63] These processions, often compared to pageantries by theater historians, appeared as early as the fourteenth century across Western Europe.[64] At some point, and for whatever reason, January 6 became a colonial holiday, and an unsupervised group of runaway slaves from two different plantations had assembled on that night to play "three drums" mentioned in the 1827 document.

By 1839, slave revolts had become endemic on the island of Cuba, and drumming was often associated with civil unrest. A consensus emerged that some allowance had to be made for religious and cultural expression, including the use of *tambores,* but that such practices should be strictly controlled. On July 23, 1839, Joaquin de Ezpleta wrote a report on behalf of the office of the governor general of Cuba about the role of *los bailes de tambores* on plantations. Despite the potential for organizing resistance, Ezpleta noted that many plantations allowed the "continuation of the slave dances known by the name *tambores*" as a means of allowing slaves some autonomy.[65]

As Elsa Goveia has argued, West Indian slave laws reflected the climate of opinion.[66] By examining the changes in the policy toward drumming, it is possible to glean information about changes in attitudes toward African music in Cuban slave society. Ezpleta expressed the opinion of the governor general that it was acceptable "to permit to the slaves of farms in the country the diversion of dances to the custom of their country on holidays." The instructions permitted slave dances with drums, but they were supposed to be supervised. The decree was first introduced in Havana and then circulated to the other provinces, reaching Matanzas by early August of the same year.[67]

It appears that this policy of permitting *tambores* on plantations on holidays was disputed the year before it was codified. In 1841, the Inspección de Policía del Cuartel de Fernando Séptimo wrote to the governor of Matanzas prohibiting "*negros*" from being able to go out in the streets with *tambores*. José Maria de Torres signed the communication on the fifth of January 1841, the day before the Día de Reyes. It read, "In your utmost compliance, I am prepared, that which orders your office, related to not permitting *negros* from going out onto the streets with *tambores* tomorrow."[68]

The following year, the infamous *Reglamento de Esclavos* was implemented across the island as the legal code to control the slave population.[69] Of the 260 articles in the code, 3 were related to the Día de Reyes festival. Article 51 was identical to the 1839 document and stipulated that "slave dances with *tambores* could be permitted at fiestas during afternoon hours provided they are supervised by some white person, and no slaves from any other estate attend." Article 87 stated, "Negro *cabildos* should only be held on Sundays and on other days of important fiestas." Finally, Article 88 declared "that the Negroes require special permission to march with flags and native costumes. Such marches can be held twice a year, and during daylight hours." One is once again reminded of the significance of the date of 1820 on the Santa Barbara *cabildo* banner.

The process of the symbolic reestablishment of the Òyó Empire in colonial Cuba was complex. Brown examines Havana *barrios* (neighborhoods) in two spatial contexts, the spaces within Havana's fortress walls (*intramuros*) and the spaces outside the walls (*extramuros*). *Cabildos* were located within the *intramuros* until 1792, when they were banished outside the walls. From then on, *barrios extramuros* were "dangerous incubators of *la hampa cubana* [the Cuban underworld] and its *mala vida*, or socially unhygienic 'bad life' of *delincuencia* [delinquency]."[70] On the Día de Reyes, carnival processions were granted permission to enter the fortress gates of the *intramuros*. Brown states, "They marched through the business and residential thoroughfares of Mercaderes, Obispo, and O'Reilly Streets toward the central Plaza de Armas, the site of the palace, as at other stops along the way, procession members performed dances, ritually demanded and received *aguinaldo* (money gratuities), and then returned home."[71] Drumming would have been performed, and the 1820 *bandera* suggests that the Cabildo Santa Barbara or Changó was involved in this procession. Brown continues: "*Cabildo* processions took over the main thoroughfares of the Old City's *intramuros* to such an extent that bourgeois families stayed inside. Genteel spectators watched and delivered *aguinaldo* from balconies or from behind barred windows. The ritualized exchange of *aguinaldo* exemplified the ways in which carnival could be an arena of contested meanings."

Those "meanings," as I have now interpreted beyond what Brown has intended, lead back to Africa and the annual rites and rituals associated with Ọ̀yọ́. The Aláàfin was subject to a number of ritual restrictions, mainly in his confinement to the palace within the city walls of Ọ̀yọ́. He appeared in public only on three major annual festivals: the *Bẹẹrẹ*, the *Mọlè*, and the *Ọrun* festivals. In all three, *bàtá* drums and Ṣàngó were heavily involved. *Bàtá* drums serve as an excellent model that can be projected backward into early-nineteenth-century references, such as "the chief was seated outside of his house, surrounded by about a hundred of his wives, and musicians with drums."[72] I will now examine an important annual festival in Ọ̀yọ́ where *bàtá* drums were heavily represented.

According to Johnson, the *Bẹẹrẹ* festival took place toward the end of the agricultural year, between late February and early March. It was an important annual festival for three reasons: First, the *bẹẹrẹ* grass was a form of tribute paid to the Aláàfin. The grass was used to thatch the roofs of houses and to feed the horses of the royal cavalry. According to Babayemi, "from the middle of the nineteenth century till around 1936, there are traditions that almost all Yorùbá speaking peoples brought tributes to Alaafin during Bẹẹrẹ festival."[73] Second, it marked the new agricultural year for the *bẹẹrẹ* grass. And third, it marked the time of year when the king would add another year onto his total reign.

As noted by Law, the earliest firsthand observation of the festival appears to be in Clapperton's journal. He described a festival in Òyó in 1826 that was held just before March. Clapperton's entry was dated February seventeenth, which conforms to the time and place of the agricultural New Year in and around Òyó: "A number of people arrived from different parts to pay their annual visit to the king."[74] This passage refers to the Bẹẹrẹ festival. His simple description, however, provides cultural historians with clues to identify and compare aspects associated with Yoruba cult ritual, such as his description of the royal courtyard. It was here where *bàtá* drums would have been used during the processions associated with the Bẹẹrẹ festival and the ceremonial burning of the fields, because fire was representative of Ṣàngó.

In Cuba, fires were set at the sugarcane harvest, which took place near the Christian New Year around the beginning of January, coincidentally close to the Día de Reyes. Fires had become endemic and a popular form of resistance used during the many slave revolts in the first half of the nineteenth century. According to Fraginals:

> Canefields in the Cárdenas area were in fact being set on fire so persistently around 1840 that something had to be done, and the extent to which the maintenance of discipline figured in this decision is shown by the Real Consulado's advice to the *hacendados*. A commission to study these problems reached these conclusions: The best way to avoid canefield fires was to feed the slaves better, and the bagesse-shed fires could be stopped by turning the immediately surrounding areas into corrals where the slaves could raise pigs.[75]

Bàtá drums are a noisy and an easily identifiable icon of Òyó culture. No matter where they were found, *bàtá* drums definitely belonged to Ṣàngó. They had to be in some way consecrated with *Àyàn* and were presumably a large part of annual festivals, specifically Bẹẹrẹ and Día de Reyes. *Bàtá* drums have played a central role to honor the Aláàfin because by design they are easy to carry. The differences in detailed aspects of the material culture of *bàtá* drums, such as differences in spelling, legends, and the like, demonstrate that people of Òyó descent were prominent among Yorùbá subgroups.

I have hypothesized that the Día de Reyes was appropriated in the symbolic reestablishment of the Òyó Empire in Cuba in the late 1820s and 1830s, which had particular meanings to slaves of Òyó descent. Òyó slaves apparently perceived the Día de Reyes as the Bẹẹrẹ festival, especially when fields were set on fire before what appears to have been nothing more than a big party. Ortiz portrayed the Día de Reyes as "an orgy of rites, dances, music, song, and liquor," with noises "of their bells, their drums, and the rest of their primitive instruments."[76] The Día de Reyes and colonial attitudes toward drumming were integral to the transference, accommodation, and trans-culturation of *bàtá* drums in Cuban slave society.

————

This study has been concerned with understanding the process of ethnic reconfiguration under slavery and what was meant by the emergence of Lucumí Ayllo culture in Cuba, and the extent to which Ọ̀yọ́ was a factor in this cultural transformation. In order to achieve a better historical understanding regarding the absence of closer linkages to Africa, more attention to cultural artifacts, such as *bàtá* drums, has yielded a vision of Ọ̀yọ́ paradigms symbolically interconnected across the Atlantic world. This study attempts to identify the cultural tendencies of Ṣàngó or Changó worship as revealed through the trans-culturation of rituals and ceremonies involving *bàtá* drums in West Africa and Cuba. My research into *bàtá* drums has enabled the "symbolic" identification of Ọ̀yọ́ entrenched in Lucumí culture in Cuba and demands further comparative studies with other places where Yorùbá were concentrated, especially Brazil and Trinidad.

Unfortunately, there appears to never have been any direct references to *bàtá* drums in early-nineteenth-century documentation; however, oral data, nineteenth-century written references to *drums* and *tambores,* the collapse of Ọ̀yọ́ during a regenerated peak in the slave trade, and the existence of comparable forms of *bàtá* in West Africa and Cuba have demonstrated the symbolic reestablishment of Ọ̀yọ́ in Cuba. *Bàtá* drums, or "talking drums," have tremendous implications in association with oral sources and traditions because they are mnemonic devices. More research into those traditions will help to further substantiate the hypothesis I have presented here.

NOTES

I would like to thank David Trotman, Michael Marcuzzi, Andrew Apter, Judith Bettelheim, Edward Alpers, Gad Heuman, Jane Landers, Oscar Grandío, Tóyìn Fálọlá, José Curto, Adrían López Denis, Mariza Soares, Ernesto Valdés Janet, and my father for their discussions, revisions, suggestions, criticisms, and time. I also want to acknowledge Robin Law, whose contributions to Yorùbá history inspired the ideas presented in this chapter.

1. William Bascom, *Drums of the Yorùbá of Nigeria,* CD liner notes (Washington, D.C.: Smithsonian Folkways Records, 1992).

2. "Lucumí" was used in Spanish-speaking colonies to refer to those now identified as "Yorùbá." See Robin Law, "Ethnicity and the Slave Trade: 'Lucumi' and 'Nago' as Ethnonyms in West Africa," *History in Africa* 24 (1997): 205–19. The spelling of Yorùbá-related terms differs between West Africa and Cuba. In a West African context, I have tried to use the spelling from West Africa, for example, Ṣàngó. In the Cuban context I have tried to use spelling from Cuba, for example, Changó. Changó is the Cuban spelling of Ṣàngó.

3. The majority of the one million Yorùbá went to Brazil. Unfortunately this study does not address Brazil or other places, such as Trinidad and Tobago, where large concentrations of Yorùbá ended up.

4. David Eltis, "The Diaspora of Yorùbá Speakers, 1650–1865: Dimensions and Implications" *The Yorùbá Diaspora in the Atlantic World,* ed. Toyin Falola and Matt Childs (Bloomington: Indiana University Press, 2004), 17–39, especially table 2.5.

5. J. D. Y. Peel, *Religious Encounter and the Making of the Yorùbá* (Bloomington: Indiana University Press, 2000), 34.

6. Paul E. Lovejoy, "The Yorùbá Factor in the Trans-Atlantic Slave Trade," *The Yorùbá Diaspora,* 40–55.

7. Fernando Ortiz, *Cuban Counterpoint: Tobacco and Sugar,* trans. Harriet de Onis (Durham, N.C.: Duke University Press, 1995), 98. Ortiz, a Cuban scholar, defines the term *transculturation* to express the highly varied phenomena that have come about in Cuba as a result of the complex transmutations of culture that have taken place. This reference to "trans-culturation" highlights an insight of Ortiz, whose detailed study of drums, and *bàtá* drums in particular, was a feature in the development of his theories of cultural change in Cuban society. As is implied here, Ortiz failed to appreciate the historical significance of *bàtá* drums as part of a process in which people from Ọ̀yọ́ symbolically attempted to recreate facets of the Ọ̀yọ́ Empire in colonial Cuba, although he clearly recognized the influence of Yorùbá culture.

8. Akin Euba, *Yorùbá Drumming: The Dùndún Tradition* (Bayreuth, Germany: Bayreuth African Studies Series, 1990), p. 33.

9. Fernando Ortiz, *Los Tambores Batá de los Yorùbá* (Havana: Publicigraf, 1954). See also Robin Law, *The Ọ̀yọ́ Empire, c. 1600–c. 1836* (Oxford: Clarendon Press, 1970), 31, 32, 36, and 37.

10. Law, *Ọ̀yọ́ Empire,* 33–34.

11. Rev. Samuel Johnson, *The History of the Yorùbás from the Earliest Times to the Beginning of the British Protectorate,* ed. O. Johnson (London: Routledge and Sons, 1921).

12. Law, *Ọ̀yọ́ Empire,* 62.

13. Hugh Clapperton, *Hugh Clapperton into the Interior of Africa: Records of the Second Expedition, 1825–1827,* ed. Jamie Bruce Lockhart and Paul E. Lovejoy (Boston: Brill, 2005), 53–60.

14. Ibid., 57, 139, 140, and 167.

15. Fernando Ortiz, *Los Instrumentos de la Musica Afrocubana*, 2 vols. (Havana: Letras Cubanas, 1995).

16. Ortiz, *Tambores Batá*, 16.

17. Mauricio A. Font, "Introduction: The Intellectual Legacy of Fernando Ortiz," in *Cuban Counterpoints: The Legacy of Fernando Ortiz*, ed. Mauricio A. Font (Baltimore, Md.: Lexington Books, 2005).

18. Franklin W. Knight, *Slave Society in Cuba during the Nineteenth Century* (Madison: University of Wisconsin Press, 1970), 128–34.

19. For such descriptions of the Día de Reyes please refer to Judith Bettelheim, *Cuban Festivals: A Century of Afro-Cuban Culture* (Princeton, N.J.: Markus Wiener Publishers, 2001).

20. David H. Brown, *Santería Enthroned: Art, Ritual, and Innovation in an Afro-Cuban Religion* (Chicago: University of Chicago Press, 2003).

21. Image was taken from Bascom, *Drums of the Yorùbá*. A digital copy of the liner notes is also available online through Smithsonian Folkways.

22. Ortiz, *Tambores Batá*, 176. Note that it is considered sacrilegious to stand consecrated *bàtá* as displayed in this photo.

23. Michael D. Marcuzzi, "A Historical Study of the Ascendant Role of Bàtá Drumming in Cuban Òrìṣà Worship" (Ph.D. diss., York University, 2005), 34–35.

24. Darius L. Thieme, "A Descriptive Catalogue of Yorùbá Musical Instruments" (Ph.D. diss., Catholic University of America, 1969), 173–214.

25. As quoted, "*Abèrínkùlà* refers to drums shaped like *bàtá* which have no spiritual affiliation. In West Africa, there is no such term for non-consecrated *bàtá* drums." John Mason, *Orin Òrìṣà: Songs for Selected Heads* (Brooklyn: Yorùbá Theological Archministry, 1992), 19.

26. For a complete description of the construction and consecration process of *bàtá* drums in Cuba refer to Juan Benkomo, "Crafting the Sacred *Batá* Drums," in *Afro-Cuban Voices: On Race and Identity in Contemporary Cuba*, ed. Pedro Pérez Sarduy and Jean Stubbs (Gainesville: University Press of Florida, 2000), 140–46.

27. Ortiz, *Tambores Batá*, 34.

28. Ibid., 174.

29. Marcos Branda Lacerda, "Yorùbá Drums from Benin, West Africa," in *Yorùbá Drums from Benin, West Africa*, CD liner notes (Washington, D.C.: Smithsonian Folkways Recordings, 1996).

30. Victoria Eli Rodriguez, "Tambores Batá," in *Instrumentos de la Música Folclórico-Popular de Cuba*, ed. Victoria Eli Rodriguez, 2 vols. (Havana: Editorial de Ciencias Sociales, 1997), 1:319–43.

31. Olavo A. Rodriguez, "Introduction," in *Sacred Rhythms of Cuban Santería*, ed. Olavo A. Rodriguez, CD liner notes (Washington, D.C.: Smithsonian Folkways Recordings, 1995).

32. Laoye I. Timi de Ede, "Los Tambores Yorùbá," in *Actas del Folklore Bóletin Mensual del Centro de Estudios del Folklore* 1 (1961): 17 (my translation).

33. Bascom, "Drums of the Yorùbá."

34. Johnson, *History of the Yorùbás*, 58.

35. John Whitford, *Trading Life in Western and Central Africa, 1877*, 2nd ed. (London: Frank Cass, 1967), 72.

36. Bascom, "Drums of the Yorùbá."

37. Morton Marks, "Introduction," in *Rhythms and Songs for the Orishas: Havana, Cuba, ca. 1957*, CD liner notes (Washington, D.C.: Smithsonian Folkways Recordings, 2001).

38. Leo Frobenius, *The Voice of Africa: Being an Account of the Travels of the German Inner African Exploration Expedition in the Years 1910–1912*, trans. Rudolf Blind, 2 vols. (London: Benjamin Bloom, 1968), 204–27.

39. Joan Wescott and Peter Morton-Williams, "The Symbolism and Ritual Context of the Yorùbá Làbà Shàngó," *Journal of the Anthropological Institute of Great Britain and Ireland* 92 (1962): 23–37.

40. Law, *Òyó Empire*, 104.

41. Bruce Trigger, *Understanding Early Civilizations* (Cambridge: Cambridge University Press, 2003), 501.

42. Johnson, *History of the Yorùbás*, 57–60.

43. Law, *Òyó Empire*, 83–85.

44. Peel, *Religious Encounter*, 31.

45. Ibid., 90.

46. Ibid., 33.

47. Bolanle Awe, "Militarism and Economic Developments in Nineteenth Century Yorùbá Country: The Ìbàdàn Example," *Journal of African History* 14, no. 1 (1973): 65–77.

48. Peel, *Religious Encounter*, 34.

49. Awe, "Militarism and Economic Developments," 67.

50. Peel, *Religious Encounter*, 35.

51. Ibid., 187. "Traditional" religion should not be treated as a purely indigenous cultural baseline, but sometimes as an entity not wholly independent of Islam, Christianity, or both.

52. Peel, *Religious Encounter*, 190.

53. Lovejoy, "Yorùbá Factor," 47.

54. Euba, *Yoruba Drumming*, 66.

55. Johnson, *History of the Yorùbás*, 57.

56. Ned Sublette, *Cuba and Its Music from the First Drums to the Mambo* (Chicago: Chicago Review Press, 2004), 229.

57. Signed statement by William Marren, Havana, July 11, 1832, National Archives, London, Foreign Office (hereinafter FO), 84/128.

58. Other slave voyages were mentioned in similar affidavits between July 1828 and December 1830, FO, 84/80, FO, 84/91, and FO, 84/107.

59. Slave Schooner *Ingadadora*, Signed statement by Juan Franco Cascales, July 31, 1832, FO, 84/128.

60. Fernando Ortiz, "La Antigua Fiesta Afrocubana del Día de Reyes," *Ensayos Etnográficos* (Havana: Editorial de Ciencias Sociales, 1984), 41–78.

61. As quoted in Gwendolyn M. Hall, *Social Control in Slave Plantation Societies: A Comparison of St. Domingue and Cuba* (Baltimore, Md.: Johns Hopkins Press, 1971), 45.

62. Juan Martínez por D. Cicilio Ayllón, Matanzas, January 7, 1827, Archivo Historico Matanzas (hereinafter AHM), Gobierno Provincial "Cimarrones," legado 12, numero 17. Document taken from the *Conde de Lagunillas*, which were property registries and manuscripts from *haciendas*.

63. Brown, *Santería Enthroned*, 35.

64. Phyllis Hartnoll, *The Theatre: A Concise History*, 3rd ed. (New York: Thames and Hudson, 1998), 45.

65. Joaquin de Ezpleta to Gobierno General (hereinafter Ezpeleta), Havana, July 23, 1839, Archivo Nacional de Cuba (hereinafter ANC), Havana, Gobierno Superior Civil "Esclavitud," orden 33102, legado 998.

66. Elsa Goveia, "The West Indian Slave Laws of the Eighteenth Century," *Revista de Ciencias Sociales* 4 (1960): 75–105; see also Knight, *Slave Society in Cuba*, 124.

67. Ezpeleta, ANC, Gobierno Superior Civil "Esclavitud," orden 33102, legado 998 (my translation).

68. Comunicación al Gobernador Político y Militar de Matanzas, José Maria de Torres por la Inspección de policía del cuartel de "Fernando" [*sic*] Séptimo, Matanzas, Jan. 5, 1841, AHM, Fondo Provincial Religioso Africana, expediente 1, legado 1 (my translation).

69. Knight, *Slave Society in Cuba*, 128.

70. Brown, *Santería Enthroned*, 29.

71. Ibid., 35.

72. Clapperton, *Journal*, 57.

73. Cited July 1959 in S. O. Babayemi, "Bẹẹrẹ Festival in Ọ̀yọ́," *Journal of the Historical Society of Nigeria* 7, no. 1 (1973).

74. Clapperton, *Journal*, 158.

75. Manuel Moreno Fraginals, *The Sugarmill: The Socioeconomic Complex of Sugar in Cuba, 1760–1860*, trans. Cedric Belfrage (New York: Monthly Review Press, 1976), 100.

76. Fernando Ortiz, "La Antigua Fiesta Afrocubana del Día de Reyes," *Ensayos Etnográficos* (Havana: Editorial de Ciencias Sociales, 1984), 41–78. Originally published in 1921.

PART FOUR

The Voices of Ṣàngó Devotees

CHAPTER FIFTEEN

Ṣàngó beyond Male and Female

OLÓYÈ ÀÌNÁ ỌLỌMỌ

If you are willing to be lived by it
You will see it everywhere
Even in the most ordinary things.
—LAO TZU

The divinities of Yorùbá spirituality have aspects that are seldom discussed or taught. These aspects are what I consider their essential features. Yorùbá deities are not merely invisible entities or long-dead historical characters of legends and myths; they are the divine forces of nature that compose the planet Earth. The divine existence and power of òrìṣà permeate all living things on the earth including the sky, wind, and waters. I will delve specifically into the power of the divinity Ṣàngó and examine how he demonstrates his existence as a primary force in nature and actively participates in the physical processes of the human body. Ṣàngó's reign does not stop there; it continues to effect humanity. As a social icon his mythology affects the gender roles of his priests and priestesses. What has been overlooked is his divine nature. It is the cosmic consciousness of Ṣàngó that is the unity of opposites, the power of having two parts that can be used individually, in combination, and interchanged without notice.

In this chapter I explore the ways in which Ifá-Òrìṣà communities apply the social context of gender to the spiritual and celestial power of the Yorùbá divinity Ṣàngó. As a divine consciousness, the divinity of thunder and lightning has been bogged down by the historical antics of men of power on both sides of the sea. In the societies of Yorùbá-based traditions Ṣàngó is narrowly considered to be the driving force behind men who are womanizers, cruel leaders, and unscrupulous scoundrels. The energy of this *òrìṣà* is primarily understood as being demonstrated within the context and experience of society's masculine roles. These predominately male actions and activities are assigned to and expected of a person not because of the individual's spiritual development, but because of the individual's biology. This gendered distinction is also true of men and women who are consecrated to Ṣàngó. Men are often encouraged to be highly visible, promiscuous, aggressive, and domineering. In contrast, women who are consecrated to the god-king Ṣàngó are encouraged *not* to be leaders, *not* to speak out, and to develop a demure demeanor in the company of men.

There are two primary ways in which a devotee experiences the physical, natural, and social expressions of Ṣàngó. One is an internal individual process and the other is the external communal rite; one is knowledge-based and the other is grounded in participation. The divinity of light and sound is most deeply perceived spiritually and mentally, and this divinity also manifests his energy in the bodily functions of humanity. His visual symbol is the double-edge axe, and his character traits also come in pairs. Those who know and comprehend the nature of the dialectic space between the spiritual and the physical easily understand this ideology. This theme of dualism is visible in the artifacts that have become symbols of the divinity; his primary weapon is the double-edge axe, which swings both ways as a weapon of offensive attacks and resistance to injustice.

Ṣàngó as a Primary Force of Nature

Ṣàngó as a divinity of most Yorùbá-based traditions has been primarily mythologized through stories and artistic representations of masculine power and leadership. Ṣàngó of the Old World *and* Ṣàngó of the so-called New World are regarded as male forces that dominate and take advantage of the people under his care or within his domain. Is this divinity a character driven by the need to expand his domain, and by his unquenchable urge to acquire territory? Or is this divinity a source of male and female leadership that we have drawn from in times of persecution, oppression, and slavery, when the leaders of the people have to step away from the crowd to speak out and bring forces together for reasons that are larger than the individual and the apparent? If the focus is on the qualities of this charismatic deity as the human warlord and the womanizer in Yorùbá spiritual mythology, the power of Ṣàngó as a force of nature is being dismissed.

In contrast, the energy of the *òrìṣà* Ṣàngó as it manifests in nature approaches the human realm in the form of thunder, lightning, fire, electricity, and sound. The divine consciousness and true character of Ṣàngó exists in the appearance of his power, his movement, and his display of natural phenomena as his divine force moves from the ground to the sky through the layers of the earth's atmosphere. The celestial power of Ṣàngó is not generated by humanity. The turbulent movement of the *òrìṣà* as he travels from the heated clouds, gathering the wind of his mate, Oya, arrives on earth as sound and light. Ṣàngó's displays of power include the thunder that intrudes upon the quiet of the earth, bellowing its being out of the silence of the other-world; it is loud, interrupting, and more often than not, it is a bit frightening.

Once again, it is the dual nature of this divine force that moves from the sky and strikes the earth as he gathers positive and negative electrical charges in the clouds above and from the earth below us. Then the space between the positive and negative becomes large enough for Ṣàngó to make his move. His energy reaches down toward earth from the sky and up from the earth. When his earthly and heavenly self meet, the collision causes the sky to suddenly light up with zigzag streaks of light. His exhibition turns the darkness of the night into the celestial light generated from the earth and the sky. Lightning is electricity, and it is the electricity in our bodies that distinguishes the brain from the mind. When Ṣàngó's energy is moving through the universe it illuminates the landscape just as the electricity in our bodies illuminates our consciousness and creates human inspiration.

Although Ṣàngó has been characterized as a man who likes many women and has short sexual relationships with them, in nature he attracts, absorbs, and is absorbed by those elements of nature that are fluid, receptive, and consequently characterized as female divinities. The barometric pressure of the earth's atmosphere swells the air because of the god-king's interaction with wind (Oya), water (Òṣun), and the distance from the sea (Yemoja-Olókun). When the electricity and water buildup exceeds the capacity of the clouds, fluids are forced out, and rain falls upon the earth.

Light and Sound

In *Core of Fire: A Path to Yorùbá Spiritual Activism,* I wrote, "Àlà (white light) is the dimension where electromagnetic radiation produces visual sensations and can open our consciousness, expanding our awareness. Despite the fact that light is an electro-magnetic energy it is experienced by humanity internally and externally. The domain of light is not only an external reality; it is also an internal power that often invades our state of mind with thoughts that resemble flashes of light or moments of cognition. The amount of light that we can extract from this dimension connects us to the tools we can use to develop our character, and our understanding, enlarging our interpretations of the world."[1] Ṣàngó's light and sound intrudes upon our thought processes and supplies the necessary energy for the earth's vegetations that feed òrìṣà and us. Light is a form of energy that is visible to the human eye and experienced by the consciousness in the form of understanding, cognition, and inspiration. The only reason that the human eye can perceive it is because it is made visible due to the movement through the different realities. Light begins in the otherworld and gathers particles from the atmosphere as it makes it way to earth. It is the movement of particles in the atmosphere that brings light into our physical realm in the form of waves or sunlight. Like Ṣàngó, these particles are always on the move; they are not sedentary. For the earth, light provides the necessary energy for the vegetation to grow; it lifts the veil of darkness, slowly revealing what shares our physical space. When the external light finally penetrates our internal world, the seeds of inspiration that have lain hidden in the recesses of our mind are illuminated. It is this internal light that can ultimately guide us toward true spiritual wisdom. Lightning is a form of light that holds 10 to 100 million volts of electricity, and its heat is six times hotter than that of the sun. As it heats the air it causes it to expand. The illumination of the celestial consciousness of Ṣàngó moves from the earth to the sky, abruptly affecting us internally and externally. Ṣàngó is an òrìṣà of expansion; this expansion is not limited by territorial boundaries; his presence, as lightning, moves in an unrestrained manner across the landscape.

Once we understand the metaphysical impact of light we must, when exploring the power of Ṣàngó, also encounter thunder. The power and energy of sound is also an important aspect of Ṣàngó. Sound is important to our spiritual and physical lives because everything comes into being as a result of sound. The sound of thought and human desire and the resonance of creative inspiration whispered inaudibly by the divine consciousness of the Infinite Mystery penetrates and diffuses through the universe. Whether or not our thoughts are made audible to another human ear through speech, our thoughts produce waves of energy. This is one reason why the elders of our traditions have always told the young to be careful of what they think and what they say. Our thoughts make sounds that we cannot see; these thoughts create waves of energy that are invisible to the naked eye. The reason we cannot see these waves is that their frequency is very high and fast moving, beyond the scope of ordinary human perception. Although invisible, the geometric patterns created by sound waves carry information from its source out into the universe and affect all dimensions as they move from their origin toward infinity.

The exhibition of the thunder-god's power of light, and the induction of nonhuman sound into the physical realm, is another form of Ṣàngó's dualism. The duality of this òrìṣà is expressed in the verbal history of this divinity; it tells us he is the father of twins because of his fertility, the òrìṣà of truth, and the *one* who can make a lie become a reality. While he has gained popularity as the god of justice and truth, there are those who also accuse him of being a liar. He is the king of debate, one who is always articulate, and able to defend both sides of an argument. Ṣàngó is the ultimate lawyer.

Instead of masculine stereotypes, how do we more thoroughly and accurately experience the energy of Ṣàngó within the physical realm? It is possible to see the manifestations of Ṣàngó in the human expression of charisma, in the expansive and intoxicating forces that draw together opposites, and attract us irresistibly to the sustaining, yet dangerous, forces of fire. From the passion of the erotic to the energies that compel us to adore, venerate, and follow our leaders, Ṣàngó's power can be found. In the physical realm, Ṣàngó is charm, the irresistible intoxicant, the earthly phenomena of desire and attraction that passes only briefly through the intellectual realm of logic, and settles the super-rational logic of humanity's need to reproduce. Ṣàngó is the carrier of passion but is not an emotional divinity. There is a definite difference between the passion for truth, the passion for living, and the instinctual passion to reproduce. Let me be clear that there is a precise distinction between passion and the emotion of love.

Ṣàngó and the Physical Processes of the Human Body

How do we understand Ṣàngó within the everyday male/female relationships that we all, at one point or another, experience? Ṣàngó expresses not only the passion that humans innately have for living, but also the passion that leads to sexual attraction; it is this passion that is known as the sex drive, the libido, and the drive to fulfillment of sexual desire. Ṣàngó brings people together despite his reputation for being a divinity that displays cruelty, aggressiveness, and tyrannical behavior toward his subjects. It is his energy that plays the music that leads the ritual dance and precedes the unification of spirit with the physical body. The outcome of sexual activity between men and women is born from the unity of opposites; this unity creates the potential for new life.

Most of us experience the energy of Ṣàngó in our lives; if we are sexually active, we accumulate knowledge or skill that results from direct participation of his energy sexually, spiritually, and intellectually. Ṣàngó is the energy we feel the moment just before ejaculation and orgasm. When all of our nerve endings are vibrating, and we are immersed by the waves of heat, fluids, and the involuntary responses of our body, we know we are fully alive. Those who engage in sexual activity, both metaphorical (erotic, flirting, or suggestive behavior) and literal, tap the divine force that is Ṣàngó. Hence, Ṣàngó has been called the rain god and the god of fertility, because ejaculation, similar to the rain, is the result of interacting with the energy force known as Ṣàngó. Ejaculation is the body's rain; like rain these fluids create new life.

In nature, Ṣàngó's copulation with air and water causes fluids to be released on the earth. The same process happens in humanity's copulation. The electrical impulses of the brain signal the body fluids to gather. These fluids fill the genital vacuums in the body.[2] When these vacuums begin to exceed their capacity, like the clouds, the body releases fluids. And then BAM! . . . ejaculation and orgasm.

The electrical energies that travel through our physical bodies determine whether or not the spirit, body, and intellect are still integrated. In other words, it is the electricity in our bodies that determines if we are still alive. The body's brain stem measures electrical activity. These are the impulses that cardiologists and the electroencephalogram equipment monitor when we are sick and physically in-between worlds.

Ṣàngó as a Cultural Yorùbá Icon

Ṣàngó has been memorialized as becoming a divinity after the reign and demise of the fourth king of Nigeria's ancient city of Ọ̀yọ́. It was this Yorùbá king who became known as Ṣàngó. Just as thunder, lightning, sound, and fire existed before the fourth king of Ọ̀yọ́, so did the divine consciousness that is Ṣàngó. Ṣàngó as a force of nature existed before the fourth king of Ọ̀yọ́. There are human personality traits that can tap the energy-base divine consciousness of the thunder-god Ṣàngó. These traits, even when they are clearly given to people as a result of their relationship with the divinity, are only a micro-fraction of Ṣàngó's divine power and consciousness. There are many opinions as to the character and effect of the fourth king's rule on Yorùbáland. Some Yorùbá born on the soil of Nigeria say that this king was ruthless, without compassion, and warmongering. The Aláàfin who is attributed with being Ṣàngó ruled Ọ̀yọ́ with a force that unified the ethnic groups that lived within Yorùbáland, using many of the same techniques that Shaka Zulu used to unify the Zulu people. Both rulers had one thing in common: they were able to rule the day and command legions of warlords because of the qualities expected from their gender, such as aggression and a lack of emotion. These "masculine" techniques belong to humanity, and are not the traits of a divine force. They do not express the totality of the divine consciousness of Ṣàngó.

Although the Aláàfin, the fourth king of Ọ̀yọ́, embodied *some* of the traits of the divine force of Ṣàngó, the *divine* consciousness of Ṣàngó has traits and abilities that surpass those of the warlord and the womanizer. Additional attributes of this divine consciousness are primarily displayed in the number of female priests in Africa and the "New World" who have been consecrated to Ṣàngó. It is the dedication and submission of women to Ṣàngó on both sides of the Atlantic that opens the way for the mysteries and more complex behavior of Ṣàngó as divinity. In the African diaspora of the "New World," most women consecrated to Ṣàngó have been victims of male brutality and societal isolation, and/or have been blessed with the curse of social leadership.

Females consecrated to Ṣàngó learn the complex power of their divinity and understand that it goes far beyond sexual alliances and promiscuous behavior. Ṣàngó as divinity is concerned with female issues, women's relations to men, and occasions of abuse. He could be called the champion of the underdog. This unique relationship between Ṣàngó and women may be the reason that males in Africa must braid their hair and dress as women in order to attain status and approach the divine force that we call Ṣàngó. J. Lorand Matory made a clear distinction between Western notions of "transvestitism" and the cross-dressing of male initiates of Ṣàngó. He wrote, "Instructed by the semiotics of dress itself, we must assume that not all crossings dressed up in 'gender' are essentially about men and women. Indeed, the overwhelming authority of men in a cult that valorizes 'brideliness' in its priests seem to lie in the fact that transvestites are the most permanent emblems of the god's own dressing across boundaries—in the bodies of human beings."[3] Although it is more common to hear about the sexual exploits of Ṣàngó, Ṣàngó also rescues women from harm. In order to understand Ṣàngó as a divine force embodied on the physical plane, we must look beyond the social limitations imposed upon male and female practitioners of Yorùbá-based spirituality, and look to Ṣàngó's movement through the skies and storms of the cosmos. Without an examination of Ṣàngó in nature, an

understanding of Ṣàngó is limited to historical characters and social conditions that can be and have been manipulated and constructed to suit
the outcomes of those in positions of power and control.

Gender Constraints of Ṣàngó Worshippers

Slavery and colonization imposed Western thought upon Yorùbá people, and redefined roles and designated new roles of males and females.
This shift away from African identification and classification moved the
defining principles for male and female away from lineage, intellect, and
achievement to a reliance on physicality as the basic component of maleness and femaleness. In essence, the experience of gender moved from
invisible or spiritual acuity to the realities of biology. The Westernization
of Yorùbá tradition has changed the experience of gender and how we
relate to each other as spiritual communities. Colonized gender roles are
a primary example of how this transformation has altered our course.

Seekers of Yorùbá spirituality in the Western world have maintained
an eagerness to incorporate Yorùbá language into their ceremonies and
daily communications. Despite this eagerness, most Yorùbánists in the
West are not aware of how many Yorùbá words reflect the societal structures of cultures other than Yorùbá. Bishop Crowther documented many
cultural intrusions on the Yorùbá language by other groups in his book,
Yorùbá Vocabulary, written in 1843.[4] Crowther translated one of the
earliest books documenting the Yoruba language for Yorùbá speakers
in Freetown. He translated prayer as *irong* (*ìrun*), the Muslim term for
communal prayer, but by 1850, in his translation of *The Book of Common Prayer,* he had decided that its specific connotations could not be
transferred to Christian practice and settled on another Muslim term,
àdúrà, which denotes individual petitionary prayer.[5] There are many
other words that are now considered as having a Yorùbá origin, but they
actually come from the Hausa and Arabic languages. For example, there
was no Yorùbá word to describe "evil." Therefore, when discussing the
Yorùbá *òrìṣà* Èṣù, the closest word decided upon was *túláàsì,* in a word
imported from the Hausa language, meaning "trouble." This word was
used interchangeably with other Hausa words such as *bìlísì* (Satan).[6] The
connection between words, actions, and status incorporated into Yorùbá
language has not been explored by the Western faithful. Women, men,
and the youth of "New World" traditions continue to be limited in their
experience of the spirituality and culture of Yorùbá beliefs before colonialism. Consequently the current applications of Yorùbá language in

the West do not support many of the gender designations now applied in Yorùbá spiritual communities.

Our spiritual communities mirror the societies that house them, and in the United States male energy is dominant; men determine the application of ritual and law. Men in the West have primarily been the ones who interpret the sacred texts and set the standards that communities must follow. Women can do most of the fundamental ritual work that prepares men and women to become the new adherents of the tradition, but they must do this work according to the interpretations and policies set by men. When the understanding of these men is grounded in biological realities, the theological and philosophical participation of the women is limited. In other words, men *and* women in Western populations should assume more responsibility for cultural *and* theological correctness. There is spiritual uniqueness to both sexes, and one gender should not bear the sole responsibility of having to dictate the *official* word on theological conformity. When one group dominates or suppresses another, the growth of the community-at-large is stunted. Both genders will need to come together to create a long-term vision that is more inclusive, and more reflective of the ways of nature.

Practitioners of the various traditions agree that the sacred texts, or *odù*, of Ifá tell us the destiny we chose before being born, the talents we carry, and the lessons we must learn. This theological principle is not grounded in gender-biology. When practitioners of Yorùbá-based traditions visit an elder for a spiritual consultation, the interpretations of the sacred text of Ifá can be totally dependent on biological gender. This difference in interpretation not only affects the individual, it also affects, by extension, the life of the community of which the person is an integral part. For example, there are verses of Ifá oracle known as *odù* that clearly state the person consulting should continue on their spiritual journey and become an initiated devotee of Ifá. However, in some lineages, Ifá initiation for a woman is not an option. Instead women in such lineages receive taboos that preclude them from taking on spiritual students. They can also be forbidden to use the technologies of divination, even of the *òrìṣà* they are consecrated to, making them indefinitely dependent on male skill and interpretation.

On the other hand, men who receive these same *odù* are also forbidden to have students prior to being initiated into Ifá, but their restriction is only temporary. Once they have been initiated into Ifá, their status in the tradition takes a major leap forward. Not only may they have students, but they may also be permitted to be policymakers of the tradition, based on their gender. This creates a state of imbalance that is solely based on gender-biology.

Among the Yorùbá, red is the color of power and strength. It is no mistake that the colors attributed to Ṣàngó are red and white. White is the color that represents the desired state of "coolness." Without the cool and cunning acts of diplomacy that evolve from the "hot" desire of courage and the "coolness" of those who assume leadership roles, it would be difficult to correct the injustices of society. Themes of "hot" and "cold" run throughout Western and Central Africa and the spiritual beliefs of various tribes. Women are viewed as "hot" because they contain the menstrual blood that ultimately forms an embryo, and men who commit sexual acts outside of the tribal social sanctions are also considered hot and dangerous to the tribal norms. Women are considered to be biologically "hot" because they can bear children. The capacity that human beings have for channeling and releasing the energies of Ṣàngó has propelled human development forward and been the fuel for elevating the human consciousness. Ṣàngó awakens our innate passion for living and loving against the odds. Ṣàngó's irresistible and intoxicating method of presenting the truth causes our bodies to overpower the intellect, discard logic, and step away from the crowd, creating heroes and heroines.

Ṣàngó as a divine force is neither male nor female; he remains neither "hot" nor "cold." Ṣàngó's "hot" power as expressed by fire and his ability to be the calm cool master strategist during war conveys the dual nature of some of his attributes. Eugenia W. Herbert describes fire and the mastery of it in the following way: "[F]ire was so often identified with the force of life itself and with prosperity. The method of making fire by friction has commonly had explicit sexual overtones, paralleling those of iron smelting."[7] Fire is essential and problematic. Fire is a tool that humanity has learned to use to improve the quality of life, but fire can also start on its own, rage out of control, and destroy human life. Because of the two-sided nature of this divine consciousness, Ṣàngó should never be taken for granted; nor should humanity take for granted what direction he might take next. The dualities of Ṣàngó's manifestations are ever-present.

Because of gender-based interpretations of the spiritual texts, the contributions that men and women can make to the larger community are limited. This is true primarily because of biology and culture, not because of their character or spiritual development. Women will need to develop more confidence in their ability to sustain culture and widen their comfort zone in terms of their connection to spirit. The desired ritual state among those who follow Yorùbá spirituality is a "cool" head. Females as a gender are thought to be "hot" more often than males; consequently they are barred from participating in most rituals during their menstruation. Women are restricted because some practitioners believe they radiate heat. Others say it is because women are infertile during the time of their menses. Eugenia W. Herbert argues "that any process where these exclusions and taboos are operative implies that the process is seen within a reproductive paradigm."[8]

Unfortunately, in Western society the usual way to capture and restrict our understanding of the essence of fire and sound is to gird its loins with restricted notions of gender. When we limit the understanding of Ṣàngó to mere "masculine traits," his duality is never fully explored. Despite the fact that male and female initiates of Ṣàngó have been taught that Ṣàngó is the womanizer of the goddesses of Yorùbá tradition, he is truly the lover of women. This restricted understanding diminishes the depth of the potential relationship that we can have as we participate in Ṣàngó's energy internally and communally. The nature-based force of Ṣàngó cannot be adequately interpreted through these distorted notions of gender. One thing becomes very clear when natural law is applied to the movement of Ṣàngó through the universe: Ṣàngó's energy is not static, nor can it be contained. Its very nature causes the darkness to be illuminated, even when it is the darkness of our prejudices and ignorance about gender roles—Káwo Kábíè Yèsí, Ọba Kòso— Hail the king, he is not dead.

> Ṣàngó ohún tíń dún nínú aginjù
> Ṣàngó tó ń la òpè l'ójú
> Ṣàngó tó ń gbé ìmọ́lẹ̀ fún òpè
> Ṣàngó olùfà òkùnkùn
> Ṣàngó tó ń fún àwọn ọmọdébìrin rẹ
>   ní okun ọkùnrin mẹ̀wàá
> Àti ìgboyà ọpọ́ ènìyàn
> Ṣàngó ohùn Olódùmarè
> Ṣàngó ẹni tí iná kò kí ń jó

Ṣàngó husband of Mother Nature
    Ṣàngó brings light to the ignorant
    Ṣàngó brings light to the ignorant
    Ṣàngó the dispeller of darkness
    Ṣàngó who gives his daughters
        the strength of ten men,

And the courage of the multitudes
Ṣàngó the voice of Olódùmarè
Ṣàngó who does not burn

NOTES

1. Aina Olomo, *Core of Fire: A Path to Yorùbá Spiritual Activism* (Brooklyn: Althelia Henrietta Press, 2003), 101.

2. Èṣù Ẹlẹ́gbá is also involved in copulation. He is the erect penis, or the promise that leads to sexual fulfillment. He is always ready whenever the opportunity presents itself. While Èṣù Ẹlẹ́gbá is the promise, Ṣàngó is the release and completion.

3. J. Lorand Matory, *Sex and the Empire That Is No More: Gender and the Politics of Metaphor in Ọ̀yọ́ Yorùbá Religion* (Minneapolis: University of Minnesota Press, 1994), 215.

4. J. D. Y. Peel, *Religious Encounter and the Making of the Yorùbá* (Bloomington: Indiana University Press, 2000), 195.

5. For Crowther's input on Yorùbá language and importation from other cultures, see J. F. A. Away, "Bishop Crowder: An Assessment," *Odu* 4 (1970): 3–17.

6. Peel, *Religious Encounter,* 195.

7. Eugenia W. Herbert, *Iron, Gender, and Power, Rituals of Transformation in African Societies* (Bloomington: Indiana University Press, 1993), 119.

8. Ibid.

CHAPTER SIXTEEN

Searching for Thunder

A Conversation about Changó

MICHAEL ATWOOD MASON AND ERNESTO PICHARDO

The Lucumí religious tradition emerged in Cuba and came to the United States with Cuban immigrants beginning in the 1950s. Its practice revolves around devotion to the *orichas* (divinities who embody one aspect of God).[1] In the tradition, people routinely assume and assert that the children of a particular divinity or *oricha* know more about their own *oricha* than anyone else. Ernesto Pichardo is a child of Changó, initiated as an *olocha* (priest or priestess dedicated to a particular *oricha*) in 1971. Since that time, he has studied the religion and the *orichas* in a wide variety of contexts. Widely recognized as an *obá oríaté* (ritual expert, master of ceremonies, and cowry-shell diviner) by both younger generations of priests and elders, he, with his family, started the Church of the Lukumí Babalú-Ayé in 1974.

When the church opened a public venue in 1987, the City of Hialeah, Florida, moved to close it down. Pichardo led the fight and the federal litigation that resulted in a Supreme Court ruling in 1993 providing constitutional protections for *oricha* religion in the United States. Pichardo has earned a position of public prominence in the *oricha* community in the United States and Cuban Diaspora in Latin America. Since the court battle, Pichardo continues to lead ceremonies around the world, teach students of the religion, and provide guidance to academics and believers alike.

Pichardo and I met in 1994 at a conference on the religion in Puerto Rico. Soon thereafter he became my teacher in the religion and later my friend. In 1998 he became my godfather when he "gave me" the *oricha* of illness and healing, Babalú-Ayé. A great deal of my practical and theoretical understanding of the tradition comes directly from conversations with him over the years. In the beginning, he would call me out of the blue, drill me with questions till he found one that I could not answer to his satisfaction, then say, "That's your homework," and hang up. I never had the nerve to call back until I had some kind of answer, however incomplete. Now I tend to call him to ask specific questions about theology, practice, history, or politics—all key aspects of the religion. These interviews convey some of the back-and-forth conversations among scholars such as Dwyer, Hastrup, and Jackson that characterize the transfer of knowledge within the Lucumí *oricha* tradition and anthropological research.

When Pichardo and I discussed the possibility of collaborating on these interviews, we agreed that we would try to go beyond the generalized characteristics usually used to describe the *orichas* in general and Changó in particular. Instead we have tried to explore Changó as he affects individual people's lives and manifests in specific circumstances, which change according to personality, historical epoch, and regional location. We hope to provide a philosophical approach to Changó that is completely in line with the practice of the religion and beyond what most academic writing has presented.[2]

The Text

MASON: It is important for people to understand who you are and how you became so involved in the religion.

PICHARDO: It all started with my mother, who was supposed to avoid getting pregnant to stay healthy. Changó through her godfather Felix—he was a Changó [priest]—said she was going to have another boy and he would be a son of Changó. When I was born, my mother was fine and I had no health issues. One day at Felix's house, when I was still a baby, he got possessed by Changó, and his Changó took me and threw me into the air. He raced all over the house and kept saying I was his son. Then came the Cuban Revolution, so our access to Felix and the island was cut off because we had to leave.

In Miami, no one knew those stories. In 1971 when I was sixteen, Romelio Pérez, who was later my *oyugbona* [second ritual sponsor at initiation], got possessed by his *batá*Obatalá [cool-headed *oricha* of creativity] and picked me out of 300 people. He threw the *collar de mazo* [multi-stranded beaded necklace used to make sacred vessels] over my head, picked me up, and danced all over the house. He said I could not leave the house without being made to Changó. That was my first contact with the *orichas* with full awareness. It seemed right to me. It felt right. Once *batá*Obatalá did that to me in front of everybody, the *babalawos* went to their room—that was their old tradition—and divined to see if *batá*Obatalá was really there. That was affirmed, and the *odu* [divination sign that affirmed the presence of *batá*Obatalá] had to do with the coming of a new king. At least that's the phrase I remember. *Batá*Obatalá put me down and said to everyone that this was a new king waiting to be born. He presented the mandate that everyone present should donate something right then and there for my initiation. Those that doubted that he was really present and speaking the truth would be dealt with by him later. Then came the *babalawos* saying the same thing based on their *odu*. The next day, Orestes Menéces—Baba Eyiogbe—came in and took out a hundred-dollar bill. And everyone followed leaving twenty- or ten-dollar bills. It was the *babalawos* who were dropping the big money. I don't know what happened to that money, it never got to me. Then my mother, with her mediumship with the ancestors [she is a spiritist and receives spiritual directions directly from the spirits], says to the elders, "We will go ahead and make my son." But the owner of that house, Carlos, had a taboo against making any Changó in his house. So she put up our house and said, "Others will also appear and they will all get made at the same time." Well, they made five of us in sixteen days. My Changó was made with two *batá*Obatalás, a Yemayá [maternal *oricha* of the sea], and an Ochúnochún [sensual *oricha* of love and rivers].

This was historic. Literally everyone who was in Miami and knew the religion was there. It took a lot of hands. There was a lot of gossip going on, and people were saying that I would be the one to die. *Así ya puedes ver que en mis dos nacimientos me quisieran perjudicar* ("so now you can see that in both of my births, they wanted to mess me up"). Plus there was always controversy. All five of us have lived very long lives, so the rumors were just nonsense. Just to give you an idea, we started the initiation at 5 AM and we went for twenty-four hours straight to do it all. Imagine five *matanzas* [sacrifices of five or six four-legged animals and more than twenty-five birds]. On the *día del medio* [semi-public, middle day of the initiation] and throughout the week, hundreds of people came through the house.

In the eleventh grade, they threw me out because I was a *santero* [priest of the *oricha*]. I was out of school for about thirty days. First I was grounded as we prepared for my initiation. Then we did the ceremony and waited a couple weeks. When I went back to school, the assistant principal had already done the paperwork to expel me from school. I was already sixteen, and, under the policy there, he could do that. I went through half the eleventh grade. So there I was out of school. People in the neighborhood saw me in the street dressed in white and knew what it was, they knew I was an *iyawó* [new initiate, who dresses in white]. Neighbors would hide or not say anything. Zero contact. People—parents would call their kids indoors when I came out. My social life went away! Gone! All that was replaced by the religious community. That became the family . . . the friends . . . the all. It was a new life, for sure, even the surroundings and the people.

It [my life] became the religion twenty-four hours a day and seven days a week. As an *iyawó*, you're restricted and cannot go out after 6. After the first three months, I had to be home by midnight. My elders were very strict. There was so much religious activity going on, I could just go and work and learn. Now of course, early on, the *babalawos* said I had to pass to Ifá, going back to the first *odu* they had cast. So, three-fourths of the time I was with the *oricha* people learning and working, but everything that related to the work of the *babalawos* I was called over to see. The first ceremony I learned was with a *babalawo*, feeding the front door and the corners of the house, the street corners, the roof, and the garbage. It was not, "Hold this water." It was, "Grab that rooster."

My religious education early on took place in the house. There were daily religious activities with group participation. I was part of this small group of *iyawós*, and new ones were coming in rapidly. We were learning in a group how to respond to the needs of the day. It was a constant. Plus I was getting additional tidbits here and there. We were making another *ocha* [initiation], and Romelio would show me the making of the clothing and buying cloth for the thrones.[3] I was learning to make the *collares* [necklaces for the *orichas*] and sitting down and stringing stuff. Learning the art was part of it. It was a constant. If you were there, you were doing something. They would say, "You're here. Work." So there was constant practice. Practice, practice, practice. Learn, learn, learn. I would participate in the preparations prior to the initiation ceremonies, building the throne and preparing the room and making the *machuquillo* [crushed sacred herbs used for the initiation]. Romelio was training me on that, but others were not. The *babalawos* would call me over to work the *matanza* and have me open the animals. I learned that whole process.

In that period I was learning everything—through observation—with Ocha Inlé, the only *obá* present in Miami at the time. A few years later, my true in-depth apprenticeship began with Jimagua [Roque Duarte]. I can point to specific people that I have learned things from: Romelio, Ocha Inlé, Jimagua, my mother. What have I learned from Changó, *batá*Obatalá, Elegguá, Yemayá? Now, who has been the real teacher? Life. Life and the community.

MASON: I remember you had some interesting remarks about the Ogún and Ochún books that came out over the years. Could you comment on the notion of a book about Changó?

PICHARDO: When some Yorùbá elders began to come to Miami and see our Cuban model in the 1970s, they were amazed to find that our ordination leads to about six *orichas*, because theirs generally only leads to one. The remarks I heard early on showed they were confused by what they saw. They said, "We can worship our head *oricha* for an entire lifetime and not fully understand him. How then is it possible to focus on six and understand them all?" These remarks I heard as an *iyawó* from two Yorùbá priestesses in 1971. As an *iyawó,* we went home from our ordination with six sets of physical objects representing different *orichas* and a consuming, overwhelming amount of information—only to learn later that all we had learned did not even scratch the surface.

We must realize that we can learn generalities and interpretations from *odu*s. We can learn rituals, procedures, ceremonies, songs, chants, and the so-called paths of certain *orichas*. We can go out and learn the sequences of the different paths. We can concern ourselves with all of that. If we do it intensely, ten to fifteen years later we feel like we know something, until we ask ourselves, "What do I know? Who is Changó? What is Changó? Or any other *oricha* for that matter?"

We find ourselves then trying to answer this bigger question. The more we try to answer, the more we realize that we know nothing. To say that we know Changó is to say that we know with precision all the possible characteristics of Changó and how they manifest in every life circumstance as characterized in 256 *odu*s. That does not include Changó's association in all those circumstances to other *orichas*. So then, after over three decades of priesthood, I ask the question, "Who is the human expert in these matters?" Nobody. I haven't met him yet. I have not met that person yet. I doubt that anyone will ever reach a level where we can say, "This person is an expert on this subject." Such claims of expertise are not appropriate. We can say that this person knows more about this particular *oricha* than I do. I go back to what those priestesses said. We can and do spend a lifetime trying to understand who and what our head *oricha* is. At the end the question is "How much did you learn?

How much do you still have to learn?" Claims to expertise are irrational, because when we are speaking of these character traits and their manifestations, it's a fact that they evolve over time. So then you have to learn its new manifestations as they appear.

Since fire is associated with Changó, take that as an example. Fire has not changed. Fire is fire, but its manifestation has changed and will continue to change: fire on plastic, fire on fiberglass, fire from explosive devices. These sorts of fire and many more did not exist a hundred years ago. But the fire is still fire. How has fire evolved over the centuries? During one lifetime, we can look to the past and to the present situation to understand how fire has manifested. Yet a week from now, a new explosive device is created by some scientist, and we are forced to learn again about fire and how it manifests in that new context. So it is impossible to fix it, to nail it down once and for all. You can never master it because it is always taking on new forms that make you go right back to square one. You start over. Trying to answer, "Who is Changó?" or "What is Changó?" is like going to a university and never being able to graduate in this lifetime.

MASON: As we have talked over the years, you have often made a distinction between thinking about the *orichas* and living with the *orichas*. This idea seems widespread among elders in the religion. Could you explain this notion?

PICHARDO: We have been laying out the philosophical basis for what the thought process should be, but we still have not made it individual. We need to take it from the broad, abstract view to the narrow, where the individual person lives with the *oricha*. Within the life of the individual, we have to look at matters beyond the home and matters in the home. Why? Although in American culture we tend to see ourselves as individuals, we are losing track of a larger reality. The individual is born into a world of already existing complexity. In this culture, the tendency is to view ourselves starting with matters of the home and moving outward. This religion says it is the opposite. It is the individual emerging into the larger world outside. What will that individual face day in and day out for a lifetime? "Individual" here means preservation within a huge, broad, and already extant complexity that constantly places the individual in harm's way and makes him or her vulnerable to danger. So it is about preservation and perseverance.

In principle, this means that accessing *oricha*—whether through divination or trance possession or any other form where there can be communication and the exchange of information—becomes most relevant to the all, everything outside the individual. The individual is a compound of physical and spiritual realities as she faces her journey on the earth in this lifetime. The divination sign given at initiation by the principal, crowned *oricha* shows the person's destiny and fate. That compound sign is lived by the individual, and she must survive that journey and make the best of it that she can. Although as a priestess, an individual may have an *itá* that reveals *odu*s from various *orichas*, which are fixed and unchangeable—those are our DNA—it is how all of that applies and is connected to her head *oricha*.[4]

There is another component to this. While we can spend a lifetime trying to learn the relationship between ourselves, our head *orichas*, and ever-evolving manifestations of the *odu*, we also have the short-term divination readings that we do. These narrow down time, space, and circumstances, so we can better understand the moment. Once we modify or change behavior, whether an outright change or a ritual, and once we take some action to remedy our situation, we have already changed the circumstances and how it manifests. We can actually look at those transitory readings addressing the here and now, but the teachings can be linked to our original *itá*. Why? Because they are just small fractions of the same, larger picture. So when we say Changó, then we must ask ourselves, who and what we are talking about? Not only in our *itá* at ordination, but in that long lifetime, accounting for every circumstance that ever arises where we need to go back to divination for a narrower understanding of how to micro-manage the circumstances. Once we act, we are able to learn a little more about the domain of Changó.

How can we address and characterize Changó, when to truly do so with any justice we would have to understand that force in the life of an individual—in his or her *itá*—and how, in that life journey, each circumstance was handled and what the outcome was for every individual for the full lifetime from life to death? Thinking in this way moves us out to other individuals and the *odu*s from their *itá*s, the components of their *odu*s. We would want to measure that by gender, by profession, by different age groups and their different problems, by geography. Add to that the social and economic conditions.

In other words, we could have two individual sons of Changó with the same identical *odu*s, born in the same city and country, but in two different generations, and the outside conditions would not be identical, and therefore the manifestations of the *odu* would not be the same, even though it is still the same *odu*.

MASON: If I understand you correctly, you are talking about Changó's actions in a given situation. This leads to the key questions here. What are you really dealing with when you engage Changó? What is the agency called Changó?

PICHARDO: Where is the formula to understanding this equation? This is the philosophical side that is not taught or documented. When we speak of any *oricha*, we have to understand its complexities: what are the common, known *odus* associated with its traits and in what contexts do they appear? Then we begin to review that context and see the *oricha*'s manifestations. That moves us to begin to understand who they are or what they are or what they stand for. You have to approach it from the thought process we use in divination. The *odus* explain the roles of the *orichas* in context and give us the formula to understand the equations. That's what I do when I do *itá*. Let's say the reading comes *iré elese Changó* [with blessings from Changó],[5] but in what *odu*? To contextualize it, you have to know what the sign is. The influence of Changó's blessings will vary from *odu* to *odu*, not in principle but in form. Its cause and effect change. Take the principle of gossip. What *oricha* deals with gossip? Something moved to produce gossip, and that gossip has the potential to manifest in many ways, constructive and destructive. And that's when we have to find where Changó is. And who else is working there? Is he working alone or with one or more other *oricha*? We take that simple thought and then ask, "What does it evolve into?" Discord? Quarrels? If so, what does that new thing turn into?

In understanding *oricha*, we must look at their generalized traits in each *odu*, but we must also consider their *iré* and *osobo* possibilities. Each idea or value has its polarity. Gossip can be constructive or destructive. The opposites are built into these words. Take quarrels. They are not always negative. In the divination sign Eyioco,[6] from quarrels comes *iré*: With a heated debate, truth is revealed. The quarrel was necessary to find the truth and establish a new peace. There are circumstances where we can look back and say that *osobo* brought forth resolution and truth.

If we take the same idea and move it into the divination sign *Obara*,[7] you have what? You have gossip, which is common in *Obara*. You have discord, quarreling, misunderstandings, and confusions. All that is *Obara*. But *Obara* is a sign that moves you to face the *osobo* and reveal its truth, and so then it becomes *iré*. The negative things could become other things which are much more destructive. If gossip becomes quarrels and it does not get resolved, then it can become hostility and violence and hatred and rancor. It can escalate to tragedy. To best understand how to describe who and what an *oricha* is in its manifestations—how it functions, affects life, and becomes real in everyday life—it must be seen through the *odu*s. That is the only source we have with tangible language to scrutinize and rationalize and then reach certain conclusions. The *odu*s give some basis for knowing and not just random speculation.

Let's take Changó and his common association with fire—*la candela*.[8] We can take our current knowledge and the material we have learned, and we can look at fire and rationalize its workings as an element. What is fire composed of? What causes fire? After a fire starts, how does it behave and what does it do? We apply fire. Fire is destructive, but again it's polarized. So we have to go further, we understand the circumstances. Consider fire in bushes, over water, over plastic, over a wooden frame home. How does fire move? What does it do? That's where we begin to understand the complexity of fire. Fire is still the principle, but it is applied in so many different ways. Its effect manifests in so many different ways.

If we follow the principles and elements associated with each specific *oricha* and we begin to understand *oricha* in this way, then we begin to know *oricha*. *Òrìṣà* does not stand on its own.[9] As soon as it becomes active, it comes into contact with the realm of others. For example, consider fire again and consider Olorun, Aganyú, and Changó as a trinity. Fire is the principle in Olorun as the sun. There is the principle of fire in Aganyú in volcanic eruptions. And then you have Changó spitting fire. None of that can manifest or move without Elegguá, because he is always necessary for anything to move. Fire is the substance, but Elegguá carries it. This is the idea of Elegguá as the *ebocero* [the one who carries sacrifices and gets things moving in rituals] as a messenger. He is the one who moves it. He is the force that guides destiny. He goes along with it. We must have oxygen, wind, that is fire's source of life. Otherwise it extinguishes itself. This is a natural example.

MASON: Is that example reflected in *odu* or *oricha*?

PICHARDO: Here is where the idea of "there is no Changó without Oyá" comes in. She is the wind. Changó is also the master of Osain [*oricha* of herbs and plants]. The plants of Osain are the source of oxygen. We are back to the simple explanations straight out of nature, but people have not considered the depth behind it and therefore they do not usually teach that depth either. We are describing the presence of Changó in fire. Where do we find fire? We find it in the divination sign *Iroso,* in *Obara,* and in *Eyilá*.[10]

MASON: To help people understand how Changó manifests in different specific contexts, let's talk about how he manifests in specific *odu*s. How would you expect to see him in *Iroso Meyi*?

PICHARDO: You look at characteristics that are natural to the *odu,* and you can condense them into keywords. Then you ask, "Where is Changó" in each case. You also begin to see where his presence or action may include one or more other *orichas,* where he is working in concert with others as well.

What is basic to *Iroso Meyi?* The sign is life difficulties, obstacles, and obstructions. It is deception, falsehood, hypocrisy, and indiscretion. It is disillusionment, it is curiosity. There is also slander and aggression, stubbornness and revenge. What do we have there? We have very common life situations reflected in these keywords with a very specific negative feeling. To look at this, we would ask, "What about Changó is revealed to us as we try to understand these key words?" We could look at it from the point of view of Changó's fire or thunder and lightning. When thunder and lightning appear in human life, it has a sudden effect on us. It forces us to focus on it all of a sudden, and it certainly catches our attention. It impacts our awareness. It is a sudden realization and sudden fear. It gives us a sense, a sudden sense of this mess we are in and the power that is beyond our human control. So it suddenly changes how things are at the moment that it appears. It changes how we see the situation. Thunder and lightning are very powerful symbols that show how massive danger presents itself very quickly. So we look at this power and we look at the key words, and we ask, "Where is that power present in the various life difficulties surrounding these key words?"

MASON: Can you talk it through using the specific example of disillusionment?

PICHARDO: Disillusionment is key to *Iroso Meyi* because the sign deals with the unknown. The person sees the world in a particular way that is not realistic. He does not see things as they really are. So *Iroso* is falling through a trap door, where the individual was far from thinking it was a trap door. Otherwise he would have paid attention and not fallen through it. Once he falls through, here comes the disillusionment. How can people be so cruel? How could he deceive me? I thought this person was my friend. So Changó comes in and says, "I represent fulfillment, realization, satisfaction, honesty, integrity, discretion. I stand for truth and praise." So the presence of Changó here says, "You may be in *osobo* living one of these negative experiences, but I represent the opposite of these negative experiences and I have the ability to show you that opposite and put you in a position to live out the *iré.*"

Now in general terms, if we find Changó in the *osobo arayé* [negativity from malefactors], then we will find him in these key words. What is fundamental to Changó is the difficulties commonly found in human life and in human relationships. He is less about plants or the challenge of building a bridge. Instead, he is more about what is natural to humans and the dynamics of their relationships. When we read about Changó, what do we find in these *patakís* [mythic narratives associated with specific *odu*s]? There is always a human difficulty that relates to another person or city or people. It is not Ogún where he pulls out his machete and cuts the way through for everyone. Ogún is cutting a path for people, which is not typical of Changó. Changó is always in the way of direct human conflict. In the case of *Iroso*, it is also common for people to fall into deep depression. Disillusionment can easily move a person into depression. Then we have Babalú-Ayé and illness. The human relationship brings out disillusionment, which is Changó. This brings on the depression, which is Babalú-Ayé. This is where they meet. Changó can show the individual realization and satisfaction, and Babalú-Ayé can remove the depression. They combine to reverse the negativity.

MASON: This is reflected in the myths of Changó and Babalú-Ayé working together, but you seem more concerned with how they work together, how they function to change a person's situation.

PICHARDO: We know that is true. We are not so concerned with the question, "Who is Changó?" We can break it down to value, power, and order. In the *patakís* we will look at virtues and morals in order to stay in sync with the *aché* of the ancestors.[11] We can look at power and ask what is power in this story? The power we look for is the power of resolution. Where is the resolution? Where does it come from in the story? And then how does this relate to the spiritual world and the divinities? We know that everything that exists is linked to a particular divinity. What the story gives us is the means to take in an *odu* that allows us to rationalize the situation, so we can [have] the difficulty or misfortune or chaos and find a sense of order to it. This understanding gives us the tools to bring back order and stability to the individual. So in *Iroso*, we ask, "What is the power of disillusionment? How did we get there? What experiences got us to the point that we felt disillusioned?" It does not just happen. There are actions that precede it. All those aspects are in the *odu*. It tells us how the person was a victim or victimizer, or how he has become both. And so we can then address the power of disillusionment in all its complexity. Though its essence does not change—it is what it is—its power has a broad range of manifestations. And we have to figure out how it is manifesting here and now in a particular person's life. We have to understand how disillusionment is manifesting in this specific situation.

MASON: Following this example of disillusionment and then working with Changó, what do you expect after the sudden change begins?

PICHARDO: First you have to cause a realization. The diviner is the interpreter. As the diviner, you have the knowledge of the sign and present it to the client in an orderly conversation. You have the capacity to talk about the *odu* in language that allows the person to move through the confusion and see the light. It is just like a psychologist who takes in information, processes it, and restates it in an orderly way. They learn to think about it in that way, and the person walks away with a sense of order and control. The person is less confused. The first step is the realization.

The proverb of *Obara* says, "He who knows does not die like he who does not know." This means realizations. If you are confused and don't understand the situation, you don't have the capacity to change. We also find depression in *Obara*. That's the lightning bolt. It says, "Wake up!"

If you worked Changó against disillusionment, what would you expect after realization? First realization has to cause acceptance, in the sense that if you were outfoxed, what is the use in becoming aggressive and seeking revenge? Where does this acceptance come from? This becomes the *odu Oché* that says, *Perdiendo se gana* ["losing you win"].[12] It says, "So everyone makes mistakes. Move on. What did you learn?" There it is another sign, *Ogbè-Sá*,[13] that says, "Don't repeat your past mistakes and you'll be okay. What did your life *pataki* teach you that it drew you into this disillusionment? So learn from it and don't repeat the mistakes. That's your responsibility. Accept it and learn from it." That's the result of realization. That's the importance of the value. We ask, "Where is the value here?"

Are we concerned with the legend or myth? Is it literally telling us about a character? Is it Changó or another character? We are not concerned with the literal. What are we really talking about? We are talking about symbols. What do we associate with Changó or his leopard?

The best way to understand what we are saying is this: Our ancestors left us a story, but today we can look at it and see a whole conversation contained in that story. We end up with a story, but when we consider it carefully, we just see a progression of symbols, one after another. We don't get bogged downed with the storytelling or the form. While an outsider will do that, an insider will start interpreting it. There is meaning to these stories. We read a story and find a character, we try to understand the significance of the character—not the character itself—the significance of the character.

Changó falls down and breaks his arm. Do we know that is true? In *Iroso,* Orula [*oricha* of Ifá divination], or his son, falls in the pit. Do we know that Orula fell in this pit for a fact? No, we don't. We can classify it as a myth or legend or a folktale and then discuss our interpretations. But we don't know if the story is true. What we know is true is when we interpret its meaning. We are talking about an authority figure and his child and the fact that people fall into pits. It does not really matter to me that it was Orula, except that I ask, "Why was it Orula? What does that add to the moral of the story?" It says that we have a respected authority figure that has certain human characteristics, and those characteristics drew him to fall into this pit out of his ignorance. While in the pit, people walk by, and no one will help him to get out. What we see there is how certain human beings—because they are in a position of authority—become so selfish and self-centered and greedy that they create their own sense of reality. They become indifferent to the rest of the world to the point that they become isolated. Only when they experience something like this fall do they become vulnerable and have the opportunity to realize that we all rely on someone else to exist. Here the powerful becomes powerless, and he has to rely on those "beneath him" to pull him out.

Now what happens? Depending on the *iré* or *osobo,* the diviner must determine if the client is represented by Orula or is the client someone else in the story? You have to place the client in the story. You see if the person is the victim, the victimizer, or both. Those who do nothing to help him are acting out their revenge. That's in *Iroso.* Being hardheaded is part of *Iroso.* Orula is in the hole demanding to be pulled out, acting like he always does. He is hardheaded, and unless there is a change and he gets humble, no one will throw him a rope. Those looking at his arrogance might be pleased to see him down there. They enjoy seeing him powerless and they enjoy feeling powerful: "We don't have to throw you a rope." Kindness comes in, saying, "We can help. We can throw you a rope." Each character is a symbol. Many stories include animals. We ask, "What is the significance here of the elephant? The leopard?" The turtle came in contact with the snake. Everything that lives has its own *eledá* [spiritual essence from the Creator] and its own *aché.* That is what we look for and that is what we interpret and that is what we apply to the here and now for the client. It is the symbol and its character—and not the specific identity or name of the character— that becomes important. In the story, we are not concerned with Orula. We ask, "What character did Orula display that got him in the hole and what did it take to get him out of the hole? What did he sacrifice to get out?" Aspects of his bad character got him in the hole in the first place, and the client is likely going through something very similar.

We have to step back. We can characterize Changó, which happens a lot. *Aleyos* [uninitiated people] come and ask, "Who is Changó?" Academics too. That is fine, but the real question is "What is Changó known for? How does he manifest in the *odu*s in the here and now?" You can look at Changó. Why does he have red and white associated with him? What does that mean? Why not pink? Why are some *orichas* associated with red and white and others are not?

MASON: Since we have come back around to the uninitiated, I want to pose some simple questions. How would you describe Changó to someone new to the religion?

PICHARDO: I hate the superficial definitions. How can you describe in a paragraph a divinity that represents such a broad aspect of human life? How do you do that? Aside from what others have already done, that does not do it justice. Thunder and lightning. Justice and truth, warrior and king. Dancer, owner of the sacred *batá* drums, original diviner who gave up the divination board to Orula. Excellent strategist in warfare. Excellent governor of people. Always present where there is injustice. Brings order where there is confusion. These are the ways people describe him, but they are a simplistic injustice to his depth.

MASON: Why is Changó called the king of the religion? Why do you think he is so adored by so many people? Why is he so central to the religion?

PICHARDO: First there is the historical fact that he was the King of Òyó. It starts there. When people are in serious trouble, they know that this *oricha* deals with that realm of difficulties, and he comes in and brings peace and order. So he is known to take on the challenging human issues of conflict and difficulty. At the same rate, there is the image of Changó as a true, just leader of a prosperous community. He is the counterbalance to Ochún. They were married and she was his queen. Changó is associated with overcoming difficulty, which makes the rest possible. Imagine a community dominated by poverty and trouble and vicissitudes. Changó is the one who comes in and takes that on head on, breaks it down, so the merriment and riches of Ochún can come in. Changó makes the change possible. In essence, they remove the difficulty and allow the prosperity to take over.

MASON: In the famous story where Changó becomes an *oricha*, he plays with lightning, destroys his palace and his family, and then hangs himself in a tree in the forest. Only the *oricha* Oyá remains loyal to him, and she says that he did not hang but rose up to heaven. How would you help someone understand this story?

PICHARDO: We say, "*Obá Koso*. The king did not hang." This story shows that an individual must be completely at one with his destiny above and beyond anything else. The "I Am" becomes the identity of the person and teaches that our identity in some way includes the surrounding world. It teaches about self-identity and shows that who you are includes those around you. It is not an individual alone in the world, but rather an individual as a part of the world. It teaches many things regarding leadership, such as the role of leadership in the context of community. In essence, that individual identity is community. There is no separate entity. If you analyze the story with this principle in mind, you will find that it lasts even after death. After death, Changó becomes deified. That link to community does not end at death. Death becomes the start of something else, a new kind of community.

People expect that identity of the person to reflect the identity of the *oricha*. So in my case, they expected me as a child of Changó to be concerned with issues in the community. My family and I started the Church of the Lukumí Babalú-Ayé to provide some education and some legal protection. Then the City of Hialeah tried to close us down, and we took the case to the Supreme Court. Ever since the church battle, some of the old folks I have met ask, "You did all that? What *oricha* do you have? Changó? That figures." Changó takes us back to community, confronting the hard issues that need to be addressed and pushing against those things that need to be changed. Changó is always looking for improvement. He is the idea of justice beating back injustice, but as we discussed, the fight against injustice will manifest in different ways at different times for different individuals.

NOTES

1. See Miguel "Willie" Ramos, "Afro-Cuban Òrìṣà Worship." In *Santería Aesthetics in Contemporary Latin American Art,* ed. Arturo Lindsey (Washington, D.C.: Smithsonian Institution Press, 1996), for a good concise introduction to the religion.

2. We held these conversations via telephone over several weeks in late 2004 and early 2005. I posed questions and Pichardo responded. Through transcriptions, I recreated the conversations as a single text, adding parenthetical and footnoted clarifications. Pichardo then read and edited the text to be certain that it accurately reflected his thinking.

3. The initiation ritual requires two sets of ritual clothing for the initiate,

and it requires a large three-dimensional cloth altar in which the initiate lives during most of the week-long ceremony. For detailed descriptions of these forms, see David H. Brown, *Santería Enthroned: Art, Ritual, and Innovation in an Afro-Cuban Religion* (Chicago: University of Chicago Press, 2003). For a detailed description of the initiation process, see Michael Atwood Mason, *Living Santería: Rituals and Experiences in an Afro-Cuban Religion* (Washington, D.C.: Smithsonian Institution Press, 2002), chapter 4.

4. *Itá* refers to any divination reading that is expected to pertain to the long term of an individual's life. It is most commonly applied to the reading that is done as part of an initiation ritual, but it is also used to describe when an *oricha* receives a large offering—usually a four-legged animal—and then speaks to an individual.

5. In practice, all divination readings determine if the client is experiencing the blessings (*iré*) or negativity (*osobo*) of the given sign. This kind of binary thought process pervades the ritual workings and practices of the religion.

6. In cowry shell divination, *Eyioco* is the name of the sign that appears when two cowries land with their serrated "mouths" up. Like all divination signs, it evokes a wide array of allegorical stories, proverbs, sacrifices, prayers, and potential ceremonies. For a fuller description of cowry shell divination, see William Bascom, *Sixteen Cowries* (Bloomington: Indiana University Press, 1980) and Mason, *Living Santería,* chapter 1.

7. *Obara* is the name of the divination sign when six cowries appear "mouth" up.

8. *Candela* is a Spanish word that literally means "fire," but in Cuba, it is used figuratively to mean "trouble." This discussion merges those two meanings in an inventive way.

9. Notice here that the word *oricha* is used sometimes as a descriptor for a specific deity, sometimes as a name for the religion, and sometimes as reference to the more abstract quality of divinity itself.

10. *Iroso* is the divination sign generated when four cowries land "mouth" up. *Eyilá* is twelve cowries "mouth" up.

11. *Aché* is one of the most essential concepts in the religion and one of the hardest to define. It usually refers to the power to make things happen, especially in relation to the spirits. It sometimes refers to a specific talent, knowledge, or style that an individual possess; one often hears things like "He has *aché* for singing to the *orichas.*" So taken together, *aché* implies performative knowledge and expertise. See Mason, *Living Santería,* chapter 5, for an extensive discussion of *aché,* including Pichardo's remarks on it.

12. *Oché* is name of the divination sign when five cowries land "mouth" up. *Meyi* means "two" and denotes a compound *odu.* Although often contemplated as single signs, in divination ritual, the signs come in a composite form, with one sign following another.

13. *Ogbè-Sá* is the name of a composite sign, where the first cast brought eight cowries "mouth" up, and the second cast brought nine.

Contributors

Àrìnpé Gbẹ́kẹ̀lólú Adéjùmọ̀ is a senior lecturer in the Department of Linguistics and African Languages, University of Ibadan, Nigeria. Her academic background and research interests include studies in satire, gender, and folklore.

Dúrótoyè A. Adélékè is a senior lecturer in the Department of Linguistics and African Languages at the University of Ibadan, Nigeria. His area of research includes Yorùbá film studies, mythology, material culture in literature, and peace and conflict management studies.

George Olúṣọlá Ajíbádé is a senior lecturer in the Department of Linguistics and African Languages at the Ọbáfẹ́mi Awólọ́wọ̀ University, Ilé-Ifẹ̀, Nigeria. Ajíbádé's research interests are in African cultural studies, critical social and literary theories, and folklore. He has recently published a book titled *Negotiating Performances: Òsun in the Verbal and Visual Metaphors* and is preparing another book manuscript on "A Sociocultural Study of Yorùbá Nuptial Poetry."

Akíntúndé Akínyẹmí is associate professor of African and Asian Languages and Literatures at the University of Florida in Gainesville, Florida. He is author of *Yorùbá Royal Poetry: A Socio-Historical Exposition and Annotated Translation,* a book on the oral historical tradition of the famous city of Ọyọ.

Diedre L. Bádéjọ is professor and dean of the College of Letters, Arts, and Social Sciences at California State University East Bay. She is author of *Ọ̀sun Ṣèègèsì: The Elegant Deity of Wealth, Power, and Femininity.*

Kamari Maxine Clarke is associate professor of anthropology at Yale University, senior research scientist at Yale Law School, and director of the Center for Transnational Cultural Analysis at Yale University. She is the author of *Mapping Yorùbá Networks: Power and Agency in the Making of Transnational Communities* and *The International Criminal Court in Question: Beyond Legal Pluralism,* and editor of *Globalization and Race: Transformations in the Cultural Politics of Blackness.*

Laura Edmunds is a Ph.D. candidate in comparative literature at the University of Georgia in Athens. Her dissertation applies Yoruba analytical paradigms to Black literatures of Brazil and the Anglophone Caribbean. Her research interests also include Anglophone and Lusophone Africa and Diaspora, Black literary aesthetics, and Black science fiction and fantasy.

Tóyìn Fálọlá is University Distinguished Teaching Professor, University of Texas at Austin. He is the author of various books, including the edited collection *The Yorùbá Diaspora in the Atlantic World* (Indiana University Press, 2005).

Stephen Fọláránmí teaches drawing and painting at the Ọbáfẹ́mi Awóló-wọ̀ University, Ilé-Ifẹ̀. His research interests include African traditional murals and architecture. He has participated in several exhibitions in Nigeria and London, and recently co-curated the traveling exhibitions "Ife Art School in Retrospect" and "Faces of the Gods," an exhibition of photographs by Ulli Beier.

Stephen D. Glazier is professor of anthropology and graduate faculty fellow at the University of Nebraska, Lincoln. He served as general editor of *The Encyclopedia of African and African American Religions.* His other publications include *Marchin' the Pilgrims Home: A Study of the Spiritual Baptists of Trinidad; Caribbean Ethnicity Revisited;* and *Anthropology of Religion: A Handbook.*

Henry B. Lovejoy is a doctoral student in Latin American history at the University of California, Los Angeles. He studies the relationship between African drums and drumming and the political, religious, and cultural composition of slave society in Cuba, Brazil, and Suriname.

Michael Atwood Mason is an anthropologist and exhibit developer at the Smithsonian Institution. He has studied the cultures of the African diaspora since 1987, when he began his field research on Afro-Cuban religious traditions. He is author of *Living Santería: Rituals and Experiences in an Afro-Cuban Religion.*

Olóyè Àìná Ọlọmọ is a Yorùbá priestess of Ifá and Ṣàngó, is an ordained interfaith minister, and has been installed as Chief Àjídakin of Ilé-Ifẹ̀, Nigeria, Oloye Iyagan of Trinidad, and Her Excellency, Igbo Iyalase for Agba Kosare, Republic of Benin. She is currently the spiritual leader for Orilé Olókun Sànyà Awópéjú of Texas and Trinidad, and she is author of *Core of Fire: A Path to Yorùbá Spiritual Activism.* She is committed to social change and interfaith sharing of Yoruba universal theological concepts. In addition to decades of spiritual work, Olóyè Àìná currently teaches Yoruba religious studies at the John L. Warfield Center for African and African American Studies at the University of Texas at Austin, and is a faculty member of the Women's Thealogical Institute.

Luis Nicolau Parés is a professor in the Department of Anthropology at the Federal University of Bahia, Brazil. A specialist in the history and anthropology of African and Afro-Brazilian religions, he is author of *A formação do candomblé: história e ritual da nação jeje na Bahia* and co-editor of the journal *Afro-Ásia.*

Marc Schiltz is visiting senior research fellow at Queen's University, Belfast. He earned his Ph.D. in sociocultural anthropology at University College London. He has carried out long-term fieldwork among the Yorùbá, the Kewa of Papua New Guinea Highlands, and "rascal" gangs in Port Moresby, New Guinea.

Joel E. Tishken is assistant professor of African and world history at Washington State University in Pullman, Washington. His research interests include Central and Southern Africa, African religious history, prophecy, Christianity, and the theory and pedagogy of religion.

Bibliography

Abimbola, Wande. *Àwọn Ojú Odù Mẹ́rẹ̀ẹ̀rìndínlógún*. London: Oxford University Press, 1977.

———. "The Bag of Wisdom: Ọṣun and the Origins of the Ifá Divination." In *Òṣun across the Waters: A Yorùbá Goddess in Africa and the Americas,* ed. Joseph M. Murphy and Mei-Mei Sanford, 141–54. Bloomington: Indiana University Press, 1998.

———. *Ifá: An Exposition of Ifá Literary Corpus*. Ibadan, Nigeria: Oxford University Press, 1976.

———. *Ìjìnlẹ̀ Ohùn Ẹnu Ifá*. Glasgow: Collins, 1973.

——— "Introduction." In *Yorùbá Oral Tradition, Poetry in Music, Dance and Drama,* ed. Wande Abimbola, 11–48. Ilé-Ifẹ̀, Nigeria: Department of African Languages and Literature, University of Ifẹ̀, 1975.

———. *Proceedings of the First World Conference on Òrìṣà Tradition*. Ilé-Ifẹ̀, Nigeria: Ọbáfẹ́mi Awólọ́wọ̀ University, 1981.

———. "The Yorùbá Traditional Religion in Brazil: Problems and Prospects." In *Seminar Series,* number 1.1, ed. O. Oyelaran, 1–64. Ilé-Ifẹ̀, Nigeria: Department of African Languages and Literatures, University of Ifẹ̀, 1976–77.

Abiodun, R. "Ifa Art Objects: An Interpretation Based on Oral Tradition." In *Yorùbá Oral Tradition: Poetry in Music, Dance and Drama,* ed. Wande Abimbola, 421–66. Ilé-Ifẹ̀, Nigeria: Department of African Languages and Literature, University of Ifẹ̀, 1975.

Abrahams, R. C. *Dictionary of Modern Yorùbá*. London: Hodder and Stoughton. 1962.

Addie, O. O. "Colour Symbolism, with Special Reference to Ṣàngó Shrine in Ibadan." Unpublished B.A. long essay, Ọbáfẹ́mi Awólọ́wọ̀ University, Ilé-Ifẹ̀, 1990.

343

Adebisi, S. "Shrine Painting in Ilé-Ifẹ̀." Unpublished B.A. long essay, Ọbáfẹ́mi Awólọ́wọ̀ University, Ilé-Ifẹ̀, 1986.

Adedeji, J. A. "The Place of Drama in Yorùbá Religious Observance." *Odu* 3 (1966): 88–94.

Adegbile, Isaiah O. *Yorùbá Names and Their Meanings plus Proverbs with English Translations.* Ibadan, Nigeria: Taa Printing and Publishing, 1999.

Adelugba, D. "Trance and Theatre: The Nigerian Experience." In *Drama and Theatre in Nigeria: A Critical Source Book,* ed. Yemi Ogunbiyi, 203–18. Lagos: *Nigeria Magazine,* 1981.

Adeoye, C. Laogun. *Àṣà àti Ìṣe Yorùbá.* Oxford: Oxford University Press, 1979.

———. *Ìgbàgbọ́ ati Èsìn Yorùbá (Yorùbá religious belief systems).* Ibadan, Nigeria: Evans Brothers Nigerian Publishers, 1985.

Afolabi, Niyi. "Beyond the Curtains: Unveiling Afro-Brazilian Women Writers." *Research in African Literatures* 32, no. 4 (Winter 2001): 117–35.

Afolayan, Funso. "Kingdoms of West Africa: Benin, Ọ̀yọ́, and Asante." In *Africa:* vol. 1, *African History before 1885,* ed. Tóyìn Fálọlá, 161–89. Durham, N.C.: Carolina Academic Press, 2000.

Ahye, Molly. "Ṣàngó in Trinidad: Its Survival and Retention." In *Proceedings of the First World Conference on Òrìṣà Tradition,* ed. Wande Abimbola, 130–91. Ilé-Ifẹ̀, Nigeria: University of Ifẹ̀, June 1–7, 1981.

Aiyejina, Funso, and Rawle Gibbons. "Òrìṣà (Òrìshà) Tradition in Trinidad." Paper presented at the Ninth International Òrìṣà Congress. Port of Spain, Trinidad, 1999.

Ajayi, J. F. Ade. "The Aftermath of the Fall of Ọ̀yọ́." In *History of West Africa,* ed. J. F. Ade Ajayi and Michael Crowder, 129–66. London: Longman, 1974.

———. "Development Is about People." In *Humanity in Context,* ed. Ayo Banjo, 1–31. Ibadan, Nigeria: Nigerian Academy of Letters, 2000.

Ajuwon, Bade. "Ògún: Premus Inter Pares." In *Proceedings of the First World Conference on Òrìṣà Tradition,* ed. Wande Abimbola, 425–50. Ilé-Ifẹ̀, Nigeria: Ọbáfẹ́mi Awólọ́wọ̀ University, 1981.

Akinjogbin, I. A. "The Expansion of Ọ̀yọ́ and the Rise of Dahomey, 1600–1800." In *The History of West Africa,* vol. 1. New York: Columbia University Press, 1972.

Akinyemi, Akintunde. *Yorùbá Royal Poetry: A Sociohistorical Exposition and Annotated Translation.* Bayreuth African Studies Series (BASS), number 71. Bayreuth, Germany: University of Bayreuth, 2004.

Alade, C. A. "Aspects of Yorùbá Culture in the Diaspora." In *Culture and Society in Yorùbáland,* ed. Deji Ogunremi and Biodun Adediran, 203–11. Ibadan, Nigeria: Rex Charles Publication and Connel Publication, 1998.

Apter, Andrew. *Black Critics and Kings: The Hermeneutics of Power in Yorùbá Society* Chicago: University of Chicago Press, 1992.

———. "Notes on Òrìshà Cults in the Èkìtì Yorùbá Highlands." *Cahiers d'Études africaines* 35, nos. 138–39 (1995): 369–401.

Armstrong, Robert. "Traditional Poetry in Ladipo's Opera Ọba Kòso." *Research in African Literatures* 9, no. 3 (Winter 1978): 363–81.

Atanda, J. A. *An Introduction to Yorùbá History*. Ibadan, Nigeria: Ibadan University Press, 1980.

———. *The New Ọ̀yọ́ Empire*. London: Longmans, 1973.

Awe, Bolanle. "Militarism and Economic Developments in Nineteenth Century Yorùbá Country: The Ìbàdàn Example." *Journal of African History* 14, no. 1 (1973): 65–77.

Aweda, Sangodara (Ẹ̀ẹ̀rìndínlógún priest). Interview conducted by the author at Alubàtá Compound, Èkọsìn, Odò-Ọ̀tìn Local Government, Ọ̀sun State, Nigeria, 2002–2003.

Awolalu, J. Omosade. *Yorùbá Beliefs and Sacrificial Rites* (1979). Brooklyn: Athelia Henrietta Press, 2001.

Babalola, S. A. *Content and Form of Yorùbá Ìjálá*. London: Oxford University Press, 1966.

Babayemi, S. O. "Bẹẹrẹ Festival in Ọ̀yọ́." *Journal of Historical Society of Nigeria* 7, no. 1 (1973): 121–23.

Babayemi, Samuel. "The Fall and Rise of Ọ̀yọ́ c. 1760–1905." Ph. D. diss., University of Birmingham, 1979.

———. "The Myths of Ọ̀rányàn in Yorùbá Historiography." M.A. thesis, University of Birmingham, 1976.

Badejo, Diedre L. Field Notes, Nigeria, 1982.

———. "Methodologies in Yorùbá Oral Historiographies and Aesthetics." In *Writing African History*, ed. John Edward Phillips, 348–73. Rochester, N.Y.: University of Rochester Press, 2004.

Balderson, David, Mike Gonzalez, and Ana M. Lopez, eds. *The Encyclopedia of Contemporary Latin American and Caribbean* Cultures. New York: Routledge, 2002.

Bamidele, L. "Ṣàngó Myth and Its Challenges in Science, Art and Religion." In *IBA: Essays on African Literature in Honour of Oyin Ogunba*, ed. W, Ogundele and O. Adeoti, 178–86. Ilé-Ifẹ̀, Nigeria: Ọbáfẹ́mi Awólọ́wọ̀ University Press, 2003.

Barber, Karin, "Como o homem cria Deus na África Ocidental: atitudes dos Yorùbá para com o òrìṣà." In *Meu Sinal está no teu corpo*, ed. C. E. M. Moura, 142–73. São Paulo, Brazil: EDICON-EDUSP, 1989.

———. "How Man Makes God in West Africa: Yorùbá Attitudes towards the Òrìṣà." *Africa* 51, no. 3 (1981): 724–45.

———. "Oríkì in Òkukù: Relationships between Verbal and Social Structures." Ph.D. diss., University of Ifẹ̀, 1979.

———. "Yorùbá *Oríkì* and Deconstructive Criticism." *Research in African Literature* 15, no. 4 (1984): 501–29.

Barnes, Sandra T., ed. *Africa's Ògún: Old World and New*. Bloomington: Indiana University Press, 1989.

Bascom, William. *African Art in Cultural Perspective: An Introduction*. New York: W. W. Norton, 1973.

———. *Drums of the Yorùbá of Nigeria*. CD liner notes. Washington, D.C.: Smithsonian Folkways Records, 1992.

———. *Ifá Divination: Communication between Gods and Men in West Africa.* Bloomington: Indiana University Press, 1969.

———. *Shàngó in the New World.* Austin: African and Afro-American Research Institute, University of Texas at Austin, 1972.

———. *Sixteen Cowries: Yorùbá Divination from Africa to the New World.* Bloomington: Indiana University Press, 1980.

Bastide, Roger. *Images du nordeste mystique en noir et blanc* (1945). Paris: Pandora Editions 1978.

———. *Sociologia de la Religion [Les religions africaines au Brésil]* (1960). Gijón, Spain: Ediciones Jucar, 1986.

Baudin, Paul. *Fetichism and Fetich Worshippers* (1884). New York: Benziger Bros., 1885.

Beier, Ulli. *The Return of Shàngó: The Theatre of Duro Ladipo.* Bayreuth, Germany: University of Bayreuth, 1994.

———. *A Year of Sacred Festivals in One Yorùbá Town.* Lagos: Nigeria Magazine, 1959.

———. "A Year of Sacred Festivals in One Yorùbá Town (ẸDẸ)." *Nigeria Magazine* (Special Production), 3rd ed., (1959): 72–79.

———. *Yorùbá Myths.* Cambridge: Cambridge University Press, 1980.

———. "Yorùbá Wall Paintings." *ODU: Journal of Yorùbá and Edo Related Studies* 8 (1960): 36–39.

Benkomo, Juan. "Crafting the Sacred *Batá* Drums." In *Afro-Cuban Voices: On Race and Identity in Contemporary Cuba,* ed. Pedro Pérez Sarduy and Jean Stubbs, 140–46. Gainesville: University Press of Florida, 2000.

Bettelheim, Judith. *Cuban Festivals: A Century of Afro-Cuban Culture.* Princeton, N.J.: Markus Wiener Publishers, 2001.

Biobaku, S. O. *The Ẹ̀gbá and Their Neighbours 1842–1872.* Oxford: Oxford University Press, 1975.

Birth, Kevin. *Any Time Is Trinidad Time: Social Meanings and Temporal Consciousness.* Gainesville: University Press of Florida, 1999.

Bomfim, Martiniano Eliseu do. "Os Ministros de Xangô." In *O Negro no Brasil: trabalhos apresentados ao 2° Congresso Afro-Brasileiro, Bahia 1937,* 233–36. Rio de Janeiro: Civilização Brasileira, 1940.

Borghero, Francesco. *Journal de Francesco Borghero, premier missionnaire du Dahomey (1861–1865)* (1865). Ed. Renzo Mandirola and Yves Morel. Paris: Karthala, 1997.

Bourguignon, Erika. "Relativism and Ambivalence in the Work of M. J. Herskovits." *Ethos* 28, no. 1 (2000): 103–14.

Bowen, Rev. T. J. *A Grammar and Dictionary of the Yorùbá Language.* Washington, D.C.: Smithsonian Institution, 1858.

Braga, Júlio. *Ancestralidade Afro-Brasileira: o culto de babá egum.* Salvador, Brazil: CEAO-Ianamá, 1992.

———. *Na Gamela do Feitiço, Repressão e Resistência nos Candomblés da Bahia.* Salvador, Brazil: EDUFBa, 1995.

Brain, R. *Art and Society in Africa*. New York: Longman Group, 1980.

Brereton, Bridget. *Race Relations in Colonial Trinidad, 1870–1900*. New York: Cambridge University Press, 1979.

Browker, John, ed. *The Oxford Dictionary of World Religions*. New York: Oxford University Press, 1997.

Brown, David H. *Santería Enthroned: Art, Ritual, and Innovation in an Afro-Cuban Religion*. Chicago: University of Chicago Press, 2003.

Burkert, Walter. *Greek Religion*. Trans. John Raffan. Cambridge, Mass.: Harvard University Press, 1985.

Cabrera, Lydia. *El Monte*. 1954. Miami, Fla.: Ediciones Universal, 1983.

Campbell, V. B. "Comparative Study of Selected Shrine Paintings in Ilé-Ifẹ̀ and Ilésà." Unpublished M.F.A dissertation, Ọbáfẹ́mi Awólọ́wọ̀ University, Ilé-Ifẹ̀, 1989.

———. "Continuity and Change in Yorùbá Shrine Painting Tradition." *Kurio Africana: Journal of Art and Criticism* 1, no. 2 (1992): 110–23.

———. "Images and Power in Sixteen Yorùbá Sacred Paintings." *Ife: Annals of the Institute of Cultural Studies* 6 (1995): 25–38.

Canizares, B. R. *Shàngó: Santeria and the Òrìshà of Thunder*. Plainview, N.Y.: Original Publications, 2000.

Capone, Stefania. *La quête de l'Afrique dans le candomblé. Pouvoir et tradition au Brésil*. Paris: Karthala, 1999.

Carneiro, Edison. *Candomblés da Bahia* (1948). Salvador, Brazil: Ediouro, 1985.

Carroll, K. With foreword by William Fagg. *Yorùbá Religious Carving: Pagan and Christian Sculpture in Nigeria and Dahomey*. London: Geoffrey Chapman, 1967.

Castor, Nicole. "Virtual Community: The Òrìsà Tradition in the New World and Cyberspace." Paper presented at the Ninth International Òrìsà Conference, Port of Spain, Trinidad, 1999.

Catholic Community Forum. "Patron Saints Index: Saint Barbara." N.d. (accessed Jan. 30, 2005) http://www.catholic-forum.com/saints/saintb01.htm.

Clapperton, Hugh. *Hugh Clapperton into the Interior of Africa: Records of the Second Expedition, 1825–1827*. Ed. Jamie Bruce Lockhart and Paul E. Lovejoy. Boston: Brill, 2005.

Clarke, Kamari M. *Mapping Yorùbá Networks: Power and Agency in the Making of Transnational Communities*. Durham, N.C.: Duke University Press, 2004.

Comaroff, Jean, and John L. Comaroff, eds. *Millennial Capitalism and the Culture of Neoliberalism*. Durham, N.C. : Duke University Press, 2001.

Conner, Randy P., and David Hatfield Sparks. *Queering Creole Spiritual Traditions: Lesbian, Gay, Bisexual, and Transgender Participation in African-Inspired Traditions in the Americas*. New York: Harrington Park Press, 2004.

Courlander, Harold. *Tales of Yorùbá Gods and Heroes: Myths, Legend and Heroic Tales of the Yorùbá People of West Africa*. New York: Crown Publishers, 1973.

————. *A Treasury of African Folklore.* New York: Crown, 1975.

Daramola, O., and Jeje, A. *Àwọn Àṣà àti Òrìṣà ilẹ̀ Yorùbá.* Ibadan, Nigeria: Oni-bon-oje Press, 1967.

Dlamini, I. *Speaking for Ourselves.* Braamfontein, South Africa: Institute for Contextual Theology, 1985.

————. "Zionist Churches from the Perspective of a Zionist Leader." In *Religion Alive,* ed. G. C. Oosthuizen, 209–10. Johannesburg: Hodder and Stoughton, 1986.

Drewal, Henry John. *African Artistry: Technique and Aesthetics in Yorùbá Sculpture.* Atlanta: High Museum of Art, 1980.

Drewel, Henry John, and John Pemberton III, with Rowland Abiodun. *Yorùbá: Nine Centuries of African Art and Thought.* New York: Center for African Art in association with Harry N. Abrahams, 1989.

Drewal, Margaret T. *Yorùbá Ritual: Performers, Play, Agency.* Bloomington: Indiana University Press, 1992.

Dwyer, Kevin. *Moroccan Dialogues: Anthropology in Question.* Baltimore, Md.: Johns Hopkins University Press, 1982.

Egonwa, D. Osa. "Patterns and Trends of Stylistic Development in Contemporary Nigerian Art." *Kurio Africana: Journal of Art and Criticism* 2, no. 1 (1995): 1–15.

Ehret, Christopher. *The Civilizations of Africa: A History of 1800.* Charlottesville: University Press of Virginia, 2002.

Ellis, A. B. *The Yorùbá-Speaking Peoples of the Slave Coast of West Africa: Their Religion, Manners, Customs, Laws, Language, Etc.* (1894). Oosterhout, Netherlands: Anthropological Publications, 1970.

Eltis, David. "The Diaspora of Yorùbá Speakers, 1650–1865: Dimensions and Implications." In *The Yorùbá Diaspora in the Atlantic World,* ed. Toyin Falola and Matt Childs, 17–39. Bloomington: Indiana University Press, 2004.

Euba, Akin. *Yorùbá Drumming: The Dùndún Tradition.* Bayreuth, Germany: African Studies Series, 1990.

Fadipe, N. A. *The Sociology of the Yorùbá.* Ibadan, Nigeria: Ibadan University Press, 1970; reprint, 1991.

Fakeye, L., M. Bruce, and H. David. *Lamidi Olonode Fakeye: A Retrospective Exhibition and Autobiography.* Holland, Mich.: De Pree Art Center and Gallery, 1996.

Falola, Toyin, and Matt D. Childs, eds. *The Yorùbá Diaspora in the Atlantic World.* Bloomington: Indiana University Press, 2004.

Falola, Toyin, and Ann Genova. *Òrìṣà: Yorùbá Gods and Spiritual Identity in Africa and the Diaspora.* Trenton: Africa World Press, 2005.

Fatunsin, A. K. *Yorùbá Pottery.* Lagos: National Commission for Museums and Monuments, 1992.

Ferreira, Pai Euclides Menezes. Interview with Luis Nicolau Parés. June 25, 2003.

Folaranmi, S. "The Importance of Oríkì in Yorùbá Mural Art." *Ijele: Art e-journal of the African World* 2, no. 4 (2002). Available at www.africaresource.com.

———. "Òrìṣà Pópó Shrine Painting in Ògbómọ̀ṣọ́." Unpublished B.A. long essay, Ọbáfẹ́mi Awólọ́wọ̀ University, Ilé-Ifẹ̀, 1995.

———. "Ọ̀yọ́ Palace Mural." Unpublished M.F.A. thesis, Ọbáfẹ́mi Awólọ́wọ̀ University, Ilé-Ifẹ̀, 2000.

———. "Ọ̀yọ́ Palace Mural: A Symbolic Communication with Symbols." *Journal of Art and Ideas* 4 (2002): 93–105.

Font, Mauricio A. "Introduction: The Intellectual Legacy of Fernando Ortiz." In *Cuban Counterpoints: The Legacy of Fernando Ortiz,* ed. Mauricio A. Font, 1–27. Baltimore, Md.: Lexington Books, 2005.

Forbes, Frederick E. *Dahomey and the Dahomeans.* 2 vols. London: Longman, Brown, Green, and Longmans, 1851.

Fosu, K. *20th Century Art of Africa.* Vol 1. Zaria, Nigeria: Gaskiya Corporation, 1986.

Foucault, Michel. "Governmentality." In *The Foucault Effect: Studies in Governmentality,* ed. G. Burchell, C. Gordon, and P. Miller, 87–104. London: Harvester Wheatsheaf, 1991.

Fraginals, Manuel Moreno. *The Sugarmill: The Socioeconomic Complex of Sugar in Cuba, 1760–1860.* Trans. Cedric Belfrage. New York: Monthly Review Press, 1976.

Frobenius, Leo. *The Voice of Africa: Being an Account of the Travels of the German Inner African Exploration Expedition in the Years 1910–1912.* Trans. Rudolf Blind. 2 vols. London: Hutchinson, 1913; Benjamin Bloom, 1968.

Gibbons, Rawle. "Introduction and Welcome." Paper presented at the Ninth International Òrìṣà Congress, Port of Spain, Trinidad, 1999.

Glazier, Stephen D. *Marchin' the Pilgrims Home: A Study of the Spiritual Baptists of Trinidad.* Salem, Wisc.: Sheffield, 1991.

———. "New World African Ritual: Genuine and Spurious." *Journal for the Scientific Study of Religion* 35, no. 4 (1996): 420–31.

———. "The Religious Mosaic: Playful Celebration in Trindadian Shàngó." *Play and Culture* 1 (1998): 216–35.

———. "Responding to the Anthropologist: When the Spiritual Baptists of Trinidad Read What I Write about Them." In *When They Read What We Write: The Politics of Ethnography,* ed. Caroline B. Brettell, 37–48. Westport, Conn.: Bergin and Garvey, 1993.

———, ed. *Encyclopedia of African and African-American Religions.* New York: Routledge, 2001.

Gleason, Judith. *Òrìshà: The Gods of Yorùbáland.* New York: Atheneum, 1971.

Gotrick, Kacke. *Apidán Theatre and Modern Drama.* Stockholm: Almovist and Wiksell International, 1984.

Goveia, Elsa. "The West Indian Slave Laws of the Eighteenth Century." *Revista de Ciencias Sociales* 4 (1960): 75–105.

Greenfield, Sidney M., and Andre Droogers. *Reinventing Religions: Syncretism and Transformation in Africa and the Americas.* New York: Rowman and Littlefield, 2002.

Grimes, Ronald. *Beginnings in Ritual Studies.* Columbia: University of South Carolina Press, 1994.

Hall, Gwendolyn M. *Social Control in Slave Plantation Societies: A Comparison of St. Domingue and Cuba.* Baltimore, Md.: Johns Hopkins Press, 1971.

Hardt, Michael, and Antonio Negri. *Empire.* Cambridge, Mass.: Harvard University Press, 2000.

Hartnoll, Phyllis. *The Theatre: A Concise History.* 3rd ed. New York: Thames and Hudson, 1998.

Hastrup, Kirsten. "Writing Ethnography: State of the Art." In *Anthropology and Autobiography,* ed. J. Okely and H. Callaway, 116–33. New York: Routledge, 1992.

Henry, Frances. "The Òrìshà (Shàngó) Movement in Trinidad." In *Encyclopedia of African and African-American Religions,* ed. Stephen D. Glazier, 221–23. New York: Routledge, 2001.

———. *Reclaiming African Religions in Trinidad: The Socio-Political Legitimization of the Òrìshà and Spiritual Baptist Faiths.* Mona, Jamaica: University of the West Indies Press, 2003.

———. See also Mischel (Henry), Frances.

Hernandez-Reguant, Ariana. "Radio Taino and the Globalization of the Cuban Culture Industries." Ph.D. diss., University of Chicago, 2002.

Herbert, Eugenia W. *Iron, Gender, and Power, Rituals of Transformation in African Societies.* Bloomington: Indiana University Press, 1993.

Herskovits, Melville J. *Culture Dynamics.* New York: Alfred A. Knopf, 1947.

Herskovits, Melville J., and Frances Herskovits. *Trinidad Village.* New York: Alfred A. Knopf, 1947.

Hethersett, A. L., ed. *Ìwé Kíkà Èkerin Lí Èdè Yorùbá.* Lagos, Nigeria: Church Missionary Society, 1941.

Higginbotham, Joyce, and River Higginbotham. *Paganism: An Introduction to Earth-Centered Religions.* St. Paul, Minn.: Llewellyn Publications, 2002.

Horn, Andrew. "Ritual, Drama, and the Theatrical: The Case of Bori Spirit Medium." In *Drama and Theatre in Nigeria: A Critical Source Book,* ed. Yemi Ogunbiyi, 181–202. Lagos: Nigeria Magazine, 1981.

Horton, R. "African Conversion." *Africa* 41 (1971): 85–108.

Houk, James T. *Spirits, Blood, and Drums: The Òrìshà Religion in Trinidad.* Philadelphia: Temple University Press, 1995.

Hucks, Tracey E. "Trinidad, Africa-Derived Religions." In *Encyclopedia of African and African-American Religions,* ed. Stephen D. Glazier, 338–43. New York: Routledge, 2001.

Idowu, E. B. *Olódùmarè: God in Yorùbá Belief.* London: Longman, 1962; New York: Frederick A. Praeger Publisher, 1963; rev. and enlarged ed., London: Longman, 1996.

Ifaoogun, Adeboye Babalola (*Ifá* priest). Interview conducted by the author in Ìlobùú, Ọ̀sun State, Nigeria, in 2001.

Isola, Akinwumi. "Èdè-àìyedè tí ó rọ̀ mọ́ orírun Ṣàngó." In *O Pegedé: Àkójọpọ̀ Àwọn Àròkọ Akadá fún yíyọ̀nbó Ọ̀jọ̀gbọ́n Adébóyè Babalọlá,* ed. O. Olutoye, 113–19. Ikeja, Nigeria: Longman Nigeria Plc., 2000.

———. "The Living Power of Ṣàngó." *Proceedings of the First World Conference on Òrìṣà Tradition,* ed. Wande Abimbola, 338–46. Held at the University of Ifẹ̀, Ilé-Ifẹ̀, Nigeria, June 1–7, 1984.

———. "Orin Etíyẹrí." Unpublished paper.

———. "Religious Politics and the Myth of Ṣango." In *African Traditional Religion in Contemporary Society,* ed. Jacob K. Olupona, 93–99. New York: Paragon, 1991.

———. "The Rhythm of Ṣàngó Pípè." In *Yorùbá Oral Tradition: Poetry in Music, Dance and Drama,* ed. Wande Abimbola, 762–93. Ilé-Ifẹ̀, Nigeria: Department of African Languages and Literature, University of Ifẹ̀, 1975.

———. "Ṣàngó-pípè, One Type of Yorùbá Oral Poetry." M.A. thesis, University of Lagos, 1973.

———. "Yorùbá Beliefs about Ṣàngó as a Deity." *Orita: Ibadan Journal of Religious Studies* 11, no. 2 (1977): 100–20.

Itacy, Jorge Oliveira. *Orixás e voduns nos terreiros de Mina.* São Luis, Brazil: VCR Produções e Publicidades, 1989.

Jackson, Michael. *Minima Ethnographica: Intersubjectivity and the Anthropological Project.* Chicago: University of Chicago Press, 1998.

Jakuta, Chief. Personal Communication to Diedre Badejo, 1982.

Johnson, John William, and Fa-Digi Sisoko. *Son-Jara: The Mande Epic.* Bloomington: Indiana University Press, 2003.

Johnson, Samuel. *The History of the Yorùbás: From Earliest Times to the Beginning of the British Protectorate* (1921), O. Johnson, ed. London: Routledge and Kegan Paul, 1966; Lagos: C.S.S., 1960, 1976.

Kerenyi, C. *The Gods of the Greeks* (1951). London: Thames and Hudson, 2000.

Kirsch, Jonathan. *God against the Gods: The History of the War between Monotheism and Polytheism.* New York: Viking Compass, 2004.

Klass, Morton. "When God Can Do Anything: Belief Systems in Collision." *Anthropology of Consciousness* 2 (1991): 3–34.

Knight, Franklin W. *Slave Society in Cuba during the Nineteenth Century.* Madison: University of Wisconsin Press, 1970.

Koch, K.-F. *War and Peace in Jalemo.* Cambridge, Mass.: Harvard University Press, 1974.

Lacerda, Marcos Branda. "Yorùbá Drums from Benin, West Africa." In *Yorùbá Drums from Benin, West Africa.* CD liner notes. Washington, D.C.: Smithsonian Folkways Recordings, 1996.

Ladipo, Duro. *Ọba Kòso (The King Did Not Hang).* Ibadan, Nigeria: Macmillan Nigeria, 1970; Institute of African Studies at the University of Ibadan, 1972.

Ladipo, P. A. "Ṣàngó Shrine Painting in Ẹdẹ." Unpublished B.A. long essay, Ọbáfẹ́mi Awólọ́wọ̀ University, Ilé-Ifẹ̀, 1992.

Landes, Ruth. *City of Women* (1947). Albuquerque: University of New Mexico Press, 1994.

Lanternari, Vittorio. *Religions of the Oppressed*. New York: Alfred A. Knopf, 1963.

Law, Robin. "Ethnicity and the Slave Trade: 'Lucumi' and 'Nago' as Ethnonyms in West Africa." *History in Africa* 24 (1997): 205–19.

———. *The Ọ̀yọ́ Empire, c 1600–1836: A West African Imperialism in the Era of the Atlantic Slave Trade*. Oxford: Clarendon Press, 1970, 1977.

Lépine, Claude. "Análise formal do panteão Nàgó." In *Bandeira de Alairá: outros escritos sobre a religião dos orixás*, ed. C. E. M. de Moura, 13–70. São Paulo, Brazil: Nobel, 1982.

Leuzinger, E. *The Art of Black Africa*. London: Cassel and Collier Macmillan Publishers, 1976.

Lewis, I. M. *Ecstatic Religion*. Middlesex, England: Penguin Books, 1971.

Lima, Maria Helena. "Introduction." In *Mulheres Escrevendo: Uma Antologia Bilingüe de Escritoras Afro-Brasileiras Contemporáneas*, ed. Miriam Alves and Maria Helena Lima, 17–23. London: Mango Publishing, 2005.

Lima, Vivaldo da Costa. *A família-de-santo nos Candomblés Jeje-Nagôs da Bahia: um estudo de relações intra-grupais*. Salvador, Brazil: UFBa., 1977.

———. "Ainda sobre a nação de queto." In *Faraimará—o caçador traz alegria: Mãe Stella, 60 anos de iniciação*, ed. Cléo Martins and Raul Lody, 67–80. Rio de Janeiro: Pallas, 2000.

———. "Os Obás de Xangô." *Afro-Asia* 2–3 (June–Dec. 1966): 5–36.

Lloyd, P. C. *The Political Development of Yorùbá Kingdoms in Eighteenth and Nineteenth Centuries*. Occasional Paper, no. 31. London: Royal Anthropological Institute, 1971.

Lody, Raul. "O rei come quiabo e a rainha come fogo. Temas da culinária sagrada no Candomblé." In *Leopardo dos Olhos de Fogo: escritos sobre a religião dos orixás VI*, ed. C. E. M. de Moura, 145–64. São Paulo, Brazil: Ateliê Editorial, 1998.

Lovejoy, Paul E. "The Yorùbá Factor in the Trans-Atlantic Slave Trade." In *The Yorùbá Diaspora in the Atlantic World*, ed. Toyin Falola and Matt Childs, 40–55. Bloomington: Indiana University Press, 2004.

Lucas, J. O. *The Religion of the Yorùbás*. Lagos: C. M. S., 1948.

Lum, Kenneth A. *Praising His Name in the Dance: Spirit Possession in the Spiritual Baptist Faith and Òrìshà Work in Trinidad, West Indies*. Amsterdam: Harwood Academic Publishers, 2000.

Marcelin, Louis Heins. "A Invenção da Familia Afro-Americana. Familia, Parentesco e Domesticidade entre os Negros do Recôncavo da Bahia, Brasil." Ph.D. diss., Universidade Federal do Rio de Janeiro, 1996.

Marcuzzi, Michael D. "A Historical Study of the Ascendant Role of Bàtá Drumming in Cuban Òrìṣà Worship." Ph.D. diss., York University, 2005.

Marks, Morton. "Introduction." In *Rhythms and Songs for the Orishas: Havana, Cuba, ca. 1957.* CD liner notes. Washington, D.C.: Smithsonian Folkways Recordings, 2001.

Mason, John. *Orin Òrìṣà: Songs for Selected Heads.* Brooklyn: Yorùbá Theological Archministry, 1992.

Mason, Michael Atwood. *Living Santería: Rituals and Experiences in an Afro-Cuban Religion.* Washington, D.C.: Smithsonian Institution Press, 2002.

Matory, J. Lorand. *Black Atlantic Religion: Tradition, Trans-nationalism, and Matriarchy in the Brazilian Candomblé.* Princeton, N.J.: Princeton University Press, 2005.

———. *Sex and the Empire That Is No More: Gender and the Politics of Metaphor in Oyo Yorùbá Religion.* Minneapolis : University of Minnesota Press, 1994.

McAlister, Elizabeth. *Rara! Vodou, Power, and Performance in Haiti and Its Diaspora.* Berkeley and Los Angeles: University of California Press, 2002.

McDaniel, Lorna. *The Big Drum Ritual of Carriacou: Praisesongs in Rememory of Flight.* Gainesville: University Press of Florida, 1998.

McLeod, Patrica (Ìyá Ṣàngó Wùmí). "World Congress—Caribbean Report." Paper presented at the Ninth International Òrìṣà Congress, Port of Spain, Trinidad, 1999.

Mintz, Sidney. *Caribbean Transformations.* 1974. New York: Columbia University Press, 1989.

Mischel (Henry), Frances. "African Powers in Trinidad: The Shàngó Cult." *Anthropological Quarterly* 30 (1958): 45–59.

Morton-Williams, P. "An Outline of the Cosmology and Cult Organization of the Òyó Yorùbá." *Africa* 34, no. 3 (1964): 243–61.

Murphy, Joseph M., and Mei-Mei Sanford, eds. *Òṣun across the Waters: A Yorùbá Goddess in Africa and the Americas.* Bloomington: Indiana University Press, 2001.

Nasiru, B. "Ṣàngó Ritual Pots." Unpublished M.F.A. thesis, Department of Fine Arts, Ọbáfẹ́mi Awólọ́wọ̀ University, Ilé-Ifẹ̀, 1989.

Niane, D. T. *Sundiata: An Epic of Old Mali.* London: Longman Group, 1965.

Newson, Linda A. *Aboriginal and Spanish Colonial Trinidad: A Study in Culture Contact.* New York: Academic Press, 1976.

Obafemi, Olufemi. *Contemporary Nigerian Theatre: Cultural Heritage and Social Vision.* Bayreuth, Germany: Bayreuth African Studies Series, 1996.

Ogunbiyi, Yemi. *Drama and Theatre in Nigeria: A Critical Source Book.* Lagos: Nigeria Magazine, 1981.

Ogunbowale, P. O. *Àwọn Irúnmọlẹ̀ Ilẹ̀ Yorùbá.* Ibadan, Nigeria: Evans Publisher, 1962.

Ogundeji, Philip A. "The Image of Ṣàngó in Duro Ladipo's Plays." *Research in African Literatures* 29, no. 2 (Summer 1998): 57–75.

———. "A Semiotic Study of Duro Ladipo's Mythico-Historical Plays." Ph.D. diss., University of Ibadan, 1988.

Ogungbile, David. "Ẹẹ̀rìndínlógún: The Seeing Eyes of Sacred Shells and

Stones." In *Ọ̀ṣun across the Waters: A Yorùbá God in Africa and the Americas,* ed. Joseph M. Murphy and Mei-Mei Sanford, 89–121. Bloomington: Indiana University Press, 2001.

Ogunmola, M. O. *A New Perspective to Ọ̀yọ́ Empire History: 1530–1944.* Ibadan, Nigeria: Vantage Publishers, 1985.

Ojo, G. J. A. *Yorùbá Culture.* London: University of Ifẹ̀ and University of London Press, 1966.

Ojo, J. R. O. *A Short Illustrated Guide of the Museum of the Institute of African Studies.* Ilé-Ifẹ̀, Nigeria: University of Ifẹ̀, 1969.

Okediji, M. "Òrìṣà Ìkirè Painting School." *Kurio Africana: Journal of Art and Criticism* 1, no. 2 (1989): 120–31.

———. "Yorùbá Paint Making Tradition." *Nigerian Magazine* 54, no. 2 (1986): 19–26.

Olajubu, O. I. "*Ìwì: Egúngún* Chants in Yorùbá Oral Literature." M.A. thesis, University of Lagos, 1970.

Olajubu, Oludare. "The Sources of Duro Ladipo's *Ọba Kòso.*" *Research in African Literatures* 9, no. 3 (Winter 1978): 327–62.

Olatona, Oyegbade (*Ifá* and *Ẹ̀ẹ̀rìndínlógún* priest). Interview conducted by the author with the Ojùgbọ̀nà Awo of Oṣogbo in Nigeria in 2001–2003.

Olatunji, O. Olatunde. *Features of Yorùbá Oral Poetry.* Ibadan, Nigeria: University Press, 1984.

Olomo, Aina. *Core of Fire: A Path to Yorùbá Spiritual Activism.* Brooklyn: Althelia Henrietta Press, 2003.

Olunlade, Chief. *Ẹ̀dẹ: A Short History,* ed. Ulli Beier, trans. I. A. Akinjogbin. Ibadan, Nigeria: G. P. S. Ministry of Education, 1961.

Olupona, Jacob K. "Introduction." In *Beyond Primitivism: Indigenous Religions and Modernity,* ed. Jacob K. Olupona, 1–19. New York: Routledge, 2004.

———. *Kingship, Religion, and Rituals in a Nigerian Community: A Phenomenological Study of Oǹdó Yorùbá Festivals.* Stockholm, Sweden: Almqvist and Wiksell International, 1991.

Ortiz, Fernando. *Cuban Counterpoint: Tobacco and Sugar.* Trans. Harriet de Onis. Durham, N.C.: Duke University Press, 1995.

———. "La Antigua Fiesta Afrocubana del Día de Reyes." *Ensayos Etnográficos* (1921).Havana: Editorial de Ciencias Sociales (1984), 41–78.

———. *Los Instrumentos de la Musica Afrocubana,* 2 vols. Havana: Letras Cubanas, 1995.

———. *Los Tambores Batá de los Yoruba.* Havana: Publicigraf, 1954.

Oyewumi, Oyeronke. *The Invention of Women.* Minneapolis: University of Minnesota Press, 1997.

Palmié, S. "Against Syncretism: 'Africanizing' and 'Cubanizing' Discourses in North American Òrìṣà Worship." *Counterworks* (1993): 73–103.

Parés, Luis Nicolau. *A Formação do Candomblé: História e Ritual da nação Jeje na Bahia.* 1st ed. Campinas, Brazil: Editora Unicamp, 2006.

————. "The Nagôization Process in Bahian Candomblé." In *The Yorùbá Diaspora in the Atlantic World,* ed. Toyin Falola and Matt D. Child, 185–298. Bloomington: Indiana University Press, 2004.

————. "Transformations of the Sea and Thunder Voduns in the Gbe-speaking Area and in the Bahian Jeje Candomblé." In *Africa and the Americas: Interconnections during the Slave Trade,* ed. José C. Curto and Rene Soulodre-La France, 69–93. Trenton, N.J.: Africa World Press, 2005.

Peel, John D. Y. *Religious Encounter and the Making of the Yorùbá.* Bloomington: Indiana University Press, 2000.

Pemberton, John, III. "Divination in Sub-Saharan Africa." In *African Art and Rituals of Divination,* ed. Alisa LaGamma, 10–21. New York: Metropolitan Museum of Art, 2000.

Picton, J. "The Horse and Rider in Yorùbá Art: Image of Conquest and Possession." *Nigeria Field* 67, no. 2 (Oct. 2002): 111–38.

Pierson, Donald. *Brancos e Pretos na Bahia.* São Paulo, Brazil: Editora Nacional, 1971.

Prince, Raymond. *Ifá: Yorùbá Divination and Sacrifice.* Ibadan, Nigeria: Ibadan University Press, 1964.

Ramos, Arthur. "Os mythos de Xangó e sua degradação no Brasil." In *Estudos Afro-Brasileiros: trabalhos apresentados ao 1er Congresso Afro-Brasileiro reunidos no Recife em 1934,* 49–54. Rio de Janeiro: Ariel Editora, 1935.

Ramos, Miguel "Willie." "Afro-Cuban Òrìṣà Worship." In *Santería Aesthetics in Contemporary Latin American Art,* ed. Arturo Lindsey, 51–76. Washington, D.C.: Smithsonian Institution Press, 1996.

Reis, João José. *Rebelião Escrava no Brasil. A história do Levante dos Malés em 1835.* São Paulo, Brazil: Companhia das Letras, 2003.

Reis, João José, and Eduardo Silva. *Conflito e negociação. A resistência negra no Brasil escravista.* São Paulo, Brazil: Companhia das Letras, 1989.

Ribeiro, Esmeralda. "A procura de uma borboleta preta." In *Mulheres Escrevendo: Uma Antologia Bilíngüe de Escritoras Afro-Brasileiras Contemporáneas,* ed. Miriam Alves and Maria Helena Lima, 26–39. London: Mango Publishing, 2005.

————. "A escritora negra e o seu ato de escrever participando." In *Criação crioula, Nu elefante branco.* São Paulo: Impr. Oficial do Estado, 1987.

Rodrigues, Nina. *Os Africanos no Brasil* (1906). São Paulo, Brazil: Companhia Editora Nacional, 1977.

Rodriguez, Olavo A. "Introduction." In *Sacred Rhythms of Cuban Santería,* ed. Olavo A. Rodriguez. CD liner notes. Washington, D.C.: Smithsonian Folkways Recordings, 1995.

Rodríguez, Victoria Eli. "Tambores Batá." In *Instrumentos de la Música Folclórico-Popular de Cuba,* ed. Victoria Eli Rodriguez, 2 vols., 1:319–43. Havana: Editorial de Ciencias Sociales, 1997.

Sansi, Roger. *Fetishes and Monuments: Afro-Brazilian Art and Culture in 20th Century Bahia.* New York: Berghahn Books, 2007.

Santos, Deoscóredes Maximiliano dos. *História de um terreiro Nagô: crónica histórica*. São Paulo, Brazil: Carthago and Forte, 1994.

Santos, Juana Elbeim dos, and Deoscóredes Maximiliano Santos. "O culto dos ancestrais na Bahia: o culto dos eguns." In *Oloorisa: escritos sobre a religião dos orixás*, ed. C. E. M. de Moura, 153–88. São Paulo, Brazil: Ágora, 1981.

Santos, Maria do Rosário Carvalho. *O Caminho das Matriarcas Jeje-Nagô: Uma contribuição para a história da religião afro no Maranhão*. São Luis, Brazil: Func, 2001.

Santos, Maria Rosario Carvalho, and Manoel Santos Neto. *Bomboromina: Terreiros de São Luis - Uma interpretação sócio cultural*. São Luis, Brazil: SECMA/SIOGE, 1989.

Schiltz, Marc. "Habitus and Peasantization in Nigeria: A Yorùbá Case Study." *Man* new series 17 (1982): 728–46.

———. "Rural-Urban Migration in Ìgànná." Ph.D. thesis, University of London, 1980.

Silveira, Renato da. "Jeje-Nagô, Iorubá-Tapá, Aon Efan, Ijexá: Processo de constituição do candomblé da Barroquinha—1764–1851." *Cultura Vozes* 6, no. 94 (2000): 80–100.

———. Personal communication to Luis Nicolau Pares. May 3, 2004.

Simpson, George Eaton. *Religious Cults of the Caribbean: Trinidad, Jamaica, and Haiti*. Rio Piedras: Institute of Caribbean Studies, University of Puerto Rico, 1980.

Smith, R. S. *Kingdoms of the Yorùbá*. London: Methuen, 1969.

Soyinka, Wole. *Myth, Literature and the African World*. London: Cambridge University Press, 1976.

Sublette, Ned. *Cuba and Its Music from the First Drums to the Mambo*. Chicago: Chicago Review Press, 2004.

Tavares, Idálsio. *Xangô*. Rio de Janeiro: Pallas, 2000.

Thieme, Darius L. "A Descriptive Catalogue of Yorùbá Musical Instruments." Ph.D. diss., Catholic University of America, 1969.

Thompson, Robert Farris. *Flash of the Spirit: African and Afro-American Art and Philosophy*. New York: Vintage Books, 1984.

———. "The Sign of the Divine King: An Essay on Yorùbá Beaded-Embroidered Crowns with Veil and Bird Decorations." *African Arts* 113 (1970): 8–17.1.

Thornton, John K. *The Kingdom of Kongo: Civil War and Transition, 1641–1718*. Madison: University of Wisconsin Press, 1983.

Timi de Ede, Laoye I. "Los Tambores Yoruba." *Actas del Folklore Bolétin Mensual del Centro de Estudios del Folklore* 1 (1961): 17–31.

Tishken, Joel E. "Ethnic vs. Evangelical Religions: Beyond Teaching the World Religions Approach." *History Teacher* 33, no. 3 (May 2000): 303–20.

Trigger, Bruce. *Understanding Early Civilizations*. Cambridge: Cambridge University Press, 2003.

Trotman, David. "The Yorùbá and Òrìshà Worship in Trinidad and British Guiana, 1938–1970." *African Studies Review* 19 , no. 2 (1976): 1–17.

Tsing, Anna. "The Global Situation." *Cultural Anthropology* 15, no. 3 (2000): 327–60.

Van Deport, Mattijs. "Candomblé in Pink, Green, and Black: Re-scripting the Afro-Brazilian Religious Heritage in the Public Sphere of Salvador, Bahia." *Social Anthropology* 13 (2005): 3–26.

Verger, Pierre. *Notas sobre o culto aos Orixás e Voduns na Bahia de Todos os Santos, no Brasil, e na antiga Costa dos Escravos, na África* (1957). São Paulo, Brazil: Edusp, 1999.

———. *Orixás.* Salvador, Brazil: Corrupio, 1981.

Visona, M. B. With introduction and preface by Rowland Abiodun and Suzanne Blier. *The History of Art in Africa.* New York: Hany Abram, 2000.

Wafer, James Walter. *The Taste of Blood: Spirit Possession in Brazilian Candomble.* Philadelphia: University of Pennsylvania Press, 1991.

Warner-Lewis, Maureen. *Trinidad Yorùbá: From Mother Tongue to Memory.* Tuscaloosa: University of Alabama Press, 1996.

Welch, David B. *Voice of Thunder, Eyes of Fire: In Search of Shàngó in the African Diaspora.* Pittsburgh: Dorrance Publishing, 2001.

Wescott, Joan, and Peter Morton-Williams. "The Symbolism and Ritual Context of the Yorùbá Làbà Shàngó." *Journal of the Anthropological Institute of Great Britain and Ireland* 92 (1962): 23–37.

Whitford, John. *Trading Life in Western and Central Africa, 1877.* 2nd ed. London: Frank Cass, 1967.

Wood, Donald. *Trinidad in Transition: The Years after Slavery.* New York: Oxford University Press, 1968.

Yai, Olabiyi Babalola. "Yorùbá Religion and Globalization: Some Reflections." *Cuadernos Digitales* 15 (October 2001): 1–21.

Young, Robert J. C. *Colonial Desire: Hybridity in Theory, Culture and Race.* London: Routledge, 1995.

Index

CPSIA information can be obtained
at www.ICGtesting.com
Printed in the USA
BVOW04s0517271216

471879BV00033B/366/P